# On Account of Sex

# On Account of Sex

## The Politics of Women's Issues, 1945–1968

CYNTHIA HARRISON

UNIVERSITY OF CALIFORNIA PRESS
Berkeley    Los Angeles    London

The publisher wishes to acknowledge with gratitude the generous
support given this book by Peg Yorkin, Los Angeles.

University of California Press
Berkeley and Los Angeles, California

University of California Press, Ltd.
London, England

First Paperback Printing 1989

*Library of Congress Cataloging-in-Publication Data*

Harrison, Cynthia Ellen.
On account of sex : the politics of women's issues, 1945–1968 /
Cynthia Harrison.
p.  cm.
Bibliography: p.
Includes index.
ISBN 0—520—06121-7 (cloth)(alk. paper)
ISBN 0—520—06663-4 (pbk)  (alk. paper)
1. Women's rights—United States—History—20th century.
2. Women—Legal status, laws, etc.—United States—History—20th
century. 3. Sex discrimination against women—United States—
History—20th century. 4. Feminism—United States—History—20th
century. I. Title.
HQ1236.5.U6H37 1988
305.4'2'0973—dc19      87–25550

Printed in the United States of America

Cloth Edition
2 3 4 5 6 7 8 9


Paperback Edition
1 2 3 4 5 6 7 8 9

*For Richie*

# Contents

COMMISSION

9.   A Model for Action                                      169

10.  A New Women's Movement                                  192

CONCLUSION. Political Strategies and Outcomes                211


     Appendix 1: Text of the Equal Pay Act of 1963           223

     Appendix 2: Executive Order 10980 Establishing
                 the President's Commission on the
                 Status of Women                             225

     Appendix 3: Members of the President's
                 Commission and Its Committees               229

     Abbreviations                                           237

     Notes                                                   239

     Bibliography                                            309

     Index                                                   327

# Preface

In 1960 a female newspaper reporter covering the presidential campaign pressed John Kennedy to compare his wife, Jacqueline, to Eleanor Roosevelt. Kennedy responded with an accusation: "Oh," he parried, "you're one of those feminists!"[1]

The future president had resorted to an epithet; no matter how devoted to the quest for women's rights and improvements in women's status, female leaders between World War II and the mid 1960s shunned the label *feminist*. At the end of the war, the National Federation of Business and Professional Women's Clubs was supporting a program comprising the Equal Rights Amendment, equal pay legislation, the abolition of employment discrimination, and the appointment of women to high governmental positions. Yet in 1945 its president, Margaret Hickey, announced, "The days of the old, selfish, strident feminism are over."[2] Even the National Woman's party, the militant wing of the suffrage movement that had formulated the Equal Rights Amendment, employed the word *feminism* cautiously, generally restricting its usage *en famille*.[3] Not until the appearance in 1966 of the National Organization for Women, the first of the modern feminist organizations, did women fighting on behalf of women reclaim the word. In March 1968 a writer in the *New York Times Magazine* declared, "Feminism, which one might have supposed as dead as the Polish question, is again an issue."[4]

The emergence of a broadly based feminist movement at the end of the sixties produced legislation mandating equal treatment for women in education and in credit, eliminating criminal penalties for abortion, changing prejudicial rape laws, banning discrimination against pregnant women, equalizing property distribution at divorce, and offering tax credits for childcare. Local consciousness-raising groups made innumerable women aware of the social and political forces that had constrained the roles they had "chosen." In August 1970, tens of thousands of women marched in support of women's rights, a public demonstration unseen since the suffrage parades. Advocates of feminism ushered in an age of reordered relationships between the sexes and endorsed a striking transformation of the educational and employment patterns of women.

Yet the first federal legislation to prohibit sex discrimination in employment was enacted in 1963, three years before the founding of the National Organization for Women (NOW). A presidential order to eliminate selection by sex in the federal civil service, the nation's largest employer, predated the feminist organization by four years. And the first "consciousness-raising" group, a presidential commission to investigate the status of women, began its activities five years before the founding of NOW. All these events took place during the presidency of John F. Kennedy, a man not heretofore characterized as an advocate of women's rights and, by his own disclaimer, no feminist.

The Kennedy administration's agenda for women was rooted in the post-war era fifteen years earlier. World War II had infused discussion of women's roles with new energy. Throughout the war, in order to win support for the defense effort, the government had emphasized national ideals of justice and equality. The contributions of women made many believe that the nation owed them a share in these ideals, some gesture of recognition in the particular form of legislation—an equal rights amendment to the Constitution or, less radical, an equal pay law.

But a longing for the social stability that had supposedly characterized the prewar world dominated the national consciousness and worked against the impulse to recognize women's individual achievements. Americans wanted to reestablish traditional family arrangements at work and at home. Government policy, implemented midwar, turned from urging women to take war jobs toward ejecting women from those places so that they—both the jobs and the women—would be available to the homecoming soldiers.

Economic events sabotaged these plans. Postwar inflation led even married women to want to remain in the labor force, despite their having to move to lower-paying sex-segregated work to do so. Because the clerical and service sectors of the workforce, reserved largely for women workers, expanded more rapidly than the population of young single women, employers gave up their long-standing objection to hiring married women. And married women, for their part, eagerly accepted the places. In 1940, 15 percent of wives worked outside the home; by 1960, 30.5 percent of them would hold jobs.[5]

Postwar politics concerning women reflected the ambivalence in espousing one set of goals (reinstatement of the "traditional" family) and acting on another (using the employment of married women to improve family financial security). Married women moved into the public arena with determination, both during the war and after, but confronted legal and economic discrimination. Leaders of women's groups sought to help, and policy measures to assist working women, to eliminate legal disabilities, and to study the "problems" caused by new styles of family living won more support than ever before. But they also elicited significant opposition.

The fifteen-year period of postwar consolidation proved inhospitable to policy initiatives on women's issues. By 1960, however, the anxiety associated with wartime dislocation which had so hobbled women had been replaced by a new set of fears. When in 1957 the U.S.S.R. orbited Sputnik, the first space satellite, the feat crystallized national apprehensions stemming from the long-standing suspicions between the two world powers. Americans worried whether their nation would be able to meet the challenge of its chief international rival. Had devotion to a stable family life resulted in a complacent and insular society vulnerable to the threat of Russian domination? The energetic liberalism of the administration of John F. Kennedy, elected in 1960 on a pledge to "get the country moving again," promised to meet the challenge, both at home and abroad. If America was to prove superior in the contest for the planet, all its resources would have to be exploited—including, as it turned out, the capacities of women.

Kennedy's commitment to orchestrate and direct social change provided the setting for the policy departure in women's issues but did not determine its specific nature. For these particulars he relied on his team in the Department of Labor, a group who in turn took their lead from the coalition of women's organizations and labor unions that had formulated a plan following

World War II to integrate women into the peacetime labor force. Their program dovetailed with the administration's other goals: U.S. international security through the use of American talents, revitalization of the economy by increasing the purchasing power of workers, and equal opportunity in both private and public sector for all Americans.

When he was inaugurated, Kennedy himself did not specifically intend to implement a program that would initiate federal intervention on behalf of women's equality in the private sector, raise their expectations, create activist networks, and legitimate women's demands for action. But the actions of his administration had that impact. The Kennedy administration provided both a psychological foundation and a structural basis for the organization of the first women's rights group of the new era. The movement for women that blossomed at the end of the sixties sprang from the combination of long-standing discrimination in the law and in practice, changes in women's lives brought about by increasing experience in the workforce, the activism of civil rights advocates, and liberal politics.

This book looks at the evolution of policy concerning women's issues in the period between World War II and the rise of the women's movement at the end of the 1960s—an era in which women's issues were not "salient." During this time the federal government experienced virtually no outside political pressure or any extenuating circumstance that forced attention to programs for women. Yet between 1961 and 1963 a departure in policy took place, marked by a sudden aggressive implementation of specific initiatives designed to enlarge opportunities for women.[6]

Examination of this issue can be taken as a case study of sorts, one that demonstrates that important policy changes can occur, given an appropriate political and social context and savvy political actors, even if no widespread social movement demands them, and that these changes can then encourage the development of such a movement. Without broad-based support, however, the dimension of such changes will be limited. The study also reveals how political tactics can take advantage of historical moments to foster the attainment of specific goals; conversely, we see that maladroit political decisions can retard their achievement. This book examines the specific case of policy measures on behalf of women's rights, but at the same time it evaluates generally the practicality and impact of a variety of strategies common to groups seeking to improve their own condition.

Although this study takes policy making on all women as its subject, the actors in the story are primarily educated, middle-class white women. From this group came those who were able to procure the skills, the position, and oftentimes the leisure to address policy questions, either as officials of civic organizations representing similarly placed women or as unionists championing women they perceived to have fewer advantages than themselves.

In seeking measures to help women, these leaders followed the pattern of black activists fighting for constitutional amendment, legislation, executive orders, and court decisions. During World War II the hypocrisy of a nation that fought the notion of racial superiority abroad while upholding a system of racial stigmatization at home had grown too apparent to ignore. That black and white Americans were doing the fighting in racially segregated battalions only heightened the irony. After the war a vigorous civil rights movement emerged that, with few overt connections to the interest groups acting on behalf of women, provided models of strategies and opportunities for policy change.

Black women leaders participated in the deliberations about women's issues at crucial points, but they in general saw racism as the chief foe. Ideas, more than individuals, linked the civil rights movement and the small group of women working for women's rights in Washington between 1945 and 1968. White policy makers recognized that black women suffered from discrimination based on race and class as well as sex, and they framed a few measures directed specifically to the plight of black women. All assumed, however, that, by and large, policy initiatives phrased neutrally would help black women as well as white. A few measures did aim specifically at the plight of black women.

The story begins in 1945, with Part One, "Consolidation and Stalemate," describing the ambivalent impact of World War II on legislative measures of significance to women. Chapter 1 looks at the renewed fight for the Equal Rights Amendment (ERA) in the immediate postwar period, chapter 2 at one alternative suggested by ERA opponents, and chapter 3 at the proposal for equal pay legislation, offered by ERA adversaries as an appropriate approach to women's employment problems. All these efforts were unsuccessful. Chapter 4 discusses the strategy of executive appointments employed by Presidents Harry Truman and Dwight Eisenhower, by which they hoped to persuade women that the party in power had a genuine interest in their welfare.

Part Two, "Moving Again," presents the consequences for women's issues of the end of "postwar politics" and the resurgence of liberalism. Chapter 5 analyzes Kennedy's politics and his administration's approach to formulating policy about women. The policy change had its source in the Women's Bureau, which determined the content of the new program. Only one measure required the cooperation of Congress: chapter 6 details the administration's achievement of an equal pay law, the first piece of legislation to limit sex discrimination in private employment.

The President's Commission on the Status of Women, the centerpiece of Kennedy's program on women's issues and its most significant outcome, is the subject of Part Three. The commission finessed the problem of the Equal Rights Amendment that had divided women's organizations for forty years, a story told in chapter 7. As a result, women leaders could forge a unified agenda for action on behalf of women, as chapter 8 describes, for the first time since suffrage. The president's commission proved to be the starting point for governmental discussions of women's status that continued for at least two decades.

Part Four surveys the impact of the president's commission. The viewpoint of Kennedy's successor, the implementation of the commission's proposals, and the forging of a women's network are discussed in chapter 9. Chapter 10 describes the interaction of the many events that led to the creation of the National Organization for Women. The combination of federal solicitude toward women, a strategic opening provided by a civil rights measure, conflicts in attitude among key players, and

rising expectations for women led to an unanticipated consequence: the rise of a women's movement that became one of the
hardiest outgrowths of liberalism.

The conclusion considers the impact of federal policy on
social change and of political pressure groups on federal policy.
It also offers an assessment of political strategies that seek to
encourage social change in inhospitable times.

# Acknowledgments

Throughout the writing of this book I have been the recipient of the generosity of dozens of colleagues and friends. It gives me great pleasure to acknowledge them here.

Archivists and librarians across the country helped with proficiency, cheer, and patience to fill seemingly endless requests for documents quickly and accurately. These include John Caldwell, Carl Albert Center Archives, University of Oklahoma; Cathy de Lorge, Oregon Historical Society; Deirdre Malarkey, Oregon Collection, University of Oregon; Dionne Miles, Walter P. Reuther Library, Wayne State University; and Mary Jo Pugh, Michigan Historical Collections, Bentley Historical Library. I would like to give particular thanks to the staffs of the Franklin D. Roosevelt Library, the Harry S. Truman Library (especially Elizabeth Costin Safly and Dennis Bilger), the Dwight D. Eisenhower Library, the John F. Kennedy Library (especially William Johnson), the Lyndon Baines Johnson Library (especially Rod Soubers), the George Meany Memorial Archives, the Schlesinger Library (especially Kathy Kraft and Elizabeth Shenton), the National Archives (especially Jerry Hess), and the Library of Congress. The Women's Bureau of the U.S. Department of Labor provided desk space and good company for many months while I went through the papers of the President's Commission on the Status of Women. I am deeply appreciative to its devoted personnel, particularly Ruth Shinn.

Many scholars freely shared their work in progress with me: Carl Brauer, D'Ann Campbell, Jo Freeman, Vivien Hart, Frances Kolb, Judith Patterson, Leila Rupp, Verta Taylor, and Patricia Zelman.

For comments and suggestions on various stages of the manuscript, I owe thanks to Marsha Adler, Annette Baxter, Susan Porter Benson, Alison Bernstein, William Chafe, Cynthia Costello, Martha Feldman, Constance Gilbert-Neiss, Charles Hamilton, Anne Hastings, Robert Katzmann, Deborah Kelly, Linda

Kerber, Sheilah Mann, John Morgan, Joyce Murdoch, Marian Palley, Richard Pious, Donald Ritchie, Rosalind Rosenberg, Leslie Rowland, Catherine Rudder, Kathryn Kish Sklar, R. Kent Weaver, Judith S. Weis, Joan Hoff Wilson, and Thomas West.

A number of particularly kind colleagues deserve special thanks for the heroic effort of reading more than one draft of this manuscript and enduring extended discussions about it: Cindy Aron, Patricia Cooper, Jo Freeman, Barbara Melosh, and Leila Rupp. John Gist not only read and commented; he also made the unique sacrifice of listening to several sections read aloud. Rovilla McHenry typed a large part of the final manuscript under pressure of time, but with abundant good humor and consummate skill. I am very grateful to her and to Judy Caruthers, who solved a major production problem.

During the last five years I have worked for the American Historical Association and the American Political Science Association as the Deputy Director of Project '87. They have assisted my revision of this manuscript through their liberal contribution of equipment and space, as well as by providing an intellectually stimulating and supportive collegial environment.

My gratitude to the Brookings Institution is profound. As a research fellow, I received both its financial and intellectual support. The staff in the library (Laura Walker and Susan McGrath), the computer center, and the administrative offices made every effort to accommodate my many requests. I wish above all to thank Martha Derthick, Gilbert Y. Steiner, James Sundquist, and Diane Hodges for countless instances of assistance and encouragement. Generous financial aid came also from the U.S. Department of Labor, which funded many of my traveling expenses, and from the Harry S. Truman Institute, the Eleanor Roosevelt Institute, and the Lyndon Baines Johnson Foundation.

William E. Leuchtenburg directed the dissertation from which this manuscript has emerged. He paid the closest attention to my work, improving it in every respect. His consistent responsibility to his students in his efforts to teach them to write history reveals the highest devotion to his calling as a teacher.

Naomi Schneider at the University of California Press has shepherded this manuscript through the editorial process with singular sensitivity and warmth. I am indebted to her for her encouragement and her friendship. I also want to thank Ruthanne Lowe for preparing the index and Anne Geissman Canright for her exceptionally careful and intelligent editing— and her tact. Barbara Ras has overseen the production with kindness and efficiency.

Peg Yorkin, in a wonderful gesture of support for scholarship on the history of women, made a gracious donation to the University of California Press to assist its publication of this book.

I wish also to express my deep appreciation to the women and men who played a part in the story I tell and who generously made available to me their written records and their recollections.

Dear friends helped me through the thickets with lots of laughs, lots of solace, and some distance on this enterprise: Cindy Aron, Marsha Adler, Patricia Cooper, Cynthia Costello, Sam Goodman, Rebecca Hirsh, Diane Hodges, Kathryn Allamong Jacob, Elizabeth and Ronald Lantz, Glen Marcus, William Martineau, Barbara Melosh, Lois Rosenblatt, Ruth Ross, Catherine Rudder, Judy Weis, and especially John Gist, who made it possible, for a few crucial weeks, for me to "Write at the Beach," really the only place anyone should write.

My parents, Herbert and Jean Harrison, sustained me with their love and pride, as have the rest of my family: Miriam, Marla, and Leo Seiden; Hannah and Harold Shapiro; Betsy, Gordon, Merissa, and Joshua Bocher; Martin and Anita Harrison; Heidi, Herb, and Bradley Chain; and Louis Hacken, Rose Aronson, and Israel Hacken, whom I keep in memory.

No one helped me more than Richard J. Peppin. From the beginning, he valued my work and he sustained this endeavor in countless ways. I dedicate this book to him with deepest thanks.

# Abbreviations

| | |
|---|---|
| AAUW | American Association of University Women |
| BPW | National Federation of Business and Professional Women's Clubs |
| CACSW | Citizens' Advisory Council on the Status of Women |
| CEA | Council of Economic Advisers |
| CSC | Civil Service Commission |
| DACOWITS | Defense Advisory Committee on Women in the Services |
| DNC | Democratic National Committee |
| DOL | U.S. Department of Labor |
| EEOC | Equal Employment Opportunity Commission |
| FLSA | Fair Labor Standards Act |
| ICSW | Interdepartmental Committee on the Status of Women |
| NAWSA | National American Woman Suffrage Association |
| NCCW | National Council of Catholic Women |
| NCJW | National Council of Jewish Women |
| NCL | National Consumers League |
| NCNW | National Council of Negro Women |
| NOW | National Organization for Women |
| NWP | National Woman's Party |
| NWTUL | National Women's Trade Union League |
| PCSW | President's Commission on the Status of Women |

RNC   Republican National Committee

UAW   United Automobile, Aerospace, and Agricultural Implement Workers of America [name changed in 1962 from United Automobile, Aircraft, and Agricultural Workers of America]

YWCA  Young Women's Christian Association

# 1

# CONSOLIDATION AND
# STALEMATE, 1945–1960

# 1

# THE EQUAL RIGHTS AMENDMENT AND THE AMBIVALENT LEGACY OF WORLD WAR II

World War II put women into work they had never done before. Highly skilled and highly paid, women workers producing war materiel demonstrated that they could do virtually any job. The information proved unsettling. American tradition dictated that women, especially married women, keep house and raise children, not put rivets into airplane fuselages. The nation was at once grateful to its women for their help and unnerved at how well they performed.[1] Women activists with political agendas of long standing sought to capitalize on the feelings of gratitude, proposing federal measures to protect women from discrimination. But they faced a resistance strengthened by the anxieties of wartime dislocation.

## POSTWAR BACKLASH

The federal government had enticed women into the labor force for war work. Federal funds helped communities take care of the children, and the National War Labor Board promised equal pay with men, declaring wage differentials based on sex impermissible (partly to lure women to work and partly to keep wage rates up in preparation for the GIs' return).[2] A massive public relations campaign sang the praises of "Rosie the Riveter." Magazine story writers began to portray married women workers favorably, able to handle their jobs competently while meeting their family responsibilities. Work and love went together—but only for the duration. Advertisers who included working moms in their ads made it clear that Mom was

3

serving because it was her duty but that she would be home again full-time as soon as she could. Now, she had to take care of her kids not directly but by doing war work. As Maureen Honey describes it, "The role allocated to women in wartime propaganda, then, was a complicated mixture of strength and dependence, competence and vulnerability, egalitarianism and conservatism."[3]

In response to patriotism and new opportunities, the female labor force swelled from thirteen million in 1940 to nineteen million and more in 1944. By March of that year, almost one-third of all women over the age of fourteen were in the labor force, and the numbers of women in industry had increased almost 500 percent, to one woman worker in three. The opportunities created by the war allowed women to leave domestic service jobs: between 1940 and 1944 the percentage of working women who held domestic jobs dropped from 17.7 to only 9.5. Still, more than half of women who worked during the war held clerical, sales, service, or domestic jobs. These women did their duty, but they faced many burdens. The number of childcare facilities never approached the need, areas with military personnel lacked adequate schools, housing was scarce near military installations and defense plants, and few businesses adjusted hours to accommodate women workers.[4]

Even with all these difficulties, however, policy makers were concerned that women in nontraditional jobs would not willingly relinquish them at the end of the war. As a result, government propaganda, midwar, did an about-face. Because the original exhortations to women to do war work had never challenged the core of ideas about femininity, because no one had suggested that work was more than a sacrifice women had willingly made for the most motherly of reasons, the shift was an easy one. The message was clear: although women *could* do anything, authentic women would choose to be home with their families. Women's magazines fell in line with the government's efforts and spotlighted articles on the importance of mothers caring for their children.[5]

Public opinion polls, however, revealed that between 60 and 85 percent of women engaged in war work did not want to leave their nontraditional jobs at the end of the conflict.[6] Out of anxiety that women workers might tenaciously hang on to their jobs, the federal government terminated daycare funding and gave veterans the right to displace wartime workers. The contraction of war materiel manufacturing alone displaced workers, male and female, without further ado. Within one month of V-J day, the government canceled $35 billion worth of defense contracts. Employers also began now to revise their judgment of their women workers: in the postwar version of the tale, they had not been very good after all, prone to high absenteeism and "bad attitudes." Women's organizations of all stripes worked against the notion that employers should force women out of jobs, but to little avail.[7]

Those women who had them lost their high-paying, high-skilled jobs, but the attempt to get women out of the workforce entirely did not succeed. The dismantling of war industries merely consigned these women once again to traditionally female occupations. Companies laid women off at a rate 75 percent greater than that for men, and the returning veterans reassumed the traditionally male jobs. The director of the Women's Bureau, Frieda Miller, suggested that women who had been laid off from the munitions industry look to the (lower-paying) service sector for employment[8]—which, given no other options, they did. Thus, although 3.25 million women either quit or were fired during the period from September 1945 to November 1946, nearly 2.75 million women assumed jobs, making the net decline only 600,000 women. But Rosie the Riveter had become a file clerk.[9]

Practical considerations had dictated the ejection of women from wartime employment: returning soldiers needed jobs. Americans worried about the return of the biting depression that had preceded the war. Then, jobs for "heads of households" had taken priority. Intense opposition to married women workers had resulted even in occasional legal bans against hiring them, and in some families in which the wife had been the sole wage earner husbands had suffered acute emotional distress.[10] No one wished to contemplate the recurrence of such a phenomenon. In the twelve months following June 1945, nine million military personnel were discharged, and policy makers now sought to ensure that the former GIs would not be displaced by women from jobs they had a right to as "breadwinners." With the contraction of defense manufacturing, the economic dislocation of the postwar period added to the pervasive strain that had attended the war years.[11]

But a still more insidious backlash emerged following the war, separate from the economic considerations resolved in part by women's relinquishing their jobs. As the psychiatrist Edwin Krause and the novelist Pearl Buck had both warned, by making them the beneficiaries of the heroic male warriors, the war caused a major setback for women. Popular literature counseled women to forget their own needs in order to make their beaux more comfortable, and articles advised them to cultivate feminine characteristics, eschewing the independence, assertiveness, and competency they had acquired from their experiences on the home front.[12] Government planners had defined the major postwar domestic problem as the readjustment of sixteen million veterans, and they believed that readjustment would come sooner if the vets found their girls as they had left them, not as independent working women.

The anxiety of readjustment translated into a desire for the reinstitution of traditional family life supported by traditional sex roles. Everyone wanted to forget the trauma of the war, including the evidence that women could perform the work of men. A survey of women's roles as portrayed in magazine fiction in 1945 showed careers for women depicted more unsympathetically than since the turn of the century. Women themselves sought the peace and pleasures of marriage and motherhood. The marriage rate, which had averaged 121 per thousand during the war, peaked at 148 per thousand in 1946, and the median marriage age for women fell more than a year, from 21.5 to 20.3. More than ever before, women were trying for both work and love. Pushed out of high-paying "men's jobs," they acquiesced to doing women's work at home and in the office.[13]

## WOMEN LEADERS AND WOMEN'S ISSUES

One group of women—the small and elite cadre that composed the leadership of national women's organizations—recognized both the vulnerability that women workers labored under and the possibility of doing something to ameliorate it. If World War II created a backlash that coerced women out of war jobs and into white-collar work, it also generated a feeling of gratitude toward these women for the contribution they had made to the war effort, one no less essential than the military commitment. In October 1945, President Harry Truman offered them some recognition:

> Since the earliest days of settlement and the beginnings of this great Republic of ours, American women have built for themselves a proud record of achievement, of unselfish devotion to the public welfare, of courageous industry in advancing every good cause. And never have they done a more magnificent job than during the crisis of recent years, both as private citizens and responsible public officials. To the women of America, I say—your untiring efforts to speed the winning of the war, your tender care and skilled nursing of those struck down on the battlefield, your passionate belief in the possibility of a just and lasting peace, and your effective work in advancing that great cause, need no tribute from me to make them shine as one of the glorious pages in our history.[14]

Women leaders hoped to capitalize on such gratitude to win at least some protection for the worker once heralded as "the woman behind the man behind the gun."

But these activists disagreed about the best goal to pursue, a controversy already more than two decades old. The break among women's groups had taken place shortly after women, in 1920, won the right to vote. By 1945 the old suffrage coalition had split into three separate, though overlapping, interest groups, each with a different (but not necessarily incompatible) agenda determined by ideology and class identification: one group pursued legislation for working women, one sought an equal rights amendment to the Constitution and the third aimed at securing a more prominent place for women in political parties.

The first group had roots going back to the settlement movement of the 1890s and the Progressive-era push for protective labor legislation for women. Middle-class women concerned about the welfare of their underclass sisters working in factories had formed organizations to improve conditions for industrial

laborers, in some cases joining forces with the women they hoped
to help. These organizations—especially the National Women's
Trade Union League and the National Consumers League—
persuaded the federal government to undertake a massive study
of working conditions of women and children, which was published in 1910. They used the data collected to promote state laws
applying to women establishing minimum wages, maximum
hours, weight restrictions on lifting, and prohibitions against
night work. This effort to prevent employers from mercilessly
exploiting women workers succeeded to some degree in nearly
every state. Sustained by a liberal ideology of participation in
government, active public intervention to assist those in need,
and a firm belief in the American institutions of enlightened and
regulated free enterprise, these reformers fought for suffrage as
a means by which women could protect themselves and their
families. This same group also persuaded federal administrators
to establish a "Women in Industry Service" during World War I
to protect women who entered defense work, and in 1920 Congress responded to pressure to make the new agency permanent:
it became the Women's Bureau, located within the Department
of Labor. With all players believing that both government and
private industry would respond to demonstrated needs of workers, the bureau's function was restricted to the collection of information about women workers.[15]

Yet the organizations that had been instrumental in creating
the Women's Bureau looked to it to provide not only information but also leadership. In 1945 the "Women's Bureau coalition" (as it will be called in the following pages) included the
following associations: the National Women's Trade Union
League (which would disband in 1950), the National Consumers
League, the Young Women's Christian Association, the National
Council of Jewish Women, the National Council of Catholic
Women, the National Council of Negro Women, the League of
Women Voters (although the league became less interested in
women's issues as the decade progressed), the American Associa-
tion of University Women, and various women's affiliates of the
American Federation of Labor and the Congress of Industrial
Organizations. Not every organization was involved in every is-
sue, and other groups occasionally participated on specific mat-

ters, but in general it was these associations that the bureau staff
most often consulted and that usually rallied to the Women's
Bureau positions. The coalition lacked key groups, however,
especially major labor organizations and political clubs. Isolated
from power centers both inside the government and outside and
handicapped by a politically maladroit director, Mary Anderson
(who headed the bureau for almost twenty-five years), the bureau had difficulty swaying policy makers.[16]

During World War II, the Women's Bureau coalition had
sought essentially to make sure that employers did not use the
war emergency as a way of vitiating standards for women workers. At the end of the war, although they looked with some
distress on the wholesale dispatch of the female labor force, these
organizations agreed with the general goal that married women
should be supported by their husbands, who would be earning
decent salaries doing men's work. For the women who had to stay
in the labor force, the coalition sought to maintain or expand
laws regarding work hours and minimum wage protections.

The second group of women activists, smaller and more
elite, grew out of the last stages of the suffrage fight in the
1910s, when it splintered from the National American Woman
Suffrage Association (NAWSA), the group leading the battle
for the vote in the mainstream liberal political tradition.
Headed by Alice Paul, a charismatic militant suffragist, the
National Woman's party (NWP) used highly visible and inflammatory demonstrations to get suffrage on the front pages of
the nation's newspapers. The more traditional-minded leadership of the NAWSA feared that such actions would hurt the
cause by creating a backlash, but sheer rivalry also played a
role in the antagonism between the two groups.

Friction appeared again early in the 1920s over Paul's decision
to introduce an amendment to the Constitution to guarantee
women complete legal equality with men. The Women's Bureau
coalition objected that the amendment would decimate the protective labor laws they had worked so hard to obtain, thus leaving
working women defenseless. The NWP was not unsympathetic;
composed largely of women of wealth and unusual educational
attainment and concerned chiefly about the right of women to
work as professionals, it initially sought a compromise that would

have excluded labor laws from the purview of the Equal Rights Amendment (ERA) it proposed. But these attempts proved futile, and the NWP ultimately took the position that laws only for women did more harm than good. The party argued variously that all labor laws should apply to both sexes or that labor laws were flat-out undesirable, the latter view reflecting the conservative political philosophy of many NWP members who opposed government interference in private enterprise. In 1928 the party endorsed the Republican Hoover-Curtis presidential ticket, primarily because Charles Curtis had been a sponsor of the ERA but also because many NWP officers were Republicans. (Neither presidential candidate had announced in favor of the ERA, although the Democratic candidate, Al Smith, was certainly against it, being an ardent enthusiast of protective labor laws.)[17]

Throughout the 1920s and 1930s, the NWP persuaded several women's organizations to support the ERA and to separate themselves from the advocates of protective legislation. By the 1940s, the National Federation of Business and Professional Women's Clubs (BPW), the General Federation of Women's Clubs, the National Association of Women Lawyers, the National Education Association, and various other smaller professional women's organizations had endorsed the Equal Rights Amendment and agreed to work with the NWP in pursuit of that goal.

But the NWP insisted on retaining leadership in the battle. Paul was not interested in a mass-based group; rather, she sought to create a Washington-based "elite vanguard," single-mindedly devoted to the pursuit of the ERA and willing to follow her directions. The membership of the NWP endorsed her design. Almost all had participated in the suffrage battle, and the group made little attempt to recruit new members. By 1945 party membership—which, it claimed, had numbered ten thousand in the 1920s—had fallen to four thousand, even by its own highly inflated figures; only some six hundred paid annual dues. The party's intense devotion to its single cause did indeed make it influential out of proportion to its numbers.[18]

Meanwhile, the NWP and the Women's Bureau coalition had become archenemies. The Women's Bureau coalition continued to cooperate, if uneasily, with other pro-ERA organizations, like the BPW and the General Federation of Women's Clubs, on specific projects such as equal pay legislation; but after World War II the fight for the ERA constituted almost the entire program of the National Woman's party, and its defeat the major consolidated effort of the Women's Bureau coalition.

A third group of political women held itself somewhat aloof from this battle, pursuing a different goal. This contingent had appeared after the achievement of suffrage in 1920—in fact, in response to it. These women had become active in the national political parties' governing bodies, the Democratic National Committee (DNC) and the Republican National Committee (RNC), and they were committed to seeing that women quickly attained their share of power within these political structures. Moreover, they wanted women appointed to government positions because they believed both that women appointees would improve government and that appointments of women would potentially benefit all women. They were supported by women in state party organizations and by female journalists, who viewed the number of women political appointees as an index of an administration's interest in women's advancement. In the 1930s the political party women were indistinguishable from the Women's Bureau coalition, and both they and the ERA proponents opposed the discriminatory features of the National Recovery Administration codes and discrimination against women workers during the Great Depression.[19] By the 1940s, however, political party women had gone one of two routes: either they openly espoused the Equal Rights Amendment, reflecting their own constituency of middle-class professional women, or else they simply tried to minimize potential fallout from the conflict by giving their party enough female appointments to counteract accusations of indifference to women's issues.

If class made a difference in support for the ERA, race apparently did not. Black women's organizations split over the amendment along the same lines white women's associations did. The National Association of Colored Women, under the influence of Mary Church Terrell, a wealthy militant suffragist, endorsed the ERA, but the National Council of Negro Women, founded by Mary McLeod Bethune in 1935, voiced concern for protective labor legislation and in 1944 went on record opposing the amendment. One member warned against the council's being led astray by the promise of equal rights: "We are being rocked to sleep by a trick phrase—one dear to us as to other under-privileged groups, and therefore calculated to dull our ability for discriminating between what is good and what appears to be good."[20]

Representatives from black women's organizations often took part in meetings arranged by the Women's Bureau coalition and were more visible fighting the amendment than favoring it. Many factors were at work here. The Women's Bureau coalition was more hospitable to black women than was the National Woman's party, which purposively narrowed its membership and its goals. The Women's Bureau coalition identified black women, as it did working women, as a special group requiring its assistance in the fight for economic opportunities. On some occasions, the white, middle-class women's organizations making up the Women's Bureau coalition even undertook to combat racism as a separate endeavor. Thus, black women felt more empathy from these white women. The NWP, in contrast, had no interest in civil rights for blacks, except when it could insist that women be included, for the sake of equity, in governmental measures aimed at racial discrimination. Further, the NWP, which accepted ERA proponents of all persuasions, had a wide tolerance for racists, and Paul herself frequently expressed racist sentiments. When convenient, the NWP used racist arguments to persuade Southerners to favor the ERA—that white women should not be denied rights accorded to black men. Such a ploy would hardly make the organization appealing to black women.[21]

But these considerations had a secondary role in determining black women's response to this struggle. Their position was clear: equal rights for women was a secondary issue; every black women's group considered the fight against racism its primary battle, more so since World War II, which had offered unprecedented opportunities for black women and men, as for white women. Black women were able to give up domestic jobs for higher-paying factory positions, and the number of black workers in government service more than tripled. War jobs encouraged blacks to move from rural areas in the South to Northern cities, and although the new mix of population often elicited antagonism, the economic benefits were significant. The clashes brought the endemic problem of racism once again to the foreground, however, as did the treatment of black men in the armed services. Blacks disproportionately joined the military, and discrimination there seemed scorchingly hypocritical in view of the fact that American troops were fighting German racial supremacists. In 1942, James Farmer founded the Congress for Racial Equality; the National Association for the Advancement of Colored People increased its membership ninefold during the war.[22]

The fight for civil rights for blacks and the struggle on behalf of women remained separate, however. Little overlap existed in the personnel engaged in these efforts, although both drew on the same liberal ideology. ERA supporters saw opportunities whenever the government appeared to move toward helping blacks, and both the Women's Bureau coalition and the National Woman's party found useful models for federal action in black activist strategies. But virtually everyone engaged in these efforts in the postwar period saw crucial distinctions between discrimination based on sex and that based on race.

All women activists shared the view that discrimination against women based on crude ideas of masculine superiority had to be eliminated, but the split between the ERA advocates and the Women's Bureau coalition itself reflected the general ambivalence toward women's roles. Both groups were trapped by the apparent verity that only women could care adequately for children. The Women's Bureau coalition tried to resolve the conflict between independence for women and motherhood; the NWP did not address it. The intensity of the disagreement between them came less from practical considerations than from the difference in the way each group handled this issue.

Although both sought to improve the way that women were treated in the public arena, the people associated with the Women's Bureau argued that women's special function in the world—to nurture families and society—ultimately took precedence over the need for individual opportunity. In their view, the American legal tradition rightly acknowledged the unique role of women by differentiation in the law. Ideally, this group believed, no married woman with small children would work.

Rose Schneiderman of the National Women's Trade Union League had remarked in 1908 that women who wanted to work under the same conditions as men "might be putting their own brothers or sweethearts, or husbands out of a job."[23] In establishing the Women's Bureau in 1920, Secretary of Labor William Wilson stated: "All will agree that women in industry would not exist in an ideal scheme."[24] Although necessity sometimes forced women into industrial occupations, the Women's Bureau coalition judged such work to be inappropriate for women, and the state within its rights to limit female activity in this kind of employment.

Inside these boundaries, however, the Women's Bureau coalition sought to expand opportunities for women and to eradicate many forms of outright economic and legal discrimination. They advocated entrance into the professions on an equal basis with men and asserted that the state had an obligation to guarantee the right of women to be rewarded according to their merits. (They did not, however, concern themselves with the problems of women professionals, whom they believed could fend for themselves.)

The National Woman's party, conversely, believed that every public activity befitting men was acceptable for women and that, indeed, it was desirable for all women to have careers. The party did not view woman as frail, in need of special protection, and largely passed over the fact the most women worked in low-paying jobs and had neither the resources nor the education to become professionals. Since many in the NWP's leadership were conservatives who opposed statutory interference in private enterprise, they further contended that the ERA rendered any additional legislation for women unnecessary. Like the Women's Bureau coalition, the NWP considered childrearing a woman's task, but it did not address the problem of how a woman could reconcile motherhood and professional responsibilities. Many party members had simply chosen not to marry; others ran households with the assistance of paid help.[25]

The internal contradictions within each group's philosophy, created by the intractable problem of childcare responsibility, undermined the possibility that either could succeed in gaining its objectives, even if the social setting were receptive, which it was not. The Women's Bureau coalition sought equal wages for women workers and access to higher-paying jobs, but at the same time it claimed a need for special protection for those workers. Employers quickly agreed that women workers needed special consideration, but they used that rationale to discriminate against them in wages and responsibility. For its part, the NWP asserted without convincing evidence that the ERA would eliminate the need for further legislation to give women equality of pay and job opportunity. The NWP took no account of extralegal causes of discrimination. So long as social norms decreed that women held the chief responsibility for childrearing and homemaking—a point the NWP did not contest—employers could justify differential treatment on the basis that a woman's commitment to work was limited as a man's was not. Thus, each plan of action addressed only a portion rather than the whole of the complex problem of women's status.[26]

In the postwar period the argument over women's roles played itself out in Congress as well. The National Woman's party, advocating the Equal Rights Amendment, took the offensive, while the Women's Bureau coalition played defense.

## THE EQUAL RIGHTS AMENDMENT ASCENDANT, 1946

The battle over the Equal Rights Amendment dominated the politics of women's rights and opportunities in postwar Washington. Interested players either took sides in favor or against or else they ducked by supporting ostensibly neutral alternative measures that were in fact thinly disguised attempts to scuttle the amendment. But one way or the other, the ERA held center stage. For both adherents and opponents, a bold question awaited decision, especially in the aftermath of women's wartime contribution: were women now to be viewed as autonomous individuals, or did they remain tied in a special way to the family, essentially dependent on the protection of both husband and state?

Shortly before the war, the ERA had made some significant progress. In July 1937, the National Federation of Business and Professional Women's Clubs, a prestigious organization of politi-

cally active women numbering sixty-five thousand, established
the ERA as a legislative priority. The following year, the Senate
Judiciary Committee reported it, although without recommendation, to the floor of the Senate, the first time the amendment
had reached the floor of either house since its introduction in
1923. It was quickly recommitted.[27]

In May 1942 the Senate Judiciary Committee, under the leadership of chairman James Hughes (D-Del.), voted nine to three
to report the amendment favorably, and in 1943 the ERA was
the first resolution introduced in the House, cosponsored by
forty-two members. The Senate Judiciary Committee again approved it, twelve to four, in May 1943, with a request for early
and favorable action. The original amendment considered in
1923 had read: "Men and women shall have equal rights
throughout the United States and in every place subject to its
jurisdiction"; in order to bring the language in line with the
Nineteenth Amendment (granting women the right to suffrage),
the Judiciary Committee adopted alternative wording provided
by Alice Paul. The new proposed amendment ran: "Equality of
rights under the law shall not be denied or abridged by the
United States, or by any State, on account of sex." The House
Judiciary Committee, after heavy lobbying by Catholic organizations committed to women's traditional roles, voted fifteen to
eleven against reporting the ERA to the House, but proponents
of the measure were increasingly hopeful that it would carry on a
wave of wartime enthusiasm.[28]

The amendment's advocates exploited the wartime esteem
for the competent woman and stepped up their lobbying efforts. Alice Paul revamped the organization of the National
Woman's party and enlisted such luminaries as Mary Woolley,
former president of Mount Holyoke College, the artist Georgia
O'Keeffe, and the birth control reformer Margaret Sanger to
stand up for the ERA. Other notable women also responded to
Paul's entreaties: Pearl Buck, Helen Hayes, Katharine Hep-
burn, Judge Sarah Hughes, Margaret Mead, and Congresswomen Margaret Chase Smith and Clare Boothe Luce.[29]

The NWP kept itself a small, elite vanguard, but to benefit
from the power of numbers it created an umbrella organization,
the Women's Joint Legislative Committee (WJLC). A coalition of

all the organizations that endorsed the ERA, the combined membership of the WJLC totaled between five and six million members, a formidable constituency. The NWP orchestrated an intense lobbying campaign in Congress and within the political parties, dominating the movement for the ERA—sometimes to the annoyance of the other organizations involved. But if the NWP insisted on the authority, it also shouldered most of the administrative and financial burden.

The Women's Bureau led the counterattack. The ERA angered bureau director Mary Anderson, who had headed the bureau since its founding. Anderson had begun her working life in 1889, at age sixteen, as a stitcher in a shoe factory. By 1900 she had been elected president of her local, and in 1911 she gave up her factory job to become a full-time organizer.[30] Devoted to laws protecting women workers, she viewed the ERA as an absurd theoretical pronouncement, unrelated to the realities of women's lives and natures. The bureau had been created to help women function as wives and mothers even if their economic circumstances drove them into the workforce; Anderson saw the defeat of the ERA as her first responsibility.

A legal treatise drawn up at her request by the solicitor of the Department of Labor, Douglas B. Maggs, became the department's fundamental position paper on the subject. It warned of injury to women as wives and mothers should the ERA be added to the Constitution. Ratification of the ERA, Maggs admonished, would unsettle the law for years. The extensive litigation would result, he was sure, in "highly undesirable" changes in the Social Security system; equal induction into the armed services; changes in workmen's compensation laws; upheaval in laws requiring husbands to support their families; and repeal of "reasonable protective legislation" with "consequent social loss." Moreover, Maggs argued, the attempt to extend such laws to men would render the statutes subject to constitutional attack. He concluded his paper by asserting that a constitutional amendment that would nullify statutory differences "having a reasonable and rational factual basis" would lead to "social and legal consequences which even the proponents of the proposal would deplore if they had the candor to recognize them." Maggs added in a footnote: "Fanatical adherence to a doctrinaire principle or dogma such as the theoretical equality of rights of men and women is foreign to the spirit of Anglo-American legislation and jurisprudence. If the proposal is ratified it should be regarded as an unwholesome original development in the law."[31] His characterization of the amendment's advocates as "fanatical" indicated accurately that the bureau did not foresee the possibility of compromise. Indeed, the two visions were irreconcilable.

When Frieda Miller assumed leadership of the Women's Bureau after Anderson's retirement in 1944, she pledged to continue the fight "with all the resources" at her command.[32] Miller had begun her career in public service in 1929 under Governor Franklin D. Roosevelt, as head of New York State's Women in Industry Service. Before joining the government, Miller had worked in organizations concerned with the protection of working women, particularly the Women's Trade Union League. Her antipathy to the Equal Rights Amendment was therefore of long standing. Out in front on the issue, she called the amendment "radical, dangerous and irresponsible," its potential effects "calamitous."[33]

Both she and other ERA opponents recognized, however, that they stood on vulnerable ground with only a negative campaign. Acknowledging that some laws did discriminate against women and that some labor statutes had outlived their utility, the bureau began to examine state codes. Its mission was to find laws that needed to be eliminated and to identify those that continued to protect women but that would be at risk under the ERA. The bureau uncovered several categories of laws it defined as harmful to women; many limited the right of married women to own and convey property, to make contracts, to establish domicile, to control bequests, and to exercise parental authority. The bureau recommended that state legislatures repeal these statutes.[34]

The National Woman's party contended that elimination of laws one by one would take too long. It also attacked as a limitation on women's freedom such regulations as laws restricting work hours for women. Good labor laws should be extended to both sexes, the NWP insisted, bad ones simply expunged. In response to the bureau assertion that the Fourteenth Amendment prohibited "unreasonable" laws, the NWP pointed out correctly that the Supreme Court had never interpreted the Fourteenth Amendment to prohibit discrimination against women.[35]

The momentum seemed to be with the National Woman's party and its wealthy, influential, single-minded members. In 1944 the Republican National Convention included a plank supporting the ERA, as it had in 1940. Indeed, from its inception enthusiasm for the amendment had been stronger among Republicans, and the argument that protective labor legislation would be affected won less sympathy from probusiness Republicans than from liberal Democrats. In 1940 representatives of the League of Women Voters, who had lobbied against the proposal in the platform committee, had dubbed its inclusion "the shock of the century," and a reporter for the *New York Times* had called the argument "the most extensive and portentous feminine controversy in the history of the country."[36] Now in 1944, however, the fight over the Democratic platform resulted in victory for ERA advocates as well. The Democrats, too, saw women earning a place for themselves as independent individuals and needed to encourage that position—at least for the duration of the war. Eleanor Roosevelt failed to speak against the amendment as she had in 1940, citing the confusion of the war and the uncertainties of the peace. It was difficult to argue in favor of labor legislation to limit women's hours when men were dying on foreign battlefields. The Democrats also felt the pressure of the Republican pronouncement. Were Democrats less committed to equality for women? The general disorganization of the opposition allowed ERA supporters, among them Perle Mesta and Emma Guffey Miller, a Democratic committeewoman from Pennsylvania and the sister of Senator Joseph Guffey, successfully to capitalize on women's war efforts. The Democratic plank finally read: "We recommend to the Congress the submission of a constitutional amendment on equal rights for women."[37]

## THE NATIONAL COMMITTEE TO DEFEAT THE UNEQUAL RIGHTS AMENDMENT

Alarmed by the successes of ERA advocates, especially the platform victories, and fearing a Senate vote, the Women's Bureau coalition called a meeting in September 1944 "to organize a National Directing Committee to oppose the Equal Rights Amendment." Twenty-seven groups decided to coalesce under the rubric of the "National Committee to Defeat the UnEqual Rights Amendment" (NCDURA). The membership consisted principally of labor organizations and the national women's organizations making up the Women's Bureau coalition. NCDURA decided that in addition to lobbying against the ERA, it would set up local branches in each state to combat the ERA directly and to undermine its support by eliminating discriminatory state laws. Because even members of this committee could not agree on which laws genuinely discriminated against women, that determination was left up to the state organizations.[38] By June 1945 fifteen state committees had been formed, and the group, which had initially planned to operate for only six months, decided to continue functioning "until the end of the emergency." NCDURA's roster was a veritable roll call of liberal organizations, now comprising forty-three national organizations, including the American Civil Liberties Union.[39]

Although advocacy of individual rights had become identified, since the New Deal, with the liberal wing of the Democratic party, support for the Equal Rights Amendment in Congress came mostly from Republicans and conservative Democrats from the South and the Southwest. On its face, the ERA was appealing—after all, it mandated equal treatment under law for half the population. Opposition to it, rather than support of it, required explanation, especially now that both parties had endorsed it. In their own defense, opponents cited the threat to protective labor laws; but those legislators who were indifferent to the labor law question had little reason to contest their party's official position. So probusiness Republicans and antilabor Southern Democrats found themselves on the same side of the issue. Advocacy of the Equal Rights Amendment served, too, as a defense against the accusation that the South opposed civil rights: some Southern legislators held that equality for white women ought to come before, or at the very least with, equality for black men and women.[40] Some liberals accepted the argument that women deserved constitutional equality and that government regulation of the workplace could extend to both men and women workers. The array of arguments concerning the ERA resulted in peculiar alliances on the issue: both the vigorously liberal Claude Pepper, a Democratic senator from Florida, and the ultraconservative Howard W. Smith, a Democratic representative from Virginia, favored the amendment. But in general, conservatives, finding the arguments in favor of free enterprise and individual opportunity especially appealing, tended to favor the amendment, whereas liberals, who espoused the idea that government had a positive responsibility to protect women and the family through regulation, were more likely to oppose the ERA.

For the moment, ERA advocates continued to carry the day. Citing the party platform pledges, the House Judiciary Committee in July 1945 reported the amendment favorably (by a vote of fifteen to seven) for the first time since its introduction twenty-one years before.[41] The NWP's revelation of support from Cardinal Dennis Dougherty "caused a minor sensation" in the Senate subcommittee hearing, and, primed by vigilant lobbying on the part of NWP workers, it voted in favor of the ERA four to one.[42]

In an effort to quell the tide of support, Frances Perkins urged President Truman to meet with the opponents of the ERA; he agreed to see them in September. In 1944 then Senator Truman had written to Emma Guffey Miller: "I am in sympathy with [the] fight for the Equal Rights Amendment because I think it will improve the standard of living." Despite Miller's entreaties, however, Truman had not reiterated his favorable statement.[43] Now confronted with a contingent of well-known liberal women, Truman was hardly willing to disavow his support for protective labor legislation. Administration aides trying to craft a position for the president felt besieged. "This is a tough baby," presidential aide William Hassett observed to David Niles, an administrative assistant. Niles concurred: "This Equal Rights thing is dynamite which ever way you place it." Matthew Connelly, the president's secretary, finally signed the letter to NCDURA chair Dorothy McAllister. The president, he wrote, "plans to give some thought to the Equal Rights Amendment in the near future and is grateful for the careful analysis you have made of this problem." Aware that the issue was both complex and charged, President Truman issued no further public statements for or against the Equal Rights Amendment.[44]

The Senate Judiciary Committee, voting eleven to four, reported the ERA favorably on January 21, 1946. The measure now stood ready for a vote in both houses of Congress. Supporters and opponents lobbied vigorously. Under the letterhead of the Industrial League for Equality (an NWP creation designed to suggest labor support for the amendment), Congress members received a copy of a 1913 editorial by American Federation of Labor president Samuel Gompers asserting that the "industrial problems of women are not isolated, but inextricably associated with those of men." An excerpt from the Supreme Court's 1941 decision upholding the Fair Labor Standards Act noted that hours and wage laws could now safely be applied to both men and women.[45] The other side sent a letter opposing the amendment, signed by Eleanor Roosevelt, Frances Perkins, Carrie Chapman Catt (the leader of the National American Women Suffrage Association when the suffrage amendment was ratified), and several other notable American women.[46]

When the roll was called in the Senate on July 19, 1946, the amendment won a majority—thirty-eight to thirty-five—but not the two-thirds majority needed for victory. With twenty-three of the favorable votes Republican, plus two absentee Republicans recorded in favor, the total was one shy of two-thirds of the thirty-nine Republican senators. Democrats made up fifteen of the pro votes, with two absent Democrats indicating their approval as well, accounting for less than a third of the fifty-six Senate Democrats. Only four of the assenting Democrats were from states outside the South or Southwest.[47]

Crushed by the loss, the NWP complained that the vote had come without advance notice, when several pro-ERA senators were away from Washington. But opponent Senator Carl Hayden (D-Ariz.) insisted that many ERA supporters had voted in favor only because they knew the measure would fail.[48] The conflict had taken a toll, as later events showed: it was long before support gained such strength again. Several senators had promised that they would not vote in favor of the amendment in the future, NCDURA informed its membership, now that they knew more about its implications.[49] The *New York*

*Times* expressed its pleasure in an editorial: "Motherhood cannot be amended, and we are glad the Senate didn't try."[50] The measure never came to a vote in the House.

The *Times* rightly marked motherhood as the central issue. The failure of the ERA hinged not on the chance absence of its supporters but on the unwillingness of the nation as a whole to affirm the independent equality of women at a moment when the restoration of "normal" family life constituted a preeminent objective. Still reeling from wartime and conversion upheaval, with industry unsettled by strikes and families fighting inflation, equal treatment for women in the public sphere seemed beside the point. Women were needed at home.

But the impulse that had led to the ERA vote could not be entirely submerged. Both equity and the place women had gained in the workforce supported the call for some response from the federal government. The battle over the ERA went on through the next decade, a metaphor for the largely unacknowledged struggle being waged as women attempted to reconcile their home and public lives. For activist women in Washington, the amendment continued to dominate the political scene, generating alternative legislative proposals, all of which suffered from the difficulty of coming to terms with the changing role of women.

# 2

# "REASONABLE DISTINCTIONS": AN ALTERNATIVE TO THE ERA

In 1945 and 1946, the respect engendered by women's performance during World War II had lent unprecedented energy to the fight for the Equal Rights Amendment. Even after Congress decided not "to amend motherhood," the *New York Herald Tribune,* calling the amendment "a measure of simple justice that is not to be denied,"[1] predicted rightly that the ERA would reappear on the legislative docket. Without missing a beat, the National Woman's party had begun to collect new statements of support from political figures, and in January 1947 John Robsion (R-Ky.) introduced the measure in the House, declaring its passage by Congress to be "at hand."[2] But the political climate had already begun to change in the mere year and a half since the war's end. The impulse toward women's equality, which had never really held the field, continued to dissipate, and the backlash, with its insistent message that women stay home, took stronger hold. If the ERA was out of step with that prescription, alternative proposals appeared no more effective at resolving the tension between women's two roles.

As part of the conservative reaction, women's magazines launched an attack on feminist ideas, following the lead of a 1947 book, *Modern Woman: The Lost Sex.* Its authors, Ferdinand Lundberg and Marynia Farnham, described feminism as a "deep illness," characterized by a hatred of men and a taste for lechery. Women's quest for education, employment, and political power represented, they asserted, an attempt at symbolic castration. Rather than pursue such misbegotten goals, the healthy woman would choose to create a rewarding life for herself based on mothering and dependency, in tune with her biological and psychological destiny. Although sociologists offered thoughtful counterarguments, these usually appeared in inaccessible scholarly journals. In any case, Lundberg and Farnham had struck the note of the times: women belonged at home.[3]

After fifteen years of depression and war, American women *and* men sought a haven in the home—stability, security, and the warmth of family in the place of uncertainty, fear, and loneliness. No one had to force women into marriage and motherhood.[4] The marriage rate, 84.5 per thousand women in 1945, shot up to 120.7 in 1946 and 106.8 in 1947; fluctuating between 78 and 98 per thousand for the next ten years, it fell off again only in 1958.[5]

Yet with only the briefest dip in the immediate postwar period, the number of women employed continued to rise. Many women did not want to, or could not, leave the labor force to be full-time wives and mothers. They voted with their feet in the postwar period and throughout the 1950s, taking jobs in the face of public disapproval but in the solid company of their peers. Between 1951 and 1963, married women with husbands present and children between the ages of six and seventeen increased their labor force participation rate from 30.3 percent to 41.5 percent. They worked to buy food and pay the rent in the face of a staggering inflation rate, but they also sought an education for their children and a higher standard of living for the entire family.[6]

Women also went back to school. Although the GI bill offered educational opportunities almost exclusively to men, and so the proportion of women in schools declined *compared to men* in several years, women made substantial gains. The number of women Ph.D.'s, though small, doubled between 1948 and 1960, and the number of women who held master's degrees (thirteen thousand in 1948) increased by 80 percent in the same period. More than 103,000 women earned bachelor's degrees in 1950; by 1959 the number had risen to over 127,000.[7]

Under penalty of being labeled neurotic (à la Lundberg and Farnham), women workers declined to offer a feminist defense of their right to work. Their families, they insisted, needed the money they earned. They did not challenge male prerogatives in the prestigious professions, nor did they overtly demand a redefinition of sex roles within the home. Although many states gave husbands control of the earnings women brought home and some barred women from certain occupations, working women in general took little notice of legislation concerning their right to jobs, to equal pay with men, or to constitutional protection against discrimination.[8] Women leaders were therefore hard pressed to argue that such legislation demanded immediate attention.

Advocates of civil rights for black Americans had no such problem. Faced with public demonstrations, retaliatory violence, and pressure from notable Americans, President Truman had taken a number of steps to improve the lot of black Americans. In December 1946 he had created a presidential committee on civil rights, which issued a report the following year; in 1948 he banned discrimination based on race in federal employment, and barred segregation in the armed services. In December 1951 the newly formed Committee on Government Contract Compliance began to monitor federal contractors for discrimination. The National Woman's party demanded that women be included in Truman's executive orders, but the request was ignored. None of the largely white women's organizations interested in the Equal Rights Amendment or other measures had tried to forge an alliance with civil rights groups; the NWP did not usually even support measures seeking to eliminate racial discrimination. Worse, it responded in anger to the notion that blacks would have rights denied to women. Still, the federal measures undertaken on behalf of blacks served as models in the fight to eradicate similar problems for women. Only months after Truman named his presidential committee on civil rights some women leaders made much the same proposal for women, as a way to meet the threat of the ERA.

## THE "STATUS BILL"

Aware of the activity of the National Woman's party and anxious about the continuing strength of the constitutional amendment, ERA opponents in 1947 decided to follow Eleanor Roosevelt's advice to construct a positive alternative piece of legislation, one that would eliminate "unfair" discrimination in the law without the supposedly deleterious effects of the ERA. The proposed joint resolution became known as the "Status Bill" or the Taft-Wadsworth bill (after its sponsors Senator Robert A. Taft [R-Ohio] and Representative James W. Wadsworth [R-N.Y.]).[9] Seeking a less negative image, the National Committee to Defeat the UnEqual Rights Amendment, which had drafted the bill, changed its name to the National Committee on the Status of Women (NCSW).[10]

The members of the NCSW chose to offer an alternative "joint resolution" rather than a constitutional amendment for several strategic reasons. First, they believed that because a resolution required only a simple majority in each house of Congress, it would be easier to obtain than a constitutional amendment, which required a two-thirds majority in Congress and then approval by three-quarters of the state legislatures. Second, they feared that any amendment they offered might itself be amended to resemble the ERA more closely than they would wish. Finally, they felt that any constitutional amendment concerning women would invite litigation, and the outcome of a court fight could jeopardize the legislation they wished to safeguard.[11]

The Status Bill had two main components. The first was an unusual statement of "policy" for the United States, one that sought to acknowledge the desire both to enhance women's autonomy and to reaffirm their connection to the family. Apparently presuming that the two aims were reconcilable, the Status Bill declared that "in law and its administration no distinctions on the basis of sex shall be made except such as are reasonably justified by differences in physical structure, biological, or social function." The proponents of this bill noted approvingly that, although such a section "prohibited" sex discrimination, it permitted differentiation on "reasonable" grounds, such as those underlying protective labor legislation only for women and military service only for men, "based on rational and commonly accepted assumptions and beliefs."[12]

The other key section seemed more unambiguously aimed at change. It created a Commission on the Legal Status of Women, composed of seven members appointed by the president, to "make a full and complete study . . . of the economic, civil, social and political status of women, and the nature and extent of dis-

criminations based on sex throughout the United States, its Terri-
tories, and Possessions." The bill also required federal agencies
to comply with the policy statement and urged that states take
similar actions.[13]

According to its drafters, the bill constituted a compromise
with the ERA. They knew that the National Woman's party
would not accept it: "Frankly [the bill] is not framed to win the
support of individuals who would seem to be satisfied with nothing less than a declaration, in fundamental law, that women,
however different from men in their physical structure, biological or social function, must be accorded, by governments, identical treatment with men." But they argued that "all who earnestly
desire to remove outmoded sex discriminations in law can at long
last unite" behind their "practicable working program," whether
or not they supported the ERA.[14]

With its policy statement, however, the bill could not serve as a
compromise. If the law could take note of social function as well
as physical structure and biological characteristics, virtually any
discrimination could be justified. Even committed members of
the Women's Bureau coalition took exception. The executive
secretary of the New York Women's Trade Union League wrote
to its national office, which supported the bill: "Please tell me,
what is a social function of women as distinguished from a social
function of men? If you are implying that it is the social function
of women to rear the children . . . , keep the home fires burning
and to be supported by their husbands, then I say to you that you
have opened wide and fastened back with iron bars the door to
eliminating by law all married women from employment. . . . A
continuation of this reasoning takes us into the question of equal
pay."[15] Several members of the Labor Advisory Council of the
Women's Bureau also felt uneasy about the phrasing. Esther
Peterson of the Amalgamated Clothing Workers and Katherine
Ellickson of the research department of the Congress of Industrial Organizations requested that a preliminary definition of
"reasonable distinctions" be made to guide the presidential commission the bill proposed to establish.[16]

ERA proponents expressed markedly less enthusiasm. The
General Federation of Women's Clubs asserted that enough
data on women existed to make the commission superfluous,

and the National Federation of Business and Professional Women's Clubs characterized the Status Bill as "sniping at the Equal Rights Amendment." The NWP issued a statement labeling the bill "unnecessary and unjustified," opening the "floodgates" to discrimination against women through the policy statement.[17]

Nevertheless, proponents of the Status Bill regarded it as a method "to break the deadlock over the so-called Equal Rights Amendment." Eager for some movement, Eleanor Roosevelt, all seven women members of Congress, the League of Women Voters, and former directors of the women's divisions of both party national committees endorsed it. So did some ERA supporters, such as the *New York Herald Tribune,* which argued that the commission would "inevitably" reach the conclusion that protective labor laws should be extended to men. The Women's Bureau lobbied actively for the bill, although the White House remained silent.[18]

The Status Bill failed as an effort of conciliation. Solidly identified with anti-ERA forces, the paradoxical policy statement engendered enough controversy that Congress could hardly enact it in the interest of accommodation. The ERA had been in both platforms, and both House and Senate judiciary committees were on record in favor of it. Thus, in the spring of 1948, both committees once again reported the amendment favorably and postponed consideration of the Taft-Wadsworth measure. Action to remove the ERA from the parties' platforms also proved unavailing, thanks to the efforts of prominent party women in support of the measure.[19]

The ERA was not an issue during the 1948 campaign. Beset within his party by objections to his civil rights measures and assaulted by Henry Wallace's new Progressive Party for his belligerent stance toward the Soviets, Harry Truman's defeat seemed assured. But much to everyone's surprise, Truman pulled the election out of the grasp of Republican Thomas E. Dewey, and the Democrats regained control of both houses of Congress (although by only twelve votes in the Senate). India Edwards, who, as head of the Women's Division of the Democratic National Committee, had planned the program to get out the women's vote, emphasized inflation, not women's rights. Relatively few women held or ran for public office. In

1949, fewer than 3 percent of the nation's state legislators were women: only one woman sat in the Senate, and eight in the House of Representatives.[20]

The new count revealed, however, that the ERA stood a reasonably good chance of passage in the Senate. In view of the lack of enthusiasm for the Status Bill, ERA opponents looked around for another measure that would provide either a positive alternative, or at least a way to maintain the status quo with respect to protective labor laws. They devised such a safety catch in the Hayden amendment.[21]

## THE HAYDEN AMENDMENT

In 1921, when the National Woman's party first proposed a constitutional amendment guaranteeing equal rights for women, it had considered a proviso to exempt laws that applied to conditions of women's work, hoping to win support from the women's groups who advocated those laws. It was a compromise unacceptable to both sides. The members of the Women's Bureau coalition found it insufficient protection, and the NWP, irritated by the coalition's response, declared that special laws for women ought to be eliminated because they restricted women's right to employment on their own terms. A Wisconsin decision concerning an "equal rights" law passed in that state substantiated this view. That law had included a clause exempting "special protections and privileges" for women, and in 1923 the state attorney general had ruled that the state could continue to forbid women to work as employees of the Wisconsin legislature because that job required "unseasonable" hours of work.[22]

Nevertheless, adversaries of the ERA held to their view that the addition of a section to the ERA expressly exempting protective labor legislation would not prove adequate. In 1944 the solicitor of the Department of Labor had warned that too many kinds of protective laws existed—an amendment could not exempt them all: no matter how carefully such a provision were drafted, some desirable laws might yet be vulnerable to elimination through the ERA. Moreover, the possibility existed that such an amendent to the ERA could be adopted by one house of Congress and then eliminated by the other. Still, in the face of the apparent popularity of the ERA, the National Committee on the Status of Women had decided that it had no choice but to support a safeguarding clause.[23]

The Senate debate on the ERA in the Eighty-first Congress began on January 23, 1950, and continued for three days. Proponents cited platform pledges, favorable committee reports, the support of well-known women's organizations, and the unfairness of discrimination based on sex. Opponents defended protective laws for women, cited labor opposition, and expressed fear of unknown consequences. Senator Estes Kefauver (D-Tenn.), an ERA opponent and introducer of the Status Bill, claimed that the ERA could "eliminate rape as a crime" and lead to joint bathroom facilities. Senator Andrew Schoeppel (R-Kans.) argued on the other side that giving women constitutional equality would help counter Communist propaganda (a salient issue with the intensification of fighting in Korea).[24]

On January 25, near the close of the debate, Carl Hayden (D-Ariz.) offered his amendment. Following instructions from the Women's Bureau, Hayden proposed that a new section be added to the ERA: "The provisions of this article shall not be construed to impair any rights, benefits, or exemptions conferred by law upon persons of the female sex." Hayden offered the following explanation: "In the beginning, God made them different when male and female created He them." He went on in a personal vein, noting that his mother had borne and breastfed him, that his father had built them a home and provided food and clothing on the "wild Apache-infested frontier," and that neither could have played the other's role. In the few minutes remaining for debate, Claude Pepper (D-Fla.) protested that Hayden was "emasculating" the ERA. The senators, however, eagerly took advantage of the opportunity to go on record in favor of both equal rights and special laws for women. They voted for the Hayden rider fifty-one to thirty-one and the ERA sixty-three to nineteen, well over the two-thirds vote required for a constitutional amendment.[25]

The Hayden amendment caught ERA adherents by surprise. Because of the short time between Hayden's motion and the vote, ERA backers Sen. Margaret Chase Smith (R-Me.) and Rep. Katharine St. George (R-N.Y.) had no opportunity to approach their colleagues and explain that they wanted the rider defeated. Thus the ERA went to the House with the Hayden rider attached.[26]

ERA adversaries considered the amendment with the Hayden rider only slightly less objectionable than the unaltered version, but ERA proponents repudiated it completely: in their view, the rider effectively negated the body of the amendment. NWP leader Alice Paul stated flatly, "It is impossible to imagine the Constitution containing two such paragraphs."[27] If given no other choice, they preferred the bill dead.

In the House, the ERA faced not only the threat of the Hayden rider but also the unshakable antipathy of House Judiciary Chairman Emanuel Celler. The liberal New Yorker had become committee chair in 1949, and he had no intention of allowing the ERA to reach the House floor even in its amended form. Katharine St. George had collected enough signatures of representatives to discharge Celler's committee, but fear of the Hayden amendment led her to withdraw her petition.[28]

ERA opponents had succeeded in finding a technique to undercut the ideal of complete legal equality for women. The Hayden amendment proved unbeatable, so long as no outside social or political impetus pressured Congress to choose unequivocally between equal treatment for women or a legally defined special family responsibility. If forced to vote on the measure, members of Congress could now have it both ways: equality *and* special privileges for women. Moreover, with the Hayden rider, the ERA proved unacceptable to its initial backers, making it unlikely to pass—the outcome the anti-ERA forces desired most. If it were to pass, the rider offered a safeguard for the legislation they deemed essential to the welfare of women workers.

ERA advocates were stymied. Eleanor Roosevelt, now at the United Nations and sensitive to the international implications of constitutional equality for women, backpedaled on her longstanding objection to the amendment, but it made no difference. President Truman stayed out of the crossfire. With no genuine support for an amended ERA, and with no grassroots enthusiasm for a radical change in women's legal status, stalemate was a foregone conclusion. The NWP therefore looked to the 1952 election, hoping for a Republican presidential victory to move the amendment forward.[29]

## EISENHOWER: FOR . . . BUT NOT QUITE

The NWP and other ERA supporters were optimistic after the 1952 Republican victory because they believed that Republicans would be less sensitive to pressure from women labor activists. Indeed, retention of the antilabor Taft-Hartley Act had been a campaign issue, with the Republicans coming out in favor of keeping it. In addition, Republicans had a longer history of support for the ERA, as the first party to introduce it in Congress in 1923 and the first, in 1940, to include support for the amendment in its platform.

But President Eisenhower held very conservative social views, and the Eisenhower period was profoundly one of social consolidation. Eisenhower eschewed a deliberately conceived and openly executed program aimed at social reform. In 1954 the Supreme Court decreed, in *Brown* v. *Board of Education,* that states could no longer segregate children by race in the public schools. Rather than welcoming this overdue gesture in support of racial equality, Eisenhower was angered by the decision and its intentional initiation of such broad social change by federal action. Confronted with overt resistance to the federal system on the part of some Southern states, Eisenhower took action against the segregationists only when national integrity appeared genuinely threatened.[30]

Eisenhower disliked overt social manipulation by the federal government, but measures passed by Congress—as federal aid for education and home and highway construction—wrought extraordinary alterations in the country's landscape and demographics. Government support of industry included a massive influx of federal dollars, all in the name of defense, into the chemical, aerospace, electronics, and computer industries, creating thousands more white-collar jobs for women to fill. The money built the economy. Between 1945 and 1960 the GNP increased more than twofold, and per capita income rose 35 percent. By 1960 nine million families had become new homeowners. More than ever before, Americans were suburban white-collar workers, well educated and well off.[31]

Although Eisenhower insisted that government should be restrained, he did give small signs of promise to ERA supporters. For one, he replaced the Democratic Women's Bureau director, Frieda Miller, with a Republican state official, Alice Leopold. Miller had been only the second director in the bureau's thirty-year history, and by tradition bureau directors did not change with a change in administration. Mary Anderson, appointed by the Democratic president Woodrow Wilson, had stayed through three Republican administrations. The Women's Bureau had long been the exclusive terrain of the liberal reformers and labor women who had lobbied for its creation, and Miller and her colleagues were not only hurt when she was replaced but also alarmed. Eisenhower's action suggested that the bureau would become less closely tied to its constituents and, therefore, presumably less a champion of women's welfare and more a tool of the administration.

Mary Anderson had been a trade unionist; Miller had worked with the National Consumers League before accepting an appointment as Industrial Commissioner in the New York State government (a post Frances Perkins had filled before her). Each represented a wing of the Women's Bureau coalition, devoted to the welfare of working-class women.

Leopold's career differed sharply. A businesswoman, she had started out as personnel director for a department store and then had owned a children's toy company. Active in Republican politics, she had won a seat in the Connecticut state legislature and gone on to become Connecticut's secretary of state in 1950. She was not unsympathetic to women's labor issues and had in fact authored Connecticut's equal pay law; she had also championed protective labor legislation. But she shifted the perspective of the Women's Bureau. For the first time, the bureau devoted part of its resources to the examination of issues concerning professional women. And as the Women's Bureau coalition feared, Leopold took the bureau out of the ERA fight.[32]

Alice Paul thought that Leopold herself supported the amendment but that she could not make an unambiguous statement in favor of the ERA because of opposition from the Women's Bureau staff. Leopold never did champion the measure, but she did consistently refuse to take any action to oppose the bill, and by stating on several occasions to ERA opponents and supporters, as well as to members of Congress, that the bureau no longer took a position against the ERA, she left a gaping hole in the leadership against the measure.[33]

To the disappointment of ERA sponsors, however, her position made little difference with respect to the fate of the measure. The Hayden amendment had become an effective weapon in the anti-ERA arsenal, and with little pressure on Congress outside of the small group of Washington lobbyists the ERA had no real chance. The National Committee on the Status of Women, whose agenda had narrowed to the Status Bill, disbanded when the Hayden rider proved more successful in scuttling the ERA.

ERA adversaries easily maintained the upper hand, even after the Republicans had gained control of both houses of Congress in 1953. In May the Senate Judiciary Committee reported the bill favorably, and by July 64 senators had pledged to vote for the amendment on the floor, as had 255 members of the House. But Carl Hayden offered his proviso on the Senate floor when the measure came up in mid-July, and once again the Senate approved both Hayden's clause (by a vote of 58 to 25) and the ERA (73 to 11).[34]

As before, the amended ERA created not a measure tolerable to both sides of the women's political community but one acceptable to neither. When NWP sleuths determined that the House would endorse the Senate "compromise," they directed their supporters to kill the hybrid creation. Janus-faced, the ERA with the Hayden amendment incorporated two contradictory views of women—equal but not equal. So long as the nation remained divided, the Congress would not choose.

Likewise, administration signals on this issue remained ambiguous throughout the decade. The Department of Labor, under the direction of James P. Mitchell, had held steady in its opposition to the ERA, but the White House had begun to give other indications. In a 1954 meeting with Katharine St. George Eisenhower had, according to her report, offered his private support. (The fall elections, however, put the Democrats back in control in both houses, vitiating Eisenhower's backing, even such as it was.) National Woman's party members began to receive invitations to Women's Bureau meetings, and in December 1955 Gerald D. Morgan, special counsel to the president, had written to Nina Price of the NWP that, because it had been included in the party platform, the ERA would continue to be part of the Republican program and that Eisenhower was "encouraged by the number of sponsors of the amendment in the House and Senate."[35] (Secretary Mitchell countered, when he received a copy of Morgan's letter, that the platform did not commit the administration to a particular bill.) Notes of a pre–press conference White House briefing in April 1956 suggest that the White House staff did not itself truly understand the basis for the dispute. A memorandum remarked: "Equal Rights for women came up, but nobody seemed to know exactly what was meant."[36]

In 1956 the ERA stayed in both party platforms, and a high-placed Eisenhower campaign official succeeded in arranging what all regarded as a coup for ERA supporters. Dorothy Houghton, cochairman of the Citizens for Eisenhower campaign, pledged that she would try to get the president to make a statement of support for the amendment. To the satisfaction of ERA enthusiasts, in an address given to a packed house at Madison Square Garden in New York City on October 25, a mere twelve days before the election, Eisenhower uttered these words: "And we shall—with intelligence and sympathetic understanding—do all in our power to make more secure, for all citizens, their civil rights. And, as a special item of this matter, we shall seek, as we promised in our Platform, to assure women everywhere in our land equality of rights."[37] Although the candidate had not in fact promised with this pledge support for any specific measure, it gained him much affection from Republican women. Eisenhower won a personal landslide (which probably did not owe much to this particular statement), but the Democrats retained their control of both houses of Congress.

Neither his campaign promise nor his 1957 budget message, which also referred to equal rights for women, made a difference in the amendment's fate—nor could it have. Moreover, Eisenhower's sincerity in championing the women's cause, even if in fact he favored the ERA, seemed questionable in light of his other behavior. The minutes of a February 1957 meeting of the secretary of labor's policy committee noted that the secretary inferred a lack of whole-hearted commitment to the ERA on the president's part: "Pres. for—but not quite." In view of his own reservations and the president's recent messages, his own posture, he decided, would be cautious: "Secretary will fudge."[38] The White House indeed responded to letters assuring the inquirers of the president's continuing interest in the subject of equal rights for women, but without specifically mentioning the Equal Rights Amendment.[39] Eisenhower further unsettled ERA advocates by his response to reporter May Craig at an August press conference. When the well-known correspondent for the Portland, Maine, *Press-Herald* asked the president why he had not worked harder for the ERA, Eisenhower replied, laughing: "Well, it's hard for a mere man to believe that woman doesn't have equal rights. But, actually, this is the first time that this has come to my specific attention now since, oh, I think a year or so. . . . I just probably haven't been active enough in doing something about it."[40] ERA supporters were shocked at both the president's response and his laughter; they had been under the impression that he had received and read their letters. Administration support was tepid, the Hayden amendment seemed unbeatable. The unadorned Equal Rights Amendment did not express the national sentiment, and it remained an unachieved objective.

The AFL-CIO Department of Legislation, headed by labor lobbyist Andrew Biemiller, maintained a cursory anti-ERA lobbying effort in the absence of effort from the Women's Bureau and other groups. The labor federation recognized that many legislators were sympathetic.[41] As lobbyist Hyman Bookbinder put it, being for the ERA "is like being against sin, I suppose";[42] AFL-CIO officials even admitted that "many of our own people . . . are surprised [*sic*] to find labor opposed to it."[43] But the labor organization had no internal qualms about its position or its support for protective labor laws. In fact, a half-hearted attempt by the American Civil Liberties Union to craft yet an-

other compromise on the ERA elicited derision. One labor official responded: "If the ladies who are now worrying about this
did not have this to worry about they would find something
else. Vive le (sex) difference!"[44] Biemiller made it clear to Senator Hayden that the organization was depending on him to
continue to introduce his proviso. The Industrial Union Department urged affiliate unions to "keep up a constant barrage of
communications to members of Congress," a campaign coordinated by legislative representative Esther Peterson.[45] Although
the Senate Judiciary Committee reported the amendment favorably in May 1959, by a vote of nine to three, the Senate in July
1960 voted both to adopt the Hayden rider and to recommit the
bill to committee.

The course of the amendment's fortunes suggested that defeat of the measure throughout the decade rested on a national
unwillingness to restructure sex roles, an unwillingness revealed
in the success of the Hayden rider to the otherwise ideologically
appealing amendment. The ERA stood little chance of passage
because it represented an affirmation of absolute equality for
women at a moment when heightened recognition of sex roles
served a number of national functions, most important of which
was the re-creation of a stable and familiar society in the wake of
the social chaos of wartime. Engaged in the contest, some ERA
opponents argued that only a more sharply focused piece of
legislation would avoid the conflict that the ERA engendered.
They proposed an equal-pay law.

# 3

## "SPECIFIC BILLS FOR SPECIFIC ILLS": EQUAL PAY LEGISLATION

The cardinal premise of the Women's Bureau coalition held that the Equal Rights Amendment would do little to help women; discrimination could be eliminated only by the prudent enactment of "specific bills for specific ills." The "specific bill" offered by ERA opponents in 1945 sought to protect equal pay for equal work for women in private employment. Such a strategy possessed several advantages: it gave opponents of the ERA a positive goal rather than a negative one; it took advantage of the wartime impulse to recognize the contribution of women in jobs traditionally done by men; it allowed a focus on unfair practices that genuinely harmed women and their families, sidelining discussion about whether "theoretical" statements of equality were of value; it proposed a change in the law that was less unsettling than the ERA because it was so much narrower; and it placed ERA adversaries squarely in favor of eliminating discrimination.

But this bill faced a major problem in the postwar world. Higher wage rates would draw more women into the workforce, not encourage them to stay home. Thus the impulse to reward women for their wartime efforts ran counter to another current: the fear that returning soldiers would face job shortages. Making it more lucrative for women to stay in the workforce would hinder men's efforts to find jobs. Moreover, federal support, in the form of legislation guaranteeing equal opportunity in the workplace, would appear to confirm the social shifts the war had produced. The war had made working women visible—and that visibility made people nervous. The fight for equal pay once again played out the tension between institutionalizing the wartime gains of women in the public arena and reinstalling them as keepers of the hearth.

In addition, the quest for equal pay legislation was hampered by the ERA struggle. Because it had been proposed by ERA opponents, some advocates of the amendment viewed the legislation with suspicion. The ERA continued to be the chief legislative goal of the groups that favored it, and the primary supporters of equal pay never devoted equivalent resources to getting their bill through. The split between the pro- and anti-ERA forces made it more difficult for women to overcome both the "back to the home" sentiment and the conservative animus against business regulation in general.

By the end of the following decade, however, both the economic and the social context had changed. Women had clearly become a permanent part of the labor force—bound securely to women's jobs. The expanding peacetime economy, in fact, had created more service and clerical jobs than ever before, so employers welcomed—indeed, sought—women workers. In assuming these jobs, women continued to bear the major responsibility for their families' welfare, so the burden on husbands of working wives was small. With the newly generated need for women workers, the sentiment in favor of equal pay legislation began to grow, and it soon stood a real chance of passage. But social and economic supports were necessary, not sufficient, conditions. Real success required a more favorable political situation.

In the postwar period, President Truman gave the reformers seeking an equal pay law reason to believe he would support such an effort. After assuming office on Franklin Roosevelt's death, he made clear gestures to identify himself with his predecessor's liberal program, designed to encourage growth and progress in the postwar period. He promoted national health insurance and aid to education and, in particular, took a stand against discrimination by issuing executive orders banning prejudicial actions against black Americans in the civil service and in the military. Such efforts made it plain that discrimination against any group in the United States—even women—could be combatted through federal measures.[1]

At the same time, though, the government had focused its sights on trying to cap the skyrocketing inflation rate and maximizing the employment of former GIs. Yet President Truman seemed unable to craft an effective program to meet these needs, or to deal with labor unrest that led to strikes in the steel, automobile, electric, coal, maritime, and railroad industries.[2] In the 1946 elections Republicans took control of both houses of Congress for the first time in fourteen years. The Taft-Hartley Act, passed over the president's veto in June 1947, circumscribed the right of unions to control hiring. Policy goals sought to keep wage rates down and the employment of males up. Nevertheless, women activists in Washington, interested in advancing women's status even while maintaining "reasonable distinctions" between the sexes, worked to raise women's wages and assert their right to jobs.

The quest began in February 1945 when the National Committee to Defeat the UnEqual Rights Amendment drafted a bill to be introduced by Senators Wayne Morse (R-Oreg.) and Claude Pepper (D-Fla.). NCDURA's desire to eliminate a prevalent and serious problem for women workers was geniune, and it solicited the backing of all women's organizations, both favorable to and hostile toward the ERA. In order to separate equal pay from its opposition to the ERA, NCDURA established an independent national equal pay committee, which the pro-ERA BPW quickly agreed to join.[3]

But however sincere the motives of supporters of equal pay, the impetus for the measure was the desire to divert attention from the ERA. NCDURA counseled its members to urge legislators to vote both in favor of the equal pay bill and against the ERA, and Mary Anderson, the ERA's archfoe (who had resigned the year before, at age seventy-two, as director of the Women's Bureau), herself chaired the new equal pay committee and drew up the bill. The bill thus got hit from two sides— by those who favored the ERA and did not want what they saw as a more important effort vitiated by a narrower one, and by those who opposed any interference in the workplace and wanted no law at all.

Often both these opponents were conservatives, either Republicans or conservative Democrats. Although the liberal-conservative split was muddled in the ERA battle, on the question of equal pay it stood out clearly. Equal pay legislation came out of the protective labor law tradition, and the original version of the bill protected only women's wage rates. Liberal organizations lined up behind the bill, but conservatives who supported independent free enterprise opposed an equal pay law. Those conservatives who also supported the ERA thus had two "good" reasons to fight equal pay legislation.

In proposing to protect women's wage rates, the liberals were arguing not in favor of new roles for women but for recognizing the reality, however undesirable it might be, of women in the workforce. Working women had taken jobs because they needed the money. Equity and decency demanded that employers pay them a fair wage—that is, the rate a man earned for the same job.

The argument might have carried the day, but in drafting the bill, Anderson, never politically astute, ignored important political considerations and made several inflammatory moves. She modeled the bill after the sweeping coverage of the National Labor Relations Act, which applied to employers engaged in businesses "affecting" commerce, rather than following the narrower coverage of the Fair Labor Standards Act, which applied only to those actually participating in interstate commerce. The bill protected the pay only of women; a man earning less than a woman at a particular job (assuming such a person existed) had no recourse. Although not important from a practical point of view, the exclusion of men from the law's protection gave the bill's opponents a powerful "equal treatment" argument to use against it. The bill also forbade employers to discharge women without cause, a provision intended to help women keep wartime employment (a goal few endorsed in 1945). Anderson went so far as to vest enforcement power in the director of the Women's Bureau. A fact-finding agency, the bureau had never had this kind of enforcement authority and had no machinery to perform it. The provision of the bill that sparked the most opposition provided for an "advisory committee" that would establish wage differentials among different types of work. Opponents could thus contend that the bureau had aims completely apart from the mere protection of women's wage rates. Finally, the bill permitted the blacklisting of employers found guilty of wage discrimination, a red flag to business interests whose cooperation the bill's supporters needed. Said one partisan, in something of an understatement: "With the enactment of this law, we will be entering [an] . . . unchartered [*sic*] field."[4]

The chances for some kind of equal pay legislation looked promising because of patriotic sentiment in its favor and because studies done during World War II had documented an authentic problem of widespread wage discrimination. "Women in producing the weapons of war have, in many industries and occupations, demonstrated their ability to turn out the same day's work as do men," Senators Pepper and Morse asserted when they introduced Anderson's bill; employers should not treat them like "second class workmen."[5] The Women's Bureau representatives had indeed discovered a large war plant where women instructors got sixty cents an hour, whereas the men they were teaching received seventy cents. In the small arms and artillery ammunition plants the bureau representatives visited, entering wage rates were found to be at least ten cents an hour higher for men than for women; in gun manufacturing men began at sixteen cents an hour more. The *New York Herald Tribune* pointed to the war widows, now the sole support of their families, and urged no further delay of "so just a measure" as the equal pay bill.[6]

Congress responded apathetically. Mary Norton (D-N.J.), chairman of the House Labor Committee, told Women's Bureau director Frieda Miller that no legislation would be enacted without an active campaign revealing "intense interest" on the part of women's organizations, labor unions, and the administration.[7] In response, Mary Anderson expanded the equal pay committee she had formed, now called the National Committee on Equal Pay. Labor and women's organizations came on board, and the CIO replied: "[We] are anxious to work with you."[8]

Not surprisingly, the National Woman's party hung back. Its response to a Supreme Court decision in 1936 on a wage and hour case had revealed its antipathy to labor legislation in general; now, although it declined to oppose this bill overtly, its members complained to congressional backers about several of the bill's features. They objected first to a special bill pertaining only to women rather than mandating equal pay for equal work regardless of sex. But even more, they rejected the bureau as the law's enforcement agent. As the chairman of the National Advisory Council of the NWP, Nora Stanton Barney, wrote to Senator Claude Pepper: "We do not want women to have any more legislation setting them apart from other workers, and sincerely wish the Women's Bureau did not exist. We certainly do not want it given any more power over the lives of women."[9] The party feared that, at worst, Anderson's plan would work and Congress, instead of enacting the Equal Rights Amendment, would use equal pay legislation to mollify women.

Equal pay advocates took no pains to conceal this possibility; indeed, they regarded it as a selling point. Elizabeth Magee, general secretary of the National Consumers League, issued a press release observing that the equal pay bill "may lead to the shelving of the proposed Equal Rights Amendment," and Dorothy McAllister, the head of NCDURA, told her committee members that passage of the equal pay bill "would greatly weaken the interest some Senators have in the [Equal Rights] Amendment."[10]

At the end of October 1945, the Senate Education and Labor Committee held hearings on the bill. Labor unions, including the AFL, offered support, as did the administration in the person of the secretary of labor. (The president said he endorsed the "principle" but no particular bill.)[11] Speakers emphasized equity, the protection of wage rates for male workers, the needs of widows, and postwar purchasing power to sustain the economy. The BPW and the General Federation of Women's Clubs spoke in favor, also emphasizing their support of the ERA, and the NWP kept mum. No one testified against the bill.[12]

The committee took seven months to report the bill. It had eliminated the provision against firing women (even Frieda Miller had testified against this provision) and vested enforcement in the secretary of labor. Even so, labor subcommittee chairman James Tunnell (D-Del.) seemed only mildly interested in the bill, and committee members Robert Taft (R-Ohio) and Joseph Ball (R-Mich.), who had strong business constituents and conservative economic principles, opposed it. The measure did have a good friend on the House side however. Mary Norton saw to it that in July the House Labor Committee, which she chaired, reported a similar bill, without hearings to create delay.[13]

The bill went no further. Because the Senate committee had taken so long, the bill reached the Senate floor near the close of the session. Robert Taft took to the floor against hasty consideration: "The bill involves a major interference with the freedom of American industry. Certainly it ought not to come up during the last days of the session."[14] With the assistance of Joe Ball, who leapt to his defense against charges of indifference to women's rights, they scuttled the measure for 1946.

This first defeat undid the bill. The ERA had gone down the previous July, so the chief impetus for the coalition backing equal pay legislation had withered. The wartime contributions of women were beginning to fade from memory, as was the desire to reward those efforts. Sympathetic Congress members continued to introduce the bill, but without an outside lobbying effort the cause was futile.[15] In subsequent hearings industry lobbyists, emboldened no doubt by the earlier failure, argued that federal legislation was unnecessary and intrusive—a position supported, to the dismay of equal pay advocates, by the AFL. The labor federation had reversed its position in 1947, arguing that collective bargaining was a more effective tool for securing pay equity for women, a position it took despite the fact that many labor unions continued to include dual pay scales in their contracts.[16]

With the Korean conflict some supporters became hopeful that Congress would use equal pay to encourage women to do war work. Mary Norton, now in the Department of Labor, asked Representative John F. Kennedy (D-Mass.) to introduce an equal pay bill to support defense production. Kennedy acquiesced, as did a number of other House members, but the war did not replicate either the massive production effort of World War II or the labor shortage of that era, and the bill got nowhere. Wayne Morse complained in August 1951 that the "reactionary coalition," supported by the AFL, put the kibosh on the bill.[17]

Indeed, the AFL now vehemently objected to the possibility that, through the equal pay law, the government might play a role in job evaluation or setting wage rates. Said one member of its legislative committee:

> Private property is the foundation of economic freedom. . . . It has been found desirable to keep decisions on economic matters in the hands of economic organizations, limiting the political to the formulation of objectives and basic principles. Administrative regulation of the economic order limits economic freedom and with increasing scope and degree may destroy it. . . . To attack the problem as an issue of social justice to be cured by legislation is to perpetuate a principle based upon the assumption that women are wards of the state.[18]

This argument seemed a bit disingenuous in view of the AFL's opposition to the ERA based on the amendment's threat to protective labor laws for women. Laws limiting women's hours of employment or barring women from certain jobs entirely certainly seemed to imply that women were wards of the state. To object to laws protecting women's rates of pay, but not those limiting their hours, lent credence to the NWP's claim that male unionists opposed the ERA for self-interested reasons rather than for the sake of women.

The NWP, itself uninterested in governmental intrusion into business matters, also continued to fight the bill's backers. The animosity between ERA supporters and equal pay advocates broke into the open again in March 1952, at a Women's Bureau conference designed to generate enthusiasm for the measure. Mildred Palmer of the National Woman's party crashed the conference and, during the question period, asked Frieda Miller why the bureau did not support the Equal Rights Amendment if it wished to expedite the matter of equal pay. With "unrestrained hatred," according to Palmer's account, Miller told her she was out of order.[19]

Effective coalition now seemed less rather than more likely, and the situation deteriorated further when Graham Barden, the new head of the House Education and Labor Committee, made it clear he had no use for the equal pay bill. The next year, 1953, AFL president George Meany affirmed that organization's position: "We feel that in a free competitive economy, the task of establishing and safeguarding the principle as well as the practice of equal pay to women workers is properly within the province of collective bargaining and not of police action by the government."[20] The National Association of Manufacturers and the U.S. Chamber of Commerce agreed that government interference was unwarranted,[21] and Alice Paul, the founder of the National Woman's party and the nation's chief exponent of the Equal Rights Amendment, joined them: "The building up of a new, far reaching system of inspection on the question of equal pay, with power to investigate every business in the United States, administered by a colossal new government agency with vast enforcement powers, would not be helpful to women, as far as I can see."[22]

The National Committee on Equal Pay (NCEP), which the Women's Bureau tried to resurrect after several years of inactivity, served as a clearinghouse of information. It had no power over its member organizations, many of which differed over the best strategy to pursue. Some members were frankly opposed to legislation and belonged to the group only to monitor its activities. The member organizations that were in accord with the objective of legislation all had many other time-consuming items on their agenda—including opposition to the Equal Rights Amendment, a big drain on energy and resources. Thus, the NCEP could hardly overcome the obstacles against the bill: an array of powerful organizations opposed to it, and a leadership vacuum and political inactivity on the part of the working women who presumably favored it.

The Republicans, elected in 1952, introduced yet another wrinkle. All the proposed bills had followed Anderson's model and covered employers "affecting commerce." Republican representative Frances P. Bolton from Ohio introduced equal pay legislation in January 1954 that would amend the Fair Labor Standards Act to narrow coverage considerably from the other bills and give enforcement to the Wage and Hour Division of the Department of Labor, which had power only to mediate disputes, not to issue "cease and desist" orders. By way of compromise, Bolton later submitted a different bill, which, although still modeled on the FLSA, broadened coverage a bit. To enforce the law, the secretary of labor would have to file suit.[23]

Advocates of the original bill refused to consider Bolton's approach, unwilling to foresake coverage for any group of women workers. Bolton retreated and introduced a bill proposing "study" of the problem, while Edith Green (D-Oreg.) went to bat for the original bill. Green reintroduced the blacklist provision for guilty employers but permitted enforcement through the courts.[24] The Department of Labor, representing the administration, insisted on the Bolton bill, and the NCEP maintained its support for the Green bill. The Women's Bureau, estranged from its traditional consistency by Leopold's appointment, also had little clout within the administration; it could influence neither side.

Meanwhile, support outside Congress was mounting. Equal pay had gone down in 1945, at a time when almost everyone agreed that women should leave the labor force. By the end of the 1950s, however, public policy had taken a new tack: concern now focused on the appropriate use of womanpower, both to fill the needs of businesses seeking white-collar workers and to meet the international challenge posed by the ostensible threat from Moscow—a challenge that highlighted the need to devote more human resources to science. In 1957 the National Manpower Council (NMC), a Columbia University panel funded by the Ford Foundation, published a landmark study entitled *Womanpower*. A comprehensive look at the experience of women in the labor force, current employment needs, and the implications of both for education, training, and public policy, the NMC analysis called women "essential" and "distinctive" workers.[25] Attracting women to work had become a matter of national interest.

Moreover, women themselves had indicated that they intended to be a permanent part of the labor force regardless of policy incentives to stay home; now no one could accuse the government of wrecking homes by improving conditions of women's work. The sex segregation of the labor force safeguarded jobs for men, so the government could not be charged with threatening the "breadwinners," and business prosperity indicated that the nation no longer needed to fear the return of the prewar depression and job scarcity. Public opinion polls consistently supported equal pay for equal work for women.[26]

President Eisenhower was the most prominent new proponent of the equal pay bill. The administration had consistently favored an equal pay law, and in 1956 Leopold persuaded Eisenhower, via the secretary of labor, to mention it in the State of the Union message. On January 5, 1956, Eisenhower told Congress: "Legislation to apply the principle of equal pay for equal work without discrimination because of sex is a matter of simple justice. I earnestly urge the Congress to move swiftly to implement these needed labor measures."[27] Women's organizations were encouraged, and the president subsequently included equal pay recommendations in all his budget messages and four of his economic reports to Congress during the rest of his term. But the Women's Bureau did nothing else with these statements.

Important backing came from another source in 1956. Since 1947, the American Federation of Labor had opposed the equal pay bill, insisting that union membership and collective bargaining constituted a preferable route—even though in a number of unionized plants sex-segregated pay scales granted skilled women workers no higher wages than male common laborers. The Congress of Industrial Organizations, however, had steadily endorsed equal pay legislation, and when the two federations merged in 1956 the AFL-CIO adopted the CIO position, swayed by the measure's popularity: both parties had endorsed it, as had the president, and women's organizations were virtually unanimous. The AFL-CIO endorsed the Green bill, not the Bolton, and insisted on an amendment to provide for administrative enforcement by the secretary of labor. Although publicly the organization expressed its concern that employees should not be forced to undergo the expense of legal action, the choice of administrative, rather than judicial, enforcement reflected the fear that unions would also be the target of equal pay suits. Where dual pay scales existed, some women had already sued unions, charging discrimination under collective bargaining agreements and asserting that the unions were not representing them fairly in the bargaining unit, as the law required. The labor federation assumed that the secretary of labor would give unions a more sympathetic hearing than a judge. Its anxiety over this provision meant that the group would not readily compromise on it.[28]

The AFL-CIO position was typical of the bill's supporters: backing hinged on special considerations. There was contention even within the administration, with the Commerce Department objecting to coverage broader than the FLSA and the whole notion of a separate bill.[29] With a Republican administration in power, labor was distrustful of any suggestion of compromise, and the Republicans' business constituents, for their part, did not look kindly at the "harassment" promised by the Green bill.

Powerful enemies on the Hill, especially Graham Barden (D-N.C.), chairman of the House Education and Labor Committee, made the problems in some ways moot. Barden told Green point-blank that he considered the bill "ridiculous" and that he would never pay a woman as much as he paid his male legislative assistant. Others involved in the struggle suggested that the problem with the bill lay in the lack of hard statistical data, but that gap provided only a convenient excuse.[30] For the last three years of the Eisenhower administration, the only significant action on equal pay legislation was the president's repeated counsel to Congress to enact it.

By the second half of the 1950s, the lack of a committed, sophisticated leadership that could gather convincing data, lobby effectively, and forge a compromise among the disparate elements backing the bill spelled defeat. The National Committee on Equal Pay served merely as an informational conduit; the administration stuck to its guns, as did the major labor organizations; and the Women's Bureau, with ties now principally to professional women rather than to its traditional constituency of labor union women and advocates for women in industry, and unwilling to alienate the Republicans' business constituency, gathered little data on the prevalence of unequal pay scales.

Like the Equal Rights Amendment, in the postwar period equal pay legislation had suffered from the national ambivalence toward women's roles. Introduced in 1945, the legislation was overtly a tribute to women war workers, but concern for reestablishing security in the workplace for returning veterans overwhelmed the desire to achieve either that tribute or real equity for women. Throughout the fifties, as the nation restored its emotional and economic foundations within a conservative social framework, women quietly left the home during the day for the workplace, becoming an indispensable and unique part of the labor force, no longer in competition with men for jobs but filling an almost completely separated category of white-collar and service work. By the end of the decade, anxiety over working women had subsided, but equal pay proponents, fragmented by diverse goals and political beliefs and lacking effective and appropriate leadership, could not overcome the business opposition united against the bill, now its only serious obstacle. From 1945 to 1960, therefore, women received from Congress virtually no recognition of their contribution to the war effort, their new place in the American economy, or their importance within the electorate. It remained for the White House to cover this political flank and do something for the women.

# 4

## TOKENS OF PRESIDENTIAL ESTEEM: WOMEN APPOINTEES

The defeat of the Equal Rights Amendment and the failure of equal pay legislation created problems for both Republicans and Democrats in the postwar period, leaving them open to the charge that male politicians didn't care about women voters and didn't appreciate the contribution women had made toward winning the war. Women within the major parties threatened that without some recognition, faithful female party workers would simply desert their posts.

Ever since suffrage had been won in 1920, both the Republican and the Democratic parties had religiously offered something to women. After World War I, the Democrats had created the Women's Bureau, and in 1921 Congress passed legislation setting up maternal and infant health programs. In 1922 a Republican president signed the Cable Act, which permitted American women married to foreign nationals to retain their citizenship as men did, and in 1923 Congress forbade differential pay by sex in the civil service. Both parties had created special women's divisions, and in the 1920 campaign both had adopted platform planks suggested by the newly formed League of Women Voters. As the first decade after women's suffrage wore on, however, it became clear that women, riven as they were by class interests and philosophical outlooks, were not going to form a consolidated bloc of voters, and male politicians relaxed. After that, few legislative initiatives spoke directly to women's needs, but in order not to alienate the women who were concerned about women's advancement, presidential administrations assiduously publicized the names and positions of women appointed to federal posts. Franklin Roosevelt, under the guidance of Democratic politician Molly Dewson, surpassed his predecessors by far: whereas Hoover had appointed three women to significant Senate-confirmed posts in eight years, in twelve years Roosevelt named seventeen.[1]

In the postwar period women's organizations were divided over the Equal Rights Amendment, a reflection of the nation's general ambivalence toward equality for women. The equal pay bill was stalemated, caught in the backwash of both the ERA battle and the divisions between Republicans and Democrats, business and labor forces. Women's organizations with divergent political objectives remained united on only one point: the need to have women in policy-making positions. Appointments offered an easy way out of the policy dilemma—and the first two postwar presidents eagerly took that route.

The strategy had many advantages. "Policy-making" appointments for women evinced concern for women as voters without the ugly prospect of waging a campaign for controversial legislation or choosing sides among women's organizations. Moreover, because each president could usually work his will on the subject of appointments, it was possible to obtain this objective expeditiously. Finally, appointments represented the premier item on the agenda of the women to whom the two presidents were closest: the heads of the women's divisions of the major parties. Truman and Eisenhower each had close ties to his party's national committee, and party women considered high-level positions for deserving qualified female candidates essential. By proxy, these appointments served as encouragement and reward for the campaign work of thousands of loyal women in local precincts whose efforts were becoming more important with each election.

Women's organizations, despite their disputes over other matters, agreed unanimously on the desirability of increasing the number of women in higher government positions. Women in public office, women leaders argued, would represent women's interests, show that deserving women could attain opportunities commensurate with their abilities, offer examples to other employers that women performed admirably in responsible jobs, and make available to the nation the wisdom that educated and talented women possessed.[2] At a June 1944 conference called by first lady Eleanor Roosevelt and held at the White House, two hundred women leaders had asked specifically that women be appointed as delegates to international conferences and as members of national policy-making bodies. Women's organizations undertook the development of rosters to ensure that "qualified" women would be visible, and Roosevelt herself continued to call attention to this demand, writing to the new president, Harry Truman, and to his associates that women's loyalty to the Democratic party depended on these rewards.[3]

The chairman of the Women's Division of the Democratic National Committee, Gladys Tillett, also wrote to Truman: "We should like," she reminded him, "to have women serve on all of the Peace Conferences which are to be held." She urged Truman that appointment of women to positions of power in the government would "establish the fact that the president is interested in matters pertaining to women."[4] Truman did not, however, take much of Tillett's advice. In fact, his appointment record of women in the term he served out as Franklin Roosevelt's successor was undistinguished: from 1945 to 1948 he appointed only three women to important Senate-confirmed posts;[5] Roosevelt had appointed thirteen women to such posts during his first three years in office.

But once India Edwards assumed Tillett's post in 1948, the number of female appointments jumped. Tillett had lacked effectiveness with Truman for two reasons: Truman saw her as a member of Roosevelt's team, and he felt no particular attachment to her or her proposals; and Tillett's suggestions for appointments were vague—a list of names of women she would ask the president to "consider."

Edwards, in contrast, had been a strong supporter of Truman even when FDR was president. Moreover, Edwards had pursued the course of finding a highly qualified woman for almost every available position and then making a specific pitch to the president on that candidate's behalf. She thus made it easy for Truman to fulfill her requests.[6]

India Edwards had begun her professional career as a journalist on the editorial staff of the *Chicago Tribune*, where she worked from 1918 until 1942. But when she left Chicago and moved with her husband to Washington during World War II, she gave up journalism and began to work as a volunteer at the Women's Division of the DNC. She became the division's executive secretary in 1945 and, in early 1948, its executive director. Edwards's assertive demeanor, coupled with her political know-how, elicited admiration from many of her colleagues, although others, put off by her "unladylike" behavior, called her a "battle-ax." Democratic party women, however, enthusiastically described her as powerful.[7]

Edwards had been a longtime Truman backer. During the 1944 campaign she was one of the few DNC workers who always included the vice-president's name in speeches and publicity materials. In 1948, then director of the Women's Division, Edwards was one of the few campaign workers who thought Truman would pull off the election. In support she organized campaign schools for women volunteers, "Housewives for Truman" trailers, a series of radio shows, and the distribution of many thousands of guidebooks, fliers, platforms, and voting records. Truman, who inherited an administration devoted to his predecessor, clearly appreciated her loyalty. When William M. Boyle, Jr., who coordinated the Truman Whistle-Stop Train, asked Edwards what she wanted as a reward for her work, she replied: "Nothing for myself but a lot of jobs for a lot of women."[8] From 1948 to 1952, Truman's appointment record showed a marked improvement. In addition to naming fifteen Senate-confirmed appointees, he placed two hundred more women in government.[9]

In general, Truman had firm ties to the DNC. Robert Hannegan and J. Howard McGrath, the two committee chairs during his first term, were longtime political associates. But his closest ties were to Edwards, whom he saw more frequently than even McGrath. In 1951 Truman offered the DNC chairmanship to Edwards—a first for a woman in either party—but she declined, believing that the amount of time she would have to spend protecting herself from enemies would hinder her effectiveness.[10]

As the head of the Women's Division, Edwards devised a procedure for getting women into appointment slots that served as a model for her successors. First she scouted among Democratic women's organizations for names of women able to hold government jobs and checked their qualifications; then she found jobs that they could fill. Before going to the president, she got the necessary clearances from party officials, senators from the nom- inee's state, and executive officers. After Truman made the nomination and the Senate approved it, Edwards fulfilled her share of the bargain by making sure the appointment got plenty of publicity. Women journalists, who always believed that women appointees made good copy, were willing collaborators. With regard to ambassadorships, Edwards primed Truman to appoint a woman even before a vacancy appeared. When the post of ambassador to Denmark opened, she had Eugenie An- derson ready to fill it, a special feat because Anderson was a married woman. When U.S. treasurer William A. Julian died in an accident in 1949, Edwards raced to the White House to see whether Truman would consider a woman for the position, a sinecure. When he said he would, if the woman was "qualified," Edwards came up with Georgia Neese Clark, a woman who was both a member of the DNC and a small-town banker. (Although every treasurer after Clark has been a woman, neither before nor since has the treasurer also been a banker.)[11]

In urging Truman to accept women appointees, Edwards emphasized the political consequences of ignoring women vot- ers. "I know there will be unfavorable reactions if not one woman is among the twenty-seven new judges," she wrote in 1949. "I hear often the criticism that most of the women's ap- pointments are window-dressing, not on the policy level. . . . I know this is somewhat true."[12] As a result of this particular campaign, Truman named Burnita Matthews to the district court bench.

Truman had his limits, however. For one, he intended to keep the cabinet a male preserve. He refused to consider Frances Perkins to head the Federal Security Administration because, one of his aides reported, he intended to create a Department of Welfare, and he "did not want any woman in the cabinet."[13] He also allowed Chief Justice Fred Vinson to veto the selection of the first woman on the Supreme Court. Edwards had recom- mended Florence Allen, who had received her seat on the court of appeals from Franklin Roosevelt. According to aide Matthew Connelly, Truman explained: "The Justices don't want a woman. They say they couldn't sit around with their robes off and their feet up and discuss their problems."[14] Truman also declined to appoint Florence Shientag to a vacant federal judgeship in New York, on the grounds that "her husband is already a Judge in the New York Courts and it seems to me that one Judge in the family is enough."[15] (Shientag eventually became a judge of the family court in New York City.)

Both Edwards and leaders of women's organizations constantly reminded Truman not to forget women in appointments. The Korean War inspired a special plea for women on emergency war committees, and a new showcase body, called the Defense Advisory Committee on Women in the Services, counseled the Defense Department on the use of women in the newly integrated military services. DACOWITS, as the group was known, functioned chiefly to reassure parents (in order to support recruitment) that the government had an interest in the welfare of young women enlistees. Although enlistment of women fell far below goals, DACOWITS did accord several dozen women an ongoing role in "policy making."[16]

The matter of women appointments did not concern the general public, however. Truman's appointments came in response to the requests of Edwards and other women lobbyists. Only a handful of letters arrived at the White House from outside Washington, and public opinion polls showed that the electorate did not want the president to turn over more power to women in government. In December 1945 a Gallup survey showed that only 26 percent of men and 38 percent of women agreed with the statement of "a woman leader" who said that "not enough of the capable women are holding important jobs in the United States Government." Furthermore, only 29 percent of men and 37 percent of women said they would vote for a woman for president even if she were the best-qualified candidate, 52 percent of men and 43 percent of women disapproved of having a "capable woman" in the cabinet, and 46 percent of men and 35 percent of women disapproved of a "capable woman" on the Supreme Court. In 1947, 48 percent polled believed that women should not participate more actively in politics, and only 46 percent said they should. By 1949, 51 percent of women and 45 percent of men would have voted for a woman for president, and 48 percent of men and 60 percent of women approved President Truman's choice of a woman for minister to Luxembourg. But these data hardly represented a mandate to a president interested in appointing women in order to win votes. In fact, public support for equal pay for women was much stronger: a 1946 poll showed that 71 percent of the men and 81 percent of the women surveyed endorsed equal pay.[17] If Truman displayed more interest in appointments than in equal pay legislation, his actions reflected the concerns of Democratic party women and the advantages of using appointments to recognize women instead of choosing a more problematic political route.

Between 1945 and 1952 Truman named eighteen women to positions requiring Senate confirmation, an average of 2.25 per year. Of these, nine were jobs women had never held before. Truman's appointments included one woman to a subcabinet position, Anna Rosenberg (assistant secretary of defense), and two ministers, Eugenie Anderson (ambassador to Demark) and Perle Mesta (minister to Luxembourg). (By way of comparison, Roosevelt, in twelve years, had appointed seventeen women, eleven of whom were "firsts.") A total of forty women (including those designated as regional comptrollers of customs and similar local officers) served during Truman's administrations in these Senate-confirmed positions (compared with thirty-seven in the Roosevelt years). In 1951–1952 women made up 2.4 percent of all executive appointments, excluding places on commissions (79 out of 3,273 posts). Edwards, counting members of presidential commissions, claimed that Truman had installed more than 250 women in high-level positions.[18] Adlai Stevenson, the 1952 Democratic nominee for president, promised to follow in Truman's footsteps in his "growing reliance upon qualified women for high public posts."[19]

Dwight Eisenhower, the Republican nominee, also understood the utility of emphasizing appointments for women. He wrote to the American Association of University Women: "If it should be my destiny to serve as chief executive, I would utilize the contributions of outstanding women to the greatest extent possible. Indeed, it would be impossible to carry out the responsibilities of the office without their help." He expanded on this statement in a speech in Portland, Oregon: "I want to speak for just a second about my honest belief, my deep conviction, that we should have more women in public life." Not only, Eisenhower observed, were there two million more women than men, but women more than men worried about "the preservation and strengthening" of American values. Thus Eisenhower urged the election of women to the office of governor, and he counseled Republicans to accept women as "equal partners" in the Republican party. Katherine Howard, the only woman on the Eisenhower Campaign Strategy Committee, pointedly brought these and similar remarks to the attention of the almost nine thousand Republican women leaders with whom she was in contact.[20]

After Eisenhower's election in November, Republican women, following the Democratic model, moved with dispatch. Jessica Weis, director of women's activities for the Republican National Committee, promptly formulated a plan of appointments for the president's consideration. Her list of possible "top-level" positions included director of the Mint, under and assistant secretaries of the Departments of Labor, Agriculture, and Commerce, and assistant postmaster general. The position of assistant attorney general, Weis said, "has aroused more interest than any other post among women." Weis also recommended the appointment of a White House assistant at some level—"a new job for women and one which should have priority." Furthermore, Weis advised, "the United Nations is a fertile field for women's positions as so many of them are in the area of women's traditional interests," and she urged as "a matter of policy" that women be appointed to all presidential commissions. Weis also suggested that Frieda Miller be replaced as director of the Women's Bureau. Although Mary Anderson, a Democrat, had held the office during the tenure of three Republican presidents, establishing a precedent that the director not be replaced with a change in administration, Weis stated: "An early appointment would be appreciated as Miss Miller is most unpopular with Republican women." In addition to the posts Weis specified, there were, she stressed, many more at lower levels in the departments and in the judiciary. She transmitted a list of eligible women and warned that Truman had created a record Eisenhower needed to match: "We must do better."[21]

In planning its program for 1953, the Women's Division of the RNC asserted that women in policy-making posts, accompanied by appropriate media attention, would reap rewards for both the administration and the party. Such appointments would not only inspire women campaign workers but also win favor with the leaders of nonpartisan women's groups. Indeed, in 1953 *Independent Woman* (*IW*), the magazine of the National Federation of Business and Professional Women's Clubs, featured women appointees of the Eisenhower administration in both its January and its March issues. Noting that women had been "frequently and emphatically reminded" during the campaign of the importance of their votes, the journal commented that they expected "substantial recognition" in the form of appointments to important posts. "And," *IW* stated, "the new president did make two selections that acknowledged the debt to hard campaign work on his behalf and his faith in the ability of the women chosen." *IW* highlighted the appointment of Ivy Baker Priest as treasurer, "a straight political appointment in which the honor somewhat outweighs the work involved," and of Oveta Culp Hobby as the new Federal Security administrator, and soon to be a cabinet member as the first secretary of the new Department of Health, Education, and Welfare. In March, Clare Boothe Luce, the new ambassador to Italy, appeared on *IW*'s cover, "the first woman to hold the top-ranking diplomatic post in a world power."[22]

In the appointment of women, the Republican National Committee had a freer hand than had the DNC, because Eisenhower ran the White House differently from the way Truman had. Truman, who had had a long career in politics, and some involvement with political machinery, liked to be personally involved in the selection of political appointees, and he felt comfortable with the idea of patronage. The former general, in contrast, instituted a militarylike hierarchy, making him less accessible than Truman had been to political operatives. Moreover, with no experience in running for office, Eisenhower disdained politics and turned all but the highest-level political matters over to subordinates.[23] Eisenhower's preference for leaving political decisions to politicians made the RNC the main clearinghouse for patronage selections, and Eisenhower's willingness to depend on the committee permitted Republican women to offer suggestions on a regular basis and to have them acted upon. The RNC leadership, which sought such appointments, proved generous in granting these requests. As chairman C. Wesley Roberts explained to White House aide Sherman Adams, "The thought behind this is to try to give better recognition to women during this administration than has been done heretofore, particularly in positions of importance."[24]

Bertha Adkins, assistant to the chairman and head of the RNC Women's Division, served as the chief conduit to Republican women[25] and regularly enumerated Eisenhower's appointment record to the press. By July 1953 she had a list of twenty-seven women who were "playing a real role in the daily-mounting achievements of the new Administration"—proper repayment to women campaign workers who had worked "in unprecedented numbers and zeal" for Eisenhower's election.[26] The record redounded to Adkins's credit, and she quickly became known in political circles as a powerful woman. A United Press poll named her one of the ten most influential women in Washington, because she supposedly had a "good telephone line to the White House."[27] Adkins's reputation did not, however, reach so far as Edwards's had, and after complaints from Republican women that they were being shut out, the president began to attend publicized "breakfasts" with women party and civic leaders. *Newsweek* reported that Adkins had "ready access to President Eisenhower, who calls her by her first name and quotes her views to male politicians,"[28] a clear attempt to evoke Edwards's relationship to Truman. RNC campaign films narrated Eisenhower's achievements in appointing women to important jobs, a theme Adkins sounded repeatedly.[29]

In April 1957 Eisenhower appointed a woman to the White House staff. In a surprise announcement to the fifteen hundred women attending the fifth annual Republican Women's Conference in Washington, he named Anne Wheaton, who had held the post of director of women's publicity of the RNC for eighteen years, as associate White House press secretary. The appointment was a public relations stroke, and the audience responded with "cheers and applause," according to newspaper accounts.[30] Adding this one to the other slots arranged by Adkins and the RNC, Adkins claimed by 1958 that Eisenhower had appointed "more women to key posts in the Federal Government, in International Affairs and on important committees and commissions than any other Chief Executive in the Nation's history."[31] Shortly thereafter Adkins herself assumed the position of under secretary of the Department of Health, Education, and Welfare (another "first"), thus becoming the top-ranking woman in the government.

Eisenhower's record of appointments of women did exceed Truman's. In roughly the same amount of time, Eisenhower named twenty-eight women to Senate-confirmed posts, compared to twenty for Truman. Even excluding such positions as collector of customs for localities, Eisenhower still could claim twenty-two such appointments to Truman's eighteen. Eisenhower also edged Truman out slightly in first appointments: ten for the general and nine for Truman. Each president had a woman in the cabinet; Truman, however, had not chosen Frances Perkins, a Roosevelt holdover who stayed only briefly after he took office, but Eisenhower himself selected Oveta Culp Hobby, who served until July 1, 1955. Both presidents had named one woman to the subcabinet (under and assistant secretaries), but whereas Eisenhower designated three women to serve as agency heads, Truman appointed none. Eisenhower also appointed one minister more than Truman (three to Truman's two), although Truman installed one more woman on a federal court than did Eisenhower. The Republican bested Truman's annual average of Senate-confirmed appointments by 0.5 percentage points: 2.75, up from 2.25 (84 out of 3,491 positions). With members of commissions, Eisenhower's distaff contingent numbered over four hundred.[32] Although the actual number of women named to important positions was in fact small, it satisfied the political women who themselves took pride in their access to the chief executives. Of the three groups competing for federal attention, only the party women could claim success.

But however commendable—or unsatisfactory—the records of Truman and Eisenhower, their appointments of women to government posts stood as a symbolic gesture more than an effective method to improve women's economic or legal position. Women's groups sought these appointments on the premise that just having women do their job properly would set an example for other employers, which in turn would expand opportunities for women at all levels. Certainly the women appointees of Harry Truman and Dwight Eisenhower, all highly qualified and competent, vindicated those who had advocated their advancement. But these appointees, as one observer noted, "did not herald a new . . . tradition in which increasing numbers of women occupied ever higher governmental positions, nor did they advance the status of women either significantly or lastingly."[33]

Nor could they have done so. Chosen principally for their sex, not their qualifications, these women were vulnerable. India Edwards later recalled that Truman had paid her "what men have always considered the ultimate compliment to a female: that I operated like a man." In the absence of a movement for women's rights, when "operating like a man" was the standard of excellence, no woman in an important governmental job could become the champion of the women's cause without calling her legitimacy into question—unless that position dealt exclusively with women's issues.

Mary Anderson, director of the Women's Bureau, which was under the aegis of the secretary of labor, encountered this problem with regard to Frances Perkins. Anderson wrote:

> When Frances Perkins came in as Secretary of Labor, we were all jubilant, because we thought that at last we would have someone who really understood our problems and what we were up against and who would fight for us. . . . But it did not turn out to be that way. . . . The terrible publicity she was subjected to because she was the first woman cabinet officer was a great handicap. . . . It was especially discouraging to me to find that the Women's Bureau was not of great interest to her though I understood that she was preoccupied with other things and did not want to be thought of as a woman who was too closely identified with women's problems.[34]

Perkins, herself in part a token, understood the difficulties common to token appointees. Often highly qualified, but selected because of their sex or because they possess a specific

visible racial, ethnic, or physical characteristic essentially irrelevant to the execution of their job—selected, that is, for the
specific political purpose of recognizing the group they
represent—token appointees are expected to ignore in the fulfillment of their duties the very attribute for which they were
chosen. Tokens have the responsibility of proving that the trait
that identifies them does not in fact constitute a handicap.
They thus labor under the burden that their mistakes impugn
not only their own abilities, but those of all members of their
group as well. Conversely, of course, the successes of "token"
appointees do both confirm their abilities and confer at least a
modicum of status on the group they represent.

But the postwar experience of the pursuit of token appointments for women reveals the drawback of this strategy. By di-
verting attention from policy questions, a roster of token appointments made in response to requests from an interested
group allowed the presidents to duck thorny political problems
without serious reprisals and to evade the debate over more
significant issues. Convinced of the value of female appointments for both women and their parties, and concerned with
the publicity deriving from the appointments rather than with
policy goals, the party women who nominated the candidates
did so in general without regard to the views of the designee on
specific matters of interest to women activists. The appointees
for the most part had no policy role with respect to women's
issues.

Both Truman and Eisenhower met their obligations to their
female constituents in a way that was ultimately cosmetic, without addressing more fundamental questions regarding the position of women in America. Because token appointments represented a traditional means of recognizing groups excluded
from real power, the political system yielded willingly to the
requests of party women. The ease with which the appointments were obtained signaled the limits of appointees' ability to
alter the status of the group they personified: if these appointments had been of greater consequence, they would have been
harder to come by. Moreover, the benefits of the appointment
practice did not filter down to the women who were not direct
recipients of presidential largesse.

During World War II, American women had proven themselves heroines on the home front; afterwards, they quietly took up again the responsibility to reestablish secure and stable homes. By 1960, a supposedly grateful nation had left them without any legislative or executive protection from discrimination, as vulnerable to arbitrary treatment in the public and private sectors as ever they had been before.

# 2
# MOVING AGAIN

# 5

# A NEW FRONTIER FOR WOMEN: THE KENNEDY ADMINISTRATION

The inauguration of John Kennedy in January 1961 marked a sea change: the end of postwar politics in America. For some fifteen years, national leadership had dealt with postwar problems: the establishment of a sound national and international economy; rebuilding Europe's industrial base; ensuring jobs for breadwinners in the United States; capping inflation and ending wartime government regulation; and coping with newly organized international spheres of influence. With the nation looking over its shoulder at two decades of depression and war, both Truman and Eisenhower had confronted the task of reestablishing a stable society. Now the time had come to face the future.

Elected in 1952, the avuncular Eisenhower had presided over eight years of national consolidation; but if Eisenhower's relaxed demeanor had suited the temper of the electorate in the fifties, by 1960 problems had emerged that called for a more active approach. The GI bill, with its subsidized mortgages for veterans, and a national highway construction program had permitted young couples to leave the crowded cities and buy homes in the suburbs in which to raise their families; they commuted to work by private car. The cities they had left, however, were now disproportionately populated by the poor, who were stuck in decaying and depressing tenements. Although personal income had jumped in the decade, in 1957 a severe recession signaled an end to the feeling of national prosperity. That same year the Soviet Union further undermined national confidence by orbiting two space satellites, feats that appeared to indicate a significant advantage in technical capabilities. Other observers indicted the complacency and boredom afflicting middle-class Americans. During the last two years of Eisenhower's administration, the overwhelmingly Democratic Congress confronted an unyielding chief executive. By the time the 1960 campaign began, John Kennedy's clear liberal theme—his exhortation to "get the country moving again"—resonated strongly for many Americans.[1] His election expressed a readiness on the part of a large segment of the population to meet the challenges of the 1960s head on.

A nascent liberalism had been visible even during the 1950s. The Supreme Court had ordered the desegregation of the nation's public schools in 1954, thus fueling the civil rights movement. The Democrats had firmly regained control of Congress, although the presidency stayed in Republican hands. By 1959 several liberal Democrats—among them Kennedy, Edmund Muskie, Eugene McCarthy, Frank Church, and Philip Hart—and liberal Republicans—Nelson Rockefeller, Mark Hatfield, Clifford Case—had won election in either congressional races or gubernatorial contests. A small antinuclear movement sought the control of atomic weapons.[2]

Despite his victory, the narrow margin by which Kennedy won—two-tenths of 1 percent—hampered his efforts to enact the multifaceted program he detailed under the rubric "The New Frontier" in his nomination acceptance speech. As the days of the new administration slipped by, the Kennedy "style" occupied more newspaper space than the Kennedy accomplishments. Indeed, his administration terminated so abruptly that many have since claimed that the Kennedy administration was mostly style and that, if his foreign affairs decisions were misbegotten and dangerous, his domestic efforts had hardly any substance at all.

But style and substance are not unrelated phenomena. Kennedy's call to public concern—"Ask not what your country can do for you, ask what you can do for your country"—represented a new dedication to an aggressive liberal politics, and it served as a national inspiration. After the election Michael Walzer, writing in the left-liberal periodical *Dissent,* observed: "There is an openness to new ideas probably unlike anything since the thirties."[3] In March 1961 a *New York Times* reporter described the change in the White House: "In two short months President Kennedy has set for the White House a physical and mental pace unmatched in modern times . . . in an urgent effort to solve or alleviate accumulated domestic and foreign problems."[4] Seven major pieces of legislation had been sent to Congress: aid to depressed areas, extension of unemployment benefits, a 25 percent increase in the minimum wage, medical care for the aged, federal aid to education, urban renewal, and commodity control programs. The development of the Peace Corps, Kennedy's sympathy with Martin Luther King, his public appreciation of the arts reverberated with the young. Even many of those who did not join the Peace Corps or engage in voter registration drives in black communities felt imbued with a sense of possibility and the expectation that Americans would do more and become better— that problems existed to be solved, not endured, that poverty, racism, war, Communism, illiteracy, hunger, and ugliness could and therefore should be eliminated by national dedication to a public purpose.[5]

It was a legacy that had both good results and bad. Most of the domestic legislation that Lyndon Johnson succeeded in getting through Congress in the terrible aftermath of Kennedy's assassination had already been initiated by the Kennedy team. So had the extended war in Vietnam. But in both cases the "style" was an authentic political event. It encouraged national energies that continued beyond Kennedy's life, through the 1960s, facilitating movements for women's rights, consumers' rights, ecology, and mental health services. It also produced, in the words of historians David Burner and Thomas West, "some of the finest social legislation . . . of the century."[6]

Kennedy's style inspired Americans who saw him only from a distance or through the cool medium of television, but his impact on his own team was even more intense. During the transition, Kennedy's staff drew up extensive programs for each department, and his appointees all recognized that for the first time in years proposals for federal action were welcome.

It was characteristic of Kennedy's pragmatic liberalism, however, that the proposals sought not the ideal but the feasible. His liberalism lacked the fervor of Eleanor Roosevelt's and Adlai Stevenson's, and Kennedy distrusted fanaticism. Respectful of intellectuals but impatient with excessive deliberation, he favored "technical" solutions over ideological ones. Thus, aware of his razor-thin electoral victory, and preferring movement to inertia, Kennedy often chose executive action when it was a possibility. This strategy allowed him to avoid confrontation with an unintimidated Congress, whose Republican—Southern Democratic majority stood able to turn back any Kennedy initiative, especially in civil rights.[7]

So, in response to a burgeoning civil rights movement, the Justice Department under Attorney General Robert Kennedy brought suits to protect black voting rights, and Kennedy appointed blacks to executive positions to compensate further for the lack of legislation. He also appointed a committee on equal employment opportunity to replace two existing but ineffective committees. The order banning discrimination in housing came in November 1962, and in June 1963, only two and a half years into his term, Kennedy told the nation that his administration had aligned itself with a civil rights revolution. As white-run governments in the South responded with violence to black demands for decent treatment, the Kennedy administration employed conciliation, exhortation, political pressure, litigation, and ultimately federal troops to persuade racist opponents to obey the law. In 1963, after a review of federal government and federal contractor employment practices, the administration introduced an omnibus civil rights bill to mandate equality in employment and public accommodations. John and Robert Kennedy did not keep all their promises to black civil rights leaders, and often the administration's dilatory responses indicated grudging acceptance of political realities rather than a spontaneous sense of moral outrage. Still, the Kennedy administration offered more support to black activists than any previous administration, and many black Americans regarded the Kennedy brothers as heroes.[8]

If Congress viewed the civil rights measures with mixed emotions, they welcomed Kennedy's proposals concerning the economy. When Kennedy took office, 7 percent of the labor force was looking for jobs. Even with the sometimes controlling influence of conservative Southern Democrats, Kennedy succeeded in extending Social Security benefits, raising the minimum wage, and procuring federal monies for housing and public works. Economic bills had two purposes: to revitalize the economy and lift poor Americans out of poverty, and to exploit national human resources in order to achieve a stronger position with respect to the Soviet Union. Expanding opportunities for women would further both those goals.[9]

## DEMOCRATIC PARTY WOMEN ON THE OUTS

Kennedy started with no particular public agenda for women.[10] Like most other male politicians, he was aware that women voted, but in the absence of a broadbased movement for women's rights he did not devote much attention to winning their votes as a bloc. As always, his mother and sisters figured prominently in his campaign, and, although he did not seek out women as advisers, he had accepted the assistance of Marjorie Lawson, a prominent black attorney, in his 1958 senatorial race. In 1960 she became director of the civil rights section of the presidential campaign. Congresswoman Edith Green ran Kennedy's campaign in Oregon.[11] Few top political party women played a role in Kennedy's presidential campaign, because few had joined him for the primary battles. After he won the nomination, the reception from the Kennedy campaign was lukewarm for most of the women who had supported his opponents. (Despite Kennedy's overtures, Eleanor Roosevelt chose to keep her distance.)[12]

Margaret Price of Michigan, a close associate of Michigan governor G. Mennen Williams, represented virtually the only Democratic committeewoman who had any clout within the Kennedy camp. The Michigan Democratic party had identified itself with the Kennedys early in the campaign and had offered effective assistance. Williams himself recommended that Price, whom many Democrats regarded as the most competent woman politician in the country, become part of the Kennedy entourage. Price worked closely at the Democratic convention with Kennedy's aide Myer Feldman. After his nomination the candidate rewarded Price for her efforts by giving her the Democratic National Committee position held by Katie Louchheim, vicechairman of the DNC and director of women's activities.[13] (Incensed at being shunted aside, Louchheim nevertheless accepted a minor post at the State Department.)

From that position Price tried to influence the candidate with regard to women's issues. In a campaign memorandum, Price counseled that "women (particularly organization and leadership women) respond to being 'included in.'" Price promised that if Kennedy offered evidence that qualified women were welcome, he would gain "enormously" in respect and allegiance from women community leaders. At the moment, she observed, "the absence of professional women in any staff capacity in the Kennedy entourage has led to an initial impression that his is an all-male cast." The presence of women would "give an incentive" to women throughout party ranks, she said. Price recommended that Kennedy present her to the press to emphasize the importance of women in policy-making roles and urged him to hire more women "onto his inner circle." Moreover, she advised, women party leaders needed to be integrated into the campaign and invited to party conferences, which at the moment were all male.[14]

But Kennedy preferred his largely male coterie, and he ignored her recommendations. He also declined to give Price a visible role in the campaign. Instead of including her in the group that traveled with the candidate, campaign manager Robert Kennedy recommended that Price go on independent campaign trips. She objected, saying that party leaders disliked making the additional arrangements. Kennedy refused to acquiesce; of the more than five hundred campaign stops Kennedy made, Price appeared with him on only twenty-one occasions.[15]

After he won the party nomination Kennedy did make an increased effort to attract the women's vote, but not by wooing party women or promising stepped-up efforts to improve women's status. The campaign formed two committees: the Committee of Labor Women, which included such notable reformers as Mary Anderson, Elizabeth Christman, Gladys Dickason, and others and was run by Esther Peterson of the Industrial Union Division of the AFL-CIO, and the Women's Committee for New Frontiers, which also boasted prominent liberal women, including Frances Perkins, Eleanor Roosevelt, Eugenie Anderson, Anna Rosenberg, and Agnes Meyer. These committees served in publicity and fund raising, not policy: they were intended to indicate the candidate's sympathy for the causes for which these women were known. Thus, they made special efforts to call women's attention to programs regarding medical care for the aged, federal aid to education, and full employment, issues that Kennedy's staff believed concerned female voters.[16]

On only a few occasions did Kennedy address proposals aimed specifically at the position of women. He hinted at one female appointment, saying that a consumer counsel in the Office of the President would be "perhaps a woman familiar with consumer problems." In a letter to daycare advocate Elinor Guggenheimer, a member of the Women's Committee for New Frontiers, he endorsed federal aid for childcare. Finally, to the surprise of many, including members of his own staff, he also appeared to have signed a letter endorsing the Equal Rights Amendment, which he had never before supported; although this statement turned out to have been a campaign blunder, it remained the official stance. (This incident is discussed in full in chapter 7.) The Republican candidate, Richard Nixon, paid hardly more attention to the status of women; his promises tended to concentrate on appointing women to top-level positions, but his endorsement of the ERA was genuine, in keeping with Republican tradition.[17]

After Kennedy's hairbreadth victory, Price, following her predecessors, encouraged the president to include women in his administration. In a transition memorandum she maintained that, although "women should not be appointed to high public positions simply because they are women, . . . pressures are strong for the appointment of women to top level public office. Millions of citizens . . . will give close attention to these appointments and the serious waste of manpower that would result if such appointments are not made." Price recommended that the new president appoint women to posts not previously held by women and briefly reviewed for him the records of Presidents Wilson, Roosevelt, Truman, and Eisenhower. She then enumerated, department by department, the jobs in which she thought a woman could appropriately serve: secretary of labor, ambassador, delegate to the United Nations, assistant secretaries of the

Treasury, defense, and labor, treasurer, and director of the Mint. Unlike Edwards, Price did not fight for specific women to fill specific positions; instead, she attached to her memorandum the résumés of some two dozen women.[18] Of this group, only four eventually received Senate-confirmed appointments: Esther Peterson, as assistant secretary of labor and director of the Women's Bureau; Eugenie Anderson, as minister to Bulgaria; Elizabeth Smith, as treasurer of the United States; and Lucia Cormier, as collector of customs for Portland, Maine. Of these, Peterson would clearly have gotten her position without Price's efforts; treasurer had been a "woman's job" since Harry Truman named Georgia Neese Clark to the post; Anderson had first been appointed an ambassador in 1949; and collector of customs of Portland, Maine, was a position of no policy-making significance. Twelve other women received minor or temporary appointments. Price, who had also vainly sought an administration job, was disappointed in the small numbers.[19]

Displeased party women attacked Kennedy on Price's behalf as well as their own. After Kennedy selected his cabinet, Doris Fleeson, a well-known journalist, commented scornfully in her column: "At this stage, it appears that for women the New Frontiers are the old frontiers."[20] A month after the inauguration, Emma Guffey Miller told Kennedy: "It is a grievous disappointment to the women leaders and ardent workers that so few women have been named to worthwhile positions. . . . As a woman of long political experience, I feel the situation has become serious and I hope whoever is responsible for it may be made to realize that the result may well be disastrous." A reply came not from the president himself, but from presidential aide Lawrence O'Brien, which offended Miller further. Such a thing, Miller complained, "never would have happened under Franklin D. Roosevelt or President Truman."[21] When the list of the fourteen top assistants to Peace Corps director Sargent Shriver included not a single female name, Fleeson again lambasted the President, declaring it "ludicrous" that of two hundred appointments he had made so far, only eight had gone to women.[22] Even Eisenhower, wrote Fleeson, had done better than that.

Margaret Price loyally tried to redeem the Kennedy appointment record. On November 1, 1961, she published a list of the eighty-eight women named to administration posts, but, rather than helping, the enumeration merely called attention to the problem. Of that number, fifty-four had received appointments to minor committees and commissions or to positions such as collector of customs, fourteen became special assistants to executives (probably named by other government officials, not by the president), and eight of the others were simply reappointed to jobs such as emergency planning office directors or representatives to various United Nations bodies. Only a few held positions of real visibility or had the ability to make policy: Anderson, Peterson, White House physician Dr. Janet Travel, Frances Willis as ambassador to Ceylon, and Marie McGuire as commissioner of the Public Housing Administration. Esther Peterson was the only woman in the subcabinet.[23] Genevieve Blatt, secretary of the Pennsylvania Democratic State Committee, wrote to Emma Guffey Miller a month after the list came out: "Things do seem to get worse and worse, so far as women in Washington are concerned, don't they?"[24]

In July 1963 one man did seem finally to get the President's attention. Clayton Fritchey, former publicity director of the Democratic National Committee, serving the Kennedy administration at the United States mission to the United Nations, put his thoughts in writing at the president's request. Fritchey began by reminding the president of the growing numbers of women voters and the fact that in many suburbs the women were "virtually running local politics." Fritchey cautioned against thinking that these women failed to notice female appointments. "Consciously, or not," he argued, "women naturally seize on any evidence that tends to dispel the age-old image of an inferior sex," which accounted, said Fritchey, for Eleanor Roosevelt's popularity and influence. With Roosevelt gone (she had died in 1962), the administration lacked any "notable" or "really famous" women, like Anna Rosenberg, Frances Perkins, India Edwards, or Oveta Culp Hobby, in its service. Happily, Fritchey remarked, it would take fairly few appointments "to create a favorable new impression." Fritchey recommended the appointment of an assistant attorney general ("the woods are full of capable women lawyers"), either a White House special assistant or an assistant secretary of commerce specializing in consumer affairs, another women ambassador, and a new secretary of Health, Education, and Welfare, "the ideal post." Appointment of an "outstanding Negro woman" would help as well. Such a program would guarantee the president favorable publicity—politically, it was a case of "everything to gain and nothing to lose," according to Fritchey. In addition, such a strategy was equitable. He urged speedy action "to avoid the appearance of political motivation."[25] Although he had personally solicited Fritchey's memorandum, Kennedy ignored the advice. He also disregarded the counsel of Emanuel Celler, the powerful chairman of the House Judiciary Committee. Celler, who abhorred the Equal Rights Amendment, considered appointments an appropriate way to elevate the status of women, and he had written twice to chide the president for failing to name women to the bench.[26]

The Kennedy record of appointments that provoked these complaints did compare unfavorably with that of his predecessors, but not overmuch. Kennedy made only ten Senate-confirmed appointments of women to policy-making executive and judicial posts, where in a comparable period Truman, who won extravagant praise for his record, had made fifteen, and Eisenhower fourteen. No president, Kennedy included, utilized the talents of women significantly. Women held 2.4 percent of all executive positions in the Kennedy administration, the same percentage they had held under the two previous presidents.[27]

But the problem was more than mere numbers. Kennedy also neglected visible appointments, becoming, moreover, the first president since Herbert Hoover never to have had a woman in his cabinet. He also appointed fewer "first women" to positions formerly held exclusively by men, thus forfeiting the good publicity that kind of nomination always received. Kennedy's admirers had anticipated that he would exceed the performance of his predecessors; their expectations were unmet, and they responded with vocal protests.[28]

But the displeasure Kennedy elicited came more from his neglect of women party leaders than from his record. These leaders had expected to control appointments of women, as they had in the Roosevelt and Truman years. Thwarted, they resented both their loss of influence and their lack of access to the president. India Edwards remarked that, with the Kennedy administration, "there was no one at the DNC . . . who had any influence . . . when it came to women's affairs."[29] Emma Guffey Miller voiced dismay over the exclusion of Price from White House inner circles: "The administration has been lax in recognizing Democratic women. . . . In the Roosevelt and Truman Administrations, the Vice Chairman [and head of women's affairs] was always consulted when women were being named to important posts, but now all Margaret Price knows is what she sees in the newspapers. This is not going to help the party."[30]

Indeed, the White House appointment procedures excluded Price, as Kennedy broke away from past methods of operation and instituted an ongoing, systematic talent hunt for "the best and the brightest." "Kennedy," wrote Theodore Sorensen, "wanted a ministry of talent." Both before the inauguration and after, the Kennedy search for people to staff his administration claimed to ignore considerations of campaign contributions or political benefits in favor of ability. The president would not, Sorensen boasted, "name a woman or a Negro to the Cabinet merely for the sake of show."[31] A decision to seek excellence did not, of course, automatically exclude women (or blacks); clearly, women (and blacks) could be found among the "best and brightest" minds in the nation. Yet the process Kennedy created to find his appointees not only omitted Margaret Price and insulted Democratic Party women, but it also actually worked against potential women nominees.[32]

Because the Kennedy staff conducted the search from the White House, women lost the use of traditional procedures which had been sensitive to the political utility of women party workers, and which had included a well-established role for them to play in appointments. Except for minor patronage positions, the White House paid no attention whatever to the DNC, figuring that it would not be a source of likely candidates, male or female, and suggestions sent by Congress members, too, were usually discarded.[33] Dan Fenn, who headed the talent search, observed: "It is a rare guy who comes up through a party or campaign organization who can be Assistant Secretary of Defense for Procurement." This view represented a departure from the position of earlier administrations, which often filled such posts with party faithful. The talent search Fenn conducted instituted no compensatory method of including women; Fenn said he experienced no pressure at all to pay special attention to the appointment of women, evidence that Price was not playing her traditional role.[34]

Women, moreover, were not likely to be found in the places the Kennedy staff did look. The search centered on elite universities, boards and executives suites of major corporations, and prestigious law firms, where women were few in number. This effective reduction of the pool of acceptable women candidates made their selection proportionately less likely. The blatant discrimination that kept women out of high-level jobs did not have to come from the Kennedy team; it had already taken place.[35]

The Kennedy team shared a bias against women, to be sure. A memorandum from Dan Fenn concerning the post of commissioner of education listed Mary Bunting, the president of Radcliffe College, as eighth choice, citing as handicaps both her lack of public education experience and her sex.[36] Fenn would later explain that he had viewed her gender as a drawback because of a "silly social assumption," which he shared, that women were less likely to have managerial talent and staff would be unhappy to work under a female supervisor.[37]

It was improbable, however, that Kennedy was more prejudiced than Truman or Eisenhower had been. Kennedy's appointment of Janet Travell as his personal physician and the testimony of Esther Peterson, whom he named assistant secretary of labor, Representative Edith Green, who managed his campaign in Oregon, and Senator Maurine Neuberger (D-Oreg.) argue against the premise put forth by some writers that the reason Kennedy did not appoint women was that he categorically disliked working with them and failed to respect their ability or judgment.[38] Bill Lawrence, a journalist who had been president of the National Press Club, complained that Kennedy pressured him repeatedly to get the club to admit women journalists as members, a change Lawrence opposed.[39] More plausibly it was the Kennedy search method, rather than an overt Kennedy intention, that excluded women more completely than in previous administrations.

Nothing impelled Kennedy to adopt a strategy of recognizing women voters through appointments. His association with the

DNC, which emphasized political patronage, differed from that of former presidents and their national committees. Kennedy's political organization had been largely an independent creation, based on developing contacts in local areas and run by close personal associates. With no particular attachment to the DNC, he had little reason to rely on its officers for counsel. In fact, the power of both national committees had begun generally to decline as primaries and television advertising assumed an ever greater role in candidate selection. In addition, Margaret Price was herself deferential, unwilling to press her views on Kennedy or threaten retaliation for being overlooked. (When Kennedy, for example, declined to address the biennial Campaign Conference for Democratic Women, a gathering of more than three thousand, Price accepted the decision; only when India Edwards wrote to the president threatening to cancel the meeting did Kennedy capitulate.) But also, as a member of the reform wing of the Democratic party in Michigan, Price felt little commitment to the patronage aspect of party politics. Viewing herself less as an advocate for women within the Democratic party than an advocate among women for the Democratic party, she did not work as hard for women's appointments as Edwards had.[40] "The surest way for a group to shut itself out of the appointment process is for it to blunder into a strategy of reticence," one political scientist has observed—which is just what Price unwittingly did.[41]

But appointments for women fell by the wayside primarily because Kennedy preferred another route: the fulfillment of the agenda of the Women's Bureau coalition of women's liberal and labor organizations, a course charted by Women's Bureau director Esther Peterson. The implementation of the Women's Bureau program constituted a New Frontier for women. Unlike token appointments, the new plan directly addressed the problem of women's status in American society, and its impact was far-reaching.

## WOMEN'S BUREAU ASCENDANCY

Throughout the fifteen-year struggle over equal pay legislation and the Equal Rights Amendment, the members of the Women's

Bureau coalition had looked to the bureau to provide, in the words of the second bureau director Frieda Miller, both "factual information and leadership."[42] In general, the "leadership" the bureau provided was disappointing. Although the bureau accepted the mandate, and although it saw itself as the bulwark against "extremist feminist" organizations that promoted the "so-called Equal Rights Amendment," none of the bureau's first three directors had been in a position to provide effective direction to the bureau's supporters. In 1961 the situation finally changed. During the Kennedy administration, thanks to the president's interest in an activist program and his reliance on the team in the Labor Department, the Women's Bureau at last assumed the role it had claimed for the previous decades.

Directors of the Women's Bureau had always been low-level appointees. Mary Anderson, the bureau's first chief, received her position from a Democratic president and then served three Republican presidents; none sought her advice. In Franklin Roosevelt's administration, Anderson was far outclassed by Eleanor Roosevelt, Molly Dewson, and Frances Perkins.[43] As secretary of labor, Perkins downplayed women's issues in order to minimize her own vulnerability, and the Great Depression made special claims for women inopportune with so many male "breadwinners" out of work. Anderson played a small role within the Roosevelt administration.

Frieda Miller had come to the Women's Bureau in 1944 from the post of industrial commissioner for the state of New York, a job she had had since 1938. Her background included little lobbying experience. Although she had been executive secretary of the Philadelphia Women's Trade Union League in the early twenties and a factory inspector for the International Ladies' Garment Workers' Union before becoming the head of the Women in Industry Division of New York State in 1929, she also had no influence with labor unions. Once in federal office, Miller indulged her predilection for the international aspects of the bureau's work, including extensive participation in the activities of the International Labor Organization. Because she was interested in maintaining peace, she restrained assertive behavior on the part of the bureau's advisory committees, comprising women's organizations and labor union groups. Truman, on record as favoring the Equal Rights Amendment but unwilling to alienate labor groups, relied on appointments of women to let him steer clear of the dispute. He had little to say to Miller, and her role of policy maker within the Truman administration was minor.[44]

Alice Leopold's problems were even more acute than Miller's, whom she succeeded in 1953. Leopold, too, had been a state executive (secretary of the state of Connecticut), but unlike Miller she had had few connections to working-class women or their middle-class protectors. When Leopold took over, she saw no need to convene the bureau's advisory groups on a regular basis, and so communications with the Women's Bureau coalition members became sporadic and formal. In addition, her apparent willingness to soften the bureau's anti-ERA stance made the coalition distrustful of her motives, with many inside and outside the bureau believing that Leopold's primary interest concerned professional women rather than the lower-paid working women the bureau had traditionally championed.[45] Leopold could hardly function as a good leader of the Women's Bureau coalition, or serve as an effective liaison among the various groups supporting equal pay legislation. In 1954 Labor Secretary James P. Mitchell alienated women's organizations further when he "promoted" Leopold nominally to be his special assistant for "Women's Affairs," because the Republicans linked the change to a suggestion that the Women's Bureau, the symbol and vehicle of the protection of women, be abolished.[46]

The Kennedy administration took a different tack, elevating the position of Women's Bureau director and granting her a genuine role in policy making—a departure having its roots in the Kennedy administration's affinity for its labor constituency. Kennedy's liberalism had found its most consistent expression in relationship to labor issues. While he was a member of the House, representing a working-class district of Boston, his voting record on bills of interest to labor had been virtually perfect: 100 percent for four of the six years, 90 percent and 88 percent in the remaining two.[47] As a member of the House Labor Committee, Kennedy had also taken an active part in opposing the Taft-Hartley Act, an unusual step for a first-term congressman. Although he butted heads with some union leaders for refusing to oppose all reforms, he spoke effectively in favor of the union shop, industry-wide bargaining, and the right to strike. Unable to get Taft-Hartley modified, he voted against the final bill and supported President Truman's unsuccessful veto of it.[48]

In the Senate, where his ties to a working-class constituency were looser, Kennedy continued to display commitment to rank-and-file workers as well as to the concerns of union leaders, winning respect even when he took an opposing view. As chair of the Senate Subcommittee on Labor, Kennedy deftly conducted hearings on a bill to extend minimum wage coverage, confronting Eisenhower's labor secretary, James Mitchell, and publicly forging an alliance with George Meany on the issue. In March 1958 Kennedy played a crucial role in enabling Walter Reuther, the president of the United Auto Workers, to testify before the McClellan Committee investigating corruption in labor unions ("labor rackets"); in response, Reuther labeled him "a real saint towards the UAW." Kennedy won still more publicity as the author of legislation to reform the practices that the rackets committee had uncovered, a strategy Meany opposed and tried to head off by instituting internal policing procedures. When Kennedy insisted on going through with a bill to require labor unions to disclose their finances, Meany publicly rebuked him. Both agreed to negotiate their differences privately, and Meany subsequently lauded Kennedy's openness to and respect for opposing arguments. Kennedy included the recommendations of AFL-CIO special counsel Arthur Goldberg in the next version of the bill, and the relationship between the senator and his labor constituents prospered. At the opening of the 1960 Democratic presidential convention, Communications Workers chief Joseph A. Beirne told a reporter that a majority of the AFL-CIO union heads favored Kennedy.[49] After Kennedy's nomination, organized labor pursued its customarily vigorous support for the Democratic candidate in a presidential election.

Kennedy named Arthur Goldberg secretary of labor, and Goldberg almost immediately assumed a unique role in the administration. One of the stars of the cabinet, Goldberg impressed Kennedy with his intellect and his professional competence. Goldberg had joined the Kennedy campaign early, so the president had no doubt of his loyalty, and he consulted him on a wide range of domestic policy issues. Moreover, Goldberg surrounded himself with extremely capable associates; AFL-CIO people filled out his staff, and Goldberg worked hard to maintain not only his fine reputation at the White House but also his close connection to George Meany. In August 1962 Meany commented that at no time had there been closer co-operation between the labor movement and the administration in power.[50]

As part of that alliance, John Kennedy named Esther Peterson director of the Women's Bureau. A native of Provo, Utah, raised in a Republican Mormon family, Peterson had been introduced to the labor movement at Columbia University in 1929, when she enrolled at Teachers College for graduate training after receiving a bachelor's degree in physical education from Brigham Young University. During the 1930s she taught in schools for workers, including the Bryn Mawr Summer School for Women Workers in Industry, and helped to organize teachers' unions in Massachusetts. In 1939 she joined the Amalgamated Clothing Workers Union (ACW) as assistant director for education under the wing of ACW leaders Sidney Hillman and Jacob Potofsky; in 1944 the ACW sent her to Washington as its legislative representative. As a labor lobbyist, she participated in the National Committee on Equal Pay, the National Committee on the Status of Women, and the Labor Advisory Council of the Women's Bureau. She also initiated her association with labor lawyer Arthur Goldberg and John Kennedy, in 1947 a freshman representative from Massachusetts, whom she was assigned to lobby. In 1948 she went abroad with her husband, Oliver Peterson, a labor attaché in the Foreign Service, and spent the next decade participating in the international union movement in Sweden and Belgium. When she returned to the United States in 1957, Peterson became a legislative representative in the Industrial Union Department of the AFL-CIO, which Arthur Goldberg served as special counsel, and she resumed her professional relationship with Kennedy, now a senator and a member of the Senate Labor and Public Welfare Committee. Peterson had a reputation as a consummate lobbyist; she in turn admired Kennedy's willingness to ask questions and his ability to absorb answers and approach issues in new ways. Following labor's position, while in the Senate John Kennedy supported equal pay legislation and refused to endorse the Equal Rights Amendment, citing the hazard to protective labor laws.[51]

Peterson joined Kennedy's campaign as soon as he announced his intention to run for the presidency. Robert Kennedy, the candidate's brother and campaign manager, offered Peterson a full-time campaign staff job organizing labor support, but Peterson declined because family illness restricted her freedom to travel. She continued to supply advice in an informal way, however, and at the convention she worked with Kennedy forces to swing her home state of Utah into the Kennedy column. Immediately after the convention, Peterson began to work with Arthur Goldberg at the campaign headquarters under Lawrence O'Brien and Ralph Dungan, making sure that Kennedy acknowledged labor at every turn.[52]

After the election, Ralph Dungan asked her what position she wanted. Because of her interest in working women, and because the National Consumers League had asked her to, Peterson chose the Women's Bureau. Peterson's appointment had the support of virtually every member of the Women's Bureau coalition. Mary Anderson, the bureau's first director and the founder of the National Committee on Equal Pay, sent the president-elect a letter, signed by fourteen other women representing major women's organizations, seeking Peterson's selection; the letter argued that under Peterson's direction "the true purposes of the Bureau" would be realized.[53] Louise Stitt, chairman of the board of the National Consumers League (NCL), started a letter-writing campaign on behalf of Peterson, an NCL board member. With the backing, and that of the labor unions (she was the only woman on George Meany's list of desirable nominees), her selection was assured, even though the BPW, not a traditional member of the Women's Bureau coalition, preferred a different candidate. Moreover, Goldberg saw to it that Peterson got more than the directorship of a minor bureau; within eight months, Congress created a new assistant secretary position for Peterson to hold with the Women's Bureau post. With her assumption of that position, Peterson became the highest-ranking woman in the Kennedy administration.

The assistant secretary post had the "growing role of women in the work force of the nation" as its particular purview, anticipating that the number of women workers would be likely to grow twice as fast as that of male workers. As assistant secretary, Peterson had charge of the Bureau of Labor Standards, the Bureau of Employees' Compensation, and the Employees' Compensation Appeal Board. Her responsibilities therefore included policy decisions concerning male as well as female workers.[54] With more actual authority than any previous bureau director, she was able to provide to the Women's Bureau coalition effective leadership unprecedented in the history of the bureau's existence. The bureau took as its domain twenty-four million working women—a third of all American women—concentrated in clerical, service, and factory work. More than half of them were married, and one in four had children; on average they earned 60 percent what male workers did. When she came to office in 1961, Peterson did not create a new agenda—she simply sought the implementation of the program that labor women had long supported: equal pay legislation and a national commission on women.[55]

With her program and her resources, Peterson eclipsed Margaret Price and her proposals for the appointment of women. DNC member Emma Guffey Miller, who also resented Peterson's opposition to the ERA, viewed the situation with utter disgust. Writing to congratulate Katie Louchheim on her new position at the Department of State (to a slightly less trivial post than she had received at the beginning of the administration), Miller said: "We women are very proud of you and wish the President would name more women to important positions, especially women who are for women instead of the Esther Peterson type as she goes out of her way to do the contrary thing."[56]

The Kennedy years marked the transition from a procedure of marginal utility for women—token appointments—to one that addressed women's social and economic position more directly. Kennedy neglected appointments of women, but he was protected from charges of indifference by the establishment of

the President's Commission on the Status of Women and administration pursuit of equal pay legislation. On the forty-second
anniversary of the suffrage amendment, August 26, 1962, Peterson warned that the Republicans were "planning to take a
crack at the Administration" for the dearth of women appointees. She was unperturbed, however, and assured the White
House that the interim report of the new commission "would
draw the fangs of any such attack." The British publication *The
Economist,* which commended Kennedy for his creation of the
commission, accurately observed that "many women felt that
Mr. Kennedy could have supported their cause more vigorously by appointing a woman to his cabinet as his recent predecessors had done."[57] But Peterson was essentially correct. Following her advice, Kennedy got credit for a substantial record
on women's issues. Moreover, the program Peterson laid out
for him had greater potential to affect the lives of American
women than had all the female appointments of the previous
fifteen years.[58]

# 6

# THE EQUAL PAY ACT OF 1963:
# COMPROMISE AND VICTORY

The fight over equal pay legislation in the Kennedy years took place in a very different context from the earlier battles. The politics of the time welcomed new programs, and equal pay fitted into the larger program of the Kennedy administration both to revitalize the economy and to draw upon the resources women offered. By now, the question of whether working women would take jobs away from male breadwinners and set off a new depression had been answered: women worked in jobs different from those of men—jobs men didn't want.

Given the sexual segregation of the workplace, few women would benefit from equal pay legislation, but prevailing sentiment favored giving those few the protection they deserved. In the last years of the Eisenhower administration, when social and economic obstacles had dissipated, equal pay bills fell victim not only to the objections of opponents but also to differences among supporters. In the Kennedy administration, the Women's Bureau gained the strength to lead the equal pay battle effectively. Its director, Esther Peterson, was both an assistant secretary of labor and a former lobbyist for the AFL-CIO. As such, she had authority within the administration and with women's organizations and labor unions, advantages her predecessors had lacked. Both context and structure now favored the enactment of the first federal law to bar discrimination against women by private employers.

Since the Women's Bureau coalition had begun its campaign for equal pay legislation after World War II, the role of women in the paid labor force had changed and expanded dramatically. During the 1950s the demand for female workers had bur-

geoned, the result of growth in the clerical and service occupations, which employed women almost exclusively. Yet at the
same time, the proportion of young single women seeking employment in the United States declined. The low birth rate of the
1930s meant that there were fewer young women in their twenties to take all the jobs designated as "women's work." Moreover,
many young women now elected to go to college rather than
work, and more of the others were getting married, thus causing
the pool of available single women in their twenties to evaporate
further. Because the younger married women tended to stay
home to care for their infants—a commonplace phenomenon
with the explosion in the birthrate after World War II—
employers had to forgo their preference for young, unencum-
bered female workers and offer jobs to older, married women
with school-age children. Smaller families, the appearance of
convenience foods, and the availability of various household ap-
pliances made it easier for wives and mothers to choose to work
outside the home. The GI bill, which offered men incentives to
stay in school, also encouraged employment of married women
to supplement meager family allowances. Between 1950 and
1960, the number of wives at work increased by 42 percent, from
21.6 percent in 1950 to 30.6 percent in 1960. As of March 1963,
41.5 percent of mothers with children between the ages of six
and seventeen worked for wages, compared with 30.3 percent in
1950, a 37 percent increase. Mothers with children under the age
of six raised their labor force participation rate from 14 percent
in 1951 to 22.5 percent in 1963, a 61 percent jump. By 1961
approximately twenty-four million women were working, 34 percent of all workers.[1] The Department of Labor predicted that by
1970 this number would swell to thirty million. One Labor Department economist in 1963 stated that the growing incidence of
married women workers represented "the most significant employment trend in the country."[2]

The employment of wives resulted, observers detected, in
more egalitarian marriages and in greater political participation
of women, but it did not expand women's employment choices,
nor did it raise their wages. Women workers still tended to be
clerks, service workers, factory operatives, domestic workers,
nurses, and teachers. In 1960, the wages of full-time year-

round women workers averaged only 60.6 percent those of men, down from 63.6 percent in 1957. Black women fared worst of all: their earnings were 42 percent of men's.[3]

## ORGANIZING SUPPORT

Against this backdrop, the Women's Bureau staff organized the quest for equal pay legislation in the new Congress. The outgoing Eisenhower administration, which for eight years had supported equal pay bills in vain, again submitted a proposal before Kennedy's inauguration. Immediately after, Peterson arranged for meetings with Democratic congresswomen, representatives of organized labor, and the members of the National Committee on Equal Pay to review the legislative situation.[4] The retirement of Graham Barden, the unfriendly chairman of the House Education and Labor Committee, made the situation much more tractable: his replacement, Adam Clayton Powell, Jr., a black Democrat from New York, favored the bill.

As before, the conflicts about the measure focused on two items: the coverage of employees and the mode of enforcement. Several Democratic congresswomen, including Edith Green (D-Oreg.), had introduced bills modeled on the broad coverage of the National Labor Relations Act (which applied to industries "affecting" interstate commerce). These bills granted enforcement authority to the secretary of labor. Two Republican legislators, Jessica Weis and Katharine St. George (both from New York), had introduced bills modeled on the narrower Fair Labor Standards Act (FLSA, which covered employers "engaged in" interstate commerce). Their proposals provided for judicial enforcement. The AFL-CIO had cleared the Green bill before its introduction, and equal pay advocates within the Department of Labor initially wanted the administration to support it as well, a course of action urged by experienced staffers to eliminate the problem of competing bills.[5]

Under the direction of the Women's Bureau, opinion quickly coalesced around a compromise proposal. The administration bill would adopt the FLSA-based coverage of the Republican bills to facilitate administration by the Wage and Hour Division of the Department of Labor, which oversaw the FLSA; however, it would retain the provision of the Green bill that gave "cease and desist" powers to the secretary of labor, as the AFL-CIO wanted. The Solicitor's Office of the Labor Department agreed to draft the bill.[6] In the meantime, the Women's Bureau set out to accumulate statistical evidence establishing the need for federal legislation—ostensibly a major impediment in the past. J. A. Beirne, president of the Communications Workers of America, wrote to Secretary of Labor Arthur Goldberg in February 1961 informing him that at past hearings the union had been "tremendously impressed by the lack of authoritative data on male-female wage differentials for workers doing the same work in a given plant or office location." Internal studies by the CWA showed no such wage differentials, according to Beirne; rather, discrimination took place in women's not being permitted to apply for the higher-paying jobs. Beirne expressed hesitation about supporting an equal pay bill without such data, attributing past failures to this omission. Beirne recommended that the government act to equalize employment opportunities in the event that widespread wage differentials could not be found.[7]

So, while the AFL-CIO studied the administration's draft bill, the Women's Bureau wrote to dozens of women's organizations and labor unions, asking them to use their resources to supply specific examples of wage discrimination. Reluctant to employ instances only from unionized plants, Peterson requested the AFL-CIO's organization director to have his staff look for cases from nonunion shops. In addition, promising confidentiality, the Women's Bureau wrote to state labor departments, hoping for instances from adjudicated cases or settlements. Finally, Peterson wrote to women who had complained to the bureau about wage discrimination in the past, asking them about their present situation and soliciting leads to cases.[8]

With the Women's Bureau now actively engaged in shoring up the coalition and gathering data, Arthur Goldberg decided to turn over to the bureau the entire lobbying effort on the bill as well. The department's Legislative Liaison Office had no particular interest in it—it had been around "forever"—and he assumed the bureau would work harder at getting the bill through Congress. In March 1961 Esther Peterson hired Morag Simchak, a lobbyist for the United Rubber Workers, to take charge.[9]

The White House Legislative Liaison Office also left the effort to the Women's Bureau. John Kennedy had supported equal pay legislation during his tenure in Congress, but without vigor. He introduced a bill in 1951 at the request of former House representative Mary T. Norton, who was then working as an aide to the secretary of labor, but did no more than that. In 1957, when he was chairman of the labor subcommittee of the Senate Committee on Labor and Public Welfare, he cosponsored an equal pay measure with Senator Wayne Morse and others but did not hold hearings on the bill despite a request to do so. A confidential listing of the standing of White House legislative proposals omitted equal pay legislation under both "major" and "minor" headings. Thus the "administration effort" on behalf of equal pay legislation became more and more localized in the Women's Bureau office at the Department of Labor.[10]

The Women's Bureau managed at least to bring its regular constituents into line. The AFL-CIO disliked the narrowed, FLSA-based coverage of the bill, but acquiesced. The National Committee on Equal Pay, composed of many of Peterson's old colleagues, including Caroline Davis of the United Automobile Workers, Mary Anderson, the first director of the Women's Bureau, Helen Berthelot of the Communications Workers, and Olya Margolin of the National Council of Jewish Women, quickly concurred. By mutual agreement, Edith Green, who had sponsored equal pay legislation ever since her election to the House of Representatives, was named chief sponsor in that body. Wayne Morse (D-Oreg.), an originator of equal pay legislation in 1945, and Patrick McNamara (D-Mich.), whose subcommittee would consider the bill, would introduce the bill in the Senate.[11]

Although the Department of Labor and the White House expressed solid support for the bill, other administration officials tried, albeit unsuccessfully, to block the measure. Under Secretary of Labor W. Willard Wirtz wrote Goldberg in early May 1961: "Arthur: I am *not* in favor of this proposal. I think it is utterly unrealistic and that if such a bill were adopted it would be the worst failure since the 18th Amendment. Nor am I per-

suaded that this is either necessary or good public relations."
The Bureau of the Budget, too, expressed reservations about
the need for such a bill and delayed its approval while awaiting
cost estimates.[12]

Nevertheless, by the end of July Esther Peterson was able to
write to AFL-CIO legislative director George Riley that "things
are moving along at last."[13] The administration bill was sent to
the House and Senate in August 1961. In his transmittal letter
to the president of the Senate, Goldberg observed that unequal wages had an adverse impact on both purchasing power
and worker morale, which in turn hindered production, a key
concern of the Kennedy administration. Equal pay, Goldberg
contended, would prevent employers from using women to
undercut the wages of male workers and would bring the workplace closer to the ideals of American justice.[14]

Equal pay legislation also received the endorsement of the
President's Commission on the Status of Women, a move Peterson orchestrated. At its first meeting in February 1962, Eleanor
Roosevelt, the commission chairman, commented: "I should
think this was a fairly safe thing to take up,"[15] and she told the
press that the commission believed that unequal wages for comparable work were "contrary to the concept of equality and
justice in which we believe."[16]

While the Women's Bureau staff shepherded the bill through
legislative channels, data in support of the bill began to come in
from the Women's Bureau constituents. The American Association of University Women produced a study of men and women
in executive positions that disclosed discriminating pay practices
in many companies. Caroline Davis of the UAW supplied material about a recent strike that resulted in the reduction of pay
differentials between men and women, not to zero, but to ten
cents an hour. Hattie Trazenfeld of the BPW reported on cases
collected from that organization's membership, and the Wom-
en's Bureau discovered specific wage differentials in about a
dozen union contracts from 1959 to 1961.[17] Peterson herself
sought cases as she traveled around the country. At one point, a
manager told her that unequal pay scales were "equitable."
When, over coffee, she pressed him for his meaning, he offered
lame justifications, which she contended she did not understand.

Finally he said to her: "Mrs. Peterson, don't do this to me. You know we pay them less because we can get them for less," an explanation Peterson often repeated in discussions with members of Congress.[18]

Thus, proponents were well prepared for the hearings that took place in March 1962, before a select subcommittee on labor headed by Herbert Zelenko (D-N.Y.) of the House Education and Labor Committee. Arthur Goldberg led off, addressing himself to the principle of equal pay legislation, then Peterson offered individual stories and surveys of wages in particular cities, including a Women's Bureau study of work orders for public employment revealing 120 job requests that offered men higher wages than women. Representatives from both sides of the aisle spoke in favor, as did delegates of various labor unions who called for the bill's enactment in order to bring nonunion shops and less enlightened unions than their own into line with the principle. Emma Guffey Miller, now chairman of the National Woman's party, supported the bill as befitted a devoted Democrat but spent most of her testimony arguing for the Equal Rights Amendment. (Privately, Miller called the measure "the so-called equal pay bill"; another NWP member characterized it as "a smart dodge for the people who want to spike the movement for real equality.")[19] Katherine Peden, president of the National Federation of Business and Professional Women's Clubs, appeared for that organization's 175,000 members and offered examples of unequal pay from BPW files. The American Association of University Women and the National Councils of Jewish, Catholic, and Negro Women also sent contingents. The National Association of Manufacturers did not attend but filed a statement affirming its belief in equal pay and its opposition to federal "intervention." Additional hearings also took place in New York, where such notables as Eleanor Roosevelt and Bette Davis testified, along with several more organizations. No one offered opposing arguments.[20]

A clean bill incorporating changes suggested in the hearings received unanimous endorsement from the House committee. The administrative enforcement provision had been lost, which irritated the AFL-CIO, and a section excluding employers with fewer than twenty-five employees was added, but the committee included a new provision expressly forbidding employers to lower the wage rates of male employees to comply. During the House debate on the rule, Representative Katharine St. George (R-N.Y.) declared that she did not see how anyone could oppose the legislation: "It would be like being against motherhood."[21] Nevertheless, many representatives had specific objections. Chief among them was the language of the key clause, requiring "equal pay for comparable work." In response, Katharine St. George proposed substituting the phrase "equal pay for equal work."

Bills concerning equal pay for women had always used the terminology "comparable work" requiring "comparable skills," rather than "equal work." Opponents of the bill objected that comparability would prove virtually impossible to determine, but advocates feared that "equal" would mean "identical," and that "slight and inconsequential" differences might be used to justify disparate wages. Few state equal pay laws applied only to identical jobs, and General Order 16, promulgated by the War Labor Board in 1942, spoke of "comparable quality and quantity of work" in authorizing equal wages for women workers. Supporters argued that formal job analysis and rating procedures, carried on in cooperation with labor and management, would establish "comparability" if necessary. This battle went to the conservatives, however: Republicans heavily supported St. George's amendment to change the wording, and it passed 138 to 104.[22]

During the House debate on the measure, several representatives offered additional amendments. Republican representative Charles Goodell (New York) moved to eliminate the provision prohibiting compliance through a lowering of wage rates, citing the "panic" of retailers, and the amendment passed 132 to 116. An amendment to add the words *or race* to the bill everywhere that *sex* appeared, offered by Charles S. Joelson (D-N.J.), was disallowed on a point of order, raised by Edith Green, as not being "germane." At the close of the debate the House passed the bill by voice vote. No one had spoken on the floor against it.[23]

House approval surprised and alarmed business groups. Unaware of the new impetus behind the bill, they had assumed it would meet the same fate it had before. The U.S. Chamber of Commerce, realizing that it had been remiss in failing to take concerted action against the bill in the House, hastily organized a campaign to bottle up the bill in the Senate committee. "Nobody really was taking the bill very seriously, but suddenly it has become a reality," a chamber spokesman told the *Wall Street Journal*. The *Journal* attributed the bill's success to administration efforts and quoted a Senate Democrat as saying, "The Kennedy administration really wants this. They can build this up as a staggering social achievement."[24]

As part of its eleventh-hour lobbying effort, the chamber devoted an issue of its bulletin to equal pay, assuring business leaders that their fear of equal pay legislation did not mean they were prejudiced. The chamber asserted that there were in fact many arguments against "coercive" federal power: for one, pay differentials often resulted from the "added costs" of employing women, caused by their supposedly higher rates of absenteeism and turnover and by state laws requiring special benefits such as rest periods. Federal legislation to compel equal pay would undoubtedly create more problems than it would solve, the chamber insisted. That the misbegotten bill had gotten as far as it did the chamber attributed to "Mrs. Peterson's twelve-hour day."[25]

In their attempt to stall action in the Senate, business groups confronted the chairman of the Senate Subcommittee on Labor, Pat McNamara, and demanded hearings. McNamara refused. The chamber finally found an ally in the ranking minority member of the Senate Labor and Public Works Committee, Barry Goldwater (R-Ariz.), who succeeded in blocking committee approval. When McNamara finally agreed to amend the bill to permit employers to reflect "added costs" in wage differentials, Goldwater lent his support. Because it was too late to win committee endorsement, in early October McNamara offered the bill as a rider to a State Department construction bill already before the Senate, and it passed.[26]

Although the equal pay bill had for the first time won approval in both houses of Congress, McNamara's strategy ultimately failed. Because the Senate bill differed from the House bill, the legislation had to go to a conference committee. But the Senate action had created parliamentary problems: the bill to which McNamara appended the equal pay measure had been reported out of the Senate Foreign Relations Committee, whereas the House Education and Labor Committee had handled equal pay. With only nine days between the Senate vote and adjournment, committee jurisdiction could not be resolved and the bill died. The belated opposition of the business community, by stalling the bill in the Senate Committee for so long, resulted once more in the bill's demise. But this time the new backers of the bill were not so easily undone.[27]

## COMPROMISE AND VICTORY

Peterson, Simchak, and the Women's Bureau staff started on a new bill immediately. Taking into account the various amendments of the administration bill offered in each house and the recommendations of the AFL-CIO, the new draft, again modeled on FLSA coverage, included the following provisions: enforcement by the secretary of labor, exemption of employers with fewer than twenty-five employees, prohibitions against compliance by wage cutting and against labor unions seeking unequal wage scales, use of the language "equal work" rather than "comparable work," a gradual elimination of wage differentials, and exclusion of offending firms from government contracts.

The draft bill represented a compromise. The AFL-CIO objected to FLSA coverage and to permitting employers to bring wages into line gradually. The Department of Labor disliked substituting "equal work" for "comparable work." Yet advocates of the legislation took the position that, for the moment, half a loaf was better than none.[28]

With the replacement of Secretary of Labor Arthur Goldberg by Under Secretary W. Willard Wirtz in September 1962, however, new problems appeared from within the administration. Goldberg had strongly backed the bill; Wirtz opposed it. With Wirtz running the shop, other equal pay opponents became bold. In response to a request for an opinion on the new bill, Walter Heller, chairman of the Council of Economic Advisers (CEA), notified the Bureau of the Budget that the council objected to the bill, citing a lack of "convincing evidence" and the possibility that "economic" reasons, such as the "added costs" of hiring women, might account for such differentials as did exist. Heller based his letter on an internal memorandum, written by Norman Simler of the CEA staff. Simler, who warned the council that fighting the bill was like "opposing virtue," accused the Labor Department of supporting the bill for its vote-getting appeal and failing to document its contention that women were indeed paid less than men, relying on "common knowledge" rather than hard data. Simler found the bill more objectionable now that it referred to "equal work" rather than "comparable work"; he doubted that many men and women actually did "equal" jobs and feared employers could therefore easily evade enforcement efforts. He predicted that the Department would ultimately create another expensive bureaucracy that would not succeed in eliminating pay discrimination. "But even if it [the bill] could be administered and enforced," Simler argued, "no evidence is presented demonstrating a need for it."[29]

Peterson responded aggressively to the CEA's contentions, asserting that Heller's reasoning revealed "a complete lack of understanding of not only the political but the economic aspects of the bill." After a telephone conversation with Peterson, Heller agreed "to take another look at it," and to have Simler call her as well. Her conversation with Simler disclosed that his research had been limited; he had neither looked at the report of the committee hearings nor asked the Women's Bureau for additional information. The day following Peterson's conversation with the two, the Council of Economic Advisers withdrew its letter to the Budget Bureau.[30]

Both Simler and Heller remained unpersuaded, however. In a memorandum for the council, Simler summarized the evidence Peterson had offered to Congress in 1962. Although he included surveys of job-hiring orders with double pay scales, labor-management contracts that applied wage rates by sex, two private surveys of employers totaling more than two thousand firms of which one-third admitted to double pay standards, and a survey of salary schedules by the National Education Association showing one salary rate for men and and another for women teachers in sixteen school districts, he insisted that the differing wage rates could reflect disparities in job content that the titles failed to disclose. He concluded: "What this all adds up to is that the Labor Department does not have one shred of evidence, except possibly the 120 cases of job orders . . . , that there is discrimination in *wage rates* based on sex where men and women perform *equal* work on jobs requiring *equal* skill in the *same* place of employment."[31] Still, Heller said, the Council of Economic Advisers would not enter "objection" to the bill.[32]

Disturbed by the new opposition from within the administration, Peterson dealt with Wirtz directly. In a February 1963 meeting, he objected to the costs of enforcing the equal pay law. Perceiving a lack of sympathy on his part for women affected by such discrimination, Peterson argued that his objection to administrative enforcement would embarrass the administration vis-à-vis unions and women's organizations. Moreover, the amount of money requested for enforcement was small in comparison to other allocations. "It does not seem unreasonable," Peterson maintained, "to spend approximately the same amount of money the government now spends on paper clips and stapling machines in order to protect the pay of 24 million women members of the labor force." Peterson argued also from the political standpoint—that women felt that pay and job discrimination affected them seriously and that such a bill would impress groups such as the BPW, possibly breaking them away from their traditionally Republican allegiance. She recognized that the bill constituted only a first step for women: "This Bill will *not* give most of them real relief, since it does not give them equal opportunity." But it would point the way to future steps.[33]

Peterson prevailed; the Bureau of the Budget finally advised that it would not obstruct the bill. Despite the continuing objections of Secretary Wirtz and CEA chairman Heller, Peterson carried the administration bill to the Hill on February 14, 1963, where it was introduced in the House by Edith Green and in the Senate by Pat McNamara.[34] The prohibition against compliance by lowering wages had been omitted because McNamara believed the bill included the injunction implicitly. The Labor Department continued to amass better evidence of the bill's need, and the AFL-CIO Executive Council issued a statement calling for prompt action without detrimental amendments.

Frank Thompson, chairman of the House Select Subcommittee on Labor (who kept material on the bill filed under *B* for "Broads"), scheduled hearings for the middle of March, hoping that, in view of the extensive hearings held the previous year, testimony would be brief.[35]

This time, business representatives organized early. The Chamber of Commerce urged its members to write or wire their representatives telling them that the bill would give the government "sweeping powers over industry" and make the secretary of labor "PROSECUTOR, JUDGE, AND JURY."[36] Manufacturers' associations met with Labor Department officials and complained that the new bill did not take into account the "added costs" of hiring women or the fate of small manufacturers who would go out of business if they had to raise women's wages.[37]

Representative Charles Goodell (R-N.Y.) sympathized with these complaints. Goodell himself believed the administration bill to be too vague; in conjunction with labor and industry representatives, particularly officials of Corning Glass Works, an important New York employer, Goodell offered a bill simply amending the Fair Labor Standards Act. As such, the bill contained no twenty-five employee test, it narrowed coverage by excluding all the exempted occupations included in section 13 of the FLSA, and it utilized the enforcement provisions of the FLSA, which meant that only the courts could compel employers to comply.[38]

During the hearings in March and April, Peterson and the bureau's allies testified against Goodell's approach. Amending the FLSA would bring undesirable consequences, they said, particularly the unavailability of administrative enforcement and the exclusion of several categories of employees from coverage. The AFL-CIO representative argued that even the coverage of the administration bill (which followed the FLSA in affecting only employers "engaged in" commerce) fell short; the labor organization still preferred the broader scope of the National Labor Relations Act.[39]

This time, four corporate executives spoke in opposition to any equal pay law, and five more submitted written statements. Their objections rested on the powers given the secretary of labor to "harass" businesses, the supposed added costs of hiring women, the anticipated difficulty of assessing equality of work, and the lack of a need for federal legislation. Some firms, though, reflecting an awareness of the likelihood that *some* bill would pass, testified in favor of legislation if it were to be an amendment to the Fair Labor Standards Act.[40]

Business opposition to the administration measure was much more vocal than it had been in the fifties, when the bill had failed without it. After the hearings, pressure mounted to assuage business fears by enacting equal pay legislation through revision of the Fair Labor Standards Act. Although the Department of Labor feared this proposal might open up the FLSA to other less desirable amendments, advantages became apparent. By way of compromise, the administration bill had limited coverage to employers with twenty-five or more employees; because the FLSA applied to all employers with two or more employees "engaged in commerce," amending the FLSA would actually increase by about three million the number of employees covered. With business objection so strong, Peterson and others feared that administrative enforcement would be lost in the legislative process anyway, and the FLSA provided established investigative practices that often resulted in voluntary compliance before court action became necessary. Goodell's bill had the recorded support of many Republicans; it appealed to legislators because it was "simple"—it did not require new procedures or machinery. The Department of Labor began to consider any other prospect of passage unlikely.[41]

After close consultation with Peterson, Simchak and other Labor Department staff, the Senate and House committees decided to endorse amendment of the FLSA. On April 30, Pat McNamara introduced such a bill in the Senate, with Edith Green following in the House on May 6. Both bills prohibited discrimination on the basis of sex in the payment of wages for "equal work on jobs the performance of which requires equal skill, effort and responsibility, and are performed under similar working conditions," and neither permitted employers to lower wages rates to reach this goal. The act was to take effect one year from the date of passage. Both the House and the Senate committees reported the bills quickly and favorably, barely one week after their introduction, despite an attempt by the Chamber of Commerce to instigate further hearings because of "inadequate" consideration of this approach in the earlier hearings.[42] In response to the congressional committee reports, Peterson stated: "There are advantages and disadvantages to this FLSA route, but the decision was made by the Congress and we believe the bills as reported out of committee are good ones." With little debate, the Senate passed the bill on May 17.[43]

Peterson had consulted with the AFL-CIO before consenting to Goodell's proposal, and, reluctantly, the organization supported the new bill.[44] Writing to members of Congress, Andrew J. Biemiller, director of the Department of Legislation, asked for their vote in favor but observed that the bill did not meet even "minimum requirements for equal pay legislation" and cautioned against any further weakening amendments. Yet Biemiller also stated that the organization would support an amendment to delete a provision granting an extra one-year stay of the law in cases where the employees were covered by a union contract. The measures granted relief, claimed Biemiller, not to unions but to employers.[45]

During the House debate at the end of May, few representatives spoke against the bill in general, although several offered specific amendments. Motions to forbid the secretary of labor to investigate without a written complaint and to permit employers to pass along "costs of hiring women" in wage differences both met defeat. Those amendments that were adopted did not eviscerate the bill: the House spelled out that wage differentials resulting from seniority, merit, or piece rate would not be illegitimate, and added a provision making labor unions culpable if they attempted to get an employer to agree to wage differentials based on sex. Many representatives commended the choice to amend the Fair Labor Standards Act over other methods of enactment. The bill in the House passed easily on May 23.[46]

Senator McNamara, contradicting assertions made on the House floor, took pains to state for the record that the bill did not require "a pattern of violation" for an employer to be culpable and that the Senate did not construe "equal" to mean "identical." The Senate then concurred in the House amendments—

the final legislative action—on May 28. Thus, eighteen years after its initial proposal, an equal pay bill came before the president for his signature.[47]

The long fight for an equal pay law culminated in a signing ceremony in the president's office on June 10, 1963, with several congresswomen, Wirtz, Peterson, Simchak, and Labor Department staff members, representatives of women's organizations, Mary Anderson, and Frances Perkins in attendance. In his remarks, drafted at the Labor Department, Kennedy observed that despite the work still to be done, the law represented a significant moment.[48]

Although its focus was narrow, the Equal Pay Act marked the entrance of the federal government into the field of safeguarding the right of women to hold employment on the same basis as men. Traditionally, the business community had justified women's lower wages by claiming that women worked for "pin money," not for income to support their families. By making wage discrimination illegal, the federal government undermined this view and implicitly supported, for the first time, the contention that paid employment was consonant with a woman's obligations as wife and mother.[49]

Women who had worked long and hard for equal pay legislation expressed deep gratitude to Peterson. Wrote Caroline Davis of the UAW:

> It could never have happened without the tremendous effort put forth on your part and the work of the women in your U.S. Women's Bureau under your expert guidance. Believe me I know, because for 15 years that I have been on the staff of the UAW we have worked to secure passage of a law, and at a time had high expectations, only to have [them] dashed before we got very far. This is indeed a great accomplishment on your part and you can rightfully be very proud that your influence played the greatest part in securing this victory.[50]

Indeed, the leadership of the Women's Bureau proved crucial. The bureau forged a compromise by persuading women's organizations and labor groups to accept a bill lacking features they had considered vital and by quashing disunity in the administration. In its final form, the equal pay law guaranteed equal pay for "equal" rather than "comparable" work; it excluded employees not covered by the Fair Labor Standards Act; it contained no provision for administrative enforcement. Yet future amendments to the Fair Labor Standards Act extended coverage, and the procedures established by the Wage and Hour Division of the Department of Labor ultimately offered good results. Court decisions construed the meaning of "equal work" liberally, declining to apply the law solely to identical jobs: in the first ten years of its enforcement, 171,000 employees had been awarded $84 million in back pay alone under the provisions of the law.[51]

The Women's Bureau coalition had succeeded in enacting its chief legislative objective through the advantages of a sympathetic social setting, an administration tied to its labor constituency, and effective leadership in Peterson and Goldberg. This particular combination of circumstances permitted the Women's Bureau coalition to achieve yet another of its goals: a commission on the status of women that had the power to reach beyond the narrow limits of an equal pay law and examine the whole question of women's status, even while draining away the minimal energy still fueling the Equal Rights Amendment.

# 3

# THE PRESIDENT'S COMMISSION
# ON THE STATUS OF WOMEN

# 7

# THE PCSW VERSUS THE ERA

If the Equal Pay Act represented a "specific bill for a specific ill," the President's Commission on the Status of Women served as the Kennedy Administration's omnibus approach to matters affecting women's lives. Since 1946 the Women's Bureau coalition had sought such a commission, but before 1961 every attempt in Congress to create a commission to examine the status of women had been derailed by the debate over the ERA. Esther Peterson, secretary of labor Arthur Goldberg, and their associates in the Department of Labor determined that such a fate would not befall the commission they proposed. Confident of the resources at their command, they contemplated instead a commission that, by taking a fresh approach to the problems confronting women, would do in the ERA.

One of the resources they possessed was the support of the president. All the previous efforts to establish a commission had looked to Congress to enact legislation, but that strategy had allowed ERA supporters to marshal their partisans to oppose the commission. When Peterson came to Goldberg with her idea for a commission, the secretary of labor offered a different idea: that the president establish the commission by executive order. With the Labor Department running this particular show, ERA supporters would not even know about the commission until it was a fait accompli.[1]

The idea of an executive commission was not entirely new either. Several times since World War II, organizations had proposed presidential commissions to study ways to advance opportunities for women, though without success. In 1948 the American Association of University Women had asked President Truman to name a commission of outstanding men and women to recommend measures to integrate women into every phase of the preparedness program.[2] The National Security Resources Board rejected the proposal, saying: "It is recognized that there are no basic personnel techniques of unique applicability to women workers." The board insisted that the idea that women must be distinguished from other workers "represents one of the more potent obstacles to the general use of women workers."[3] After the Korean conflict began, the AAUW reiterated its request, telling the president that a commission was needed to establish policy concerning the use of women in such emergencies, and that women should be integrated in the planning for the long-range defense effort. Again administration advisers concluded that "there is no special problem of 'women power.' Problems in utilizing women are part and parcel of the total problem of utilizing human resources."[4]

The most important recommendation had come from the National Manpower Council (NMC) at Columbia University. In the 1957 study *Womanpower*, the council staff pointed out that, although the federal government had not taken a stand on the desirability of women's employment, many statutes concerning, for example, taxation and licensing, had an impact on women workers. The NMC therefore recommended that the secretary of labor establish a committee to review "the consequences and adequacy of existing federal and state laws which have a direct bearing on the employment of women."[5]

Eisenhower's Department of Labor, however, seemed loath to admit, by appointment of a commission, that it was not equal itself to the task the NMC proposed. Women's Bureau director Alice Leopold recommended that the secretary "utilize existing facilities, including both governmental agencies and interested non-governmental organizations" to look into the effect of legislation on women's employment.[6] Leopold may have doubted her ability to control a commission composed of leaders of women's organizations and notable educators with whom she had few ties; yet if the director of the Women's Bureau recommended against appointing a commission on women, no other administration official was likely to overrule her. The secretary followed her advice, and the commission was not appointed.[7]

Ideas for a commission under the Kennedy administration

came from many sources. The New York Business and Professional Women's Club had written to the president on inauguration day to request the creation of a panel to discuss the utilization of the skills of mature women. Kennedy turned the letter over to Esther Peterson, who replied that another, similar plan was being considered. With Peterson, Katherine Ellickson, formerly assistant director of the Social Security Department of the AFL-CIO, and Dollie Lowther Robinson, also a longtime union employee now at the Women's Bureau, the coalition favoring a commission had strong voices. Robinson, a black woman, urged that the president express the same concern for women's opportunities as he had about racial discrimination; the commission would be such a vehicle. Secretary Goldberg took the plan to Kennedy.[8]

Kennedy agreed to the idea, sympathetic to the general aims and recognizing that his administration needed a program for women. At the commission's first meeting, Kennedy explained his support: "Every two or three weeks," he said, "Mrs. May Craig [the Washington correspondent for the Portland, Maine, *Press Herald*] asks me what I am doing for women."[9]

The president's commission had many other appealing aspects. For one, it had the potential to do some good—the problems it pointed to were legitimate matters of concern. Kennedy was confident of the commission's leadership in the Labor Department, believing rightly that they would not allow the commission to embarrass him. The proposal also had virtually no costs to the administration. The commission's goals, so far as they were stated, were congruent with the goals of the administration, and the mere establishment of the commission committed the president only to examining the problems raised, not to a particular set of policy initiatives. Once proposals were made, he could pursue them with some insulation from criticism. They would, after all, represent the best judgment of a prestigious group of public leaders, including the most prominent exponent of the liberal Democratic position and the most highly respected woman in the country, Eleanor Roosevelt.

The former first lady's acceptance of the commission chair identified her—at long last—with Kennedy's administration, an endorsement the president had long sought. Everyone backing the plan agreed that only Eleanor Roosevelt could chair a presidential commission on the status of women. Her acquiescence gave it the seal of approval and smoothed out the long and troubled relationship she had had with Kennedy. As early as 1950, Roosevelt had opposed the then representative over a bill he was sponsoring giving aid to Catholic schools. In 1956, when Kennedy made a bid for the vice-presidential nomination, she had made much of his failure to speak out against Joseph McCarthy, the senator from Wisconsin who was wreaking havoc with unsubstantiated charges of communist infiltration in the government. Later, Roosevelt and Kennedy became embroiled in a tense exchange over an allegation Roosevelt had made on television—that Joseph Kennedy was spending lavishly to buy the nomination for his son. Intensely hostile to Kennedy's father, who had infuriated her husband when he was president, and dedicated to the candidacy of Adlai Stevenson, she had been a powerful opponent during the primary campaign. She was slow to rally to Kennedy even after he won the nomination, and Roosevelt's distance had been a constant irritant to the Kennedy team. But now she was officially on board. Apart from conducting meetings, Roosevelt did little of the actual work of the commission; she did, though, serve as an adviser, make herself available for publicity purposes, and sign letters. When she died in November 1962, the administration decided not to appoint another chair, stating simply that there could be "no adequate replacement."[10]

Under the leadership of the Women's Bureau, the plan to appoint a commission to investigate the status of women, after so many years of proposals for legislative and executive action, came finally to fruition. The Women's Bureau staff drew up a comprehensive program, and Peterson, Goldberg, and the White House staff selected the eleven men and fifteen women participants, making sure to acquire people who would ultimately develop a program the White House could endorse.[11]

Commission membership represented the mainstream opinion of the Women's Bureau coalition and included several key administration officials. Eleven members came from the government, including Peterson, who held the position of executive vice-chairman, the attorney general, the chairman of the Civil Service Commission, the secretaries of the Departments of Commerce, Agriculture, Labor, and Health, Education, and Welfare, and four members of Congress, two Republican and two Democrat. Officers of the National Councils of Jewish, Catholic, and Negro Women and the National Council of the Churches of Christ spoke for middle-class women reformers. Two more members came from labor unions. Two college presidents, Mary Bunting of Radcliffe College and Henry David of the New School for Social Research, represented the world of higher education. (Under Bunting's direction, Radcliffe had instituted a new program to permit older women to return to college, and David had been executive director of the National Manpower Council when it published *Womanpower*.)

The commission also included Caroline Ware, a historian who had been fired in 1935 from a summer teaching job at the University of Wyoming because she was married (to Gardiner Means, a New Deal economist). The incident had engendered a great deal of publicity because Ware fought the dismissal, gaining the support of the National Association of Women Lawyers, the BPW, the American Federation of Teachers, the National Woman's party, and several other organizations but to no avail. Margaret Hickey, the public affairs editor of the *Ladies' Home Journal*, also served. As a past president of the pro-ERA National Federation of Business and Professional Women's Clubs, Hickey appeared to favor the ERA, but only Marguerite Rawalt, an attorney and a member of many pro-ERA groups, endorsed the amendment openly. A representative of the progressive business firm Kaiser Industries and one political appointee placed on the commission at the request of Vice-President Lyndon Johnson made up the balance of the membership. Dr. Richard A. Lester, a Princeton University economist who had worked on the Kennedy campaign, was appointed vice-chairman.[12]

President Kennedy established the President's Commission on the Status of Women on December 14, 1961. In his executive order, written at the Women's Bureau, the president contended that "prejudices and outmoded customs" prevented the "full realization of women's basic rights" and hindered their ability to make their fullest contribution to the national welfare. He pointed out that women traditionally had "served with distinction" in times of national emergency, only to be treated as marginal in times of peace. The creation of the commission recognized, he said, that women were entitled to "develop their capabilities and fulfill their aspirations on a continuing basis irrespective of national exigencies." The twenty-six-member commission was charged with reviewing progress and making recommendations in six arenas: employment policies and practices of the federal government; employment policies and practices of federal contractors; social insurance and tax laws; labor legislation; political, civil, and property rights; and new and expanded services necessary for women as wives, mothers, and workers. The commission's report was due October 1, 1963.[13]

In his accompanying remarks, the president expressed his hope that the commission would indicate what needed to be done to demolish the barriers to women's full participation in the nation. Progress, he said, would require the "cooperation of the whole community," through legislation and the provision of needed services. He promised to make the federal government "a show case of the feasibility and value of combining genuine equality of opportunity on the basis of merit with efficient service to the public." The federal career service would henceforth be maintained, he declared, "in every respect without discrimination and with equal opportunity for employment and advancement."[14]

Because the commission met only eight times in the two years of its existence, the Women's Bureau and commission staff exerted a great deal of influence. They implemented all commission requests, planned meetings, answered mail, communicated with other government agencies between meetings, developed position papers, and reviewed recommendations. Commission staff and officials also conferred with the White House over questionable proposals.[15]

Confident that the commission would yield good results, the White House supported it enthusiastically. At the commission's first meeting, held at the Executive Mansion, the president assured the members of his backing: "I can't imagine any more important assignment—not merely for women, but for members of Congress, organized labor, women's organizations themselves, religious groups, and all the rest," he said. "I promise you that we are strongly behind you in all your work."[16] In May 1962 he reiterated his interest in the commission's work on Eleanor Roosevelt's television program, "Prospects of Mankind." Kennedy, moreover, never refused a request made of him by the commission, a happenstance undoubtedly aided by the fact that Esther Peterson cleared all such appeals with the White House before they were proffered.[17]

In order to broaden its support among women's organizations, the commission agreed at its first meeting to set up subcommittees composed of experts in various areas. The staff named seven committees after the subjects listed for investigation in the executive order: federal employment; private employment; civil and political rights; protective labor legislation; social insurance and taxes; home and community; and education. Each committee was chaired by a commission member, and most had at least one other member on its rolls. Like the commission, the eighty-nine committee members included educators, lawyers, and members of womens' organizations, labor unions, business firms, and state governments. The committee system gave many individuals and organizations a feeling of involvement in the commission's outcome.[18]

Still, Esther Peterson, who guided the development of the commission within the Kennedy administration, realized that the dispute over the Equal Rights Amendment could easily wreck this commission, as it had all the other commission proposals. She knew that if the commission opposed the amendment at its outset, pro-ERA organizations would be unwilling to cooperate, and no consensus would emerge on an effective plan to help women. Although Peterson herself opposed the Equal Rights Amendment, she wanted to keep the conflict from destroying a serious effort at addressing the many conflicts, burdens, and obstacles confronting American women. Therefore, in contrast to the 1947 bill to establish a commission, the President's Commission on the Status of Women did not begin with an overt declaration against the constitutional amendment; Peterson promised, rather, that it would examine the issue "objectively."

## THE EQUAL RIGHTS AMENDMENT
## AND THE 1960 CAMPAIGN

John Kennedy agreed with the Women's Bureau coalition on the ERA. In 1957 the then senator had told the Massachusetts Committee for the Equal Rights Amendment that he could not declare in favor of the amendment although he believed in "non-discriminatory treatment of women." He wrote: "There is still, I humbly acknowledge, some question in my mind as to the most appropriate method of insuring real equality for women."[19] In 1958 he explained to a constituent who requested his support for the resolution, "My experience in the field of protective labor legislation has made me somewhat wary about over-all solutions to problems which do not always lend themselves to easy or simple formulas."[20] He assured her, however, that he continued "emphatically" to favor equal opportunity for women. During the preconvention presidential race, the senator declined to comment directly on the ERA.[21]

Although attached to the Kennedy campaign, Esther Peterson was less circumspect. She was still working as a legislative representative for the Industrial Union Division of the AFL-CIO, and from this position she headed the alliance to prevent the Democratic convention from endorsing the amendment in the 1960 party platform. Peterson testified before the platform committee on behalf of twenty-four national organizations, contending that real equality required measures that distinguished between men and women. "Specific bills for specific ills," she declared, was the better way to go. Peterson listed three principal objections to the ERA: it would nullify protective labor legislation at a time when increasing numbers of women in the labor force made the need for such laws more acute; it would create confusion in legislation concerned with marriage, property, and personal status; and it would fail to address the major forms of discrimination that were the result of custom. She asked the platform committee instead to endorse equal pay legislation and the pursuit of equal opportunity without disturbing protective labor laws.[22]

The organized opposition surprised the National Woman's party, which had not been confronted by its opponents at the platform hearings since 1948. The NWP told the platform committee that renunciation of the ERA, in view of the Democratic party's past commitment to it, would be "unprecedented and incredible." With support from the National Federation of Business and Professional Women's Clubs and the General Federation of Women's Clubs, Emma Guffey Miller, chairman of the NWP, pointed out that past efforts showed that it would take more than a hundred years to repeal, law by law, the fourteen hundred statutes that discriminated against women. Moreover, she asserted, without the constitutional amendment subsequent state legislatures could reenact each one.[23]

To Miller's dismay, the Democratic drafting committee accepted enough of the opposing argument to endorse, not the Equal Rights Amendment, but "equal treatment" for women. Incensed, Miller labelled the language "impossible" and meaningless. Working with Representative William Green of Philadelphia, she managed to get the plank amended in the full platform committee, of which she was also a member. The plank read in its final form: "We support legislation which will guarantee to women equality of rights under the law, including equal pay for equal work." Despite the alteration, the platform represented success for opponents of the ERA. A statement in support of a constitutional amendment, which had appeared in every platform since 1944, had been eliminated.[24]

The National Woman's party simply refused to acknowledge the defeat. As a member of its national council explained, "The wording, . . . though not so specific as 'Amendment,' does we feel include an amendment as a means of bringing about 'equality under the law.'" The language of the plank, she insisted, did not represent a victory for ERA enemies. Ignoring the facts, the NWP maintained that the Democrats had endorsed the ERA in 1960.[25]

After the platform battle, the NWP sought Kennedy's personal endorsement of the ERA. Emma Guffey Miller, ultraloyal Democrat and chief advocate of the ERA within the Democratic party, wrote to John Kennedy that she was extremely concerned because Vice-President Richard M. Nixon, the Republican nominee, had delivered a prompt statement asking for "widespread support" of the Amendment.[26] Miller advised Ken-

nedy to announce quickly in favor of the ERA and to point out
publicly that the Democratic platform surpassed the Republicans' on women's rights. Labor opposition to the ERA, she
counseled him, came not from chivalrous concern for the well-
being of mothers but from male fears of lost jobs.[27]

Wringing an affirmation of the ERA from John Kennedy
proved difficult, however. Not only had Kennedy himself declined to support the ERA theretofore, but campaign letters on
women's rights had to meet Esther Peterson's approval. Kennedy's reply to Miller, which Peterson checked over, thanked her
for the opportunity to make a statement "regarding equal
rights for women." Expressing his belief in equal rights for all
"regardless of race, creed, color, or sex," he quoted the platform plank and stated his full approval of it. The letter concluded: "You have my assurance that I will interpret the Democratic platform . . . to bring about, through concrete actions, the
full equality for women which advocates of the equal rights
amendment have always sought." The letter did not contain any
statement of support for the Equal Rights Amendment.[28]

Annoyed, Miller took the matter into her own hands. Although she had few ties to the Kennedy campaign (she had
supported Lyndon Johnson in the primary battle), as a Democratic Committee member from Pennsylvania she had many
friends at DNC headquarters. Miller amended the letter in pen
and had a colleague deliver it to the DNC. There, an assistant to
the chairman of the publicity committee had it typed on the
Kennedy campaign letterhead and signed, presumably by machine, without the knowledge of the Kennedy campaign staff or
of Peterson. The new letter read: "Thank you for providing me
with an opportunity to make a statement regarding the equal
rights amendment. . . . You have my assurance that I will interpret the Democratic platform . . . to bring about, through concrete actions including the adoption of the Equal Rights Amendment, the full equality for women which advocates of the equal
rights amendment have always sought." In this manner, John
Kennedy's "support" for the Equal Rights Amendment became
a matter of official record. Peterson was outraged, but the Kennedy campaign let the matter drop, unwilling to expose internal
conflict or inefficiency.[29]

Miller won the battle, but the announcement that Esther Peterson was to head the Women's Bureau suggested that she would lose the war. When press reports intimated that Kennedy intended to appoint Peterson as Women's Bureau director, the National Woman's party was aghast. Emma Guffey Miller tried to organize a movement against Peterson and wrote to the president that this appointment was inconsistent with his stated support of the ERA, a disingenuous argument at best. Miller, who had no influence at the White House, did not succeed in harming Peterson.[30]

## THE PCSW: AN ALTERNATIVE TO THE ERA

Peterson, in the meantime, found herself in a good position to make Miller miserable. In April, with eighty-two House resolutions on the ERA in the hopper, she told a *Washington Post* reporter that rather than having the ERA she would like to see a committee of the "best brains in the country" assay the status of women and recommend ways to improve it. She expressed her confidence that if all the women's organizations, pro and con, would discuss the conflict over women's legal place, a solution would appear. "If we sit down and talk this over," she said, "I feel sure we can work out a way to achieve our goals."[31]

While the commission was being planned, Peterson cautioned presidential aide Myer Feldman to have his letter writers stick to the platform and omit any mention of the "nuisance" amendment in responding to letters from ERA supporters. She realized, she said, that the issue amounted to "peanuts," but the "pile of peanuts" was growing pretty big and the proponents were intensifying their efforts. Indeed, Miller, who scoffed at Peterson's offer of compromise, told her co-workers at the NWP to barrage Secretary of Labor Arthur Goldberg with letters in order to "counteract" Peterson's influence, a campaign doomed to fail. Miller regarded Goldberg as "very broadminded"—but Peterson authorized the secretary's answers to letters from ERA supporters, and she used the exact language of the original Kennedy campaign letter, endorsing the Democratic platform and full equality for women but not the Equal Rights Amendment.[32]

In the meantime, the ERA languished in Congress. Although 135 members of the House had introduced ERA resolutions by the fall of 1961, they did so with the knowledge that House Judiciary chair Emanuel Celler would not permit the bill to be reported. The seventeen Senate sponsors knew likewise that the upper chamber would agree to the amendment only with Carl Hayden's rider preserving "benefits" for women. Still, Miller viewed Peterson as the ERA's greatest threat.[33] "We must find some way to shut her up, at least from opposing what our platform and President have endorsed," she told a friend.[34]

Peterson did not shut up; instead, she and her colleagues used the presidential commission on women to stop the ERA dead in its legislative tracks. Peterson reasoned that Congress would not be likely to act on the amendment while the matter was under consideration by a presidential panel. In addition, she presumed that eventually the commission would offer substitute recommendations that would further stymie the amendment's progress.

But obstructing the ERA was not the commission's chief objective; the Hayden rider had already taken care of that. The creators of the commission intended it primarily to devise an alternative program to improve women's status. Unfortunately, as they saw it, the ERA dispute had always made such a goal impossible.

From the very first discussions about the commission early in 1961, its creators worried about protecting the commission from being "diverted" from its task by the argument over constitutional equality. Throughout the spring, the Women's Bureau staff, Peterson, and Katherine Ellickson of the Social Security Department of the AFL-CIO refined arguments in favor of a commission, hoping to devise a plan that women's organizations would deem acceptable, regardless of their position on the ERA.[35] One staffer observed that "there is a good bit of evidence to suggest that the objectives of most women's groups with respect to women's status are the same, despite differences expressed by those who favor or oppose the Equal Rights Amendment."[36]

When Peterson presented the plan to the White House, she began by arguing that "the appointment by the President of a

Commission on women in our American democracy would substitute constructive recommendations for the present trouble-
some and futile agitation about the 'equal rights' Amendment."
But more than that, she asserted, the commission would "help
the nation to set forth before the world the story of women's
progress in a free, democratic society, and to move further
towards full partnership, creative use of skills and genuine
equality of opportunity." Peterson told White House aide Myer
Feldman that trade union women, professional women, and
congressional staff had all greeted the idea with enthusiasm.
But the commission could succeed only if the ERA dispute did
not undermine it.[37]

Therefore, Peterson decided, the PCSW would, in contrast to
past commission proposals, begin without taking an overt stand
on the issue. In her remarks at the announcement ceremony,
Peterson paid tribute to Emanuel Celler, who had first introduced a bill proposing a national commission on women in
1947—but the Celler bill had included a policy statement endorsing statutes that distinguished women from men if the laws
were "reasonably based on differences in physical structure,
biological, or social function." This statement established before
the fact that such a national commission would necessarily oppose the ERA, which was designed to strike down laws based on
just such characteristics. The executive order creating the President's Commission on the Status of Women contained no such
phrase indicating a preconceived position.[38]

Peterson's plan paid off. The president's commission won
enthusiastic support from the influential BPW, as well as from
many pro-ERA organizations. Congress members and women's
organizations joined the BPW in expressing widespread interest in the commission, and women in the federal government
felt encouraged by the new policy the president had enunciated. Caroline Davis, director of the Women's Division of the
United Automobile Workers, wrote to Peterson: "Congratulations[;] you did it. This is a victory that we have long waited
for."[39] In an editorial, the *Washington Post* praised Kennedy for
creating the "blue ribbon panel," declaring that the country
could not afford to waste the trained talent of women.[40] The
*Christian Science Monitor*, observing that Kennedy had been criti-

cized for failing to appoint women, crediting him with launching a "distaff 'fair deal.' "[41]

Not everyone shared the enthusiasm, however. Despite Peterson's expression of esteem and a letter from Arthur Goldberg telling him that the presidential commission represented the "fruition" of his efforts, Emanuel Celler took the commission to task. He noted its appearance with interest, he said, but he wanted to "sound a warning" that he would oppose "any effort on the part of this group to revive any campaign for the adoption of the so-called Equal Rights Amendment which is an 'Unequal Rights Amendment.' " Celler, perhaps because of the absence of the biological function clause, apparently did not recognize the commission's origins in his own proposal. He went on to vilify the amendment, declaring that "mores have set off women from men and no constitutional Amendment could alter them." He expressed his hope that the commission would not be "pressurized" to raise the "specter" of the ERA.[42]

The National Woman's party also viewed the commission with suspicion, but for reasons more realistic than Celler's. Emma Guffey Miller correctly judged that the commission arose partly from Peterson's distress over Kennedy's "endorsement" of the ERA during the campaign, and Miller saw to her own dismay that Peterson was now "riding high, wide and handsome" within the administration.[43] Alice Paul presciently explained to a questioner that the commission had been set up to prevent the adoption of the amendment and that ERA opponents would urge Congress members to delay action on the amendment until the commission had issued its report.[44]

Opponents of the amendment did just that. The White House reported that the president would not comment on the amendment until the commission had concluded its work, and Arthur Goldberg asked Emanuel Celler to defer House Judiciary Committee activity on the ERA until the commission report was submitted. Celler in turn recommended to the Senate Judiciary Committee that it wait for the report, and Carl Hayden made the same request to the full Senate. Although the Senate Judiciary Committee reported the ERA favorably in August 1962, the Eighty-seventh Congress took no further action on it.[45] An NWP member reported to Miller that both adversaries and advocates of the ERA in Congress with whom she had spoken "say frankly that they are not going to 'jump the gun'" on the president's commission.[46]

Of course, there was never a chance that the commission would endorse the Equal Rights Amendment, despite its claim to be approaching the study of the ERA without prejudice. By design, too many commissioners came from labor or women's groups that opposed it. Because a body with no ERA supporters would lack credibility, Marguerite Rawalt, a past president of the BPW and a member of the National Woman's party, had been appointed, but she was the only certain ERA supporter of the membership of twenty-six. In addition, Peterson, Ellickson, and the Women's Bureau staff maintained a careful watch over the commission, monitoring proposals and making the administration position clear.[47]

Although she knew Peterson would not allow many ERA supporters on the commission, Emma Guffey Miller, Democratic National Committee member and NWP chairman, did not take her exclusion philosophically. She brought her displeasure to the attention of John Bailey, chairman of the DNC, and to Governor David L. Lawrence of Pennsylvania, a state in which the Guffeys and Millers had significant political clout. Lawrence confidently wrote to the White House asking that Miller be given a seat on the commission, but to his surprise he received a letter, drafted by Peterson, regretfully denying his request but offering Miller a seat on the commission's subordinate body, the Committee on Civil and Political Rights. Even this appointment did not come to pass, because Edith Green, the committee chairman, vetoed Miller's participation. Miller continued her efforts to win a place on the commission until its conclusion, but Peterson squelched her petitions without much difficulty, explaining to the White House staff that the commission contained no political members except members of Congress and the cabinet. Furthermore, Peterson said, Marguerite Rawalt represented Miller's point of view. Miller's extended campaign to become a member of the Commission came to nothing.[48]

Understandably, tension between Peterson and the National Woman's party remained high. Miller bitterly resented Peterson's station within the administration. An informant had told her, to her disgust, that "no woman has an entree at the White House unless Esther Peterson . . . introduces her";[49] although this was an overstatement, the White House did customarily check such matters with her. Indeed, Peterson's instructions caused a White House aide to deny an appointment to an NWP member the president himself had promised to meet.[50] For her part, Peterson viewed the National Woman's party with increasing disdain. She told Assistant Secretary of Labor Daniel Patrick Moynihan and Lee White, a White House aide, that the NWP was a "paper organization, with no standing with substantial women's organizations." The ERA was introduced each session, she said—"tongue-in-cheek"—because male legislators hesitated to declare themselves against women, and the NWP consistently met with defeat despite the fact that "the little ladies marched the corridors from the first day of the session to its end."[51] Nevertheless, because the Commission was ostensibly neutral, the warfare was covert. Peterson promised NWP correspondents that the subject of the ERA would be approached with an open mind. "As a member," she wrote, "I want to take this opportunity to assure you that the Commission has undertaken a completely objective study of this question."[52]

## SEQUESTERING THE ERA

If the commission did not in fact approach the subject of the ERA with an open mind, neither did it consider the subject lightly or arrive easily at the stand it took. The Women's Bureau and the commission staff recognized that, improperly handled, the dispute over the ERA could still make the commission fruitless. Even the commission members, many of whom were not privy to Peterson's rationale for the Commission's establishment, realized the dangers. Hyman Bookbinder, representing the secretary of commerce, broached the issue at the first meeting, feeling, he said, like "the proverbial fool who likes to move in where angels fear to tread." Remarking that the amendment had "divided the country" for years, he asserted that "if this Commission does nothing else [but] get an accommodation of views on this difficult and delicate area, we will have made a substantial contribution." Viola Hymes, president of the National Council of Jewish Women, agreed that the ERA had been "the most divisive . . . issue . . . among women's organizations," which had not reexamined their positions on it for twenty-five years. The commission would, she felt, "enable the women's organizations to take a new look in the light of developments and changes which will be very helpful." "Maybe," she suggested, "the women's groups will get together." To this Peterson declared: "It will be worth the Commission if we do it."[53]

But for the commission to unite women's groups on this issue, it first had to make sure it would not itself be torn apart by it. Indeed, the planners evolved a way to prevent such an outcome—by sequestering the highly loaded discussion so that it did not supplant the rest of the commission's work. The commission turned the issue over to one of seven subunits it had established, the Committee on Civil and Political Rights. Because no public statement on the ERA would be made until the commission concluded its work, the other six committees could address the many additional problems women faced without themselves becoming embroiled in the conflict over constitutional equality.[54]

As a result of this strategy, the Committee on Civil and Political Rights became the first commission body to confront the problem of the ERA directly. It did so in an exceedingly civilized fashion. Representative Edith Green, an ERA opponent, chaired the committee, although Marguerite Rawalt, the commission's one ERA advocate, took over when Green turned her attention to her reelection campaign. Peterson had appointed Rawalt to the commission because she considered her a sensible and thoughtful advocate of the ERA; Rawalt, in her turn, respected Peterson's directness and her commitment to improving women's employment laws. Committee membership, apart from the two commission members, included two representatives of labor unions, six members of the legal profession, most of them opposed to the ERA, and three presidents of pro-ERA women's organizations. ERA supporters were outnumbered, but at least they were represented.[55]

The committee met for the first time in May 1962 and quickly established pointedly even-handed procedures for dealing with the ERA. Like the other commission subunits, the Committee on Civil and Political Rights began to accumulate data, in the form of returned questionnaires from women's organizations (on both sides of the ERA controversy), staff papers, and the findings of committee members' own research. The committee decided to invite four organizations—two groups favoring the amendment (the National Woman's party and the BPW) and two opposed (the American Association of University Women and the American Nurses Association)—to present their opinions on the ERA at the next meeting.[56]

## A COMPROMISE PROPOSAL

Unexpectedly, however, a member of the Civil and Political Rights Committee offered yet another approach to the matter of constitutional equality. Pauli Murray, a black attorney long associated with the civil rights movement, volunteered to write a memorandum detailing a strategy to get a court ruling that discriminatory state laws violated the Fourteenth Amendment. One of the few explicit connections between the civil rights movement and the federal quest for equity for women in the early 1960s, Murray's proposal offered, she said, an alternative to choosing one side or the other of the controversy. Murray thought the commission could thus avoid both conflict with the "very influential" National Woman's party and the waste of effort in attempting to win ratification of the ERA from three-fourths of the state legislatures, which she viewed as impossible. Murray suggested instead that the commission recommend a concerted effort to pursue litigation of a case involving a discriminatory state law, with the goal of having the Supreme Court decide that arbitrary discrimination against women violated the Fourteenth Amendment in the same way racial bias did. The problem, as Murray saw it, was not that some laws distinguished between men and women, but that those that did failed to take into account differences among groups of women, such as those with children and those without. A ruling under the Fourteenth Amendment would provide the flexibility to maintain appropriate laws relating to women, while abolishing those that simply hampered women's right to function in the public sphere. In reviewing previous court cases, Murray argued that past decisions had not revealed a consistent pattern and that the Court might be willing to make a ruling distinguishing among groups of women if persuaded by a "Brandeis-type brief" discussing the changing roles of women. She proposed that either the American Civil Liberties Union or the Justice Department compile such a brief with the assistance of a commission-sponsored Legal Advisory Committee.[57]

At the request of Esther Peterson, Pauli Murray presented her plan to the full commission at its October meeting. Impressed with her suggestions, the members decided to distribute an expanded version of her memorandum to attorneys in the Justice Department. Concern arose over the plan's implications for protective labor legislation, but Murray herself asserted that these laws should remain undisturbed.[58]

In the expanded version of her paper, Murray explained that a new differentiation needed to be drawn between laws "genuinely protective of the family and maternal functions" and those that discriminated "unjustly" against women as individuals. The courts, she counseled, had not theretofore made distinctions among women, assuming that all would consider their maternal and family functions primary. True freedom of choice would permit women to develop different abilities if they so chose. Murray argued that the principle developed in the 1908 case *Muller* v. *Oregon,* which permitted states to enact laws aimed exclusively at women, had inappropriately been extended to institutionalize a virtual "separate but equal doctrine" for women. Laws could appropriately classify citizens by sex, she maintained, when the law protected "maternal and family functions" and applied only to women who performed those functions, when it protected the health of women or compensated for women's traditionally disadvantaged position, or when the differential treatment did not "imply inferiority." Murray suggested that a statute to protect future mothers could legitimately single out "women of child-bearing age"; she therefore did not envision the total equality sought by advocates of the Equal Rights Amendment. Nevertheless, she still affirmed the need to proscribe arbitrary classification by sex in state codes.[59] Peterson regarded Murray's proposal with great hope.

"You must know how grateful I am to you for this work," she
wrote her. "I feel in my bones that you are making history."[60]

Aware of the controversial nature of the proposal, and therefore of the necessity of frequent consultation with interested
women's organizations, the Committee on Civil and Political
Rights invited fifteen women's organizations, including the National Woman's party, to appear before it in March to address
the Fourteenth Amendment strategy, the ERA, and the state-
by-state approach to women's legal status.[61] Murray was hopeful of reaching an accord. She observed that in the past the
advocates of both the national commission and the ERA had
*assumed* that the Fourteenth Amendment could not reach discrimination based on sex. "The controversy over the Equal
Rights Amendment seemed to force people who espoused the
same goals into rigid positions and dissipated energies which
might have gone toward a development of standards for the
concept of equal status," she said. "[This controversy] can be
avoided if we can get a consensus of sound alternatives."[62]

But agreement was hard to come by. The American Association of University Women asserted that it still preferred the
state-by-state approach. The American Nurses Association reas-
serted its stand against the ERA but said it did not feel qualified
to comment on the Murray proposal. The National Council of
Jewish Women both reiterated is objection to the ERA and took
exception to the Murray recommendation.[63] The NCJW spokes-
woman, Mrs. Samuel Brown, predicted that the procedure
would be "time-consuming, costly and laborious without any
assurance that the results will be entirely satisfactory." Brown
found the plan fundamentally lacking in two ways: it equated
racial discrimination, which was always bad, with differential
treatment based on sex, which was sometimes desirable; and it
assumed that women's organizations, which had never before
been able to agree on what constituted "discrimination," would
now unite on a definition.[64]

ERA proponents were no more enthusiastic. Although the
National Woman's party agreed to appear at the committee
hearing, the members evinced a deep distrust of the proceed-
ing. Margery Leonard declined Emma Guffey Miller's request
to represent the NWP, saying, "I wouldn't mind the time, effort

and money involved in such an undertaking if I could feel it would do any real good. [But the Commission] is controlled by our arch enemy. The Commission was handpicked." Leonard asserted that even Marguerite Rawalt—an NWP member—was not their advocate: "The fact that she is on the Commission shows she is no friend of ours."[65] Other NWP members contended that Pauli Murray, a black woman, was primarily concerned with the movement for racial equality and that she apparently intended "to hitch that wagon to our Equal Rights Amendment star," which would "spell disaster for our hopes." One party officer believed, in a staggering misperception of reality, that black civil rights groups wanted to use the ERA struggle "as a springboard for their own propaganda."[66] Finally, however, the NWP did send two representatives to the committee meeting, at which the NWP, the BPW, the American Medical Women's Association, and the National Association of Women Lawyers backed the ERA, arguing that the Supreme Court had not in the past been amenable to making the sort of ruling that Murray advocated.[67]

Of the groups asked, only the National Council of Catholic Women endorsed the Murray approach, but at the same time it emphasized the necessity of recognizing differences between men and women. It approved of wider access for women to the world of politics and paid labor, especially in the fields of education and social work, but it cautioned, "It must be remembered that the most important function of woman will always be associated with home and family." Although man and woman were equal in dignity before God, the council asserted, their natures differed and women did not have the same ability to "wage that struggle for survival which still prevails in all walks of life." Women's organizations thus seemed to feel no impulse to abandon their prior positions to unite behind Murray's plan.[68]

Nevertheless, as the discussion continued, the committee appeared convinced that, with the Fourteenth Amendment approach, women could have the protection of both the Constitution and state labor statutes. Its members felt sure that the Court would uphold statutes such as support laws requiring husbands to provide for their families—which would not be permissible under the ERA—and still strike down "unreasonable" legal distinctions. Respectful of differing viewpoints, and without an established position to defend or a history of personal antagonism, the committee could reach for a compromise.[69]

## THE ERA—"NEED NOT NOW BE SOUGHT"

But even as the committee sought a new route toward constitutionally based equality, it still felt obliged to make a statement about the Equal Rights Amendment. At the March 1963 meeting committee member Frank Sanders, a Harvard University Law School professor, insisted that, with the amendment now under consideration by Congress, they had a duty to take a stand on the controversial item. "This has been an eternal political question," he told them. "There has been no Congress when this hasn't been pending before it. . . . Here is an expert body that spent two years and a hell of a lot of the government's money." Congress, he claimed, would want to know the committee's views.[70] Esther Peterson said with Sanders that Congress expected guidance from the commission, and other committee members agreed that the situation demanded a declaration. Pauli Murray, however, demurred, still suggesting some way of dealing with the issue short of polarization, which had stymied any action in the past. She explained, moreover, that if the Court refused to rule as she hoped under the Fourteenth Amendment, she herself would advocate the ERA.[71]

Although Peterson said she was reluctant to influence the committee's position, she nevertheless made the Department of Labor's views known. Pauli Murray asked whether the Labor Department would object to mention of the ERA as one of many alternatives. Peterson initially replied: "I think you should express yourselves on this. I have tried to stay out"; but she continued, "The Department of Labor does feel that protective labor legislation is seriously threatened if an equal rights amendment were passed."[72] Peterson endorsed the suggestion that the committee approve the principle expressed in the ERA while indicating "dissatisfaction" with "any formulation presently in effect" coupled with an affirmative approach under the Fourteenth Amendment. At the end of the March meeting, the committee asked a subcommittee composed of Pauli Murray,

Marguerite Rawalt, and three others to draft a recommendation on the subject of constitutional equality, which it could
propose to the full commission.[73]

The subcommittee resolution affirmed the need for constitutional recognition of women's equality before the law and
ducked the issue of the Equal Rights Amendment. The recommendation read: "Equality of rights under the law for all persons, male or female, is so basic to democracy and its commitment to the ultimate value of the individual that it must be
reflected in the fundamental law of the land." Pauli Murray
proposed an additional statement that declared: "The Commission also believes that legal distinctions between the sexes not
reasonably justified by differences in physical structure or by
maternal function are violative of this constitutional principle,"
but the subcommittee rejected it. The subcommittee expressed
its sentiment that the principle of equality was implicit in the
Constitution and that the courts would ultimately affirm it. It
requested interested groups to take steps that would lead to a
ruling to that effect. As for the ERA, the subcommittee recommended a statement for the commission: "In view of the promise of this constitutional approach, the Commission at this time
takes no position on the proposed equal rights amendment."
The recommendation carefully refrained from criticizing the
efforts of any group with regard to improving the status of
women, remarking that the progress women had made in the
recent past was due to the work of civic and women's groups;
the statement urged that such activities continue. The subcommittee proposal went on: "[The Commission] therefore com-
mends and encourages the continued efforts of such interested
groups in educating the public to the problems and in urging
action within the . . . government to the end that full partnership of women may become a reality whether effected by federal or state legislation . . . or through appropriate federal or
state constitutional Amendment, or by test litigation within the
existing constitutional framework." Marguerite Rawalt was
deeply relieved at the recommendation.[74]

At the meeting of April 5, the committee changed the recommendation from "at this time takes no position on the proposed
equal rights amendment" to "does not take a position in favor

of the equal rights amendment at this time." The majority of the committee opposed the ERA and felt obliged to say so. But those who objected to the constitutional amendment believed they were leaving options open, both by including the phrase *at this time* and by encouraging other groups to work toward the end they considered most suitable, even including a constitutional amendment. In making this statement, the committee hoped to placate ERA supporters.[75]

The commission was not at first so cautious or so diplomatic. Far more than the committee, it seemed willing to turn the amendment down flat. Marguerite Rawalt chaired the discussion at the commission meeting of April 23–24; the lone ERA supporter, she had more at stake than any other commission member. Carefully she explained to the commission the reasoning behind the committee's delicately worded recommendation and its desire not to bar any course of action. John Macy, chairman of the Civil Service Commission, was not persuaded. Unwilling to admit even the possibility of supporting the ERA, he contended: "You weaken the basic position . . . if you also continue to ride the equal rights amendment horse."[76] Rawalt tried to persuade the commission against complete rejection of the ERA, saying it was a national commission's duty to encourage rather than to foreclose action, and she cited the support of the BPW and the General Federation of Women's Clubs and of Presidents Truman, Eisenhower, and, ironically, Kennedy for the ERA. On the other side, both Henry David, president of the New School for Social Research, and Viola Hymes, president of the National Council of Jewish Women, argued against hedging, including phrases like *at the present time*. They insisted that because the president's commission was to go out of existence in October, it could either endorse the amendment or reject it, but it could not suggest that the position might change in the future. Caroline Ware, herself a victim of sex discrimination, dissented. She suggested that if the Court refused to rule favorably in a test case, some constitutional amendment might be appropriate. Although David and Hymes repeatedly asked for a clear commission vote on the subject, vice-chairman Richard Lester, Caroline Ware, and Mary Bunting, the president of Radcliffe, seemed eager to avoid one. Ware suggested that a "pro or con" approach was "wrong" in view of Murray's new suggestion. Rawalt, who recognized the certainty of a rejection if a poll were taken, predicted that a "yea or nay" vote would result in a newspaper headline the commission might wish to avoid. The majority of the commission appeared sensitive to the prospective enmity a flat denunciation of the ERA would bring from the BPW and other pro-ERA women's groups: only three voted in favor of a substitute statement offered by Henry David and Norman Nicholson of Kaiser Industries clearly condemning the amendment.[77]

A substitute drafted by the Department of Justice that did not change the substance of the committee draft won greater favor. It read: "In view of the fact that a constitutional Amendment does not appear to be necessary to establish the principle of equality, the Commission believes that constitutional changes should not be sought unless, at some future time, it appears from court decisions that a need for such action exists." Rawalt objected to the contention of "fact" in the first part of the recommendation, and the commission eliminated that part and substituted the word *since*: "Since a constitutional Amendment does not appear to be necessary. . . ." ERA opponents then maintained that the word *since* indicated that they were not foreclosing the possibility that the amendment might become desirable under unforeseen future circumstances; they therefore moved to strike the words after *sought*. Despite Rawalt's objection, the motion carried ten to five. Rawalt, who felt sorely defeated, asked to be recorded in opposition. The other four votes opposed are unknown.[78]

On the day following the vote, Rawalt made a final attempt to modify the commission statement. She observed that deleting the words from the Justice Department recommendation— "unless at some future time it appears from court decisions that a need for such action exists"—appeared to close off the consideration of amendments in the future. Rawalt argued that many had said that the word *since* indicated a recognition that a constitutional amendment might be appropriate if the Murray approach failed, and that this position could be stated more clearly by inserting the word *now*—"the Commission believes that constitutional changes should not now be sought." Henry

David, although an enemy of the ERA, seemed eager for some
sort of compromise and suggested "need not now be sought," a
change Rawalt quickly accepted. Margaret Mealey of the National Council of Catholic Women, another strong ERA opponent, seconded the motion. The motion carried, but the vote
was not recorded, except that Henry David asked to be noted as
"not voting." Rawalt had succeeded in averting a flat denunciation of the ERA.[79]

But more important, despite lingering concern that even the
Fourteenth Amendment approach might imperil some legislation commission members thought valuable, the commission
had followed the committee recommendation and asserted that
women had to have some affirmation of their rights to equal
treatment under the Fourteenth Amendment to the Constitution. Coming from a citadel of the Women's Bureau coalition, it
was the first genuine move toward compromise since the NWP
had proposed exempting protective laws from the ERA forty
years before.[80]

## EQUALITY OF RIGHTS: "BASIC TO DEMOCRACY"

In its report the President's Commission on the Status of
Women emphasized its stand that women needed the protection of the Constitution against arbitrary sex discrimination; it
did not stress its position on the ERA. The section of the
report entitled "Women Under the Law" began with the statement that "equality of rights under the law for all persons,
male or female, is so basic to democracy . . . that it must be
reflected in the fundamental law of the land." It went on to
say that whereas the commission believed that this principle
was already incorporated in the Fifth and Fourteenth Amendments to the Constitution, but that some state laws made distinctions between men and women that "do not appear to be
reasonable in the light of the multiple activities of women in
present-day society." The commission had considered three
approaches to dealing with such laws, it said: test litigation
looking toward Supreme Court review, the Equal Rights
Amendment, and state legislative action. The report continued: "Since the Commission is convinced that the U.S. Consti-

tution now embodies equality of rights for men and women, we conclude that a constitutional amendment need not now be sought in order to establish this principle. But judicial clarification is imperative in order that remaining ambiguities with respect to the constitutional protection of women's rights be eliminated." Interested groups should, the commission said, seek appropriate test cases. In addition, the commission asked all branches of government to "scrutinize" their laws and to remove "archaic" discriminatory standards. With respect to the activity of other groups, the commission "commended" and "encouraged" education and action "to the end that full equality of rights may become a reality." No specific proposals were mentioned.[81]

On the day the commission report came out, Peterson wrote to Senator Carl Hayden to thank him for his efforts in staving off the Equal Rights Amendment. His rider, she said, had constituted "an indispensable safeguard." She expressed her hope that "active work on the E.R.A. could be deferred to allow a reasonable opportunity for testing the effectiveness of the new approach recommended by the Commission"; she was sure, she told him, that the Supreme Court would uphold protective laws for women under the commission plan. She asked him, however, to be sure to continue appending his rider if the ERA were introduced.[82]

Predictably, the National Woman's party opposed the commission's conclusion with respect to the ERA. "In our opinion," explained an NWP statement, "the fate of American women should not be left to a possible future change in the attitude of the Supreme Court." The NWP did not object philosophically to the proposed reinterpretation of the Constitution; it avowed only that the possibility was unlikely. "Such a change," the party declared, "might not come for years, or it might never come." In any case, the party expressed the hope that the president's commission would signal the end of the study of women's status, which had been investigated ever since the presentation of the first colonial petition for women's suffrage 315 years before. Adoption of the "simple, clear and comprehensive" Equal Rights Amendment constituted the next logical step, the party maintained.[83] Privately, Emma Guffey Miller called the outcome "a contradictory report from a packed committee."[84] Alice Paul proposed that the NWP simply ignore the commission report and go forward with the ERA, which again awaited action in both the Senate and the House.[85]

Congressional opponents, however, believed that the proposal of the president's commission eliminated whatever chance the ERA had in Congress. Carl Hayden sent copies of the commission report to correspondents, telling them: "In view of the recommendations . . . , I doubt that it would be possible to obtain two-thirds majority in each branch of the Congress in favor of submitting the Equal Rights Amendment for ratification by three-fourths of the State Legislatures." He suggested that persons who complained of discrimination file federal suits.[86]

Peterson herself viewed the commission suggestion on constitutional equality as a constructive plan of action, and she called a meeting ten days after the commission presented its report to discuss its implementation. She invited the National Woman's party to attend, and three representatives, including Alice Paul, participated, along with delegates from several other women's groups. Although Paul publicly expressed her hope and support for legal appeals through the courts, she continued to believe that such a strategy would "cripple the movement for the Equal Rights Amendment," which she did not intend to allow.[87] An expanded meeting of organizations willing to work on the Fourteenth Amendment approach took place two weeks later, with some seventeen groups present, including, again, the National Woman's party, which wanted to monitor the proceedings. The group elected the BPW president to chair a clearing-house for the dissemination of information, creating much the same structure as the National Committee on Equal Pay. Plans were made for future meetings. Despite the uncertainty of the outcome, and the ambivalence of the NWP, for the first time since the introduction of the ERA in 1923 women's organizations on both sides of the question were uniting to work on an alternative plan for constitutional equality.[88]

The creation of the President's Commission on the Status of Women thus succeeded in achieving one of the goals of the Women's Bureau coalition. During the commission's life it forestalled action on the ERA in Congress, and it developed an alternative that seemed likely to sap the strength of the amendment's appeal in the future.

But by agreeing that women needed to be considered "equal under law," it broke the long-standing stalemate that had hobbled concerted action on behalf of American women since the end of World War II. The President's Commission on the Status of Women had included the amendment's backers; it had further declined either to make an unacceptable policy statement at its inception or permanently to reject the amendment at the commission's conclusion. In fact, the commission's suggested alternative—"that the principle of equality [for women] become firmly established in constitutional doctrine" by means of an "early and definitive Supreme Court pronouncement"— was acceptable ideologically to the ERA's advocates; most merely thought it impractical.[89] Moreover, the amendment's opponents had even suggested that constitutional amendment might be required if the judiciary did not vindicate their belief in the Fifth and Fourteenth Amendments. The central argument over the ERA had now been sidestepped in such a way that both proponents and opponents could work together on constitutional equality and other women's issues as well. Although the NWP doubted that the Supreme Court would ever rule in favor of equal rights for women, other ERA advocates contended that a well-organized case had not before been presented, and they were willing, at least for a time, to take on the task.

The outcome of the Commission's work on this issue thus proved salutary; the way in which the commission functioned had an equally useful result. By isolating the discussion of the ERA during its life, the President's Commission on the Status of Women found itself able to embark on what it viewed as its main work: the creation of a program for women that would address the many problems that constitutional equality would not rectify.

# 8

# THE PCSW AND A UNIFIED AGENDA
# FOR WOMEN'S RIGHTS

By the 1960s, the political objective of equal treatment for women seemed more within reach than it had in the previous postwar years. The ambivalence over new social roles for women had abated as the family and the economy revealed not only the ability to tolerate women as permanent workers but also the need for women to assume this role. A president now held office who was committed to growth and the liberal agenda of government intervention on behalf of the social good. The internal politics of the Kennedy administration had given a particular shape to the development of a strategy of which the President's Commission on the Status of Women was the centerpiece. Sequestering the ERA allowed the commission to move toward developing a unified agenda to expand opportunities for women.

As soon as the commission inquiry began, however, it became apparent that it would not resolve the philosophic contradiction that had beset all previous efforts to improve women's opportunities outside the home. The commission took the stand that women had the right to be full-time permanent workers and to be treated as such according to their merits, but only so long as their traditional relationship to their children remained unchanged. As far as the commission was concerned, women's obligation to be the primary nurturers of children remained immutable, a critical difference between men and women as workers. This fundamental conflict between equal opportunity for women in the public realm and fulfillment of the role of traditional motherhood showed itself in the ambivalence that pervaded the commission's discussion and reports.

The inherent incongruity left the commission open to criticism from both sides. The executive order establishing the commission stressed employment aspects of women's status, reflecting the new social acceptance of women as workers. It charged the commission with "developing recommendations for overcoming discriminations in government and private employment on the basis of sex and . . . developing recommendations for services which will enable women to continue their roles as wives and mothers while making a maximum contribution to the world around them."[1] Because of the emphasis on work problems, some accused the commission of urging mothers to leave their children and join the labor force. Following Eleanor Roosevelt's discussion of the PCSW with the president on her television show, "Prospects of Mankind," Lee Udall, wife of the secretary of the interior and the mother of six children, told a *Washington Post* reporter that the program "didn't do a thing to elevate the profession of motherhood."[2] Letters to the president from the public made the same point. In response, Peterson drafted a reply affirming her conviction that motherhood was the "major role of the American woman" and her "primary responsibility."[3] Conscious indeed of the national commitment to women as mothers, whenever the commission encountered a conflict between the roles of mother and of worker, it usually endorsed the former at the expense of the latter.

Because it supported the general view that sex roles could not fundamentally change, the commission could not reconcile the underlying contradiction between its affirmation of motherhood and the simultaneous assertion that women shared with men "the freedom to choose among different life patterns." Hyman Bookbinder, who represented the secretary of commerce on the commission, observed: "It is a fact of life—past, present, and future—that the great majority of women either choose to, or have to, devote their energies and their talents to the rearing of children and the management of homelife during at least half of their adult years." The implication of this "fact of life" for Bookbinder followed: "We should not pretend that women as a group are equal to men as a group in qualifying for participation in the world of work and in public affairs."[4] Margaret Mealey, speaking for the National

Council of Catholic Women, of which she was executive director, cautioned that woman's nature and the well-being of her family imposed limitations on her public life.[5] The Committee on Home and Community maintained in its report: "Over and above whatever role modern women play in the community . . . , the care of the home and the children remains their unique responsibility. No matter how much everyday tasks are shared or how equal the marriage partnership may be, the care of the children is primarily the province of the mother. This is not debatable as a philosophy. It is and will remain a fact of life."[6] Logically, the commission also espoused a corollary belief, that the major responsibility for the family's financial support fell to the father. Given these assumptions and a stated objective of equal opportunity for working women, vice-chairman Richard Lester pointed out to the commission that it had a problem of "inconsistent justification for . . . different recommendations."[7] The dichotomy between the primacy of traditional sex roles and the goal of equal treatment for women at work produced a tension which the commission never satisfactorily explored or resolved. No coherent intellectual argument for women's equal treatment would emerge from the president's commission.

Not only were the commission's choices limited by its unwillingness to question the sex-role structure or prevailing beliefs about the nature of women in American society, but the commission's desire to recommend proposals that would likely be endorsed by the administration, adopted, and implemented also constrained its options. Because it coveted widespread approval, the commission rejected most potentially contentious positions, from fundamental changes in the Social Security system to endorsement of the provision of birth control information. It did not intend to begin a debate over the basic principles that sustained the social order. Hyman Bookbinder pointed out facetiously that if the commission took the position that monogamy, for example, created certain problems, the publicity directed to that opinion would overwhelm all the other material in the report and cause the public to dismiss the balance of the recommendations. Convinced that even internal dissension would vitiate the strength of the suggestions, the commission also pursued unanimity, sometimes sacrificing a majority opinion to achieve it. Both the committees and the full commission strove to produce documents acceptable to the administration, to which end Esther Peterson cleared all proposals and reports with cabinet and White House officials before their release. The President's Commission on the Status of Women very much represented a mainstream reform attempt, working for the Kennedy administration within the constraints of prevailing values and liberal politics.[8]

Because they were working within a liberal consensus, most commission members felt no need even to articulate the principles they held in common. Commission recommendations evinced a faith in the ability to make meaningful changes without radically altering the economic or political structure. With constructive leadership, the commissioners believed, the nation progressed through time toward increasing freedom and greater equality of opportunity, to the benefit of both individuals and the society as a whole. Therefore, the commission assumed, government had the right and the duty, using "expert advice," to intervene within the private sector in order to bring about desirable goals, provide services, and assist those in need. Few of the commissioners found it necessary to define their terms, although many would no doubt have differed as to what constituted appropriate federal intervention in either the private sector or the family.

No commission member grappled with the idea that business might find a marginal female labor force efficient and economical; instead, recommendations contended that better opportunities for women would inevitably result in larger profits and increasing productivity. Many did acknowledge that women should not individually have to bear all the costs of childrearing—that industry and educational institutions should seek some accommodation to the wants of women and children. But none suggested that maternity and childrearing ranked first, with employment structured to suit those needs. With certain modifications, women would still have to fit into a male-designed world.

Within its ideological and political boundaries, however, the commission made a conscientious effort to establish as expedi-

tiously as possible a record of responsible action on behalf of
women, both in the home and at work. Recommendations took
note of differences in class, race, political ideology, and individual preferences, as well as some social norms it deemed inappropriate to support. The total package of recommendations resulted in a blueprint for change that, if implemented, would
significantly enlarge the range of choices for American women.[9]

## FEDERAL EMPLOYMENT

The president's commission began its operations by addressing
employment discrimination practiced by the federal government—the obvious place to start. The nation's largest employer,
it had sixty thousand women on its payroll. Moreover, the government practiced a blatant form of sex discrimination: agency
heads by law could limit jobs to persons of one sex or the other.
Taking steps against sex discrimination in the civil service presented few procedural problems and, because the form of discrimination was so bald, few ideological problems.

Sex discrimination in the civil service had a long history. The
first women clerks had been hired specifically to provide cheap
labor. In 1864 Congress enacted a law allowing the appointment of female clerks at a rate of six hundred dollars per year,
half the lowest government wage. By 1870, however, with more
than seven hundred women employed in federal offices in
Washington, Congress passed a new provision permitting department heads to hire women to fill the regular clerkship
grades and to pay them the commensurate salary. In the revised statutes, adopted the following year, this section came to
read: "Women may, in the discretion of the head of any department, be appointed to any clerkship therein authorized by law,
upon the same . . . conditions . . . as are prescribed for men."[10]
Although clearly intended as an authority to pay women the
same rate as male clerks, the Civil Service Commission (CSC)
interpreted the provision to mean that Congress had granted
agency heads the absolute right to specify the preferred sex of a
worker for any job. Agency heads used their prerogative almost
invariably to select women for the low-paying jobs and men for
the more responsible ones. In 1919 only 5 percent of new

women federal employees received salaries over $1,299, compared to 46 percent of the men. Under pressure from the Women's Bureau coalition, the CSC that year had rescinded the rule barring women from more than 60 percent of the civil service examinations, but it maintained the right of agency heads to designate sex in requesting names from the eligibles list for employment. In 1923 the Classification Act mandated equal pay for equal work regardless of sex, but the right of federal managers to hire by sex was not addressed. Finally, in 1932, just before his term was to expire, President Herbert Hoover, acting on the advice of Republican members of the National Woman's party, issued an executive order rescinding the right of agency heads to select by sex, although reserving the right to the Civil Service Commission in the case of jobs where sex represented a bona fide occupational qualification.[11]

Although this decision pleased the National Woman's party, the Women's Bureau coalition had mixed feelings. Before the passage of the Veterans' Preference Act during the Harding administration, they too had argued for the change. But because veterans had points added to their scores automatically, women had less chance of falling among the top three eligibles from which appointments were customarily made. Therefore, the Women's Bureau preferred selection by sex, which at least gave women access to clerical positions and permitted sympathetic agency heads, like Mary Anderson, to choose women regardless of the availability of men with higher scores. The interests of each side reflected its class orientation. The NWP sought to open opportunities so that able women could move into upper-level jobs; the Women's Bureau concerned itself with the right of women to entry-level positions.[12]

Soon after FDR became president, the Women's Bureau gained enough leverage to assure the outcome it sought. The bureau pointed out that under Hoover's executive order, appointments of women to the civil service did actually decline (although the Depression, which impelled all employers to give preference to men, probably accounted for the change at least as much). Mary Anderson asked the new president to countermand Hoover's instructions. In response, the Civil Service Commission polled women's organizations throughout the country;

with six replies in favor of restoring the previous rule and two preferring the new one, Roosevelt's attorney general ruled that Hoover's executive order had been illegal. Only Congress, he said, could rescind the power it had given agency heads to select by sex. In October 1934, to the NWP's disgust, Franklin Roosevelt reversed Hoover's directive.[13]

The policy remained in force throughout the forties and fifties, although it had become increasingly apparent that, veterans preference or no, selection by sex consigned women to low-level jobs. In 1954 the median grade for women had been four; for men, seven (excluding postal employees). Out of every hundred women federal workers, 80 percent held jobs in grades one to five, compared to only 25 percent of the men; less than 1 percent of women served as administrators, as opposed to 9 percent of males. By 1959, the median for men had risen by two grades but remained at GS-4 for women; half of all women were found in the four lowest grades, compared with only one-fifth of the men. Even in professional positions, the median grade for women was lower than for men generally, GS-7 compared to GS-9.[14]

Despite these facts, repeated presidential statements about the need for women in policy-making positions, and the increasing disapproval of women's organizations, neither the Democratic nor the Republican administrations of these decades took steps to limit the right of federal managers to select by sex. Complaints and appeals to the CSC and the attorney general brought the response that only Congress could revoke this authority. But when, in 1957, Representative Marguerite Stitt Church (R-Ill.) introduced a bill to amend section 165 of the Revised Statutes to remove the discretion in appointments, the Civil Service Commission reacted unenthusiastically, and the bill died in committee.[15]

The CSC had not deemed the status of women federal employees a problem. Although a 1959 federal employment survey had found that women, still one-quarter of the federal labor force, continued to be clustered in the lowest grades, the commission failed to identify discrimination as a cause of this situation. After all, it noted, more men than women were trained professionals and therefore were naturally classified in the higher grades. Yet the Commission did concede that even in fields such as social administration, which contained as many women as men, the median grade for men was still GS-13, and that for women was GS-12. The commission suggested that still another factor might account for the disparity: the traditional employment pattern of women. Because women left the labor force to raise children, the "interruption of their careers retards their progress up the promotion ladder."[16] Nevertheless, the commission cheerfully observed, there was still room for women at the top. Out of 575,990 women federal employees, 18 had attained positions among the 1,496 employees in grades sixteen, seventeen, and eighteen, slightly over 1 percent.[17]

In seeking to eliminate so obvious a form of sex discrimination within the civil service, the President's Commission on the Status of Women did not need to address the conflict between motherhood and equal opportunities at work, and in the presence of the Civil Service Commission it did not have to draw up formal rules regarding penalties or affirmative action. In addition, John Kennedy was already on record favoring the eradication of sex bias in the civil service. When he announced the creation of the presidential commission, Kennedy (with prompting from Peterson, Senator Philip Hart [D-Mich.], and others) had expressed his belief that the federal career service should be a "showcase" of equal opportunity in employment. He at that time instructed John Macy, chairman of the Civil Service Commission, to review policies and procedures to ensure that selection was made solely on merit without regard to sex. As president, Kennedy could execute additional PCSW recommendations on the subject without further ado.[18]

The PCSW promptly recommended the policy change and John Kennedy promptly implemented it. Robert Kennedy reversed the ruling made by Roosevelt's attorney general, and the president put CSC chief John Macy in charge of eliminating the discriminatory practice of selecting personnel by sex. "Bona fide occupational qualification" exceptions would be few.[19]

Merely forbidding agency heads from excluding women did not mean that more women would be hired, and no one considered penalizing executives who did not place women in upper-level jobs; nevertheless, change was visible as early as a year later. Many agencies had appointed women to particular positions for the first time, and the CSC had instituted monitoring procedures. Although the configuration of employment did not change at once, the idea of equal opportunity for women in employment had been introduced, confirmed, and legitimated.[20]

The president's commission also addressed, albeit cautiously, the other form of federal employment of women: presidential appointments. Although no woman representative of the Democratic National Committee sat on the commission (a fact that irritated many DNC members), the PCSW nevertheless recognized administration appointments as being worthy of attention. Still, criticism of the administration would be impolitic, so the members decided to focus on the needs for the future rather than the failures of the past. The commission's recommendation on nominations read: "Increasing consideration should continually be given to the appointment of women of demonstrated ability and political sensitivity to policy-making positions."[21] The White House did not find the suggestion objectionable, and Dan Fenn, head of the administration's "Talent Search," met with Margaret Hickey, chairman of the commission's Committee on Federal Employment, to find a way to implement it. Fenn deplored the practice of merely supplying lists of names of women seeking positions. He therefore proposed a small committee of women who would help locate the right woman for a given job and lobby to appoint her—in short, that the president's commission perform the function India Edwards had fulfilled for Truman. But because the commission had less than one year to its conclusion, it could not assume such a responsibility. Kennedy's appointment record remained undistinguished.[22]


PRIVATE EMPLOYMENT


The desire to make the civil service a "showcase" reflected in part the presidential commission's belief that private employers would emulate the federal model. But if the federal government intended to take action with regard to sex discrimination in the private sector, the guidelines of enforcement and consequences of noncompliance had to be spelled out more clearly than for the civil service, where the Civil Service Commission could implement a general policy on an ad hoc basis.

Both political and philosophical considerations, however, prevented the commission from seeking to penalize business for sex discrimination. James Roosevelt (D-Calif.) proposed a fair employment practice bill in 1962 that barred discrimination based on sex as well as on race, but the NAACP and the Departments of Justice and Labor objected to including women in the bill. The House Committee on Education and Labor omitted the sex provision on the motion of Edith Green (D-Oreg.) in order to give the president's commission time to study the best methods of achieving employment equity for women. Neither the PCSW's Committee on Private Employment nor the commission as a whole believed that coercive measures would win acceptance from either the business community or Congress. In addition, because no sanctions against sex bias obtained within the federal government, it would be hard to defend punitive measures against private business for the same offense. More to the point, although they held up equal treatment as ideal, both the Committee on Private Employment and the commission, reflecting the beliefs of most Americans, regarded differential treatment in employment on the basis of sex warranted under some circumstances because of women's familial obligations.[23]

By the time the commission began to consider the attitude of business toward women, the administration had already taken executive action with respect to racial discrimination in private employment. Shortly after assuming office, John Kennedy had issued an executive order (EO 10925) establishing the President's Committee on Equal Employment Opportunity. The order required federal contractors to agree not to discriminate on the basis of "race, creed, color or national origin" and to take affirmative action to ensure equal treatment. A second executive order, issued in June 1963, extended the initial provision to federally assisted programs receiving grants, loans, insurance, or guarantees. The possibility of including "sex" in EO 10925 had been considered, but administration drafters concluded that racial discrimination constituted enough of a burden without adding other conditions, such as sex, age, or handicap. Moreover, ever since World War II a widespread social movement to end racial discrimination had been pressuring the government and seeking to change public attitudes—and with some success: race had become less and less a legitimate criterion for discrimination. Neither a social movement nor a coherent feminist philosophy existed to support the inclusion of a prohibition on sex-based discrimination in an executive order (or a bill, also considered) to ban racial bias in private employment.[24]

The president's commission considered this issue a fertile field for policy initiatives, and, although sex discrimination had been omitted from the first executive order, the commission continued to view the relationship between the federal government and its contractors as the most accessible vehicle for bringing about some change in the private sector. The president could prohibit sex discrimination merely by fiat, and an executive order pertaining to contractors would protect a significant number of workers. In 1960, the federal government bought about 20 percent of all goods and services produced in the country, and the one hundred largest defense contractors employed ten million workers.[25]

The question for the Committee on Private Employment to resolve centered on the kind of executive order to recommend. Committee member Caroline Davis, director of the Women's Division of the United Automobile Workers, strongly urged that the president ban discrimination based on sex and include penalties and machinery for enforcement. She had supported the addition of the word *sex* to EO 10925, and because of her defeat on this issue, she said, she had failed to win a prohibition against sex discrimination in the automobile industry contracts of 1961.[26]

The Private Employment Committee refused to go along with her proposal, though. As committee chairman Richard Lester explained, "There are very good grounds, apparently, for discrimination against women in connection with training, promotion and upgrading in certain lines." Because women differed from men in motivation and career aspirations, and usually interrupted their work lives to raise families, the government, Lester contended, would find it difficult "to determine the line between justified and unjustified selection of males over against females in training and promotion." Moreover, said Lester, because illegitimate sex discrimination could not at that point be specified, any executive order prohibiting it would have to depend for enforcement on "moral suasion and company consultation." The experience gained using these techniques would, he argued, permit the formulation of stronger measures later if they proved necessary.[27]

The administration stepped in to quell the dispute. The new secretary of labor, Willard Wirtz, refused to endorse an executive order that relied on more than education and moral suasion for its enforcement. At its meeting one week later, the Committee on Private Employment, in keeping with the administration's wishes, passed a recommendation for a contract clause to be specified in an executive order: "It is the policy of the Government that there should be no discrimination against women in regard to hiring, training or promotion in employment by reason of their sex. In the performance of this contract, the contractor is requested to use his best efforts to comply with this policy in order to assure that equal employment practices for women are observed." After strenuous objections from Caroline Davis and Muriel Ferris, Senator Philip Hart's legislative assistant, the committee compromised and changed *is requested to* to *shall.*[28]

In its report, the committee recounted its reasons for not recommending the amendment of EO 10925 and for preferring persuasion to compulsion. "The consensus," the report explained, "was that the nature of discrimination on the basis of sex and the reasons for it are so different [from race] that a separate program is necessary to eliminate barriers to the employment and advancement of women." Volunteerism would permit business managers to demonstrate that they could act without coercion, and a noncoercive program would therefore elicit more support from industry, Congress, and other groups, the committee asserted. Information could be collected "in a cooperative atmosphere" that would permit distinguishing "differentiation that is justifiable on the basis of sex from differentiation that cannot be justified." In cases of willful noncompliance, firms could conceivably be barred from federal contracts, and if more definite penalities turned out to be necessary they could be added later.[29] Only Caroline Ware dissented, citing experience with voluntary compliance and cases of racial discrimination.[30]

The commission would not accept Davis's proposal to add the word *sex* to EO 10925, which it believed meant ignoring the impact of family responsibilities on women workers and their employers, nor could it envision forcing private employers to share with women the costs of taking time out from work to raise families. Thus, despite initial protestations of the commission's planners that "prevailing institutions and work practices . . . largely shaped by and for men"[31] limited women's chances, the commission did not propose to forbid sex discrimination. Unable to reconcile the conflict between pursuit of equality for women and endorsement of the traditional obligations of women, the commission suggested that women's interrupted work patterns might justify exclusion from on-the-job development programs—implying that women would have to continue to pay the price of lost promotions and missed wage increases for fulfilling what the commission deemed to be their appropriate roles. Further, PCSW personnel viewed with sympathy the objections of civil servants and business people who did not want to be saddled with additional burdens in getting or offering contracts for government supplies. Finally, the commission did not want to place the White House in a position where it would refuse to comply with a PCSW recommendation. The commission had been designed to enhance the president's reputation, not embarrass him. Given the nature of the dispute, political considerations dictated leaving the recommendation vague. Interested in achieving widespread endorsement of its views, the commission, in this instance as in others, attempted to arrive at positions that would not unduly inconvenience its constituents, even at the expense of working women's opportunities. It thus wound up in large measure mirroring rather than advancing the state of national opinion.[32]

Although hardly a battle cry, the commission's statement denouncing discrimination in employment still advanced the cause of wider opportunities for women. In its report the commission called attention to the number of women employed (one worker in every three was female) and the need for their skills and their income.[33] It also decried women's low wages and countered the myths, such as increased absenteeism, that employers offered to justify discrimination. "Reluctance to consider women applicants on their merits," the commission declared, "results in underutilization of capacities that the economy needs and stunts the development of higher skills."[34] The commission enunciated for the first time a federal policy censuring discrimination against women in employment by the federal government itself, by the private sector, and by state governments receiving federal grants. Although the limits to discrimination were not clearly drawn, at least, according to the commission, there ought to be some limits.[35]

## PROTECTIVE LABOR LEGISLATION

The commission could not easily insist on full equality for women in hiring and training, but it was able to come closer to affirming nondiscriminatory treatment for women under protective labor laws, the coverage of which could be extended to men rather than withdrawn from women.

Because employers had always used labor laws to justify discrimination, advocates of the Equal Rights Amendment had for a long time urged that such legislation either apply to men as well as women or be eliminated. The Women's Bureau, in contrast, had traditionally maintained that protective labor laws helped the overwhelming majority of women and hurt only a few. When faced with the imminent threat of the ERA, advocates of protective labor legislation, fearing that the amendment would result not in extension but in obliteration of the labor laws, fought the amendment vigorously and defended the laws for women. With the Committee on Civil and Political Rights working on a method for achieving constitutional equality while still safeguarding protective laws for women, the Committee on Protective Labor Legislation was free to consider the laws themselves, undisturbed by the heated ERA controversy. By the 1960s many of those most committed to protective labor laws were willing to acknowledge that some of the more restrictive and rigid rules did more harm than good. It was up to the Committee on Protective Labor Legislation to determine the difference between the laws still useful and those now antiquated and to find a way to reconcile the demand for equal opportunity for women and the expectation of special protection.

Consideration of the laws apart from the Equal Rights Amendment produced a ready accord; in most cases the Committee on Protective Labor Legislation, and the commission as a whole, concurred in principle with ERA proponents. The most desirable outcome, committee members concluded, was the extension to men of the laws in effect protecting women. However, whereas ERA adherents saw constitutional equality as causing the beneficial changes in state laws, the Committee on Protective Labor Legislation strongly believed that laws pertaining to women should remain in force until they were superseded by better laws covering men as well.

This judgment did not present any problems for the committee in most areas of discussion, which were quickly decided by consensus. At the first meeting, members endorsed the extension of minimum wage legislation with premium pay for overtime at both federal and state levels to men and women workers presently uncovered; likewise for equal pay legislation. The committee also agreed that industrial homework should be eliminated. Later the committee voted in favor of a flexible weight-lifting law pertaining to both men and women. Cash maternity benefits under disability programs and the right to maternity leave also met with approval.[36]

The sticking point came over hours legislation. Most members concurred that state law should establish an absolute number of hours for workers, but committee member Henry David, a prominent labor historian, adamantly and successfully resisted a proposal to recommend extending prohibitions on women's hours to male workers. He contended both that the PCSW had no mandate to recommend laws for men and that proposing a limit to the number of hours men could work would elicit "howls of rage." Furthermore, David argued, hours laws for women were well established; applying them to men would raise "a whole new series of questions which we certainly are not able to deal with and on which we have seen no basic data at all."[37] Ultimately, after David's vehement argument, the committee recommended that hours laws set a definite maximum for women, that they be administered "flexibly," and that women in administrative, executive, and professional jobs be exempted.[38]

Commission members greeted the committee recommendation with varying degrees of satisfaction. Margaret Hickey said she had hoped the time had come to apply these standards equally to men. Henry David explained to her the reasoning of the committee—which was in fact his own—that hours laws for men would not gain public acceptance. Hickey responded that such a consideration did not appear to be a very good reason to burden women. Many commission members, including Peterson, expressed the view that overtime pay as a deterrent might be preferable to maximums, but David argued strongly for his position, insisting that the commission was making trouble for itself on the matter and that to come out against maximum hours for women would be breaking with "a body of history which meant something and conceivably still does mean something." Sarcastically, he admitted that the original resolution did have a weakness; it was, he said, "realistic."[39]

Faced with an apparent deadlock, Peterson had a statement drawn up before the next meeting detailing the Department of Labor's position on the issue. According to this position paper, the department desired adequate labor standards for all workers, and it judged premium pay for additional hours for both men and women as the best way to shorten the workday. The Department concluded that, where special hours laws for women represented the best attainable protection at present, they should be "maintained, strengthened and expanded."[40] The commission adopted this position almost verbatim, adding the exemption of professional and executive women from the committee's original recommendation. Although David believed that the commission had adopted his position, this statement differed in that it spoke of maximum hours laws only as interim measures, to be eliminated when states enacted laws requiring premium pay for overtime. Hours laws constituted the only area of conflict with respect to protective labor legislation and, except for pregnancy and maternity leave, became the only kind of labor legislation about which the committee and the commission proposed differential treatment of women workers—and even this remaining distinction was to be temporary. The gap between the Women's Bureau coalition and proponents of the ERA was growing smaller.[41]

Taken all together, the commission's proposals on employment revealed its ambivalence toward women's roles. While continuing to endorse equality in the civil service, in private employment, and in labor law, the commission also spoke of "justifiable" discrimination and extending and strengthening hours laws for women. Recognizing that private employers were unlikely to change their behavior without federal direction, it nevertheless declined to specify the action the White House should take. Because it was caught between the fundamentally contradictory ideals of traditional womanhood and equality, the commission could not make a clear statement.

## EDUCATION

The dichotomy of women's needing both equal and different treatment that ran through the commission's discussions on employment also weighed on the consideration of recommendations concerning education. The commission maintained that educational institutions needed to accommodate to the patterns of women's lives so that women who followed traditional paths could reenter the labor force when their children had grown. Educational programs had to be available in the community, through either local junior colleges or correspondence schools. Schools had a responsibility to offer part-time study, financial aid, and flexible academic and residency requirements.[42]

But the educational establishment had another obligation as well. According to both the Committee on Education and the commission as a whole, educational institutions needed to help women prepare for their special role. "The expectation that a woman will become a wife and mother differentiates the educational requirements of girl and boy from the very beginning,"[43] the committee report asserted. The commission cautioned that "widening the choice for women beyond their doorstep does not imply neglect of their education for responsibilities in the home." All girls and women should learn about childcare and family relations, nutrition, family finances, and "the relation of individuals and families to society." The commission did not recommend such a program for boys and men.[44]

Yet at the same time that the commission proposed educational programs to fortify prevailing sex roles, it also argued that education played a key role in expanding women's horizons. Counseling women, the commission contended, required special skills: "From infancy, roles held up to girls deflect talents into narrow channels. . . . Imaginative counseling can lift aspirations beyond stubbornly persistent assumptions about 'women's roles' and 'women's interests' and result in choices that have inner authenticity for their makers."[45] But here again, the commission refused to acknowledge the underlying problem. Many of the characteristically male-dominated fields did not mesh well with the traditional roles of women. If childcare remained ultimately a female responsibility, as the commission assumed it should, fewer women could be expected to overcome the hurdles in fulfilling both the role of nurturer and that of career professional. A young woman who received both the homemaking education the commission prescribed and counseling to become a mechanical engineer had to sort out conflicting messages. Its recommendations on both employment and education disclosed the commission's vacillation between the two ideals it professed.

## FINANCIAL SECURITY

When it came to issues of family support, however, the traditional view of women as dependent ultimately took clear precedence. Consonant with its view that women had unique responsibilities with respect to families which justified differential treatment in employment, the commission also affirmed that men had to continue to fulfill traditional support obligations. The Committee on Civil and Political Rights recommended that "in view of the childbearing and homemaking functions of the wife" the husband should continue to bear the primary burden of financial support.[46] The commission concurred in the committee's judgment, which colored many of the commission's additional suggestions.

The Commission made no recommendation for changes in the Social Security system for women workers who paid Social Security taxes and, in many cases, received no additional awards over that which they would have gotten as wives who had not made payments. The system presumed the dependency of both wives and children on male workers and so also denied benefits even for the children of working women. The commission did, however, emphasize the need for increased payments to the widows of workers and to divorced women.[47]

Part of the commission's reluctance to tackle these questions came from the complexity of the Social Security system and the expense of making changes in benefits.[48] But the Committee on Social Insurance and Taxes went out of its way to affirm that it would not "be appropriate for the social insurance program to provide a benefit so that the father could stay at home to care for the child" in the event of the mother's death.[49] Childcare, after all, was women's work. Thus, despite the assertion throughout the commission report that women worked to provide necessities for their families, the commission nevertheless failed to acknowledge that such families would continue to need the mother's income if she died—without recognizing that this omission undercut its initial premise.[50]

Although the commission declined to explore the implications for equality in employment of leaving traditional assumptions about financial support untouched, it did acknowledge some danger in the complete economic dependency of the homemaker. Most states followed the common-law precept that income belonged to the person who earned it. Thus, in a family where the husband worked for pay and the wife did not, she had no legal right to any of the family income or property. The commission took exception to this state of affairs. Calling marriage a partnership "in which each spouse makes a different but equally important contribution," it asserted that wives should have a "legally defined substantial right in the earnings" of the husband and in the property acquired through those earnings.[51] The implementation of the commission recommendation would mitigate the financial insecurity of full-time homemakers.

## CARE OF CHILDREN

In fact, the commission recognized the need to offer other kinds of help to homemakers, as well as to working women. If the commission's devotion to the ideal of motherhood tempered its commitment to equality of treatment for women, its belief in free choice moderated its stand on who could care for children. The commission understood that unless women received some help in raising their children, educational and employment opportunity had little value. Moreover, as the commission repeatedly pointed out, mothers of young children did hold jobs outside the home, and these children needed supervision. Therefore, the Commission strongly endorsed an extensive day-care program.

The last time federal dollars had been allocated for day care was during World War II, and even then the provision of services had met less than 10 percent of the presumed need. The Children's Bureau, located in the Department of Health, Education and Welfare (HEW), published a study in 1958 which asserted that four hundred thousand youngsters under the age of twelve lacked adequate arrangements for care; nevertheless, the Eisenhower administration opposed government funding of childcare centers. The National Conference on Day Care for Children, held in Washington in November 1960, recommended a comprehensive program of day care, supported by federal and state money, and during the 1960 campaign John Kennedy had promised his support in a letter to Elinor Guggenheimer, a founder of the day-care movement in New York State. Guggenheimer, now heading a group called the National Committee on Day Care, met with the new secretaries of HEW and Labor in 1961, and won a provision for funding in the administration bill regarding amendments to the Social Security Act. Peterson strongly supported Guggenheimer's goals of day care for children of working mothers and placed her on the Home and Community Committee.[52]

By the time the committee gathered for its first meeting in May 1962, however, Congress was close to enacting a day-care funding law that aimed not to care for the children of mothers already at work or to give those mothers who wished to work the opportunity to do so, but rather to force the mothers of young children into the labor force, a goal anathema to the Women's Bureau coalition reformers working with the president's commission. The Public Welfare Amendments, signed into law in July 1962, authorized money only for day care for children on public assistance and implied that the service was to be provided so that the mothers of children receiving public assistance could be forced to work for wages. Congress apparently believed that middle-class taxpayers wanted impoverished, unmarried, disproportionately black women to leave their children in the care of others and take paying jobs, although they disdained middle-class women who chose to do so themselves.[53]

The commission usually deferred to prevailing political sentiments, but it could not do so in this case because insisting that lower-class mothers work contravened the philosophy of the Women's Bureau coalition, which expressly promoted the protection of women and children. Ideally, the commission believed, mothers should care for their young children at home regardless of class. The commission came out against using day-care services to support coercion of welfare recipients to work for wages and expressed sorrow for low income women who did leave babies in the care of others. The Committee on Home and Community declared that women with small children should not "be forced by economic necessity or the policies of welfare agencies" to seek outside employment,[54] and the full commission labeled the practice "regrettable."[55]

The commission declined to support day care as a coercive measure, but still it emphasized the need for such services. Both the committee and the commission maintained that day care should be available to families at all income levels, to provide for the children of mothers already working and to permit mothers who wanted to join the labor force to do so. They also contended that full-time homemakers who desired to devote a portion of their energy to the community or who had to meet other family needs should also have access to day-care facilities.[56]

Although the provision of day-care services would help some women take advantage of the new opportunities the commission proposed, it could not completely resolve the dilemma of reconciling family obligations and equal chances for women in the public sphere—nor did the commission intend it to. Day care could assist women, especially those who needed to work, but the final responsibility for young children lay with the mother, and the commission presumed that she would still devote a large portion of her life to childrearing. The commission believed that women's maternal functions made them different from men in both motivation and career aspirations; therefore, it could not see forcing employers to invest equally in the training of women—equality at work would have to yield to a greater imperative of motherhood. Fatherhood implied not childcare but financial support.

In all its recommendations, the commission sought to correct the clearest injustices, to remove anachronistic obstacles to women's participation in public life, to affirm the desirability of equal treatment and the unfettered expression of individual talents, and to serve obvious and unfulfilled social needs. In doing so, however, the commission also resolved to remain firmly within the framework of traditional family roles. In making this choice, the commission reflected the ambivalence of the culture it served.

### THE IMPACT OF THE PRESIDENT'S COMMISSION

The President's Commission on the Status of Women took trouble to see that interest in women's status did not end with the submission of its report. In order to monitor the implementation of its proposals, and to serve as a reminder that the problems persisted, the commission asked the president in its final proposal to appoint two continuing federal bodies: an interdepartmental committee and a citizens' advisory council to "evaluate progress made, provide counsel, and serve as a means for suggesting and stimulating action."[57] John Kennedy established the two groups on November 1, 1963; it was the next-to-last executive order he signed.

The outlook seemed hopeful. The establishment of the president's commission had raised the expectations of those concerned about women. In her bestseller, *The Feminine Mystique,* published in February 1963, Betty Friedan had written: "The very existence of the President's Commission on the Status of Women, under Eleanor Roosevelt's leadership, creates a climate where it is possible to recognize and do something about discrimination against women, in terms not only of pay but of the subtle barriers to opportunity."[58]

Moreover, to ensure that its proposals would find a sympathetic response, the president's commission had made a sustained effort throughout its deliberations to reach out to those women's organizations that it viewed as its primary sources of support, the members of the Women's Bureau coalition. The commission had asked for the assistance of these organizations when searching for data to support its recommendations, requesting information about their experiences with protective labor legislation, their knowledge of employment and statutory discrimination, and their familiarity with court cases involving sex bias. The women's organizations reciprocated the commission's interest. Most responded to commission queries at length, many wrote articles in their newsletters, and the National Council of Catholic Women distributed sixteen thousand commission brochures. Only one organization had a less than satisfactory relationship with the commission. The National Woman's party, although it participated in every commission-related function to which it was invited, viewed the commission with justified suspicion about the Equal Rights Amendment; and for her part, Esther Peterson, who invited the NWP to all appropriate commission functions, regarded the organization as intractable.[59]

The recalcitrance of the NWP notwithstanding, the enthusiasm of the women's associations even outside the traditional Women's Bureau coalition had resulted in the development of an entirely new set of institutions at the state level concerned with the status of women. In November 1962, the National Federation of Business and Professional Women's Clubs notified Peterson that it wanted to undertake a program to encourage every governor to appoint a state commission patterned after the "excellent structure" of the president's commission. The leaders of the organization asked for a meeting with the president to get his approval of their plan, and, at Peterson's request, he complied, endorsing the proposal. The governor of the state of Washington was the first to respond to the federation's campaign; he appointed a commission in February 1963 based closely on the president's model. At the same time, he issued an executive order asking for a review of state employment regulations to ensure that they did not discriminate against women. The states of Indiana and Illinois quickly followed, as did many others, often with the assistance of the regional offices of the Women's Bureau. Although some other women's organizations resented the primary role of the BPW, during the presidential commission's lifetime ten state commissions on women were formed, and by 1967 every state had created one. The state commission movement indicated widespread national support for the president's commission; moreover, because the state commissions looked to it for their lead, they gave the parent body increased visibility and influence.[60]

In addition to inspiring state commissions, holding meetings with women's organizations, and inviting the participation of almost two hundred citizens on its committees, the commission had enlarged its base of support through "consultations" with special interest groups. Altogether, the commission held four such consultations; three of them, "Women in the Mass Media," "Private Employment," and "New Patterns in Volunteer Work," brought in delegates from relevant organizations in an effort to explore issues and win potential allies.[61]

Only in the fourth consultation, on the problems of Negro women, did the commission address the black woman specifically, even though it generally acknowledged in its discussions that virtually every disability affected black women more severely than white. In preparation for the consultation, the staff furnished a paper that described how pending recommendations of the president's commission, such as the extension of minimum wage laws, would assist minority women. Daniel Patrick Moynihan, special assistant to the secretary of labor, believed that the staff paper gave insufficient attention to the fact that "Negro society in America," according to his "limited understanding," was still "substantially a matriarchy," and did not address methods by which male-headed families could be established "if that is what is needed."[62] The people attending the consultation—educators, editors of black magazines, representatives of the New York Urban League, and government offi-

cials—agreed with Moynihan that the black family was matriar-
chal, a situation forced on them, they said, by lack of job opportunities for black males. They therefore advocated better,
black-run community programs and the inclusion of Afro-
American history and culture in the elementary school curricu-
lum to provide male models for black children. The participants also raised an objection to the idea of forcing mothers of
AFDC (Aid to Families with Dependent Children) families to
work. In general, the consultation revealed that black women
considered racial bias, not sex discrimination, their major handicap. For the commission, the consultation provided evidence of
its concern for the opinions of black leaders as well as white.[63]
But whereas the commission recognized the special hardships
of black women, it rejected an analogy between discrimination
based on sex and discrimination based on race, and between
remedies for racism and those for sex bias.

The commission formally ended its work with the presentation of its report to the president on October 11, 1963, Eleanor
Roosevelt's birthday.[64] Press coverage of the report was widespread. The *New York Times* gave it front-page space, the Associated Press devoted a four-part series to it, and the "Today" show
on NBC television offered a live interview with Peterson on the
day of the presentation. More than one newspaper editorial observed that the commission was inconsistent in maintaining that
a woman's first responsibility was to her family in the home and
then expecting employers to treat her the same way they did
male employees; the *Wall Street Journal* found the commission's
proposal for day care "a tinge . . . collectivist."[65] On the whole,
however, these views were exceptional. Most women's magazines
and journals of women's organizations, after summarizing the
report's contents, commended it to their readers.[66]

White House advisers concluded that, with the presentation
of the commission report, the Kennedy administration had put
together a worthy record on behalf of women, regardless of the
number of women appointees. In preparation for the presentation ceremony, Myer Feldman recounted for the president the
list of achievements. Most had proceeded from the agenda laid
out in the Women's Bureau: the presidential commission's
study; equal pay legislation; the ruling against discrimination in

the civil service; the elimination of a quota system for women officers in the armed forces (undertaken also at the request of the president's commission); and the extension of the Fair Labor Standards Act to include retail workers, many of whom were women. Feldman also included the establishment of a consumer advisory council, which Kennedy had pledged in his campaign, and the provision of money for day care.[67] The administration was justified in regarding the President's Commission on the Status of Women as the jewel in its crown for women.

Constrained by its refusal to examine the conflicts in defining roles by sex, its search for unanimity, and its desire for political acceptability, the PCSW often left the hardest problems untackled and forswore the most potent solutions; nevertheless, taken all together, the recommendations of the president's commission broke new ground. Were it brought to fruition, the agenda formulated by the commission would improve opportunities for women outside the home and enhance support within it. For the first time, a federal body examined the status of women, found it wanting, and offered prescriptions for its improvement. It decreed the problem of sex discrimination legitimate, insisting that it hurt not only the individual but also the nation. In doing so, the commission responded to a social reality and a social need. Although not far ahead of public opinion, the president's commission, by openly acknowledging the validity of the quest for equal treatment, nudged public opinion along.

Commission proposals covered the range of problems observed by each of the three interest groups of women in the fifteen years since World War II and forged them into a unified agenda. Like the Women's Bureau coalition, the President's Commission on the Status of Women suggested many "specific bills for specific ills." The committee asked the federal government to assume responsibility for encouraging private employers to treat women workers equitably and requested both public and private enterprises to provide women with the chance to work part-time so that they could acquire or use their skills while at the same time meeting their family responsibilities. Both federal and state legislation, counseled the commission, should mandate minimum wages for men and women, premium pay for overtime, and equal wages for men and women performing equal work. The commission maintained that unemployment insurance coverage had to offer women better protection and that employers, trade unions, and government at all levels should unite to develop a program of maternity benefits that would remove some of the burden from women who bore all the costs of having and rearing children. The commission advocated that the federal government permit more generous tax deductions for childcare and that local, state, and federal governments finance both educational programs and skilled counseling assistance sensitive to needs of women at all stages of their lives. The commission proposed community childcare facilities, with costs shared publicly and privately, so that women might take advantage of better educational opportunities and employment possibilities. Like ERA advocates, the commission endorsed the need for an affirmation of constitutional equality for women, as well as a movement to expunge from state legal codes antiquated laws that discriminated against women, barring them, for example, from jury service or hampering their right to own or convey property or change their domicile. Following the counsel of political party women, and to ensure that the legal system would become more responsive to women's needs, the commission encouraged women, political parties, and appointing officials to see that more women participated in government. The president's commission combined and endorsed all the separate agendas, permitting the boundaries that had separated the groups before to fade into the background.

Three weeks after the submission of the report, Kennedy completed his actions on behalf of American women by creating the continuing groups the commission had recommended: the Interdepartmental Committee and the Citizens' Advisory Council on the Status of Women. In the executive order, the president declared: "Enhancement of the quality of American life, as envisioned by the Commission's report, can be accomplished only through concerted action by both public and private groups, through coordinated action within the Federal Government, and through action by States, communities, educational institutions, voluntary organizations, employers, unions, and individual citizens."[68] Further federal initiatives would take place under a new administration.

In her memorandum to Secretary of Labor Arthur Goldberg proposing the establishment of a commission on women, Esther Peterson had argued that the commission would not only block the Equal Rights Amendment, but it also would "help the nation . . . move further towards full partnership, creative use of skills, and genuine equality of opportunity." As Peterson intended, the President's Commission on the Status of Women had important implications for the politics of women's issues in the 1960s. It drew opposing interest groups together, narrowing the gap between the Women's Bureau coalition and ERA advocates; it enunciated a federal policy against sex discrimination, affirming that women, like men, had a right to paid employment; it presented a cogent set of proposals to begin the amelioration of the difficulties women faced; it built up networks of support among women's organizations and served as the model for analogous institutions on the state level; and, at its conclusion, it provided for a continuing presence at the federal level, to ensure that the consideration of the status of women would not disappear with the termination of the commission.[69] But only indirectly did the commission foster its most important sequel: a resurgent, energetic, widespread women's movement that arose from the active politics of the 1960s.

# 4
## BEYOND THE PRESIDENT'S COMMISSION

# 9

## A MODEL FOR ACTION

After the conclusion of the President's Commission on the Status of Women, female activists within the federal government and the state commissions strove to improve opportunities for women, using the commission's agenda as a guide. The transfer of power from John Kennedy to Lyndon Johnson, who was strongly sensitive to the exigencies of political patronage, engendered new attention for appointments of women; yet Johnson strongly supported the plan of the president's commission, going so far as to mute his own endorsement of the Equal Rights Amendment. As the attempt to find a case suitable for Supreme Court adjudication languished, the success of a new civil rights bill soon presented ERA proponents with an unexpected opportunity to take a swipe at the recommendations; the result of their action was to give women new and unprecedented protection against employment discrimination. Official resistance to the new law, however, bred resentment among women nationwide—and as the number of women aware of women's equity issues grew, so did the seeds of a grassroots movement.

### LYNDON JOHNSON

Following John Kennedy's assassination, Lyndon Johnson came into office with several goals. Painfully aware of Kennedy's popularity, Johnson sought to prove himself faithful to the objectives of his predecessor and win equal affection. A Southerner, but now distanced from his Texas constituency, Johnson wanted to display his commitment to equalizing treatment for blacks, to eliminating poverty in America, and to bringing the war in Vietnam to a successful conclusion. In pursuit of these ends, Johnson presided over liberalism's "greatest triumphs and sharpest defeats," as historian William Chafe characterized the events of Johnson's tenure. Under the new president's guidance, Congress enacted path-breaking civil rights laws and produced legislation providing federal aid to education, housing, medicare, mental health programs, urban mass transit, preschool for underprivileged children, employment and training programs, environmental and consumer programs. Johnson's "War on Poverty" lifted the incomes of millions of American families.[1]

Kennedy's assassination and the murders of black leaders Medgar Evers in 1963 and Malcolm X in 1965, together with Johnson's encouragement of civil rights legislation and his pursuit of the Vietnam war, all fueled the social protest in the 1960s. In 1962, a nascent student movement emerged seeking to quell militarism and to join with the civil rights movement in the cause of racial equality; by 1968, Students for a Democratic Society counted one hundred thousand members. Peaceful demonstration proved an inadequate force for halting the war, however, and campuses exploded in protest in 1968. Meanwhile, urban ghettos were beset by waves of violence, and in the spring of 1968 civil rights leader Martin Luther King, Jr., and Robert F. Kennedy, who was running in the Democratic primaries as a peace candidate, were both murdered.

Although the national community seemed truly to be coming apart, by the mid-1970s the eruptions of angry protest had abated. The antiwar movement was defused by troop reductions and the elimination of the draft. Black leaders turned from street demonstrations to more traditional politics. Yet out of the turmoil of the 1960s, from both the government's commitment to moderate, controlled social change and the New Left's objective of radical social reorganization, was born a vital women's movement that endured for another decade.

## "CRYPTO-FEMINISM"

The policy initiatives of the Kennedy years had taken place against a backdrop of widening activity by women, continuing the trend that had intensified after World War II. Between

1960 and 1965 the number of bachelor's and first professional degrees earned by women increased 57 percent, compared with only a 25 percent increase for men. By 1968 women were earning about one-third of all master's degrees and 13 percent of doctorates. The more educated the woman, the more likely she was to work outside the home, and by 1968 women represented 37 percent of the labor force, up 3 percent since 1960. The increase for married women was even more significant: in 1960, 30.6 percent of married women worked; by 1968, that figure had grown to 37 percent.[2]

What these figures did not reveal, however, was that, relative to white men, white women had declined in economic position throughout the postwar period. Of full-time workers in 1966, women earned only 58.2 percent of the income of men, down from 63.3 percent in 1956. Women with college degrees, a growing proportion of women workers, were still earning less than men with only high school educations. As more and more college-educated women entered the labor market, they encountered opportunities far narrower than their male peers enjoyed.[3]

Working women did not suffer only economic disadvantages; they also paid an emotional price for joining the workforce. Throughout the fifteen-year postwar period, publications both popular and scholarly suggested that American women who assumed nonconventional roles were neglecting their families or losing their femininity. The country continued to prefer that women not openly challenge men professionally or intellectually. By the early 1960s, journalists were describing a "prevailing malaise" among women as a result of the conflict between women's achievements and traditional norms. Marya Mannes protested in the *New York Times Magazine* that intellectual women were victimized because American men were uncomfortable with them, and an essay in the *Commonweal* lamented that an honest, intelligent woman had inevitably to become a social rebel because American society did not really approve of forceful, thinking women. In October 1962, the editors of *Harper's* published a special supplement in recognition of the "important changes" that had taken place in the roles of women. In this issue, such authors as psychologist Bruno Bettelheim argued that women who had been educated like men experienced frustration when confronted after graduation by limitations for intellectual expression. *Harper's* called the nascent disquiet "crypto-feminism."[4]

The discussion in the popular press of the plight of the American woman culminated in February 1963 in the publication of *The Feminine Mystique* by Betty Friedan. In evaluating information garnered from a questionnaire sent in 1957 to her 1942 classmates at Smith College, Friedan had detected a "problem that has no name," which displayed itself in the breakdown of the mental and physical health of college-educated homemakers who were living through their husbands and children. Friedan argued that women needed creative work of their own and that women's life plans had to integrate marriage and motherhood with independent work in order for them to be healthy individuals.[5]

The "problem that has no name," "malaise," and "crypto-feminism" all referred to the strain between customary expectations for women and the changing circumstances of American life. Greater numbers of highly educated women, believing it to be best for their families if they did not work for pay, found themselves stultified by the lack of intellectually stimulating outlets while they were home. Then they faced three potentially useful decades after their children had grown, but often lacked skills and experience to permit an easy transition to the workplace. Those women with children who were forced to work by the exigencies of a consumer society discovered severely circumscribed possibilities for employment and advancement and in addition suffered criticism for leaving their families ostensibly without proper care.[6]

Yet women did not, in the early 1960s, organize themselves to alleviate such difficulties. As Jo Freeman has pointed out, "Social strain does not create social movements; it only creates the potential for movements." The "social strain" described had in fact characterized the entire postwar period, leading finally to the call for a national commission on women. That commission's report, *American Women,* now served as a focus of discussion for the state commissions set up to emulate the national group, a nationwide system of commissions on women that, as

Freeman described it, created a "climate of expectations" for potential action.[7]

*American Women* followed the appearance of Friedan's book by only six months, and the reaction to it, in both demand for copies and continuing formation of state commissions, indicated that the chord struck by these publications had wide reverberations. By October 1964 the government had distributed eighty-three thousand copies of *American Women* (which had also been translated into three languages: Japanese, Swedish, and Italian), and in 1965 Charles Scribner's Sons published a commercial version edited by Margaret Mead.[8]

## THE CITIZENS' ADVISORY COUNCIL AND THE INTERDEPARTMENTAL COMMITTEE ON THE STATUS OF WOMEN

President Johnson was eager to capitalize on the good will engendered by the commission. As vice-president, Johnson had made known his strong support of the commission's objectives and had often attended commission functions; following the group's first meeting it was Mrs. Johnson, not Jacqueline Kennedy, who hosted the reception for the assembled representatives. Shortly after Johnson took over, Elizabeth Carpenter, Mrs. Johnson's press secretary, called Esther Peterson to ask her advice on how to win for the new president the support of the women's organizations that had so enthusiastically backed the president's commission. Peterson replied that Johnson should appoint commission member Margaret Hickey to chair the Citizens' Advisory Council on the Status of Women (CACSW)—a decision John Kennedy already made but not implemented—and that this appointment would signal his intention to stand behind the commission's work. Johnson dutifully followed the advice, and both he and Mrs. Johnson attended the council's first meeting. In Women's Bureau releases, Esther Peterson moved quickly to identify Johnson with the Kennedy policy initiatives on women.[9]

The Interdepartmental Committee on the Status of Women

(ICSW) and the CACSW were continuations of the president's commission not only in spirit but also in personnel. The executive order establishing the ICSW and the CACSW placed in the former group all the cabinet members who had been on the president's commission, plus the secretaries of state and defense. John Kennedy named to the CACSW all the nongovernment members of the presidential commission, adding Eleanor Roosevelt's daughter, Anna Halsted, and the president of the Trenton Trust Company, Mary Roebling. The support of the two continuing groups, with membership almost identical to that of the president's commission, signified that there would be no sharp departure in the Johnson administration from the agenda described in the commission report.[10]

The new president chose, however, to highlight one particular recommendation in order to differentiate himself from his predecessor and to win some new and exciting publicity before the 1964 election. His decision provided a momentary return to the modus operandi of Kennedy's predecessors. In January 1964, Lyndon Johnson declared to a *Washington Post* reporter that he intended to appoint fifty women to significant policy-making positions within thirty days; the story appeared on the front page. Johnson, a longtime party man, endorsed the notion that the appointments were good politics, and he responded to the suggestions of party women with whom he had long been associated—and whose counsel, to their delight and relief, was once again welcome in the White House. The president's closest female adviser, Elizabeth Carpenter, originally a journalist, saw good public relations in the campaign to appoint women and encouraged the president to do so.[11]

Indeed, Johnson's actions led to a sharp increase in the number of women serving in Senate-confirmed positions, with ten such appointments in his first thirteen months in office—excluding local customs office jobs, the same number as Kennedy had named during his whole three years. Of these ten, six represented "firsts" for women, compared to four for Kennedy. During the balance of his term, Johnson appointed another seventeen women. Of the twenty-seven total appointments, sixteen were firsts, and the number of women serving in the administration rose from thirty in 1963 to fifty-two in 1968.

Although Johnson did not name a woman to his cabinet, he was not criticized for this omission—an indication that his overall record, with due attention given to breaking new ground, contented Democratic women. Moreover, thanks to Liz Carpenter, Johnson accompanied his appointments with the fanfare political women thought appropriate. Yet unlike Truman and Eisenhower, Johnson also took an interest in the civil service efforts the presidential commission had instigated. Rapid gains in high-level jobs for women took place at the beginning of 1964.[12] Party women were very pleased, and the journalist Isabelle Shelton recalled more than a decade later: "There's never been anything like it—before or since."[13]

But Johnson's burst of interest in appointments created some unforeseen consequences that affected the status of women more significantly than the mere numbers of nominees. By pledging a larger role for women in his administration, Johnson raised expectations that he then failed to fulfill. The appointments campaign ended with the 1964 presidential election, and by March 1965 Margaret Price complained once again that women were dissatisfied with the number of staff appointments. This time the displeasure spread through the state commissions, gaining attention from many more women—women organized and focused on the status of women—than ever before.

A second outcome of Johnson's appointments concerned the Women's Bureau. The president designated Esther Peterson to be his special assistant on consumer affairs, the single highest post to which he named a woman. (India Edwards and Liz Carpenter both observed the irony in giving this post to Peterson, who already was the ranking female member of the administration as assistant secretary of labor, a job she retained. Both women pointed out that Johnson would be able to name more women to important jobs if Peterson did not get them all. In fact, Peterson became one of the few Kennedy appointees Johnson continued to trust.) With the new appointment, Peterson decided to relinquish the directorship of the Women's Bureau, the least prestigious of the three jobs she held, and Johnson replaced her with Mary Dublin Keyserling, an economist active in Democratic politics.

Keyserling was not pleased by the new position of concilia-

tion the president's commission had crafted.[14] A longtime
worker with the National Consumers League, Keyserling maintained a firm commitment to its philosophy that working
women required protection, a point of view she had expressed
emphatically while serving on the Committee on Protective Labor Legislation of the commission. Secretary of Labor Willard
Wirtz shared Keyserling's view, as expressed in the president's
commission report, that hours laws for women should be expanded until they could be replaced by laws requiring premium
pay for overtime. As Peterson and Catherine East, formerly the
technical secretary of the Committee on Federal Employment
and now the executive secretary of the Citizens' Advisory Council on the Status of Women, moved away from the idea of maintaining laws that protected women and not men, they came into
increasing conflict with Keyserling and Wirtz.[15]

## TITLE VII

The issue became of great moment with the consideration of
the 1964 omnibus civil rights bill. Introduced by Representative
Emanuel Celler (D-N.Y.) in June 1963, the comprehensive civil
rights bill strengthened voting rights and access to public education for black Americans and prohibited discrimination based
on race in places of public accommodation, in federally assisted
programs, and in employment. The House Judiciary Committee held hearings on the bill for twenty-two days, reporting it
favorably on November 20, 1963, two days before President
Kennedy was assassinated. Sex discrimination had not been
mentioned.[16]

The National Woman's party reacted to the committee report with a resolution, passed in December, that bemoaned the
fact that the bill "would not even give protection against discrimination because of 'race, color, religion, or national origin,'
to a *White Woman,* a *Woman of the Christian Religion,* or a *Woman
of United States Origin.*" With this statement, the NWP began its
campaign to amend the bill to include a prohibition against sex
discrimination.[17]

Although the party maintained that the ERA constituted all
the protection women needed, given that such an amendment

did not exist, party members had always sought to have women included in fair employment practices legislation and executive orders applying to minorities. The NWP did not initiate such legislation, because its largely privileged and conservative membership generally believed that the government should not intervene in private enterprise. However, if the federal government insisted on offering protection to black workers, the NWP did not want women placed at a relative disadvantage by being denied similar assistance.[18]

The party quickly turned to a powerful ally, Representative Howard Smith (D-Va.), the chairman of the House Rules Committee and a longtime proponent of the Equal Rights Amendment. An archconservative Southerner, Smith, in common with many NWP members, opposed the whole idea of the bill. If the addition of *sex* to Title VII, the employment title of the pending civil rights statute, were to result in the bill's demise, Smith, and several NWP members, would be satisfied. Yet if the bill were to pass, Smith agreed with the NWP that it had to include women in its scope: otherwise white women would lack an advantage granted to black men. In addition to seeking Smith's backing, the NWP also approached women members of Congress. The party met resistance, however, either because the women representatives perceived a lack of support from other members or because they had promised the administration not to offer amendments on the floor. Finally Representatives Martha Griffiths (D-Mich.) and Katharine St. George (R-N.Y.), both strong supporters of the ERA, decided to back the amendment but to let Howard Smith introduce it, pointing out that his endorsement would bring many votes they themselves could not acquire. During the hearings on the rule, Smith quizzed Celler about the omission of sex as a prohibited basis for discrimination and warned that he intended to offer an amendment to eliminate the gap. On January 26, White House correspondent May Craig raised the issue with Smith on the television show "Meet the Press," and Smith agreed again to consider it.[19]

The Women's Bureau coalition opposed adding sex as a prohibited basis of discrimination on two grounds. For one thing, the President's Commission on the Status of Women had asserted that race and sex discrimination were best treated separately, and the coalition continued to endorse this view. Banning sex discrimination in the same way as racial bias threatened protective labor laws. Then, like most liberal reformers, the members of the coalition believed that the fight against racism had prior claim. The year 1964 was, once again, the "Negro's hour," and many liberal women believed that the issue of women's rights had been raised merely to kill the bill with another controversial clause. As before, the two factions were at loggerheads.

On February 8, 1964, as he had suggested he would, Howard Smith introduced an amendment to add the word *sex* to Title VII of the pending civil rights bill. Assuring the House that he was "very serious" about the proposal, Smith insisted that it could not do the measure any harm and that it might in fact improve it. After he discussed the issue of discrimination against women in employment, however, Smith read excerpts, with an excess of chivalry, from a letter he had received complaining that some women were cheated out of husbands because there were too few men to go around. He warned his colleagues to take note of such "real grievances." Celler responded with similar jocularity, pointing out that he usually had the last two words in his household of women, and they were "yes, dear." Other members found the exchange highly amusing. Celler then offered serious objections to the amendment, citing first a Department of Labor letter quoting Esther Peterson, who reiterated the position of the president's commission that sex discrimination was best treated separately and who argued that the addition of sex to Title VII would "not be to the best advantage of women at this time." Celler contended that the provision would reproduce the language of the pending Equal Rights Amendment, and he opposed it on that basis, referring to alimony, compulsory military service for women, custody, and rape laws—none of them relevant to the proposal at hand, which dealt only with employment. The germane point he raised concerned protective labor laws: Celler warned that enacting the proposal under discussion might result in the nullification of state legislation regulating hours and conditions of women's work.[20]

After Celler and Smith finished, all but one of the twelve women members of the House rose ("suddenly," according to the *New York Times*) to speak in favor of the amendment. Martha Griffiths, prepared for the occasion, pointed out that the laughter surrounding the introduction of the amendment exposed the second-class citizenship of American women. Her concern, she said, was that the bill as written would leave white women with no protection at all, because black women would have a cause of action against employers who hired only white men, but white women would not. She dismissed the argument concerning labor legislation; the main function of such laws, she said, had been to protect men's rights to better-paying jobs. But she suggested that a clause to save protective laws would be feasible if that were the price of labor support. Griffiths concluded by declaring that a vote against the amendment by a white man was a vote against his wife, his widow, his daughter, and his sister.[21]

The one woman legislator who spoke against the amendment was Edith Green, former member of the president's commission, who risked, she said, being deemed an "Aunt Jane." Nevertheless, she argued, discrimination against blacks was more severe than against women, and she could not support an amendment that would jeopardize the bill as a whole. Green further noted that not one organization had submitted testimony in favor of this change to the committees considering it. Later in the debate she voiced the argument that biological differences between men and women would spell trouble for employers forced to hire women. Despite Green's protest, however, after a two-hour discussion the coalition of women legislators in favor of equality for women, Republicans in sympathy with the ERA, and opponents of civil rights legislation seeking to block passage of the bill added sex discrimination to the ban in the pending legislation by a vote of 168 to 133. Two days later the House passed the entire bill 290 to 130. All the men but one who had spoken in favor of the sex amendment voted against the bill.[22]

Predictably, response to the sex provision was mixed. The National Woman's party rejoiced, as did the congresswomen who had supported the proposal. The Women's Division of the United Automobile Workers, which had always favored compulsory measures to eliminate sex discrimination, also applauded.

Esther Peterson, however, expressed fear that the amendment might hurt the bill's chances in the Senate and insisted that, in any case, discrimination based on sex warranted separate treatment.[23] A *Washington Post* editorial facetiously concluded that the vote made it "pretty plain . . . who's head of the House up there on the Hill."[24]

The newly formed Citizens' Advisory Council on the Status of Women held its first meeting two days after the House vote and, at the request of the Justice Department, made no statement. The CACSW had a commitment to implement the presidential commission's recommendations opposing such a law, but Assistant Attorney General Burke Marshall told the council that the bill's passage represented the "most important thing" and that employment opportunity for women was "a side matter," regardless of commission proposals. According to Marshall, the administration was indifferent as to whether the bill passed with the sex amendment or without it; its only concern was to decide in which form the bill's chances were best. Dorothy Height, the president of the National Council of Negro Women, spoke of a two-part dilemma: she feared on the one hand that the inclusion of sex would weaken the administration of the bill with respect to race, which clearly came first for her; but on the other she also feared that any discussion about the ill effects of the sex amendment might weaken the support for the bill as a whole, by providing an excuse for someone to vote against it. Marshall agreed, and asked the CACSW to take no position. The council readily assented, without even discussing the bill's implications for women. Because it would not meet again until the fall, the council thus played no role in the enactment of legislation prohibiting sex discrimination in employment.[25]

Eager to avoid a conference on the bill, the White House decided to seek a Senate vote on the measure exactly as it had passed the House, including the sex proviso. The women in the House of Representatives lobbied among the senators for the amendment, and Pauli Murray, as a black woman sensitive to the problems of both racial and sex-based discrimination and the dynamic between them, circulated a memorandum that maintained that the omission of *sex* would weaken the civil rights bill by once again dividing the interests of oppressed groups in the society and by neglecting the problems of black women. In support of her argument, Murray, then on the faculty of Yale Law School, quoted at length from the documents of the president's commission. Ironically, then, the discussion by the commission, which had not recommended fair employment legislation for women, of the problem of discrimination against women, together with its inclusion of dissenting opinions in its publications, furthered the cause of the new bill.[26]

The National Woman's party continued to play a major role in the controversy, forming a special emergency committee to watch over the sex provision. When Senator Everett Dirksen spoke against it, the NWP asked ERA supporter Margaret Chase Smith, the only female Republican senator, to intervene. The Illinois BPW organized an intensive lobbying campaign directed at Dirksen, who finally acquiesced. Although the attempt to have the Senate pass the House measure without any amendment did not succeed, on June 17 the Senate did endorse a substitute bill, with the sex discrimination clause included, by a vote of seventy-six to eighteen. Two weeks later, on July 2, 1964, the House adopted the Senate bill with more than two-thirds voting in favor. Lyndon Johnson signed the measure into law the same day.[27]

Thus, by 1964 a situation unique in the postwar period prevailed: in the absence of a widespread women's movement, a federal law had been passed that prohibited sex discrimination in employment, thanks to ERA advocates who took advantage of both the administration's eagerness to protect the welfare of black citizens and the desire of Southern legislators to thwart that effort. Two federal advisory groups and a national network of commissions on women, all the work of the Women's Bureau coalition, existed for the purpose of examining the status of women in the context of a stated federal policy of equality rendered first by the president's commission and now by Congress as well.

This combination of partial successes on the part of both the Women's Bureau coalition and the proponents of the ERA in the early sixties led to raised expectations and tools with which to organize. An atmosphere now obtained in which the discontent, born of the disjuncture among the ideals of womanhood, the changing conditions of women's lives, and the unrealized promise of equality, could find constructive expression. The unforeseen backlash that greeted the new sex discrimination law proved to be the catalyst for action.

## ACTING ON THE PCSW AGENDA

The President's Commission on the Status of Women had not predicted or advocated so sweeping a legal measure as Title VII of the 1964 Civil Rights Act, and at the beginning its heirs preferred to ignore it and concentrate on their more moderate agenda. As a result of PCSW recommendations, civil service health benefits were equalized, the Departments of State and Defense revised regulations on dependency allowances, and the Department of Labor amended rules for eligibility to federal apprenticeship programs to prohibit sex bias. Congress also raised the income level for tax deductions for childcare. In 1966 the Department of Health, Education, and Welfare inaugurated a policy of supplying birth control information and devices on request. Federal funds supported pilot programs in the counseling of girls and mature women. Amendments to the Fair Labor Standards Act left only 5.4 million women and 6 million men uncovered. As of November 1966, more than $3 million had been found owing in equal pay violations and the secretary of labor had brought thirty cases to court.[28]

Also in keeping with the position of the PCSW, the Johnson administration did not support the ERA, even though Lyndon Johnson had as a senator endorsed the amendment. National Woman's party members had believed that his accession to the presidency presaged a favorable change in White House policy, but Johnson could not take over for Kennedy and immediately disown the presidential commission's recommendation on so crucial a matter. He publicly backed the Fourteenth Amendment strategy the commission had ultimately proposed. In December 1963, Peterson drafted a position statement for White House letters that announced: "The President is impressed by the Commission's position and believes that this approach should be fully explored before considering a new constitu-

tional amendment on this subject."[29] To the dissatisfaction of
ERA proponents, the White House followed her line. Amendment adherents were further distressed when Johnson saw to it
that the 1964 Democratic party platform contained no reference to the ERA. Emma Guffey Miller wrote bitterly to Johnson, whom she admired intensely:

> As one who has grown old in the service of the Democratic Party
> may I tell you . . . of the deep disappointment of *many* thousands of
> Democratic women like myself who question the right of Mrs. Es-
> ther Peterson to assume the leadership of the Democratic women
> and dictate the womans [*sic*] plank in our 1964 platform. . . . Now
> [it] omits the Equal Rights plank for women, a plank which has
> been adopted by our party for two decades. This is not progress,
> Mr. President, but retrogression.[30]

Other support for the amendment rapidly declined. After 1964
the Senate Judiciary Committee ceased reporting the amendment out, and in 1968 the Republicans dropped the amendment from their platform as well. Many members of Congress
responded to letters on the ERA by informing constituents of
the PCSW plan for constitutional equality.[31]

In 1965 a case finally appeared that looked as though it
might yield the Supreme Court interpretation the commission
had sought and result in unity with ERA adherents. The hope
proved short-lived. Black residents, both men and women, of
Lowndes County, Alabama, represented by the American Civil
Liberties Union (ACLU), filed a suit in federal district court
charging that methods of jury selection in Lowndes County
contravened the Fourteenth Amendment in excluding blacks
by practice and women by state law. Mary Eastwood, Pauli Murray, Marguerite Rawalt, and Catherine East, all connected by
their association on the president's commission, worked together to obtain amicus briefs from various women's organizations, and the Justice Department intervened at Esther
Peterson's request. Pauli Murray helped draft the ACLU brief,
looking forward to Supreme Court review. When the federal
district court ruled in favor of the plaintiffs, however, the state
of Alabama did not appeal.[32] Although the Citizens' Advisory
Council on the Status of Women declared the district court

decision a "landmark victory for women's rights,"[33] the absence of a Supreme Court ruling made the event inconclusive. Proponents of the PCSW position continued to seek a Supreme Court declaration, but to no avail.

At the same time, because of the President's Commission on the Status of Women, hundreds of women and men were involved in state commissions actively fighting on local fronts for women's rights. The CACSW devoted the major part of its attention to monitoring programs of women's organizations and state commissions in fulfillment of the presidential commission's agenda for women.[34] Their activity brought results and, concomitantly, an expectation of further change. In the two and a half years after the commission's report, six states enacted minimum wage laws that applied to both men and women, and nine more states extended previously existing minimum wage laws for women to cover men as well. Eleven states took action to make hours laws for women more flexible, three repealed such laws, and six adopted laws providing for overtime pay for work in excess of a certain number of hours. Nine states enacted equal pay laws, bringing to thirty-five the number of states with some equal pay protection. Spurred by local groups and federal grants, homemaker services in local communities burgeoned. Many states took action to amend various laws that restrained the rights of women to operate as freely as men. Four states modified discriminatory jury service laws, three amended statutes limiting a married woman's right to dispose of her property, and several states strengthened child support laws or changed laws that prescribed one legal marriage age for men and another for women. Every year state commissions and women's organizations held conferences, published literature, created pilot programs in cooperation with state and local governments, conducted studies, lobbied for state and federal legislation, trained volunteers, operated day-care centers and homemaker programs, ran courses, and developed audiovisual materials for use by educators—all in the attempt to further the goals established by the president's commission. Not since World War II had women's issues received so much attention.[35]

The scions of the PCSW brought all these activists together. In 1964, in order to establish ties among the state groups, the

CACSW and the Interdepartmental Committee on the Status of Women began inviting representatives of state commissions annually to Washington for national conferences and publishing written reports of the proceedings. At the first such meeting, eighty-three representatives of commissions in thirty-one states discussed issues of equal pay, minimum wage laws, day-care facilities, equality in public employment, educational and counseling programs for women, and derisive media treatment. By 1965 the conference had grown to more than four hundred participants from forty-four states, with eleven workshops addressing legal status, Title VII, vocational guidance, educational and employment opportunities, community services, consumer education, labor standards, income maintenance, and women in public life, as well as the financing and management of state commissions. Administration support for their efforts showed in the attendance of the president, cabinet members, and other federal officials. By now, the participants in the state commissions had combined into a national watchdog agency on women's rights; they proceeded to turn their attention to the implementation of Title VII.[36]

The ICSW and the CACSW intended to have the state commissions follow their lead on Title VII and protective labor legislation—but their own position was not entirely clear. A subcommittee of the ICSW, composed of Evelyn Harrison, deputy for Civil Service Commission chair John Macy, Mary Eastwood, from the Justice Department, and Mary Keyserling, acting as the deputy of Secretary of Labor Willard Wirtz, set to work formulating a position.[37] The subcommittee could not, however, reach a consensus on how the newly formed Equal Employment Opportunity Commission (EEOC) should construe the effect of Title VII on state laws. Eastwood, who had been the technical secretary of the PCSW Committee on Civil and Political Rights and who had written the attorney general's opinion in 1962 permitting John Kennedy to ban sex discrimination in the civil service, had become convinced that protective labor laws hampered women's opportunities, and she observed that more and more state commissions had arrived at the same conclusion. The Civil Service Commission had itself ruled that women federal workers were sufficiently protected by regulations to be exempted from coverage by state laws pertaining to women's employment. Harrison and Eastwood recommended that in the case of a conflict between state laws and Title VII, the state laws should be ruled inoperative. Mary Keyserling, however, continued to be committed to the traditional posture that women needed special treatment. She contended simply that no conflict existed between Title VII and state labor laws for women. The subcommittee therefore drew up two position papers for ICSW chairman Secretary of Labor Willard Wirtz to consider.[38]

For her part, Assistant Secretary of Labor Esther Peterson was ready to concede that protective labor laws had had their day and that the Department of Labor should now move ahead to a single standard, a standard she had been ready to adopt even for the president's commission. Peterson suggested that most problems could be solved by extending protective laws to men or, where the work was of an especially heavy nature, by permitting exceptions under the "bona fide occupational qualification" provision. While Peterson admitted that the prohibition of sex discrimination in employment came before she and many others anticipated it would, it represented, to her, a "great opportunity." She proposed that the EEOC adopt the principle of a single standard and consider each law on a case-by-case basis.

Peterson, however, had moved beyond her former constituency of labor unions and traditional women's organizations, and the Department of Labor did not follow her recommendation.[39] Rather, the consensus of the Women's Bureau coalition favored retention of the laws. Yielding to the advice of Mary Keyserling and many labor union representatives, Willard Wirtz wrote to EEOC chairman Franklin D. Roosevelt, Jr., that Title VII did not require "a general invalidation" of protective laws, many of which, he counseled, were useful and reconcilable with the objectives of Title VII. "In general," he advised Roosevelt, "the Department believes that the Commission should follow a policy of protecting and preserving these laws wherever possible and practicable."[40] Women's organizations, labor unions, religious groups, and civil liberties organizations, including the AFL-CIO, expressed similar views to the EEOC. The CACSW, unable to reach a firm consensus among its members, merely issued a statement upholding the president's commission position on protective laws, while glossing over the key issue of Title VII's impact.[41]

The EEOC willingly followed the advice of the Women's Bureau coalition and the Department of Labor. At the 1965 meeting of state commissions on women, hosted in July by the ICSW and the CACSW, Roosevelt assured the participants that the commission would move "with great care" regarding protective labor laws. The commission did not, Roosevelt explained, see "any clear Congressional intent to overturn all of these laws."[42]

## THE EQUAL EMPLOYMENT OPPORTUNITY COMMISSION

The EEOC's willingness to retain protective labor laws did not stem only from its concern for the opinions of the groups lobbying it; EEOC commissioners and staff also expressed a general belief that the addition of *sex* to the law had been illegitimate—merely a ploy to kill the bill—and that it did not therefore constitute a mandate to equalize women's employment opportunities. Aileen Hernandez, the only woman on the commission, later recalled that the subject of sex discrimination elicited either "boredom" or "virulent hostility."[43] In September 1965, EEOC executive director N. Thompson Powers told Secretary Wirtz that "the Commission is very much aware of the importance of not becoming known as the 'sex commission.'"[44] By November 1965 Herman Edelsberg had succeeded Powers, and he told the press: "There are people on this Commission who think that no man should be required to have a male secretary—and I am one of them."[45]

The commission's attitude revealed itself in both its actions and its words. Title VII included a clear ban on segregated employment advertisements; the act read: "It shall be an unlawful employment practice for an employer . . . to publish or cause to be . . . published any notice or advertisement relating to employment . . . indicating any preference, limitation, specification, or discrimination, based on race, color, religion, sex, or national origin" except in the case of a bona fide occupational qualification. The EEOC quickly ruled that newspaper adver-

tisements for jobs segregated by race constituted a clear trans-
gression of the act but convened an ad hoc committee to determine whether sex-segregated want ads similarly violated the
statute, since sex would presumably be a bona fide occupational
qualification more often than race.

The committee comprised fourteen members from advertising agencies, newspapers, and business firms, two from the
Department of Labor, and one from the American Nurses Association. Not surprisingly, this group, with its disproportionate
representation of commercial interests, resolved that want ads
segregated by sex did not contravene Title VII.[46] Moreover,
Abraham Fortas, then on the Supreme Court, reportedly told
Johnson that the Court would strike down a regulation banning
sex-labeled want ads as a violation of the First Amendment's
free press clause. The EEOC had initially split three to two for
making sex-segregated want ads illegal. Commissioners Richard Graham, a white Republican from Wisconsin, Aileen Hernandez, a black woman from California, and Sam Jackson, a
black Republican from Kansas, supported the ban, with commission chairman Franklin Roosevelt, Jr., and vice-chairman Luther Holcomb opposed. After Holcomb passed along Fortas's
opinion from Johnson, Jackson changed his vote.[47] In August
1965, the EEOC issued its ruling that employers could advertise
in sex-segregated columns. The commission required only that
newspapers publish a disclaimer informing readers that the
headings were not intended to be discriminatory but only reflected that fact that some jobs were of more interest to one sex
than another. The EEOC ignored the recommendation of the
CACSW that advertising be sex-neutral.[48]

Although the EEOC had issued a regulation that directly con-
tradicted the wording of Title VII, it received criticism even for
the mild restraint it had imposed on the newspapers. The ostensibly liberal *New Republic* believed the commission would have
done better simply to have ignored the sex provision. "Why,"
asked the journal, "should a mischievous joke perpetrated on the
floor of the House of Representatives be treated by a responsible
administrative body with this kind of seriousness?"[49]

The *New Republic* spoke for many; the ban on sex discrimination elicited derision and ridicule. The *Wall Street Journal,* in an

article published a week before the effective date of the act, asked its readers to picture, if they could, "a shapeless, knobby-kneed male 'bunny' serving drinks to a group of stunned businessmen in a Playboy Club" or a "matronly vice-president" chasing a male secretary around her desk.[50] EEOC's own executive director, Herman Edelsberg, reportedly circulated a suggestion that the commission seal depict a brown rabbit, together with a white rabbit "couchant," with the legend "Vive la différence."[51] A personnel officer at a large airline described his employer as "unnerved" by the ban on sex discrimination. "What are we going to do now," the personnel officer asked, "when a gal walks into our office, demands a job as an airline pilot and has the credentials to qualify?" A manager of an electronic components company that employed only women suggested sarcastically, "I suppose we'll have to advertise for people with small, nimble fingers and hire the first male midget with unusual dexterity [who] shows up."[52]

Business attitudes placed the EEOC on the defensive. One official told the *Wall Street Journal* that the government intended to enforce the sex prohibition with great leniency "if the women's groups will let us get away with it." Nevertheless, commission staff explained apologetically, "some interpretations must be made if those provisions are to make sense and to be understandable to those covered."[53]

In November 1965, sixteen months after passage of the 1964 Civil Rights Act and four months after it went into effect, the EEOC finally issued full guidelines on sex discrimination under Title VII; the business community's fears were assuaged. The commission reiterated that it had received no help from the legislative history of the amendment; state laws, it said, constituted particularly difficult problems, but it did not believe that Congress intended to disturb laws that protected women against hazard or exploitation. The commission therefore stated that it would not consider the necessity to pay women minimum wages or premium wages for overtime as valid reasons for discriminating against women, and where the law permitted administrative exemption from state hours laws employers would have to seek them. An employer would not be breaking the law, however, if he refused to hire a woman for a job from which she was barred by state statute.[54] In a December letter to a member of the National Woman's party, commissioner Richard Graham explained: "There seems to be a widely held misconception that this Commission can or would overturn state protective legislation. This is not the case. . . . If there is a clear conflict between the laws, we would not ask that [an employer] violate the state law. Rather, we would suggest that this conflict be brought to the attention of the Governor or the State Legislature or the state commission for remedy."[55] In any case, the woman herself could bring suit, and the courts might render a judgment that essentially overturned state law. At a press conference on the new guidelines, commission chairman Franklin D. Roosevelt, Jr., assured the public that the guidelines would not result in a massive assault on sex-segregated jobs.[56] Four months later, the *New York Times* quoted a commission spokesperson as saying that the EEOC had moved cautiously on sex discrimination because of the lack of legal precedent, because of a concern for protective labor legislation, and because "it did not want this area to interfere with its main concern, racial discrimination."[57]

The following month, April 1966, the commission once again evinced its half-hearted commitment to enforcing the prohibition of sex discrimination. It yielded to pressure from advertisers and newspapers who had already breached the original ruling on want ads by failing to print the disclaimer of discrimination. Ignoring the recommendations of the ICSW and the CACSW, the Equal Employment Opportunity Commission amended its regulations to permit the placement of job notices in sex-segregated columns without any restriction, except that the ad itself could not state a preference.[58] Commission vice-chair Luther Holcomb (now acting chairman since the resignation of Franklin Roosevelt, Jr., to run for governor of New York) believed that aggressive action on the part of the EEOC would hurt President Johnson's reputation. His judgment, combined with pressure from the newspaper industry, prevailed. Executive director Edelsberg explained the commission's action by observing that the sex amendment was a "fluke" "conceived out of wedlock."[59] Esther Peterson warned Secretary Wirtz that interested women's groups might "react strongly to the abandonment of any attempt by the EEOC to enforce the sex-segregated advertisement ban of Title VII." Peterson herself asserted that "any rationale for this action on the part of the Commission is difficult to perceive."[60]

Peterson's prediction that the EEOC action would inspire protest proved correct. In June Martha Griffiths, one of the prime movers behind the sex amendment to Title VII, took to the House floor to blast the commission's decision. Griffiths accused the EEOC of a "wholly negative attitude" toward the sex provision, observing that it focused on ridiculous examples such as Playboy bunnies and male housemothers of college sororities. It had reached a "peak of contempt," she said, with the issuance of the ruling permitting sex-segregated want ads. This interpretation, Griffiths contended, bespoke on the part of the EEOC "nothing more than arbitrary arrogance, disregard of law, and a manifestation of flat hostility to the human rights of women."[61]

Convinced of the power of Griffith's speech, Catherine East saw an opportunity to build support to change the EEOC's attitude. The third meeting of delegates from state commissions around the country was about to take place, planned by the CACSW. East arranged for copies of Griffith's speech to be distributed to the participants.[62]

Although she was proud of the accomplishments of the President's Commission on the Status of Women and of the CACSW, East recognized that the ability of these bodies to make major changes was limited by their identification with the administration in power. East and her colleagues who had worked in the government had been looking for an outside group to take the lead and force the EEOC to respond seriously to the issue of sex discrimination in employment. The members of the state commissions arriving in Washington had been primed. The moment had arrived.

# 10

## A NEW WOMEN'S MOVEMENT

In October 1966, three years to the month after the President's Commission on the Status of Women presented its report to John Kennedy, the first avowedly feminist organization to emerge since suffrage held its inaugural conference. With the appearance of the National Organization for Women, women leaders outside of government, building upon the president's Commission's report, took over the creation of the policy agenda for women from those in government who had served as "midwives of the Women's Movement."[1] The new movement adopted the objectives of the activists who had laid the groundwork, but it went beyond their work in a signal way. The women's movement of the 1960s forged a new, coherent, feminist philosophy that would enable women finally to make a claim for complete equality both in and outside the home.

## THE CREATION OF THE
## NATIONAL ORGANIZATION FOR WOMEN

Martha Griffiths was not alone in her indignation at the behavior of the EEOC. Although initially disturbed by the threat to protective labor laws Title VII represented, by 1966 virtually every women's organization protested the EEOC's cavalier attitude toward sex discrimination. By June, a "proto-feminist" nucleus in Washington (Peterson, Catherine East, Mary Eastwood, and EEOC commissioner Richard Graham) had come to believe that the EEOC would not improve unless outside pressure from organized women served to heighten the commissioners' interest in enforcing the sex provision of Title VII. This cadre had begun to work toward the formation of a new outside group devoted exclusively to sex discrimination, starting with the traditional women's associations of the Women's Bureau coalition.[2] These groups were reluctant, however, to establish an activist group that would fight exclusively for women's rights;[3] as council member Viola Hymes had earlier explained, women's organizations hesitated to take the lead in the fight "for fear it would be interpreted that they were favoring women instead of looking upon everyone as having equal opportunity."[4]

But other, less familiar, avenues were being explored. Betty Friedan, author of *The Feminist Mystique,* who had begun work on a book concerning the new law on sex discrimination, was now in close touch with Catherine East, Sonia Pressman, Pauli Murray, and Martha Griffiths—part of what Friedan later described as the "feminist underground" in Washington. Pressman, an attorney at the EEOC, told Friedan that only she could start a national organization to fight for women as the civil rights movement had for blacks. Richard Graham, too, urged Friedan on, telling her that he had asked the mainstream women's associations, such as the League of Women Voters and the American Association of University Women, to develop such an organization, but they had declined. Friedan nevertheless delayed. Although East and Eastwood supplied her with lists of women likely to be sympathetic, Friedan suggested that the state commissions on the status of women take the lead. East protested that women on the state commissions were too dependent on the state governors and had too little power of their own. Over Mary Keyserling's objections, East invited Friedan to attend the Washington gathering of the state commissions in June.[5]

Friedan took the opportunity the conference provided to probe the sentiments of the state commission members. Shortly before the meeting Friedan, to her dismay, had learned through her Washington friends that Lyndon Johnson did not intend to reappoint Richard Graham to the EEOC after his initial term expired in July. (Ironically, Graham himself had no sense that he was being "dismissed" from the commission, although he was aware that Roosevelt, Holcomb and Edelsberg preferred that he not be reappointed. Graham's term on the EEOC had ended; he welcomed the White House offer of the post of director of the National Teacher Corps as a chance to work effectively for civil rights free of the energy-draining backbiting of the EEOC. He left the EEOC unaware of the controversy swirling around his departure.)[6] Mindful of East's words, Friedan invited a group of interested women participating in the state commission conference to come to her hotel room and discuss what could be done about Graham's reappointment and about the recent EEOC ruling regarding sex-segregated advertising. The women who caucused in Friedan's room agreed that a civil rights organization for women was not necessary but proposed that a resolution be offered at the conference supporting Graham and insisting on better enforcement efforts by the EEOC. Kathryn Clarenbach, chairman of the Wisconsin commission on women and known for her close working relationship with the CACSW, volunteered to speak to Peterson, Keyserling, and Hickey about the proposal.[7]

Administration officials had anticipated some expression of irritation at the conference. Esther Peterson confided to John Macy that "95 percent" of the delegates believed that the EEOC was lax about enforcing the sex provision of Title VII. Moreover, she said, a grapevine made up of "women active in women's groups, unions, civil rights groups and political parties" was communicating dissatisfaction because Lyndon Johnson's campaign to bring more women into government had lapsed.[8]

But despite Peterson's obvious sympathy with the grievances, the action she and the other conference hosts took to address them brought the annoyance to a head. When Clarenbach conferred with Hickey, Keyserling, and Peterson about offering resolutions on the subject, all three told her it could not be done because the conference participants were not official delegates and because conference organizers did not want resolutions critical of the administration emerging from a federally supported gathering. Angered by the ruling, Clarenbach reported back to Friedan and the others. Having had their request for action denied, the fifteen women who had met in Friedan's room the night before took over two tables at the conference luncheon. Within sight of the conference directors, Friedan, Clarenbach, and their colleagues planned an inaugural meeting for a new women's association. Friedan scribbled the name on a paper napkin: NOW—the National Organization for Women.[9]

In addition, disregarding the official decree, eighty representatives in the Title VII workshop voted for a resolution asking Lyndon Johnson to reappoint Richard Graham. Olya Margolin of the National Council of Jewish Women reported to AFL-CIO lobbyist Andrew Biemiller that "the most unfortunate part of these proceedings" was that some labor women joined conference participants ("equal-righters") in an attack on protective labor legislation, which "created the impression that labor is either divided or no longer concerned about these labor standards." Mary Keyserling ignored the disputes and the ire of conference participants. She reported to Secretary Wirtz that the conference had been "very successful," mentioning no disagreement of any kind.[10]

Keyserling tried to pretend that nothing had happened, but the June conference constituted a crucial point in the history of women in the 1960s. Until then, either influential individuals or official government bodies had created a federal agenda for women and moved with caution and deference to traditional views about women, carefully couching requests for specific improvements in the language of liberal ideals and obeisance to women's "natural" roles as wife and mother. The formation of NOW indicated that many women were no longer satisfied working within the constraints imposed by being official members of governments. From that time forward, the federal government would no longer control or restrain the agenda of the women's movement; NOW could take action, as official groups could not, without executive sanction. At the conclusion of the June conference, NOW officers sent telegrams to Lyndon Johnson asking him to reappoint Richard Graham to the commission and requesting the EEOC to revise its ruling on sex-segregated want ads.[11]

The target of NOW's original animus, the EEOC, was in extremis as the new group got underway. The *Chicago Tribune* alleged that Franklin Roosevelt, Jr., when he resigned in May 1966, had been "driven" from the commission over the issue of enforcing the sex provision of the civil rights law. In June commissioner Aileen Hernandez complained to the White House

about the slowness in naming commission replacements and
about the high staff turnover. Johnson did not fill Graham's
post promptly; thus, in July the commission, with only three
members, was at 60 percent of its total strength. The White
House, concerned about the controversy over the commission
and its personnel, decided to take no note of the July anniversary of the enactment of the civil rights statute.[12]

The situation continued to decline. In August the EEOC issued a new ruling backing away from a position in support of
protective labor laws, saying that it would not make decisions in
cases of alleged conflict but would wait for court interpretations.
In doing so, the commission now drew the wrath of labor women
as well as ERA advocates. In September Hernandez sent a memorandum to the commission and its staff expressing her dismay at
the long time lag in responding to complaints and at the neglect
of sex discrimination. This grievance had no effect, however,
and in October Hernandez submitted her resignation in disgust,
effective November 10. Stephen Shulman, whom Johnson appointed to head the commission in September, was not in an
enviable position. The National Organization for Women intended to make sure he took his new job seriously.[13]


## AN OUTSIDE PRESSURE GROUP

The new women's rights organization convened its inaugural
conference in October 1966, the first formal expression of the
new wave of feminism. At the meeting, the membership
elected Friedan president and Clarenbach, in absentia, chairman of the board; former EEOC commissioners Aileen Hernandez and Richard Graham both became vice-presidents.
The composition of the board of directors disclosed NOW's
origins in the discontent of elite women and their male supporters. The board included seven university professors or
administrators, five state or national labor union officials, four
federal or local government officials, four business executives,
four members with some affiliation to a state commission on
women, one physician, and three members of religious orders.
Thanks to the media experience of the professionals in the
organization, the October conference elicited a surprising

amount of press attention, which greatly enhanced NOW's impact from its birth.[14]

Although NOW appeared because its founders grew impatient with the timid posture of ICSW and CACSW officials in relation to the Equal Employment Opportunity Commission, the formation of NOW did not imply a renunciation of the President's Commission on the Status of Women or of the ongoing groups created at the commission's request to implement its recommendations. Rather, the originators of the new organization were motivated by an understanding of the intrinsic limitations of federal bodies. In the invitation to join the new organization, the creators paid respects to the president's commission, the governors' commissions, the CACSW, and the ICSW as part of the "basis" laid "for realizing the democratic goal of full participation and equal partnership for all citizens." And in the statement of purpose, adopted at the October meeting, they stated: "The excellent reports of the President's Commission on the Status of Women and of the State Commissions have not been fully implemented. . . . They have no power to enforce their recommendations. . . . The reports of these Commissions have, however, created a basis upon which it is now possible to build." The architects of NOW established the organization in order to commence "a civil rights movement for women" that would confront law and custom "to win for women the final right to be fully free and equal human beings."[15] Although upset by the decision of Peterson, Keyserling, and Hickey not to permit a resolution at the conference, NOW's founders held no grudge against the administration officials concerned with women. Friedan later referred to Esther Peterson and Eleanor Roosevelt as the "two towering figures of recent history," who had first brought together many of the new organizations' founders in the President's Commission on the Status of Women.[16]

Likewise, Peterson bore no ill will toward the organization that was preparing to wrest control of women's policy from the administration groups. In a memorandum to Civil Service Commission chairman John Macy, she described the membership list of the new organization as "very distinguished," although she found its positions "rather militant." Their governing principle, she wrote, was that sex and race discrimination were inter-

twined (many had been active in the civil rights movement) and
that the EEOC had proved consistently inadequate in righting
these injustices. Moreover, the particular incidents leading to
the group's formation were irrelevant; it was "inevitable" that
some such organization would appear. "The society," Peterson
said, "simply is not going to take women and their needs seriously until women take themselves and their needs seriously
enough to fight for them. . . . An organization is needed to
focus the underlying resentment and frustration into constructive channels. If NOW does not succeed, some other organization will take its place."[17]

Although Peterson characterized NOW's positions as "militant," in its first months NOW's program closely paralleled the
program of the president's commission. In subsequent years
NOW continued to owe to the president's commission its pen-
chant for seeking federal action to ameliorate women's problems, its emphasis on employment issues, and its attractiveness
for middle-class women who had first been sensitized to wom-
en's issues by the reports of the national and state commissions.
As "targets for action" in the first year, NOW highlighted equal
employment opportunity and the actions the federal government could take toward that end, including amendment of Executive Order 11246, which prohibited federal contractors
from discriminating on the basis of race. It also focused on full
deductability of childcare expenses, greater enforcement powers for the EEOC, the appointment of the full number of commissioners, revision of the regulations concerning advertising,
and equal attention to the needs of minority women in federal
poverty programs. The agenda was very broad and included
economic rights for homemakers, training programs for mothers reentering the labor force, projects to address discrimination in educational institutions, prohibition of distinctions based
on sex in jury service, and equal protection for women under
the Constitution. The people who founded NOW were friends
or colleagues of members of the presidential commission, or
members themselves, and they agreed generally with the commission on many of the most pressing problems and their solutions.[18]

As with the president's commission, NOW's founders did not

raise questions concerning sexual freedom. In 1966 NOW did not mention homosexuality, and a statement that women should control their own reproduction was excised from the statement of purpose as being "too controversial." NOW's creators assumed that women would continue to live in traditional families, and they did not envision or endorse a radical restructuring of most institutions.[19]

Similarly, in its founding year NOW approved the presidential commission's proposal regarding constitutional equality. Upon hearing of NOW's formation, the National Woman's party, hoping for an ally, wrote immediately asking for the organization's statement in favor of the Equal Rights Amendment. Mary Eastwood, who had been technical secretary of the PCSW Committee on Civil and Political Rights, which had formulated the commission's stance, wrote on NOW's behalf to the NWP that the ERA amendment was superfluous because the Constitution, properly interpreted, would guarantee equality without disturbing state labor laws.[20]

But if NOW considered the PCSW a model in many ways, it also differed from the governmental bodies that preceded it in two significant respects. First, unlike the presidential commission, NOW was independent of traditional political structures and owed no allegiance to a party or politician. Rather than seeking to praise members of the administration, NOW warned that "official pronouncements of the advance in the status of women hide not only the reality of [a] dangerous decline, but the fact that nothing is being done to stop it." NOW pledged to prevent the election of any public official "who betrays or ignores the principle of full equality between the sexes" by mobilizing the votes of feminist men and women. Since membership in NOW did not depend on the good favor of president or governor, NOW's freedom of action had few limits. It could afford to be, to use Peterson's term, "militant."[21]

Second, and more important, NOW declined to share the presidential commission's view that sex roles were immutable. In its statement of purpose, the organization's founders declared: "We reject the current assumptions that a man must carry the sole burden of supporting himself, his wife and family . . . or that marriage, home and family are primarily woman's world and

responsibility—hers, to dominate—his to support. We believe
that a true partnership between the sexes demands a different
concept of marriage, an equitable sharing of the responsibilities
of home and children and of the economic burdens of their
support."[22]

This renunciation of biological destiny ultimately permitted
NOW to demand a kind of equality for women that neither the
president's commission nor any other women's group preceding
NOW could have claimed. For the first time, women seeking
equal rights for women could offer a coherent and logical program, founded on an internally consistent philosophy. Women
could insist on equal treatment in the workplace because fathers,
too, had the responsibility to take care of children. With this
theoretical leap of great consequence, the feminists in NOW
anticipated, rather than reflected, the prevailing viewpoint.

Still, despite its assertion of independence, in its initial overtures to federal officials NOW assumed a very respectful attitude. Soon after the organizing conference, letters went out to
the president, the attorney general, the chairman of the Civil
Service Commission, and the EEOC commissioners, courteously
introducing the organization.[23] Emphasizing NOW's interest in
the administration of Title VII, the officers told the president:
"Our greatest concern today is that the Equal Employment Opportunity Commission should be able and willing to fulfill its
legal mandate to enforce the prohibitions against discrimination
in employment based upon sex." But NOW also asserted the
need for the appointment of women to government posts, affirmative action programs for women, and the inclusion of women
in legislation and executive orders respecting racial discrimination. The officers expressed to the president their gratitude for
his "past efforts."[24]

Administration officials recognized immediately the significance of a new organization dedicated to fighting for women's
rights. In November, Civil Service Commission chief John Macy
and three EEOC commissioners met with NOW officials to discuss the points NOW raised in its letter. EEOC chair Stephen
Shulman indicated to correspondents that he was aware of
NOW's position on the matters under discussion.[25] The Department of Labor, also the recipient of a letter from NOW, con-

gratulated the officers on NOW's objectives, which the secretary said the ICSW shared. Willard Wirtz wrote: "It is my hope that many of the advances you point to as needed can be effected."[26] Esther Peterson promised her support: "Your organization will be very useful at this moment and I am sure you know I am following it with great interest and will be helpful in any way I can."[27]

The White House reacted more guardedly. The letter to the president went to Peterson with a request that she handle it, and Shulman counseled the president not to meet with NOW's officers, advising him that the EEOC commissioners had already done so. He suggested that the president wait a year to see "whether or not they have achieved a status worthy of Presidential attention."[28]

NOW did not anticipate immediate results from the president. The group's founders recognized that the elimination of entrenched sex discrimination required a long-term educational and activist effort. "Our first order of business," Betty Friedan explained, "was to make clear to Washington, to employers, to unions and to the nation that someone *was* watching, someone *cared* about ending sex discrimination." The first goal of the organization was publicity. Many NOW actions, such as picketing newspapers and integrating men's bars, had as their rationale simply the desire for media attention to make their presence known. This goal was easily achieved: from the moment of its birth, Washington politicians knew NOW was there.[29]

Presidential acknowledgment came quickly, in fact. In March 1967 an aide advised the organization's officers that the president found their recommendations "most welcome" and that in keeping with one of their proposals he was willing to amend the executive order prohibiting racial discrimination in federal employment and contractors to include sex discrimination.[30]

Johnson's letter reflected the culmination of a series of developments. The President had issued EO 11246, which required affirmative action programs to ensure equal opportunity for all races, in September 1965. By that time, Congress had already passed the Civil Rights Act, which prohibited sex discrimination in employment, and Esther Peterson had warned that the omis-

sion of sex in the executive order "might prove embarrassing to
the President." Furthermore, she argued, if left out then, it
would create serious problems with women's organizations; it
would have to be added eventually. Secretary Wirtz had disagreed. He cautioned Peterson that it was not the "moment in
history" to press the point and that for her to do so would be
"counter-productive."[31] Peterson, outranked by Wirtz, had no
choice but to desist, but the following spring the National Federation of Business and Professional Women's Clubs wrote to
the White House to ask that sex discrimination be included in
the executive order. In February 1967 the CACSW too asked
for the addition of sex to EO 11246, and in March these organizations were joined by the Federal Women's Award Study
Group, constituting the thirty-six winners since 1960, whom
Johnson had also asked for recommendations. As support for
the change grew, Peterson turned out to be right; Johnson
asked the ICSW to recommend the form of the new executive
order. With relatively little discussion, the ICSW advised the
president simply to amend the original order to add the word
*sex* wherever the phrase "race, creed, color or national origin"
appeared. This he did in October 1967. The dispute over
whether sex discrimination should be treated like racial bias
had ended. Because the executive order mandated positive action against discrimination on the part of the government, Civil
Service Commission chief John Macy instituted the Federal
Women's Program, which was designed to upgrade efforts to
improve women's position in the civil service.[32] NOW president
Betty Friedan claimed credit for the new amendment. The discussion of sex discrimination, Friedan declared, was "out in the
clear light of day."[33]

The cordial relationship between the new organization and
the federal bodies concerned with women's status quickly became problematical with the continued equivocation of the
EEOC on protective labor legislation. Initially, NOW's founders
themselves had no unified position. Pauli Murray and Mary
Eastwood had come to the conclusion, argued in their landmark article, "Jane Crow and the Law," in the December 1965
issue of the *George Washington Law Review,* that laws for women
alone had "waning utility." Kathryn Clarenbach, in contrast,

continued to support the position espoused by Mary Keyserling and the Women's Bureau coalition that the EEOC should not overrule protective labor laws. But when a California woman filed a complaint with the EEOC against a firm that refused to promote her because of the state's maximum hours laws, and the commission declined to rule, NOW offered the woman its assistance in getting the California law nullified. Peterson suggested that the Department of Labor take a public position in favor of the plaintiff, as NOW requested; Keyserling, backed by the National Consumers League and the other members of the Women's Bureau coalition, urged the secretary not to intervene. Secretary Wirtz sided once again with Keyserling.[34]

But the administration position on the issue of protective labor legislation could no longer be addressed and decided only "in house." NOW's membership grew rapidly—one year after its creation it counted twelve hundred members, with chapters in several states—but its influence continuously outstripped its actual numbers. Access to media and legal services made NOW a force to be reckoned with from the beginning. Thus, in 1967 the EEOC felt enough pressure that it held hearings on several issues pertinent to the women's cause, including protective labor legislation, age discrimination against airline stewardesses, who also customarily lost their jobs on marriage, help-wanted ads, and pension inequality.[35]

NOW testified at the EEOC hearings against protective labor legislation, in company with Representative Martha Griffiths and representatives of the BPW and the United Automobile Workers, and together they succeeded in bringing about a change unwelcome to die-hard advocates of differential treatment for women. Katherine Ellickson spoke for the National Consumers League asking, along with some state labor officials, that the EEOC safeguard laws for women. But in February 1968, the commission overturned its 1966 decision to leave the judgment entirely to the courts or to states for reconciliation, and it announced it would consider the arguments on a case-by-case basis.[36] Labor unions objected again; the Amalgamated Clothing Workers called this application of Title VII "a modern version of the effort years ago to use the so-called Equal Rights Amendment . . . to deprive women workers of the protection of this legislation."[37] Yet as more and more groups, from NOW to state commissions to labor unions, began to endorse the position that state labor laws applying only to women did more harm than good, the advocates of special treatment became increasingly isolated, outside the mainstream.

Despite the continuation of this historic controversy among seekers of women's rights, more often than not all the groups proved to be allied on the same side of most issues, continuing in the path of the president's commission by refusing to let the differences occupy center stage. Four members of the CACSW, including Richard Lester who had been vice-chair of the presidential commission, signed NOW's petition to the EEOC to revise the ruling on job advertisements; the ICSW submitted a memorandum in support, as well as one contending that the airline industry's practice of firing stewardesses who married or who had reached the age of thirty-two constituted sex discrimination, a position NOW emphatically shared. The EEOC finally ruled in favor of the stewardesses in June 1968.[38]

Forcing a change in the want ads position proved more difficult. In December 1967 the EEOC became the target of the first feminist demonstration in five decades when NOW set up picket lines in front of EEOC offices in five cities. Still, the commission remained obdurate. In February, Marguerite Rawalt, a member of the President's Commission on the Status of Women and the Citizens' Advisory Council on the Status of Women, and now general counsel for the National Organization for Women, filed a mandamus suit in U.S. district court against the commission; the court agreed to dismiss the case only after the commission promised to improve its performance on behalf of women. Finally, in August, the EEOC promulgated the sought-after regulation that barred employers from advertising in sex-segregated newspaper columns.[39] Fortas's prediction not withstanding, the Supreme Court upheld the regulation in a 1973 decision, ruling that the First Amendment does not extend fully to commercial speech.

The issues raised by the EEOC's enforcement of Title VII of the 1964 Civil Rights Act dominated NOW's earliest days but did not consume them entirely. Once a clear position on protective labor legislation had been arrived at within the organization, NOW's endorsement of the Equal Rights Amendment followed quickly. The effort to find a good court case to test the Fourteenth Amendment strategy had come to nothing, done in partly by the decisions on protective labor laws and partly by disinterest. Many who had been persuaded by the argument that women were protected by the Fourteenth Amendment now reconsidered. Although the National Woman's party had been bitterly disappointed by NOW's initial reluctance, an NWP member organized the D.C. branch of the new group and soon won the chapter's approval of the amendment. At the 1967 national conference, NOW decided to back the ERA by a vote of eighty-two to three, with twelve abstentions. The vote cost NOW the clerical services provided by NOW members who were affiliated with the Women's Division of the UAW, which at the time still opposed the ERA (the union reversed its stand two years later). Following the vote, NOW turned immediately to the NWP. One member wrote to ask Alice Paul for a list of congressional supporters and expressed her thanks "for your patient years of striving while most of the nation's women were asleep." Carl Hayden and Emanuel Celler, unimpressed by the new movement, continued to stymie congressional action. Feminists did not succeed in freeing the ERA from the House Judiciary Committee until 1970.[40]

Despite its conversion to the amendment, NOW's insistence on a broad program of women's rights distinguished its method of operation from the one-issue approach of the National Women's party. Alice Paul's pleasure with NOW's advocacy of the ERA was therefore restrained. She took particular exception to NOW's 1967 endorsement of the movement to repeal abortion laws in recognition of women's right to control their own bodies.[41] Paul contended that taking positions on such issues as abortion "gets the men all mixed up."[42] NOW, interested in achieving equality and autonomy for women in every area of American life, as well as in drawing large numbers of women and men into the movement, saw no purpose to narrowing its focus. Still, it considered the ERA to be of major importance.

The growing interest in the Equal Rights Amendment, as evidenced by the support of NOW and a renewed commitment by the BPW and the General Federation of Women's Clubs, did not sway the CACSW. Member Marguerite Rawalt, the one PCSW member in favor of the ERA, asked that the council reconsider its position, but it declined. Catherine East told Esther Peterson that the delay in the Supreme Court case the president's commission had recommended and the negative attitude of the courts with respect to decisions under Title VII accounted for at least part of the new interest in the amendment. Rather than champion the ERA, Peterson urged the Justice Department to find a good test case. The administration maintained this position to the end, but it was soon to be in the minority on the issue.[43]

The 1968 presidential campaign took place in the midst of turmoil over racism, urban riots, the war in Vietnam, and paralyzing student demonstrations. The assassinations that year of Martin Luther King, Jr., in April and Robert Kennedy in June, the "Poor People's Campaign" in Washington in the spring, and the violent clashes between peace marchers and the police at the Democratic National Convention in Chicago all highlighted and focused the impulse toward social reform. The just-emerging women's movement was a small part of that tableau, but even so, women's issues were achieving a new salience.

In the 1968 campaign, both NOW and the National Woman's party urged all the candidates to speak on behalf of the ERA, and most did. During the New Hampshire primary Eugene McCarthy, the amendment's chief sponsor and challenger of Lyndon Johnson for the Democratic party's nomination, highlighted his support for the amendment in his campaign literature and in a special mailing to the New Hampshire Federation of Women's Clubs. Hubert Humphrey, calling the ERA a "vital issue," reminded amendment advocates of his allegiance while in the Senate. American party candidate George Wallace favored the ERA, as many conservatives always had, and held up his wife, Lurleen, as one who contributed to women's advancement in her role as governor of Alabama. Richard Nixon again affirmed his long-standing approval. Senator Robert Kennedy was less enthusiastic; he promised support only if other measures proved inadequate. Unlike the National Woman's party, however, the National Organization for Women asked the candidates to express themselves as well on a whole variety of women's issues.[44] For the first time in four decades, a genuine national women's movement was bringing a wide array of issues to the attention of a national audience.

A chain of events accounted for the appearance of the first new feminist organization of the 1960s. The civil rights movement served as the vanguard, its philosophy, tactics, and successes priming the political and social environment and providing models for action. The changing configuration of women's work lives and their now-established place in the workforce produced a disjuncture between women's lives as they were living them and the social setting that offered few supports, either ideological or material. The formation of the President's Commission on the Status of Women in 1961, in recognition of this disjuncture, had resulted in the creation of a national network of knowledgeable women concerned about their status. In 1964, the proponents of the ERA accomplished a legislative coup with the enactment of a federal law that barred sex discrimination in employment. The statute had problematical implications for the Women's Bureau coalition, but the derision exhibited by the Equal Employment Opportunity Commission, the agency responsible for enforcing the law, angered the national network of women newly sensitized to inequities confronting women. Indeed, the commission's behavior spurred the women into establishing a new association committed to fighting for women's rights. Inaugurated by women affiliated with the president's commission and the resulting state commissions, the National Organization for Women reflected both the commission's successes in bringing the status of women to the fore and their limitations in taking effective action to improve it. NOW's creation bespoke as well the short reach of the narrowly focused, ingrown movement for the Equal Rights Amendment and expressed the frustration of politically sensitive women relegated to token appointments.

After the formation of NOW, federal policy makers had to start responding to demands sustained by a high degree of public awareness rather than initiating moderate actions in the relative calm of general disinterest. The recommendations of the president's commission and the citizens' advisory council, the existence of the state commissions on women, the efforts of mainstream women's organizations, the activity of the National Woman's party, the inclusion in Title VII of sex as a prohibited basis for employment discrimination, the work of women representatives to Congress and of women within the executive branch, and NOW's overt feminist agenda became intermingled as influences on the development of federal policy, with synergistic effect. Unquestionably, by the end of Lyndon Johnson's term the federal government faced demands and expectations concerning women undreamt of at the time of John Kennedy's inauguration.

Moreover, yet another strain of active feminism emerged at the end of the decade, with the appearance of women's groups on the community level growing out of the antiwar struggle and the movement for social justice. In the fall of 1967 local women's liberation groups began to appear in several cities, as radical women recognized the futility of reform within New Left civil rights and community action organizations. Younger than the women who had formed NOW and committed to local, rather than national, activity, these small, autonomous groups developed a technique of uncovering the political nature of the oppression of women through candid discussion of women's personal lives.[45]

"Consciousness raising" became the initiation rite of the women's movement; locally focused groups went from there to organizing day-care centers, rape crisis committees, women's health collectives, and a plethora of movement publications.[46] By the mid seventies, women involved in these groups had begun to seek state and federal support for local programs, forming coalitions with staid feminist organizations such as NOW. And NOW, which had started life as a top-heavy lobbying group, itself encouraged the emergence of local chapters. The branches of the women's movement, in their essential parts, had merged. With forty thousand members in 1974, NOW offered a highly visible and respectable link to a national movement, but the diversity of smaller groups provided comfortable alternatives for almost any woman to join.[47]

The women's movement ultimately forced federal policy makers to consider action to ameliorate the disadvantages women suffered in virtually every part of their lives. But the federal initiatives taken *before* the movement's rebirth played a crucial role in forming that movement; they broke a critical stalemate among women's organizations, set much of the early agenda, legitimated the idea of women fighting for their rights, provided legislative tools, and helped to establish a network of women nationwide who could be easily mobilized for the cause of women.[48]

# CONCLUSION
# POLITICAL STRATEGIES AND
# OUTCOMES

The liberal politics of the Kennedy administration, embodied particularly in the President's Commission on the Status of Women, gave shape to the agenda of the first feminist organization of the 1960s and provided it with both a structural and a psychological underpinning. New administrations, particularly when a new party takes over, bring bursts of energy to the political process. If after the dislocations of World War II the populace had sought a return to stability, fifteen years later Kennedy's call to action tapped a wellspring of enthusiasm for solving social problems. Although no grassroots women's movement pressed for them, new frontiers opened for women.

## THE EQUAL RIGHTS AMENDMENT

Ambivalences about women's roles in the postwar period had shown themselves in national politics in the battle over several legislative initiatives. The most important measure to be entangled in these complex feelings was the Equal Rights Amendment, which served as context for most of the other legislative disputes concerning women.

The Equal Rights Amendment failed because federal policymakers would hardly approve so significant a proposal without wide and deep support for it. An amendment to grant women constitutional equality bespoke a belief in the right of women to function as individuals. But individual equality, however in keeping it was with traditional American ideals, conflicted with an ideology that considered women as responsible primarily to their families, not to themselves. Historically, the law defined women as wives, mothers, and daughters, placing them under the aegis of their husbands and fathers. Twentieth-century innovations gave the state a new role in overseeing the conditions of women's employment, under the rationale of protecting their interests as homemakers. The Equal Rights Amendment, which would remove legal distinctions between the sexes, suggested a reordering of the world, a responsibility the U.S. Congress does not readily assume. By 1960, women leaders had had little to show for their efforts except token offerings of executive appointments, tendered by presidents who were staying out of the fray.

## TOKEN APPOINTMENTS

The strategy of token appointments offered many advantages to the presidents who employed it. The women's organizations on both sides of the ERA struggle emphasized their desire for more appointments of women, persuaded that such appointments marked significant gains for the sex. Thus, presidents who followed that course won praise, especially from women journalists, who found the selections made good copy. Appointments, moreover, could be had at virtually no cost, and they were easy to effect. Unless the candidate was wildly unqualified (and women appointees tended to be overqualified), the Senate offered no opposition to a presidential choice. In many cases, Senate confirmation was not even required.

But welcomed as they were by women's organizations, the appointments had an unanticipated consequence that worked badly for women seeking substantive measures. By acceding to the request for more women appointees, the chief executive could evade much more significant policy questions. The president could state in truth to his women constituents that he had met *one* of their objectives; he could not in fairness be asked to meet them all, especially when no political pressure existed outside Washington for a comprehensive program for women. Therefore, the groups requesting appointments diminished their chances of wresting other—more important—benefits from the administration.

Moreover, the willingness of chief executives to yield to these

requests itself suggested that the appointments made little difference for the status of most women. In general, when the
standing of a particular group has been low, it has often sought
high-level appointments as a way of winning respect and recognition, and the symbolic value of a black or female cabinet officer may in fact have important psychological and sociological
implications. But in the absence of a social movement to enhance the position of blacks or women, such token appointees
can achieve few concrete gains. In order to prove the competence of both the group and the officeholder, a token appointee
is constrained to "lean over backward," as Mary Anderson observed of Frances Perkins, not to show favoritism and thereby
lose credibility with the white males who made the appointment. The ability of such a woman official in the postwar period
to assist the underprivileged members of her group was thus
severely limited. In fact, the onus on the appointee was to prove
that she was no different from the usual nominee. Under these
circumstances, only an executive whose job expressly required
her to address the status of women felt free to press for meaningful change.

When John Kennedy was elected president, he sought programs that would directly address the problems American society confronted in the 1960s. A well-developed program concerning women—one that comported with his views and the
rest of his liberal agenda and that had few political costs—
emerged from the Women's Bureau coalition. Kennedy's ties to
the progressive labor community made him especially receptive
to the coalition's plan of action (as Truman's ties to the Democratic National Convention had made him sympathetic to its
agenda). Kennedy's appointment of Esther Peterson to head
the Women's Bureau and then to assume the post of assistant
secretary of labor placed a representative of the Women's Bureau coalition in a highly strategic position. With access to the
president and to all the political resources of the administration, close ties to her own constituency, and an impressive degree of political savvy, Peterson proved to be an effective agent
for the Women's Bureau coalition, providing leadership and
crafting compromises.

## THE PRESIDENT'S COMMISSION
## ON THE STATUS OF WOMEN

The program of the Women's Bureau spoke to the unresolved problems in women's lives, and the President's Commission on the Status of Women was its centerpiece. Emerging in part from the animus of the Women's Bureau coalition against the ERA, the commission succeeded in undermining the amendment. But its role was not merely negative. Peterson, Arthur Goldberg, and John Kennedy recognized the hardships caused by the injustices that the ERA sought to correct. Women were often denied the right to serve on juries; some states gave husbands total control of family income or barred women from certain professions; the right to contract, own, and convey property or to establish domicile was available to women only within limits. In addition, women in the labor force consistently earned lower wages than did men, and they had fewer opportunities for advancement. Even the adversaries of constitutional equality recognized the need to better women's condition.

Using models provided by the civil rights movement (federal commissions, legislation, executive orders) and drawing on the same liberal ideology of individual equality, these advocates for women's rights—at a time of continuing ambivalence about appropriate roles for women—addressed many of the legal and extralegal inequities women faced. The commission affirmed the primacy of women's traditional roles, and the tension between this ideal and the simultaneous quest for expanded opportunities for women as paid workers pervaded all the commission's discussions and recommendations. At the same time, however, the commission also conferred new respect on the subject of equality for women, and it forged into one agenda the proposals of the three diverse groups fighting for women's opportunities: the proponents of constitutional equality, the advocates of increased opportunity in the workplace, and those who sought appointments for women.

At its conclusion in 1963, the commission proposed, and President Kennedy established, two continuing federal bodies to monitor action on the status of women. State legislatures and governors followed the presidential model and instituted their own commissions on the status of women, developing a national network of women and men knowledgeable and concerned about the position of women in society.

When ERA supporters succeeding in adding to the Civil Rights Act of 1964 a provision protecting the employment rights of women, many women activists responded with hesitation because of the conflict between women's role in the labor force and their responsibilities in the home, which the president's commission had left unresolved. But the disdain with which the Equal Employment Opportunity Commission treated its obligation to enforce this section of the law catalyzed the network created by the presidential commission of those involved in women's issues and led to the formation of the first women's rights group of the new wave of feminism, the National Organization for Women.

## POSSIBILITIES AND LIMITATIONS
## OF GOVERNMENT ACTION

Presidential commissions are commonly thought to be worse than useless. A rhyme that appeared in *Punch* in the 1950s expresses the common view:

> If you're pestered by critics and hounded by faction
> To take some precipitate, positive action,
> The proper procedure, to take my advice, is
> Appoint a commission and stave off the crisis.[1]

Herbert Hoover admitted creating "a dozen committees" in order to divert crusaders into research.[2]

Yet presidential commissions have often resulted in worthwhile outcomes. They have built support for controversial courses of action, helped to provide data to back up proposals for mainstream legislation, dramatized the existence of a problem, and broken policy deadlocks. Thomas R. Wolanin, investigating the policy achievements of presidential advisory commissions from Harry Truman through Richard Nixon, concluded that 68 percent of presidential commissions produced "substantial" or "major" presidential responses to their recommendations, and

59 percent elicited "substantial" or "major" responses from federal government agencies.[3]

The experience with the President's Commission on the Status of Women sustains Wolanin's thesis that commissions can meaningfully affect issues. The president's commission and its state-level offspring helped to legitimize the issue of sex discrimination, made data available to support allegations that discrimination against women constituted a serious problem, drew up agendas to ameliorate inequities, raised expectations that responsible parties would take action, and, most important, sensitized a nationwide network of women to the problems women faced. This network proved to be in the vanguard of the creation of the widespread, vocal women's movement that surfaced at the end of the 1960s. Betty Friedan, the first president of the National Organization for Women, repeatedly acknowledged the model the president's commission had provided for NOW, although she expressed disappointment with the commission's accomplishments.[4] The change in approach from highly publicized but ephemeral token appointments to a presidential commission proved beneficial.

The initiatives of the Kennedy administration anticipated, rather than responded to, the appearance of a broad-based feminist movement and ultimately helped to bring it about. Characterized by the quest not for fundamental change but for attainable goals, this significant policy shift occurred despite the absence of a grassroots movement seeking federal action.

If the fate of women's issues in the Kennedy administration demonstrates that representatives of interest groups can initiate significant policy change, it also indicates the limits of such a course of action. The president's commission proposed moderate steps, placing the responsibility for implementation on government and private institutions. But none of these institutions had strong incentives to execute the proposals on their own, and Congress was loath to establish new bureaucracies to control private businesses. New bureaucracies cost money and make people angry; employers are important campaign contributors and vigilant lobbyists. Without political pressure, legislation would be hard to come by. So the temperate federal steps taken as the result of internal policy pressures engendered expectations the federal government did not intend to fulfill.[5]

Jo Freeman has pointed out that policy is "the means by which government stimulate[s], respond[s] to, and/or curtail[s] social change."[6] It represents an attempt to channel or preempt the conflict. Yet policy can also incite reformers. By collecting information and offering modest solutions, the federal government helped to turn a latent issue into a salient one and to supply data to those who wanted to go further than the government did. In order to justify even limited steps, the president's commission and the Women's Bureau had gathered copious evidence to substantiate their proposals so that they could persuade Congress and other political actors to respond appropriately. By doing so, they pointed out problems of which the general populace had before been largely unaware. The minimal change the federal government supported could not have eliminated the pervasive problem it documented. So the government action heightened awareness, raised expectations, and then disappointed the new observers.

But in order to achieve an effective and coherent government policy concerning women's issues, women activists had not only to resolve internal contraditions within their own groups but also to reach a rapprochement with other women's organizations. The philosophies of the National Women's party and the Women's Bureau represented thesis and antithesis—two sides of the ambivalent attitude toward women in the postwar period—but a new resolution or restatement of the problem was essential if a united front was to be presented to policy makers.

That resolution grew out of the changing status of women, but it was also made possible by an ideological leap—new feminist theory separated childbearing from childraising, philosophically if not in fact, and permitted a redefinition of the "problem" of women's status. Without such a resolution, policy makers could have continued to exploit the differences in the views of women. Once NOW adopted the position that both mothers and fathers were responsible for the care of children, a coherent feminist philosophy could inform responses to questions of policy.

The new women's movement was also able to move beyond the

president's commission because by now the remedies the Commission had recommended had been tried and found wanting. As halfway measures proved inadequate, those who previously had hesitated now came to acknowledge the need for potent curatives. The National Organization for Women quickly became aware that the proposals of the president's commission, based as they were on traditional conceptions of sex roles, had no power to get at the root causes of discrimination. The group's endorsement of the Equal Rights Amendment soon followed. Thus the president's commission, formed in part to ward off the ERA, unintentionally contributed both to its endorsement by virtually every liberal group that once had opposed it and to the recognition that the sex roles on which special legislation for women had been based had limited utility for the final three decades of the twentieth century. As Sara Evans remarked: "The purpose, in fact, may have been to quell a growing pressure for an Equal Rights Amendment, but unwittingly the government organized its own opposition."[7] And Frances Kolb has observed: "The network's realization of the need for action collided with the inaction of the government agencies producing the classic revolutionary situation in which the revolution began in the government's backyard, at a government sponsored event!"[8]

Not only did federal activity assist in the development of the women's movement, it made it more broad based. The vigor of the women's movement came partly from its solid roots in traditional liberal politics. Both at its inception and at its height, the women's movement at the national level operated largely in the context of prevailing values and institutions. It was at its most effective when it sought incremental changes, invoking equality of individual opportunity, the central tenet of liberal theory. Moderate demands cloaked the magnitude of fundamental change that took place whenever women *were* viewed by the government as individuals rather than as instruments of the family.

The array of feminist organizations formed by middle-class women, in addition to the community-based groups formed by younger, more radical women, provided women across the country a site of activity on as broad or narrow a range of issues as they wished. In time, the distinctions between "radical" and "middle-class" feminists became less clear. Historically, radical organizations have not been successful in the United States, which is a system organized to sustain the politics of the center. Jo Freeman has observed that, whereas the political system rewards those who seek reform, it excludes proponents of fundamental change. Yet, ironically, the mainstream women's organizations, such as NOW, have advocated one of the most fundamental changes in American life.[9]

In short, the women who became federal policy makers during an era in which they themselves eschewed the term *feminist* ultimately helped to bring about a revitalization of feminism— to create, in the words of James Q. Wilson, an "enduring organizational base" for influencing policy.[10] These leaders, without a women's movement to back them up, forced the federal government to recognize that changes were taking place in women's lives, and they shaped the government's response. Ultimately— predictably—demands outstripped the possibilities of ready government acquiescence.

The presidential commission's report came at a critical moment. As Ethel Klein has documented, women were poised to expand their roles in the world. Between 1960 and 1970 the fertility rate declined from 118 per thousand to 87.9; mothers with preschool children increased their labor force participation rate from 19 percent to 30 percent; and the divorce rate rose from 15 per thousand women to 26 per thousand.[11] In 1966, the cumulative efforts of the President's Commission on the Status of Women and the federal agencies it spawned, the state commissions on women, ERA activists, and women both inside and outside the government culminated in the emergence of an independent women's movement. In December 1967, the *New York Times* alerted its readers to the fact that "the feminists are on the march once more."[12]

## FEMINISM

The feminism of the late sixties and seventies reaffirmed the philosophy that men and women should be politically, economically, and socially equal, but it also expanded the theory to argue that differences between men's and women's roles were culturally based rather than biologically determined. In practical terms, this new definition released women, at least in principle, from the total responsibility for childcare. It also meant that, for the first time, feminism was an internally consistent ideology, no longer rent by the contradictory demands for both equality and special privileges for women as mothers. Although consideration would still be requested for those who took care of children, now these "privileges" would be sought for male parents as well as for female ones, and employers would find that both men and women had demands on them as parents as well as workers.

Before this ideological break took place, women who fought for women struggled fruitlessly to resolve the central dilemma of women's lives: how to be at once an individual concerned with her own destiny *and* a mother (no word evokes a more laden image) entirely responsible for the welfare of her children. Some called themselves "feminists," and some did not.

Because the definition of feminism has changed, historians today writing about the history of feminism face problems. The term *feminism* is now as much normative as it is descriptive. We find it difficult to conclude that Eleanor Roosevelt, a great woman in every sense of the term, was not a feminist (a word she never would have applied to herself). So modern works often begin with a set of definitions that permit the writer to apply the label "feminist" as she or he sees fit. But the profusion of definitions is at once confusing and unnecessary. The term *feminism* as we use it was born in the 1960s. We need not ask if women were "feminists" per se in order to comprehend their behavior and motivation, or to illuminate their character. To do so, in fact, can create a diversion and may, because of the emotional content of the term, distort a viewpoint rather than clarify it.

Instead, we might ask: Which elements of women's lives appeared to a historical figure to be immutable? What aspects of women's lives did she or he question? What beliefs informed a choice of action? Did an activist favor a wider range of influence for women, or more power within a narrow one? How did class origins color political agendas? What constraints limited the selection of political strategies?

## EFFECTIVE STRATEGIES

For the purposes of this study, I have distinguished among activist women by describing the strategies they promoted. My pursuit has been to determine which strategies proved effective under which conditions. Governmental responses to social change do alter outcomes, although not necessarily in predictable or desirable ways. Political decisions can intensify, or retard, nascent social movements. Good strategies push the political system as far as possible without provoking a backlash, making the best of even inhospitable times. The story of policy for women in the premovement era suggests some approaches. In the absence of a strong social movement, we find that posing an all-or-nothing choice results in no gain at all. Conversely, incremental goals often can be achieved. If a group succeeds in gaining access to the White House, executive actions are easier to come by than legislative ones, but successful proposals are virtually always noncontroversial ones with low political costs. Neither a quest for appointments nor devotion to a single nonnegotiable legislative measure is likely to be productive. Compromises, in contrast, can elicit meaningful, if incomplete, initial efforts that can later lead to more effective policy instruments. The lesson is in fact an old one: If you want to get a camel into someone's tent, ask if you can just put its nose under the tentflap.

# Appendix 1: Text of the
# Equal Pay Act of 1963

*Be it enacted by the Senate and House of Representatives of the United States of America in Congress assembled,* That this Act may be cited as the Equal Pay Act of 1963.

## DECLARATION OF PURPOSE

SEC. 2. (a) The Congress hereby finds that the existence in industries engaged in commerce or in the production of goods for commerce of wage differentials based on sex—

(1) depresses wages and living standards for employees necessary for their health and efficiency;

(2) prevents the maximum utilization of the available labor resources;

(3) tends to cause labor disputes, thereby burdening, affecting, and obstructing commerce;

(4) burdens commerce and the free flow of goods in commerce; and

(5) constitutes an unfair method of competition.

(b) It is hereby declared to be the policy of this Act, through exercise by Congress of its power to regulate commerce among the several States and with foreign nations, to correct the conditions above referred to in such industries.

SEC. 3. Section 6 of the Fair Labor Standards Act of 1938, as amended (29 U.S.C. et seq.), is amended by adding thereto a new subsection (d) as follows:

(d)(1) No employer having employees subject to any provisions of this section shall discriminate, within any establishment in which such employees are employed, between employees on the basis of sex by paying wages to employees in such establishment at a rate less than the rate at which he pays wages to employees of the opposite sex in such establishment for equal work on jobs the performance of which requires equal skill, effort, and responsibility, and which are performed under similar working conditions, except where such payment is made pursuant to (i) a seniority system; (ii) a merit system; (iii) a system which measures earnings by quantity or quality of production;

or (iv) a differential based on any other factor other than sex: *Provided,* That an employer who is paying a wage rate differential in violation of this subsection shall not, in order to comply with the provisions of this subsection, reduce the wage rate of any employee.

(2) No labor organization, or its agents, representing employees of an employer having employees subject to any provisions of this section shall cause or attempt to cause such an employer to discriminate against an employee in violation of paragraph (1) of this subsection.

(3) For purposes of administration and enforcement, any amounts owing to any employee which have been withheld in violation of this subsection shall be deemed to be unpaid minimum wages or unpaid overtime compensation under this Act.

(4) As used in this subsection, the term "labor organization" means any organization of any kind, or any agency or employee representation committee or plan, in which employees participate and which exists for the purpose, in whole or in part, of dealing with employers concerning grievances, labor disputes, wages, rates of pay, hours of employment, or conditions of work.

SEC. 4. The amendments made by this Act shall take effect upon the expiration of one year from the date of its enactment: *Provided,* That in the case of employees covered by a bona fide collective bargaining agreement in effect at least thirty days prior to the date of enactment of this Act, entered into by a labor organization (as defined in section 6(d)(4) of the Fair Labor Standards Act of 1938, as amended), the amendments made by this Act shall take effect upon the termination of such collective bargaining agreement or upon the expiration of two years from the date of enactment of this Act, whichever shall first occur.

# Appendix 2: Executive Order 10980 Establishing the President's Commission on the Status of Women

WHEREAS prejudices and outmoded customs act as barriers to the full realization of women's basic rights which should be respected and fostered as part of our Nation's commitment to human dignity, freedom, and democracy; and

WHEREAS measures that contribute to family security and strengthen home life will advance the general welfare; and

WHEREAS it is in the national interest to promote the economy, security, and national defense through the most efficient and effective utilization of the skills of all persons; and

WHEREAS in every period of national emergency women have served with distinction in widely varied capacities but thereafter have been subject to treatment as a marginal group whose skills have been inadequately utilized; and

WHEREAS women should be assured the opportunity to develop their capacities and fulfill their aspirations on a continuing basis irrespective of national exigencies; and

WHEREAS a Governmental Commission should be charged with the responsibility for developing recommendations for overcoming discriminations in government and private employment on the basis of sex and for developing recommendations for services which will enable women to continue their role as wives and mothers while making a maximum contribution to the world around them:

NOW, THEREFORE, by virtue of the authority vested in me as President of the United States by the Constitution and statutes of the United States, it is ordered as follows:

## PART I—ESTABLISHMENT OF THE PRESIDENT'S COMMISSION ON THE STATUS OF WOMEN

SEC. 101. There is hereby established the President's Commission on the Status of Women, referred to herein as the "Commission." The Commission shall terminate not later than October 1, 1963.

SEC. 102. The Commission shall be composed of twenty members appointed by the President from among persons with a competency in the area of public affairs and women's activities. In addition, the Secretary of Labor, the Attorney General, the Secretary of Health, Education and Welfare, the Secretary of Commerce, the Secretary of Agriculture and the Chairman of the Civil Service Commission shall also serve as members of the Commission. The President shall designate from among the membership a Chairman, a Vice-Chairman, and an Executive Vice-Chairman.

SEC. 103. In conformity with the Act of May 3, 1945 (59 Stat. 134, 31 U.S.C. 691), necessary facilitating assistance, including the provision of suitable office space by the Department of Labor, shall be furnished the Commission by the Federal agencies whose chief officials are members thereof. An Executive Secretary shall be detailed by the Secretary of Labor to serve the Commission.

SEC. 104. The Commission shall meet at the call of the Chairman.

SEC. 105. The Commission is authorized to use the services of consultants and experts as may be found necessary and as may be otherwise authorized by law.

## PART II—DUTIES OF THE PRESIDENT'S COMMISSION ON THE STATUS OF WOMEN

SEC. 201. The Commission shall review progress and make recommendations as needed for constructive action in the following areas:

(a) Employment policies and practices, including those on wages, under Federal contracts.

(b) Federal social insurance and tax laws as they affect the net earnings and other income of women.

(c) Federal and State labor laws dealing with such matters as hours, night work, and wages, to determine whether they are accomplishing the purposes for which they were established and whether they should be adapted to changing technological, economic, and social conditions.

(d) Differences in legal treatment of men and women in regard to political and civil rights, property rights, and family relations.

(e) New and expanded services that may be required for women as wives, mothers, and workers, including education, counseling, training, home services, and arrangements for care of children during the working day.

(f) The employment policies and practices of the Government of the United States, with reference to additional affirmative steps which should be taken through legislation, executive or administrative action to assure non-discrimination on the basis of sex and to enhance constructive employment opportunities for women.

SEC. 202. The Commission shall submit a final report of its recommendations to the President by October 1, 1963.

SEC. 203. All executive departments and agencies of the Federal Government are directed to cooperate with the Commission in the performance of its duties.

## PART III—REMUNERATION AND EXPENSES

SEC. 301. Members of the Commission, except those receiving other compensation from the United States, shall receive such compensation as the President shall hereafter fix in a manner to be hereafter determined.

JOHN F. KENNEDY

THE WHITE HOUSE.
*December 14, 1961.*

# Appendix 3: Members of the President's Commission and Its Committees

The names of the men and women appointed to the Commission, and the posts they occupied at the time of their appointment, were:

Mrs. Eleanor Roosevelt, *Chairman*
(*deceased*)
Mrs. Esther Peterson
*Executive Vice Chairman*
Assistant Secretary of Labor
Dr. Richard A. Lester, *Vice Chairman*
Chairman, Department of Economics
Princeton University
The Attorney General
Honorable Robert F. Kennedy
The Secretary of Agriculture
Honorable Orville L. Freeman
The Secretary of Commerce
Honorable Luther H. Hodges
The Secretary of Labor
Honorable Arthur J. Goldberg
Honorable W. Willard Wirtz
The Secretary of Health, Education, and Welfare
Honorable Abraham A. Ribicoff

Honorable Anthony L. Celebrezze
Honorable George D. Aiken
U.S. Senate
Honorable Maurine B. Neuberger
U.S. Senate
Honorable Edith Green
U.S. House of Representatives
Honorable Jessica M. Weis
(*deceased*)
U.S. House of Representatives
The Chairman of the Civil Service Commission
Honorable John W. Macy, Jr.
Mrs. Macon Boddy
Henrietta, Tex.
Dr. Mary I. Bunting
President
Radcliffe College
Mrs. Mary E. Callahan
Member, Executive Board
International Union of Electrical, Radio and Machine Workers

Dr. Henry David
   President
   New School for Social Re-
      search
Miss Dorothy Height
   President
   National Council of Negro
      Women, Inc.
Miss Margaret Hickey
   Public Affairs Editor
   Ladies' Home Journal
Mrs. Viola H. Hymes
   President
   National Council for Jewish
      Women, Inc.
Miss Margaret J. Mealey
   Executive Director
   National Council of Catholic
      Women
Mr. Norman E. Nicholson
   Administrative Assistant
   Kaiser Industries Corp.
   Oakland, Calif.

Miss Marguerite Rawalt
   Attorney; past president:
      Federal Bar Association,
      National Association of
      Women Lawyers, National
      Federation of Business
      and Professional Women's
      Clubs, Inc.
Mr. William F. Schnitzler
   Secretary-Treasurer
   American Federation of La-
      bor and Congress of In-
      dustrial Organizations
Dr. Caroline F. Ware
   Vienna, Va.
Dr. Cynthia C. Wedel
   Assistant General Secretary
      for Program
   National Council of the
      Churches of Christ in the
      U.S.A.

## COMMITTEE ON CIVIL AND POLITICAL RIGHTS

Honorable Edith Green, *Chairman and Commission Member*

Miss Marguerite Rawalt, *Co-Chairman and Commission Member*

Mrs. Harper Andrews, Former President, Illinois League of Women Voters, Kewanee, Ill.

Mrs. Angela Bambace, Manager, Upper South Department, and Vice President, International Ladies' Garment Workers Union

James B. Carey, President, International Union of Electrical, Radio and Machine Workers

Miss Gladys Everett, Attorney, Portland, Oreg.

Mrs. Yarnall Jacobs, President, National Council of Women of the United States, Inc.

John M. Kernochan, Director, Legislative Drafting Research Fund, Columbia University

Judge Florence Kerins Murray, Associate Justice, Rhode Island Superior Court

Miss Pauli Murray, Senior Fellow, Law School, Yale University

Mrs. E. Lee Ozbirn, President, General Federation of Women's Clubs

Miss Katherine Peden, President, National Federation of Business and Professional Women's Clubs, Inc.

Mrs. Harriet F. Pilpel, Attorney, Greenbaum, Wolff and Ernst, New York

Frank E. A. Sander, Professor of Law, Law School of Harvard University

*Technical Secretary*, Miss Mary Eastwood

## COMMITTEE ON EDUCATION

Dr. Mary I. Bunting, *Chairman and Commission Member*

Miss Edna P. Amidon, Director, Home Economics Education Branch, U.S. Office of Education

Mrs. Algie E. Ballif, Former President, Utah School Board Association

Mrs. John D. Briscoe, Board of Directors, League of Women Voters of the United States

Mrs. Opal D. David, Former Director, Commission on the Education of Women, American Council on Education

Dr. Elizabeth M. Drews, Professor, College of Education, Michigan State University

Dr. Seymour M. Farber, Assistant Dean for Continuing Education in Health Sciences, University of California, San Francisco Medical Center

Mrs. Raymond Harvey, Dean, School of Nursing, Tuskegee Institute

Mrs. Agnes E. Meyer, Washington, D.C.

Dr. Kenneth E. Oberholtzer, Superintendent, Denver Public Schools

Dr. Esther Raushenbush, Director, Center of Continuing Education, Sarah Lawrence College

Lawrence Rogin, Director of Education, AFL-CIO

Miss Helen B. Schleman, Dean of Women, Purdue University

Dr. Virginia L. Senders, Lecturer, Former Coordinator of Minnesota Plan, Lincoln, Mass.

Dr. Pauline Tompkins, General Director, American Association of University Women

*Technical Secretary,* Mrs. Antonia H. Chayes

COMMITTEE ON FEDERAL EMPLOYMENT

Miss Margaret Hickey, *Chairman and Commission Member*

E. C. Hallbeck, Chairman, Government Employes Council, AFL-CIO

Judge Lucy Somerville Howorth, Former General Counsel, War Claims Commission, Cleveland, Miss.

Honorable Stephen S. Jackson, Deputy Assistant Secretary of Defense for Manpower, U.S. Department of Defense

Mrs. Esther Johnson, Secretary-Treasurer, American Federation of Government Employees

Honorable Roger W. Jones, Bureau of the Budget

Dr. Esther Lloyd-Jones, Head, Department of Guidance and Student Personnel Administration, Columbia University

Honorable John W. Macy, Jr., *Commission Member*

Dr. Jeanne L. Noble, President, Delta Sigma Theta, and Assistant Professor, Center for Human Relations Studies, New York University

Dr. Peter H. Rossi, Director, National Opinion Research Center, Chicago

Honorable Kathryn H. Stone, Virginia House of Delegates, and Director, Human Resources Program, Washington Center for Metropolitan Studies

Honorable Tyler Thompson, Director General of the Foreign Service, U.S. Department of State

Dr. Kenneth O. Warner, Director, Public Personnel Association

*Technical Secretary,* Mrs. Catherine S. East

## COMMITTEE ON HOME AND COMMUNITY

Dr. Cynthia C. Wedel, *Chairman and Commission Member*

Mrs. Marguerite H. Coleman, Supervisor of Special Placement Services, New York State Division of Employment

Dr. Rosa L. Gragg, President, National Association of Colored Women's Clubs, Inc.

Mrs. Randolph Guggenheimer, President, National Committee for Day Care of Children, Inc.

Mrs. Viola H. Hymes, *Commission Member*

Mrs. Emerson Hynes, Arlington, Va.

Maurice Lazarus, President, Wm. Filene's Sons Co., Boston

Mrs. Martha Reynolds, United Community Services, AFL-CIO, Grand Rapids

Charles I. Schottland, Dean of Faculty, Brandeis University

Miss Ella V. Stonsby, Dean of College of Nursing, Rutgers University

Dr. Caroline F. Ware, *Commission Member*

Dr. Esther M. Westervelt, Instructor, Guidance and Personnel Administration, Teachers College, Columbia University

*Technical Secretaries*, Miss Ella C. Ketchin and Mrs. Margaret M. Morris

## COMMITTEE ON PRIVATE EMPLOYMENT

Dr. Richard A. Lester, *Chairman and Commission Member*

Jacob Clayman, Administrative Director, Industrial Union Department, AFL-CIO

Miss Caroline Davis, Director, Women's Department, United Automobile, Aerospace and Agricultural Implement Workers of America

Miss Muriel Ferris, Legislative Assistant to Honorable Philip A. Hart, U.S. Senate

Charles W. Gasque, Jr., Assistant Commissioner for Procurement Policy, General Services Administration

Miss Dorothy Height, *Commission Member*

Joseph D. Keenan, Secretary, International Brotherhood of Electrical Workers

Norman E. Nicholson, *Commission Member*

Frank Pace, Jr., General Dynamics Corp., New York

Mrs. Ogden Reid, Former President, Board Chairman, New York Herald Tribune

John A. Roosevelt, Bache and Co., New York

Samuel Silver, Industrial Relations Adviser, Office of Assistant Secretary of Defense for Manpower, U.S. Department of Defense
*Technical Secretary,* Sam A. Morgenstein


## COMMITTEE ON PROTECTIVE LABOR LEGISLATION

Miss Margaret J. Mealey, *Chairman and Commission Member*

Mrs. Margaret F. Ackroyd, Chief, Division of Women and Children, Rhode Island State Department of Labor

Dr. Doris Boyle, Professor of Economics, Loyola College, Baltimore

Mrs. Mary E. Callahan, *Commission Member*

Dr. Henry David, *Commission Member*

Mrs. Bessie Hillman, Vice President, Amalgamated Clothing Workers of America

Mrs. Paul McClellan Jones, Vice President, National Board, Young Women's Christian Association of the U.S.A.

Mrs. Mary Dublin Keyserling, Associate Director, Conference on Economic Progress

Carl A. McPeak, Special Representative on State Legislation, AFL-CIO

Clarence R. Thornbrough, Commissioner, Arkansas State Department of Labor

S. A. Wesolowski, Assistant to President, Brookshire Knitting Mills, Inc., Manchester, N.H.

Mrs. Addie Wyatt, Field Representative, United Packinghouse, Food and Allied Workers

*Technical Secretary,* Miss Ella C. Ketchin

## COMMITTEE ON SOCIAL INSURANCE AND TAXES

Honorable Maurine B. Neuberger, *Chairman and Commission Member*

Honorable Jessica M. Weis, *Associate Chairman and Commission Member* (*deceased*)

Dr. Eveline M. Burns, Professor of Social Work, New York School of Social Work, Columbia University

Mrs. Margaret B. Dolan, Chairman, Department of Public Health Nursing, University of North Carolina

Dean Fedele F. Fauri, School of Social Work, University of Michigan

Dr. Richard B. Goode, Brookings Institution

Miss Fannie Hardy, Executive Assistant, Arkansas State Insurance Commissioner

Miss Nina Miglionico, Attorney, Birmingham, Ala.

J. Wade Miller, Vice President, W. R. Grace & Co., Cambridge, Mass.

Dr. Raymond Munts, Assistant Director, Social Security Department, AFL-CIO

Mrs. Richard B. Persinger, Chairman, National Public Affairs Committee, Young Women's Christian Association of the U.S.A.

*Technical Secretary*, Dr. Merrill G. Murray

# Abbreviations

| | |
|---|---|
| AAUW | American Association of University Women |
| ALUA | Archives of Labor and Urban Affairs, Wayne State University, Detroit, Michigan |
| BHL | Bentley Historical Library, University of Michigan, Ann Arbor, Michigan |
| BPW | National Federation of Business and Professional Women's Clubs |
| CACSW | Citizens' Advisory Council on the Status of Women |
| CEA | Council of Economic Advisers |
| CSC | Civil Service Commission |
| DACOWITS | Defense Advisory Committee on Women in the Services |
| DDEL | Dwight David Eisenhower Library, Abilene, Kansas |
| DNC | Democratic National Committee |
| DOL | U.S. Department of Labor |
| EEOC | Equal Employment Opportunity Commission |
| FDRL | Franklin D. Roosevelt Library, Hyde Park, New York |
| FLSA | Fair Labor Standards Act |
| HSTL | Harry S. Truman Library, Independence, Missouri |
| ICSW | Interdepartmental Committee on the Status of Women |
| JFKL | John F. Kennedy Library, Boston, Massachusetts |
| LBJA | Lyndon Baines Johnson Archives |
| LBJL | Lyndon Baines Johnson Library, Austin, Texas |
| LC | Library of Congress |
| NAWSA | National American Woman Suffrage Association |

| | |
|---|---|
| NCCW | National Council of Catholic Women |
| NCJW | National Council of Jewish Women |
| NCL | National Consumers League |
| NCNW | National Council of Negro Women |
| NOW | National Organization for Women |
| NWP | National Woman's Party |
| NWTUL | National Women's Trade Union League |
| NYPL | New York Public Library |
| OHS | Oregon Historical Society, Portland, Oregon |
| PCSW | President's Commission on the Status of Women |
| POF | President's Office Files |
| RNC | Republican National Committee |
| SL | Schlesinger Library, Cambridge, Massachusetts |
| UAW | United Automobile, Aerospace, and Agricultural Implement Workers of America [name changed in 1962 from United Automobile, Aircraft, and Agricultural Workers of America] |
| WBOF | Women's Bureau Office Files |
| WHCF | White House Central File |
| WHOF | White House Official File |
| WSHS | Wisconsin State Historical Society, Madison, Wisconsin |
| YWCA | Young Women's Christian Association |

# Notes

A great deal of the source material for the later chapters derives from the papers of the President's Commission on the Status of Women (1961–1963) and its seven committees. When I used these papers, they were located in the Women's Bureau in Washington, D.C., in a series of filing cabinets. The papers of each committee were kept separate from the papers of the Commission as a whole, although some committee documents were integrated with those of the commission and given commission document numbers. A set of numbered commission documents was kept in still another drawer. Committee documents with commission document numbers are so identified. Otherwise, when available, folder titles are given, followed by a committee designation:

PE    Private Employment
FE    Federal Employment
PLL    Protective Labor Legislation
CPR    Civil and Political Rights
HC    Home and Community
E    Education
SIT    Social Insurance and Taxes

The location of other manuscript collections cited in the notes can be found in the bibliography. Fuller documentation of much of the evidence in this manuscript can be found in Cynthia Ellen Harrison, "Prelude to Feminism: Women's Organizations, the Federal Government, and the Rise of the Women's Movement, 1942 to 1968" (Ph.D. dissertation, Columbia University, 1982).

## PREFACE

1. Laura Bergquist, "What Women Really Meant to JFK," *Redbook*, November 1973, 53.

2. *New York Times*, 26 February 1945.

3. Leila J. Rupp, "The Survival of American Feminism: The Women's Movement in the Post-War Period," in *Reshaping America: Society and Institutions, 1945–1960*, ed. Robert H. Bremner and Gary W. Reichard (Columbus: Ohio State University Press, 1982), 33–65.

4. Martha Weinman Lear, "The Second Feminist Wave," *New York Times Magazine,* 10 March 1968, 25, 50.

5. Abbott L. Ferriss, *Indicators of Trends in the Status of American Women* (New York: Russell Sage Foundation, 1971), 85–86, 99, 104; U.S. Department of Commerce, Bureau of the Census, *Statistical Abstract of the United States, 1975* (Washington, D.C.: GPO, 1975), 346–347; William Chafe, *The American Woman: Her Changing Social, Economic, and Political Roles, 1920–1970* (New York: Oxford University Press, 1972), 181, 218–219. For a full examination of this phenomenon, see Valerie Kincade Oppenheimer, *The Female Labor Force in the United States: Demographic and Economic Factors Governing Its Growth and Changing Composition* (Westport, Conn.: Greenwood Press, 1971).

6. The scholarly discussion over the explanation for the emergence of an energetic feminist movement in the latter part of the sixties has engaged both historians and political scientists. The two most important works on the roots of the women's movement have been Jo Freeman's *The Politics of Women's Liberation* (New York: McKay, 1975) and Sara Evans's *Personal Politics: The Roots of Women's Liberation in the Civil Rights Movement and the New Left* (New York: Knopf, 1979). Freeman, in her excellent and original study of the relationship of social conditions, social movements, and policy, described the origin of the two main branches—one reformist, one radical—of the women's movement in the sixties, their convergence, and the impact of the movement on policy. Evans details the genesis of women's liberation among radical women in the civil rights movement. Leila Rupp and Verta Taylor, in a recently published work, *Survival in the Doldrums: The American Women's Rights Movement, 1945 to the 1960s* (New York: Oxford University Press, 1987), trace the feminist impulse during the 1950s; they denominate the period before the modern grassroots feminist movement as the "elite-sustained" phase of the women's movement. In particular, they explore the dynamics of feminism within the National Woman's party, the chief proponent of the Equal Rights Amendment during this period.

Chafe, *The American Woman,* provides the best overview of women's experiences for the period between suffrage and the new feminist movement. Other helpful works include Ethel Klein, *Gender Politics: From Consciousness to Mass Politics* (Cambridge: Harvard University Press, 1984); Ellen Hole and Judith Levine, *Rebirth of Feminism* (New York: Quadrangle Books, 1971); Judith Sealander, *As Minority Becomes Majority: Federal Reaction to the Phenomenon of Women in the Workforce, 1920–1963* (Westport, Conn.: Greenwood Press, 1983); and Nancy E. McGlen and Karen O'Connor, *Women's Rights: The Struggle*

*for Equality in the Nineteenth and Twentieth Centuries* (New York: Praeger, 1983).

Susan M. Hartmann, *The Home Front and Beyond: American Women in
the 1940s* (Boston: Twayne, 1982); Leila Rupp, *Mobilizing Women for
War: German and American Propaganda, 1939–1945* (Princeton, N.J.:
Princeton University Press, 1978); D'Ann Campbell, *Women at War
with America: Private Lives in a Patriotic Era* (Cambridge: Harvard University Press, 1984); Eleanor Straub, "Government Policy Toward Civilian Women During World War II" (Ph.D. diss., Emory University,
1973); Karen Anderson, *Wartime Woman* (Westport, Conn.: Greenwood Press, 1981); and Maureen Honey, *Creating Rosie the Riveter:
Class, Gender, and Propaganda During World War II* (Amherst: University of Massachusetts Press, 1984), discuss the experience of American
women on the homefront and the impact of World War II on their
lives.

*The Torch Is Passed: The Kennedy Brothers and American Liberalism*
(New York: Atheneum, 1984), by David Burner and Thomas West, is
an especially insightful volume on the impact of the liberalism of the
Kennedy administration. Herbert Parmet's *Jack: The Struggles of John
F. Kennedy* (New York: Dial Press, 1980) and *JFK: The Presidency of
John F. Kennedy* (New York: Dial Press, 1983) and James MacGregor
Burns's *John Kennedy: A Political Profile* (New York: Harcourt, Brace &
World, 1961) help the reader understand the evolution of Kennedy's
politics. William H. Chafe, *The Unfinished Journey: America Since World
War II* (New York: Oxford University Press, 1986), is a useful survey
of the postwar period and one of the few that looks at the develop-
ment of the women's movement or at events from the perspective of
women's experience. Virtually none of the books on the Kennedy,
Eisenhower, and Truman administrations considers policy concerning women.

CHAPTER ONE

1. For a fuller discussion on the experiences of women during
and immediately after World War II, see William Chafe, *The American
Woman: Her Social, Economic, and Political Roles, 1920–1970* (New
York: Oxford University Press, 1972); Susan M. Hartmann, *The Home
Front and Beyond: American Women in the 1940s* (Boston: Twayne,
1982); Leila Rupp, *Mobilizing Women for War: German and American
Propaganda, 1939–1945* (Princeton, N.J.: Princeton University Press,
1978); D'Ann Campbell, *Women at War with America: Private Lives in a
Patriotic Era* (Cambridge: Harvard University Press, 1984); Eleanor

Straub, "Government Policy Toward Civilian Women During World War II" (Ph.D. diss., Emory University, 1973); Karen Anderson, *Wartime Women* (Westport, Conn.: Greenwood Press, 1981); and Maureen Honey, *Creating Rosie the Riveter: Class, Gender, and Propaganda During World War II* (Amherst: University of Massachusetts Press, 1984).

2. It is worth noting that federal funding for childcare was grossly inadequate and that the National War Labor Board did not enforce its equal pay ruling with any enthusiasm. The measures were designed to support the manufacture of military goods, not the advancement of women (Straub, "Government Policy Toward Civilian Women," 22, 181–194, 240–250).

3. Honey, *Creating Rosie the Riveter*, 7 (quote), 78–80, 117–123, 211–214.

4. Hartmann, *Home Front*, 86; Valerie Oppenheimer, *The Female Labor Force in the United States: Demographic and Economic Factors Governing Its Growth and Changing Composition* (Westport, Conn.: Greenwood Press, 1976), 8; Chafe, *American Woman*, chaps. 6 and 7.

5. Honey, *Creating Rosie the Riveter*, 6–7, 54, 76, 79, 97–113, 124, 167–172, 177, 181. See also Rupp, *Mobilizing Women for War*.

6. A poll taken by the United Automobile, Aircraft, and Agricultural Implements Workers of America—Congress of Industrial Organizations indicated that 85 percent of UAW women members planned to continue working after the war; Women's Bureau studies found that almost 80 percent of women working in the Detroit area and in Erie County, New York, hoped to keep their jobs (*CIO News*, 30 July 1945, 10, clipping, in folder "S. 1178," box H1, Wayne Morse papers, University of Oregon).

7. Straub, "Government Policy Toward Civilian Women," 307–331; Chafe, *American Woman*, chap. 8.

8. Frieda Miller, "What's Ahead for Women Workers," Women's Bureau press release, 6 January 1946, in folder "Press Releases," box "Women's Bureau Statements and Press Releases; Correspondence," Frieda Miller papers, SL.

9. Chafe, *American Woman*, 175–186; U.S. Department of Labor, Women's Bureau, *Employment of Women in the Early Postwar Period*, bulletin no. 211, 8 October 1946, 2; U.S. Department of Labor, *Annual Report of the Secretary of Labor for the Fiscal Year Ended June 30, 1945*, 6.

10. Lois Scharf, *To Work and to Wed: Female Employment, Feminism and the Great Depression* (Westport, Conn.: Greenwood Press, 1980), 140–149.

11. Hartmann, *Home Front*, 6–7.

12. Susan Hartmann, "Prescriptions for Penelope: Literature on Women's Obligations to Returning World War II Veterans," *Women's Studies* 5 (1978): 223–239.

13. Donald R. Makosky, "The Portrayal of Women in Wide-Circulation Magazine Short Stories, 1905–1955" (Ph.D. diss., University of Pennsylvania, 1966), 97; Hartmann, *Home Front*, 164–165, 181.

14. "Statement by the president," 17 October 1945, file 63, box 145, President's Personal File, HSTL.

15. J. Stanley Lemons, *The Woman Citizen: Social Feminism in the 1920s* (Urbana: University of Illinois Press, 1975), 25–30; U.S. Congress, Senate, *Labor Bureau Report on Condition of Women and Child Wage-Earners in the United States*, S. Doc. 645 (19 pts.), 61st Cong., 2d sess., 1910; Judith Sealander, *As Minority Becomes Majority: Federal Reaction to the Phenomenon of Women in the Workforce* (Westport, Conn.: Greenwood Press, 1983), chap. 3.

16. This is much the same group that William O'Neill has called "social feminists" (O'Neill, *Everyone was Brave: The Rise and Fall of Feminism in America* [Chicago: Quadrangle Books, 1969]).

17. Susan D. Becker, "An Intellectual History of the National Woman's Party, 1920–1941" (Ph.D. diss., Case Western Reserve University, 1975), iii, 11, 166–169; Leila Rupp and Verta Taylor, *Survival in the Doldrums: The American Women's Rights Movement, 1945 to the 1960s* (New York: Oxford University Press, 1987), 183, 349 (typescript MS).

18. Rupp and Taylor, *Survival in the Doldrums*, 171, 180, 188 (typescript MS); Nancy F. Cott, "Feminist Politics in the 1920s: The National Woman's Party," *Journal of American History* 71 (June 1984): 43–68; Leila J. Rupp, "The Women's Community in the National Woman's Party, 1945 to the 1960s," *Signs* 10 (Summer 1985): 718.

19. Scharf, *To Work and to Wed*, 134.

20. "Notes on proposed so-called 'Equal Rights Amendment' (for women) to the Constitution," by Constance Daniel, attached to Elizabeth Christman to Mary McLeod Bethune, 25 October 1944, folder 349, box 23, series 5, NCNW papers; Women's Joint Legislative Committee, minutes of meeting, 28 February 1946, folder 4, and "Report of the Convenor," 1943, folder 2, Katharine Norris papers, SL; Leila J. Rupp, "American Feminism in the Postwar Period," in *Reshaping America: Society and Institutions, 1945–1960*, ed. Robert H. Bremner and Gary W. Reichard (Columbus: Ohio University Press, 1982), 33–65.

21. Rupp and Taylor, *Survival in the Doldrums*, 383–404 (typescript MS).

22. William H. Chafe, *The Unfinished Journey: America Since World War II* (New York: Oxford University Press, 1986), 17–22.

23. Chafe, *American Woman*, 129.

24. Sealander, *As Minority Becomes Majority*, 1.

25. Rupp and Taylor, *Survival in the Doldrums*, 73–83 (typescript MS).

26. Becker, "National Woman's Party," chap. 7.

27. *New York Times*, 7 October 1938.

28. The four senators who opposed the amendment in the Senate committee were Tom Connally (D-Tex.), Abe Murdock (D-Utah), Pat McCarran (D-Nev.), and John Danaher (R-Conn.), a political combination of no particular significance. "Pro: Should Congress Approve the Proposed Equal Rights Amendment to the Constitution?" *Congressional Digest* 22, no. 4 (April 1943): 107–110; Loretta J. Blahna, "The Rhetoric of the Equal Rights Amendment," (Ph.D. diss., University of Kansas, 1973), 53; *Equal Rights*, January–March 1949, 7; Thomas C. Pardo (ed.), *The National Woman's Party Papers, 1913–1974: A Guide to the Microfilm Edition* (Sanford, N.C.: Microfilm Corporation of America, 1979), 116–119; Mary Anderson to Dean Acheson, 8 June 1943, in folder "ERA, 1938–1943," box 1, Dean Acheson papers, HSTL; *New York Times*, 12 May 1942, 7 January 1943, 22 January 1943, 13 April 1943, 25 May 1943, 6 October 1943, 8 October 1943, 25 October 1943; Chafe, *American Woman*, 187–188.

29. Pardo, *National Woman's Party Papers*, 113–115.

30. Mary Anderson, *Woman at Work: The Autobiography of Mary Anderson as Told to Mary Winslow* (Minneapolis: University of Minnesota Press, 1951).

31. Douglas B. Maggs to Mary Anderson, 29 June 1943, in folder "Bills, Equal Rights Amendment, S.J. Res. 25," box 89, RG 174 (Perkins), NA.

32. Frieda Miller to Frances Perkins, 23 September 1944, in ibid.

33. Frieda S. Miller, biographical notes, August 1956, SC 1104, WSHS; Frieda S. Miller to Frances Perkins, 23 September 1944, in folder "Bills, Equal Rights Amendment, S.J. Res. 25," box 89, RG 174 (Perkins), NA.

34. Eleanor Roosevelt to Rose Schneiderman, 11 February 1944, and Eleanor Roosevelt to Frances Perkins, 11 February 1944, folder 51, Mary Anderson papers, SL; Sara L. Buchanan to Frieda Miller and Miss Plunkett, 20 November 1945, in folder "Women's Bureau, U.N. Subcommittee on the status of Women," box "Committees—WB," Frieda Miller papers, SL.

35. Mabel Griswold, "Homemaker's Program—WHA, The Equal Rights Amendment," 22 June 1946, folder 2-6, NWP papers, WSHS.

36. *New York Times,* 27 June 1940.

37. *New York Times,* 7 May 1944, 27 June 1944, 19 July 1944, 21 July 1944; Pardo, *National Woman's Party Papers,* 120–125; Democratic National Committee, Office of Women's Activities, *History of Women at Democratic National Conventions,* in folder "Papers re: the 1964 Democratic National Convention," box 21, Margaret Price papers, BHL; 1940 Democratic Party Platform, in folder "ERA 1960–61," box "Women," Esther Peterson papers, SL; Frances Perkins to Dorothy McAllister, 8 July 1944, and L. Metcalfe Walling to Theodore Green, 14 July 1944, in folder "Bills, Equal Rights Amendments, S.J. Res. 25," box 89, RG 174 (Perkins), NA; "Memorandum Concerning the Two Major Political Parties and the Equal Rights Amendment," reel 103, NWP papers (microfilm ed.); Chafe, *American Woman,* 187–188; Alice Paul, "Conversations with Alice Paul: Woman Suffrage and the Equal Rights Amendment," an oral history conducted 1972–1973 by Amelia R. Fry, Regional Oral History Office, The Bancroft Library, University of California, Berkeley, 1976, p. 516. Courtesy of The Bancroft Library.

38. Labor organizations included the AFL, the CIO, the Amalgamated Clothing Workers, the International Ladies Garment Workers Union, and the United Electrical Radio and Machine Workers of America (National Committee to Defeat the UnEqual Rights Amendment, 28 September 1944, folder 21, box 3, Hattie Smith papers, SL).

39. National Committee for the Defeat of the UnEqual Rights Amendment, memorandum, 20 June 1945, folder 7, box 12, Helen Gahagan Douglas papers, Albert Archives, University of Oklahoma; National Committee for the Defeat of the UnEqual Rights Amendment, memorandum, 29 June 1945, folder 20, box 3, Hattie Smith papers, SL; *New York Times,* 19 November 1944.

40. Rupp and Taylor, *Survival in the Doldrums,* 398 (typescript MS).

41. The seven minority members included six Democrats and one Republican. Representative Louis Ludlow (D-Ind.) introduced the ERA as H.J. Res. 1 (*Equal Rights,* January–March 1949, 6–7; Pardo, *National Woman's Party Papers,* 128; *New York Times,* 17 July 1945). The majority report was written by Fadjo Cravens (D-Ark.).

42. *New York Times,* 29 September 1945; Pardo, *National Woman's Party Papers,* 129–130; Mary Anderson to Maud Park, 2 October 1945, folder 60, Mary Anderson papers, SL.

43. "Alice W." to William Hassett, 22 March 1947, file 120-A, WHCF, HSTL. Franklin Roosevelt had never openly committed himself on this issue, although Alice Paul claimed that the death of FDR eliminated the "greatest opposition" (Edwin M. Watson, secretary to the president, to Sen. William Langer, 9 September 1943, file 120-A, WHOF, FDRL; Alice Paul oral history, p. 511).

44. David Niles to William Hassett, 1 February 1946, and Matthew J. Connelly to Dorothy McAllister, 18 February 1946, file 120-A, WHCF, HSTL. Truman ultimately did change his mind on the ERA. In 1963 he wrote to Emma Guffey Miller, in response to a letter from her, that he did not favor too many constitutional amendments and that the goals of ERA advocates could be achieved by legislation (Harry Truman to Emma Guffey Miller, 17 May 1963, reel 108, NWP papers [microfilm ed.]).

45. Ella M. Sherwin to Each Member of the 79th Congress, 9 May 1946, folder 7, box 12, Helen Gahagan Douglas papers, Albert Archives, University of Oklahoma.

46. U.S. Congress, Senate, Letter to the Senate, S.J. Res. 61, 79th Cong., 2d sess., 18 July 1946, *Congressional Record* 42: 9401; Blahna, "Rhetoric of the Equal Rights Amendment," 64–65.

47. "Republican Record on Equal Rights Amendment," and "Democratic Record on the Equal Rights Amendment," June 1948, folder 2-8, NWP papers, WSHS; *Equal Rights*, July–August 1946, 1–2.

48. Carl Hayden to Pauline Brown, 29 July 1946, and Carl Hayden to Warda Hulsey, 4 August 1946, folder 5, box 119, Carl Hayden papers, Arizona State University.

49. National Committee for the Defeat of the UnEqual Rights Amendment, newsletter, 31 July 1946, folder 20, box 3, Hattie Smith papers, SL.

50. *New York Times*, 20 July 1946.

CHAPTER 2

1. *New York Herald Tribune*, 20 July 1946, clipping, folder 2-8, NWP papers, WSHS.

2. *Equal Rights*, January–March 1949, 7; *New York Times*, 10 January 1947.

3. William Chafe, *The American Woman: Her Changing Social, Economic, and Political Roles, 1920–1970* (New York: Oxford University Press, 1972), 202–216.

4. Susan M. Hartmann, *The Home Front and Beyond: American*

*Women in the 1940s* (Boston: Twayne, 1982), 181; Ethel Klein, *Gender Politics* (Cambridge: Harvard University Press, 1984), 71.

5. U.S. Department of Commerce, Bureau of the Census, *Historical Statistics of the United States, Colonial Times to 1970*, pt. 1 (Washington, D.C.: GPO, 1975), 64.

6. Hartmann, *Home Front*, 93.

7. Ibid., ch. 6; *Historical Statistics*, 385.

8. Chafe, *American Woman*, 202–216.

9. Status Bill sponsor James Wadsworth strongly opposed the ERA, partially because it might require women to serve in the military. "It may seem absurd," he wrote to one constituent, "but it would not be beyond the bounds of possibility that some young woman in the future would demand admission to West Point or Annapolis" (Wadsworth to Mrs. Vernon Howe, 1 February 1949, in folder "Equal Rights Amendment, January 31, 1949–February 22, 1950" box 24, James W. Wadsworth papers, LC.

10. Memorandum, 8 January 1947, and Peter Seitz (form letter), 10 February 1947, in folder "1947," ERA files, WBOF; Mary Anderson to Hattie Smith, 14 March 1947, folder 21, box 3, Hattie Smith papers, SL.

11. "Supporting Comment on Proposed Joint Resolution on the Status of Women," 21 January 1947, folder 21, box 3, Hattie Smith papers, SL.

12. Memorandum, 10 February 1947, folder 9, box 44, Helen Gahagan Douglas papers, Albert Archives, University of Oklahoma.

13. Memorandum, 10 February 1947, folder 9, box 44, Helen Gahagan Douglas papers, Albert Archives, University of Oklahoma; Memorandum, 19 February 1947, folder 21, box 3, Hattie Smith papers, SL.

14. Memorandum, 10 February 1947, folder 9, box 44, Helen Gahagan Douglas papers, Albert Archives, University of Oklahoma.

15. Blanch Freedman, Executive Secretary, New York Women's Trade Union League, as sent to National Women's Trade Union League, 24 January 1947, attached to Rose Schneiderman to Malvina Thompson, 3 February 1947, in folder "Harry S. Truman, 1945–1948," box 3765, Eleanor Roosevelt papers, FDRL.

16. Minutes of meeting, 9 September 1947, in folder "Women's Bureau Labor Advisory Committee, 1950–53," box "Committees— Women's Bureau," Frieda Miller papers, SL.

17. *Independent Woman*, March 1947, 88 (quote from BPW); "Brief Memorandum in Opposition to the Taft-Wadsworth Bill, (Commonly

called the Biological Status Bill)," folder 1-2, NWP papers, WSHS (quote from NWP); *New York Times,* 18 February 1947; "Highlights of the Women's Status Bill, 16 April 1947," in folder "1947," ERA files, WBOF.

18. "Statement in regard to Women's Status Bill, H.R. 2007 and S.J. Res. 67—80th Congress," 15 June 1947, in folder "1947," ERA files, WBOF (quote beginning "to break the deadlock . . ."); *New York Herald Tribune,* 7 April 1947; "Statement by Mrs. Eleanor Roosevelt regarding Bill on the Status of Women," 14 February 1946, and *Washington Post,* 25 February 1947, clipping, in folder "1947," ERA files, WBOF; "Brief for Action," League of Women Voters publication 91, 1 April 1947, in folder "General Correspondence, 1947," subject file, India Edwards papers, HSTL; *New York Times,* 18 February 1947.

19. The National Women's Trade Union League received information that the House committee had reported it favorably in return for "some large party contributions from 'rich ladies'" (NWTUL, legislative report, 16 August 1948, reel 10, NWTUL papers, LC). Anita Pollitzer to Members of the National Council and Others Particularly Concerned, 5 April 1948, and Anita Pollitzer to Members of the National Council and Others Concerned with the Equality Campaign, 13 April 1948, folder 1-2, NWP papers, WSHS: "JD" [i.e., J. E. Dempsey, Administrative Assistant to the Secretary] to "Judge" [i.e., Secretary L. B. Schwellenbach], 19 April 1948, in folder "Bills—Misc.," RG 174 (Schwellenbach), NA; Thomas C. Pardo (ed.), *The National Woman's Party Papers, 1913–1974: A Guide to the Microfilm Edition* (Sanford, N.C.: Microfilm Corporation of America, 1979), 147–150.

In the Senate committee, Republican senators Wiley, Langer, Ferguson, Donnell, and Cooper and Democratic senators McGrath and Fulbright voted in favor; Democratic senator James Eastland voted no. *Washington Post,* clipping, 1 May 1948, in folder "Equal Rights for Women, 1939–49," box 601, Robert A. Taft papers, LC; Louise Young to Friends of the NCSW, 6 July 1948, folder 21, box 3, Hattie Smith papers, SL; "1948 Republican Party Platform for ERA, a report to members by Anita Pollitzer, National Chairman [NWP]," [June 1948], and Emma Guffey Miller to Sally Butler, President, BPW, 6 July 1948, and "Memorandum Concerning the Two Major Political Parties and the Equal Rights Amendment," reel 103, NWP papers (microfilm ed.); *Equal Rights,* May–August 1948, 1–3.

20. *New York Herald Tribune,* 12 January 1949; "Housewives for Truman: A Program Designed to Bring in the Vote," in folder "Housewives for Truman," box 2, subject file, India Edwards papers, HSTL; Press release R-145, 9 February 1948, in folder "Women Voters," box 105, DNC papers, LBJL.

21. *New York Times,* 10 April 1949; Minutes of meeting, National Committee on the Status of Women, 5 April 1949 and 4 August 1949, in subject file "Equal Rights Amendment," SL; Olya Margolin to Elizabeth Magee, 23 November 1948, in folder "ERA, NCSW, 1947–48," box C6, NCL papers, LC; Anita Pollitzer to State Chairmen and Members of the Outgoing National Council, 31 May 1949, folder 1-3, NWP papers, WSHS; Pardo, *National Woman's Party Papers,* 152.

22. J. Stanley Lemons, *The Woman Citizen: Social Feminism in the 1920s* (Urbana: University of Illinois Press, 1975), 186–191.

23. Douglas B. Maggs, Solicitor of Labor, to Mary Anderson, 17 January 1944, folder 13, box 92, Helen Gahagan Douglas papers, Albert Archives, University of Oklahoma; Douglas B. Maggs to Mrs. Thomas F. (Dorothy) McAllister, 2 June 1945, folder 55, Mary Anderson papers, SL; National Committee for the Defeat of the UnEqual Rights Amendment, "To the member organizations and individuals on the National Committee," 20 June 1945, and Margaret F. Stone to Mary McLeod Bethune, 27 January 1945, folder 351, box 23, series 5, NCNW papers.

24. U.S. Congress, Senate, 81st Cong., 2d sess., 23, 24, 25 January 1950, *Congressional Record* 96: 738–744, 758–762, 809–813, 861, 873.

25. Ibid., 25 January 1950, 861–873 (Hayden quotation, p. 868; Pepper, 869); *New York Times,* 26 January 1950. Thirty-six Democrats and fifteen Republicans voted in favor of the Hayden amendment, and thirteen Democrats and eighteen Republicans against. All nineteen votes against the ERA with the rider were Democrats. All absent senators were announced in favor of the ERA.

26. Alice Paul, oral history, pp. 518–530.

27. *New York Times,* 27 January 1950. See also *Independent Woman,* March 1950, 85–86, for the response of the BPW to the Hayden amendment—that it "nullif[ied] and [made] ridiculous the whole procedure."

28. U.S. Congress, House, 81st Cong., 2d sess., 7 March 1950, *Congressional Record* 96: A2053–54; Alice Paul to Agnes Wells, 7 June 1950, folder 1-4, NWP papers, WSHS; U.S. Congress, House, 81st Cong., 2d sess., 6 March 1950, *Congressional Record* 96: 2855; National Committee on the Status of Women, Minutes, 3 February 1950, in folder "ERA, NCSW, 1949–50," box C6, NCL papers, LC; Pardo, *National Woman's Party Papers,* 158; *New York Times,* 26 May 1951.

29. "My Day," 25 May 1951, box 3153, Eleanor Roosevelt papers, FDRL; "My Day," 7 June 1951, from *Washington Daily News* (typescript copy), in folder "1950's," ERA files, WBOF; Harry S. Truman to Gertrude Dixon Enfield, 17 April 1952, file 120-A, WHCF, HSTL. The Senate Judiciary Committee reported the ERA favorably on May

21, 1951, by a seven-to-two vote, but the full Senate did not take the amendment up.

30. William Chafe, *The Unfinished Journey: America Since World War II* (New York: Oxford University Press, 1986), 154–157.

31. Alonzo Hamby, *Liberalism and Its Challengers* (New York: Oxford University Press, 1985), 119–125, 137–138, chap. 3; Chafe, *Unfinished Journey,* 112–127, 138–139, 144; Eugenia Kaledin, *Mothers and More: American Women in the 1950s* (Boston: Twayne, 1984), 11.

32. U.S. Department of Labor, Women's Bureau, "Biographical Sketch of Alice K. Leopold, director, Women's Bureau, U.S. Department of Labor," 11 December 1953, and U.S Department of Labor, "Biographical Sketch: Alice K. Leopold," n.d., folder 1, box 1, Alice K. Leopold papers, SL.

33. Mabel Griswold, the party's executive secretary, wrote to a comrade: "One piece of good news is that Mrs. Leopold, Director of the Women's Bureau, has withdrawn the Bureau's opposition to the Amendment. . . . Next best thing to outright support which may come some time" (Mabel Griswold to "Elda," 30 March 1954, folder 2-1, NWP papers, WSHS). Alice Paul to Mrs. George Ramey, 1 March 1954, Alice K. Leopold to Mabel Griswold, 10 March 1954, folder 2-1, NWP papers, WSHS; *Equal Rights,* October 1954 (typescript), folder 92-7, Katherine P. Ellickson papers, ALUA.

34. Martin P. Durkin to Chauncy W. Reed, 27 July 1953, in folder "H.J.R. 55," box 42, Katharine St. George papers, Cornell University. See bill files (S.J.R. 49), Committee on the Judiciary, Records of the U.S. Senate, RG 46, NA; *New York Times,* 2 July 1953. See, for example, Carl Hayden to Jacob Potofsky, 19 May 1953, and Jacob Potofsky to Carl Hayden, 22 May 1953, folder 8, box 457, Carl Hayden papers, Arizona State University; *New York Times,* 17 July 1953; Pardo, *National Woman's Party Papers,* 159.

35. Alice A. Morrison to Winifred Helmes, 23 February 1955, in folder "1950's," ERA files, WBOF; John Mitchell to Irma Piepho, 3 March 1955, in folder "Correspondence, 1955," box 5, WJCC papers; Katharine St. George to Alice Paul, 3 February 1956, James P. Mitchell to Katharine St. George, 27 February 1956, and Alice K. Leopold to Katharine St. George, 6 March 1956, in folder "H.J.R. 55," box 42, Katharine St. George papers, Cornell University.

36. Briefing, in folder "Press conference, April 25, 1956," box 4, Press Conference Series, Anne Whitman files, DDEL; Gerald D. Morgan to Nina B. Price, 10 December 1955, in folder "Equal Rights Amendment," folder 136-A, box 1059, WHGF, DDEL; Secretary of

Labor to Gerald D. Morgan, 9 February 1956, in folder "Equal Pay 1956," box 134, RG 174 (Mitchell), NA.

37. White House, press release, 25 October 1956, reel 103, NWP papers (microfilm ed.).

38. Handwritten notes on meeting #258, 4 February 1957, and notes on meeting of 22 April 1957, in folder "1957—Secretary's Policy Committee—chronological—meetings 258–277," box 75, James P. Mitchell papers, DDEL; *Washington Post,* 17 January 1957.

39. Gerald D. Morgan to Nina Horton Avery, 27 December 1957, folder 136-A, box 1059, WHOF, DDEL.

40. *Hickory [N.C.] Daily Record,* editorial, 24 August 1957, reprinted in the *Congressional Record,* 27 August 1957, A7087–7088, clipping in folder 136-A, box 1059, WHGF, DDEL.

41. AFL-CIO, memorandum on Objections to Proposed Equal Rights Amendment, and Andrew Biemiller to All Members of the 86th Congress, 11 February 1959, folder 92-8, Katherine P. Ellickson papers, ALUA; Andrew Biemiller to John F. Kennedy, 15 February 1957, in folder "Equal Rights Amendment, October 3, 1951 to February 15, 1957," Legislative Assistant's Background Files, Prepresidential papers, JFKL.

42. Hyman H. Bookbinder to Boris Shishkin, 6 November 1957, folder 3, box 17, Legislative Reference Files, Meany Archives.

43. Hyman H. Bookbinder to Helen O'Donnell, 7 January 1958, folder 4, Box 17, Legislative Reference Files, Meany Archives.

44. Tom Harris to Andrew Biemiller, 19 January 1960, folder 7, and Patrick Malin to Biemiller, 4 January 1960 (with attachments), folder 7, box 17, Legislative Reference Files, Meany Archives.

45. Jacob Clayman to Legislative Representatives of IUD Affiliated Unions, 14 June 1960, in folder "ERA 1960–61," box "Women," Esther Peterson papers, SL; Andrew Biemiller to Carl Hayden, 12 June 1959, folder 6, box 17, Legislative Reference Files, Meany Archives; Pardo, *National Woman's Party Papers,* 161.

CHAPTER 3

1. Alonzo Hamby, *Liberalism and Its Challengers* (New York: Oxford University Press, 1985), chap. 2.

2. Susan M. Hartmann, *The Home Front and Beyond: American Women in the 1940s* (Boston: Twayne, 1982), 7–8.

3. National Committee for the Defeat of the UnEqual Rights

Amendment, memorandum, 10 May 1945, folder 351, and Dorothy McAllister to Member Organizations, 15 December 1945, folder 352, box 23, series 5, NCNW papers.

4. Louise Stitt to Elizabeth Magee, 19 May 1945, in folder "Equal Pay—National Legislation, 1945," box C4, NCL papers, LC; *New York Times,* 22 June 1945; John Earner, "Equal Pay for Equal Work: Federal Legislative Activity, 1945 to 1962," pp. 1, 23, Legislative Reference Service, Library of Congress, in folder "Labor—Equal Pay for Equal Work," box 15, Maurine Neuberger papers, University of Oregon; U.S. Congress, Senate, S. Rept. 1576 to accompany S. 1178, 79th Cong., 2d sess., 21 June 1946; U.S. Department of Labor, Women's Bureau, "Analysis of Proposed Federal 'Wage Discrimination Act of 1945,'" folder 54, Mary Anderson papers, SL; National Committee for the Defeat of the UnEqual Rights Amendment, memorandum, 10 May 1945, folder 351, and Dorothy McAllister to Member Organization, 14 December 1945, folder 352, box 23, series 5, NCNW papers; Sen. Claude Pepper, diary, 22, 23 May, 20 June 1945 (in Pepper's possession).

5. Press release, 21 June 1945, folder 55, Mary Anderson papers, SL.

6. *New York Herald Tribune,* 27 June 1945; Marguerite J. Fisher, "Equal Pay for Equal Work Legislation," *Industrial and Labor Relations Review* 2 (October 1948): 50–51; *New York Times,* 18 July 1945; U.S. Department of Labor, Women's Bureau, "Differentials in Pay for Women," November 1945, box 189, RG 174 (Schwellenbach), NA.

7. Frieda Miller, memorandum, 4 July 1945, folder 55, Mary Anderson papers, SL.

8. Nathan E. Cowan to Mary Anderson, 13 July 1945, folder 55, Mary Anderson papers, SL.

9. Nora Stanton Barney to Claude Pepper, 26 June 1945, in folder "S. 1178," Records of the U.S. Senate, RG 46, NA.

10. NCL press release, 30 July 1945, in folder "Equal Pay—National Legislation—1945–48," box C4, NCL papers, LC; Dorothy McAllister to Member Organizations, 15 December 1945, in folder "Equal Rights Amendment—National Committee to Defeat Unequal Rights Amend.—Publications," box C6, NCL papers, LC.

11. Report of Equal Pay Meeting, 10 September 1945, folder 58, Mary Anderson papers, SL.

12. "A Summary of Hearings by the Subcommittee on Labor on the Equal Pay Bill (S. 1178) on October 29th, 30th and 31st (1945)," in folder "S. 1178," box H1, Wayne Morse papers, University of Oregon; *New York Times,* 30, 31 October 1945.

13. U.S. Congress, Senate, S. Rept. 1576 to accompany S. 1178, 79th Cong., 2d sess., 21 June 1946.

14. U.S. Congress, Senate, 79th Cong., 2d sess., 31 July 1946, *Congressional Record*, 92: 10547–10548.

15. Elizabeth Christman to Members of the Executive Board, 7 March 1947, reel 9, NWTUL papers, LC.

16. Dorothy McAllister to Elizabeth Magee, July 1946, in folder "Equal Pay—National Legislation—1946–56," box C4, NCL papers, LC; Minutes of meetings, 11 October 1948 and 1 March 1948, box 8, WJCC papers, LC; Press release, 2 July 1947, in folder "S. 706," box H6, Wayne Morse papers, University of Oregon; *Independent Woman*, April 1948, 117–118; "Statements in opposition to proposed federal equal pay legislation," 28 May 1956, in folder "Equal Pay 1956," box 7, WBOF; Earner, "Equal Pay for Equal Work," 2, 3, 24, 25; J. W. Grove, testimony before the Wage and Hour Subcommittee of the House Education and Labor Committee, 13 February 1948, folder 54, box 16, Legislative Reference Files, Meany Archives.

17. Wayne Morse to Mrs. O. D. Cook, 27 August 1951, in folder "S. 1374," box H9, Wayne Morse papers, University of Oregon; John F. Kennedy to Mary T. Norton, 6 June 1951, in folder "Equal Pay for Equal Work," box 3, Prepresidential papers, JFKL.

18. [William C. Hushing] to George Riley, 24 April 1951, folder 54, box 16, Legislative Reference Files, Meany Archives.

19. "Equal Pay Conference under the Auspices of the Women's Bureau, U.S. Department of Labor," report by Mildred Palmer, Executive Secretary, National Woman's Party, reel 98, NWP papers (microfilm ed.), U.S. Department of Labor, Women's Bureau, *Report of the National Conference on Equal Pay* (31 March and 1 April, 1952), bulletin no. 243, 29 August 1952.

20. Meany quoted in Alice A. Morrison to Elizabeth S. Magee, 24 December 1953, in folder "Equal Pay—National Legislation—1946–56," box C4, NCL papers, LC.

21. National Committee for Equal Pay, newsletter, 16 March 1953, in folder: "1954 Equal Pay," box 48, RG 174 (Mitchell), NA.

22. Alice Paul to Mabel E. Griswold, 19 October 1954, folder 2-2, NWP papers, WSHS.

23. Secretary of Labor to Frances Bolton, 18 February 1954, in folder "1954—Congressional—B," box 64, RG 174 (Mitchell), NA; Arthur Larson to Frances Bolton, 27 May 1954, in folder "1954—Equal Pay," box 48, RG 174 (Mitchell), NA; U.S. Congress, House, 83rd Cong., 2d sess., 19 July 1954, *Congressional Record* 100: 10951–10953.

24. U.S. Congress, House, 84th Cong., 1st sess., 13 January 1955, *Congressional Record* 101: 285; "Preliminary Report on the Legislative Program of the Department of Labor for 1955," in folder "1954 Secretary's Policy Committee—Material from the Secretary's Notebook (2)," box 70, James P. Mitchell papers, DDEL; Stuart Rothman to the Secretary of Labor, 28 February 1955, in folder "1955 Equal Pay," box 113, James P. Mitchell papers, DDEL; Millard Cass to John J. Gilhooley, 5 May 1955, in folder: 1955—Congressional—B," box 106, RG 174 (Mitchell), NA; "Summary of Action," Secretary's Policy Committee, meeting no. 121, 26 May 1955, in folder "1955—Secretary's Policy Committee—chronological (meetings 106–122)," box 72, James P. Mitchell papers, DDEL.

25. National Manpower Council, *Womanpower: A Statement by the National Manpower Council with Chapters by the Council Staff* (New York: Columbia University Press, 1957).

26. George H. Gallup, *The Gallup Poll: Public Opinion, 1935–1971* (New York: Random House, 1972), 1:322.

27. "Equal Pay—Administration Support 1956—January 1961," 24 January 1961, in folder "Equal Pay—1961," Box 7, WBOF; Alice K. Leopold to Secretary of Labor, 6 January 1956 (plus attachments), in folder "1956—Equal Pay," box 134, RG 174 (Mitchell), NA; "State of the Union Message, comments by Cabinet members, 2 December 1955," in folder "State of the Union January 1956 (3)," box 15, Anne Whitman file, speech series, DDEL.

28. Secretary of Labor to William Schnitzler, Secretary-Treasurer, AFL-CIO, 17 January 1957, and William Schnitzler to Secretary of Labor, 27 December 1956, in folder "1957—Equal Pay," box 193, RG 174 (Mitchell), NA; George D. Riley to Edith Nourse Rogers, 1 February 1957, and George D. Riley to James Roosevelt, 1 February 1957, folder 92-9, Katherine P. Ellickson papers, ALUA; George D. Riley to Wayne Morse, 1 February 1957, in folder "S. 1807," box H26, Wayne Morse papers, University of Oregon; "Files (for the record)," Alice A. Morrison, 4 January 1957, in folder "Equal Pay 4, National Equal Pay Committee," box 1096, RG 86, NA; Alice A. Morrison to Alice K. Leopold, 4 January 1957, in folder "Equal Pay 3, Federal Legislative Proposals," box 1096, RG 86, NA; National Committee for Equal Pay, newsletter, February 1957, folder 17, box 2, Hattie Smith papers, SL; James T. O'Connell, Acting Secretary of Labor to Lister Hill, 1 August 1957, in folder "Equal Pay, 1957," WBOF; U.S. Congress, Senate, S. 1807, 85th Cong., 1st sess., 4 April 1957, *Congressional Record* 103: 5091–5092; Earner, "Equal Pay for Equal Work," 11–13.

29. Stuart Rothman to Secretary of Labor, 30 January 1956, in

folder "1956—National Legislation D/L Legislative Program," box 180, James P. Mitchell papers, DDEL; Notes on Secretary's Policy Committee meetings nos. 205 (10 February 1956), 206 (20 February 1956), 216 (4 April 1956), 228 (17 May 1956), 236 (12 June 1956), 249 (30 July 1956), in folder: "1956—Secretary's Policy Committee—chronological (meetings 197–213)," Box 75, James P. Mitchell papers, DDEL; Alice K. Leopold to Secretary of Labor, 28 September 1956, in folder: "1956 Equal Pay," box 134, RG 174 (Mitchell), NA.

30. President's Commission on the Status of Women, Committee on Civil and Political Rights, transcript of the meeting of 28 May 1962, Washington, D. C., pp. 13–14, PCSW papers (Washington, D.C.); "Material on Equal Pay for Equal Work prepared by the U.S Department of Labor, Women's Bureau, January 1956," in folder: "Equal Pay 1956," box 7, WBOF; Margaret Mealey to James P. Mitchell, 19 September 1956, attached to James P. Mitchell to Margaret Mealey, 6 October 1956, in folder "1956—Equal Pay," box 134, RG 174 (Mitchell), NA; Telephone interview with Alice A. Morrison, 11 February 1981 (Alexandria, Va.); Alice K. Leopold to Irma Piepho, 30 April 1957, in folder "Equal Pay 4, National Equal Pay Committee," box 1096, RG 86, NA; Alice K. Leopold to Edith Green, 3 July 1957, in folder "Equal Pay," box 1096, RG 86, NA.


CHAPTER 4

1. Karen Keesling and Suzanne Cavanagh, "Women Presidential Appointees Serving or Having Served in Full-Time Positions Requiring Senate Confirmation, 1912–1977," Congressional Research Service Report 78-73 G, 23 March 1978, Library of Congress, Washington, D.C. "Significant Senate-confirmed posts" excludes local comptrollers and collectors of customs. If these appointments are added to the figures, Hoover appointed seven women to Senate-confirmed posts during his tenure, and Roosevelt twenty-eight.

2. *Independent Woman*, March 1947, 82.

3. Eleanor Roosevelt to Robert Hannegan, 3 June 1945, box 3756, Eleanor Roosevelt papers, FDRL; "A Summary Statement of the Conference on How Women May Share in the Post-War Policy Making," 14 June 1944, in folder "Meeting, heads of Women's Organizations," box 113, Eleanor Roosevelt papers, FDRL.

The National Council of Negro Women was particularly interested in submitting the names of black women, noting that "to date several American women have been appointed as U.S. Delegates to important international committees and conferences, but none of them were Negro women" (Mary McLeod Bethune to "Dear Council Member and Friend," [21 July 1944], folder 449, box 30, series 5, NCNW papers).

4. Mrs. Charles W. Tillett to Matthew J. Connelly, 3 July 1945, file 120, box 534, WHOF, HSTL.

5. Keesling and Cavanagh, "Women Presidential Appointees."

6. Transcript, India Edwards Oral History Interview, 16 January 1969, pp. 82–83, HSTL. Cabell Phillips, a historian of the Truman Presidency, has observed that Truman had to rely heavily on recommendations for appointments because he lacked a "broad acquaintance among the nation's elite" (Phillips, *The Truman Presidency: The History of a Triumphant Succession* [New York: Macmillan, 1966], (144).

7. Democratic National Committee, press release, 7 October 1953, in folder "Louchheim, Mrs. Katie," box 149, DNC papers, LBJL. I am indebted to James Sundquist for his recollections of India Edwards.

8. India Edwards, *Pulling No Punches: Memoirs of a Woman in Politics* (New York: Putnam, 1977), 173.

9. Keesling and Cavanagh, "Women Presidential Appointees." See G. Calvin MacKenzie, *The Politics of Presidential Appointments* (New York: Free Press, 1981), 12–14, for a discussion of the importance Truman attached to loyalty.

10. Harry S. Truman, *Memoirs* (New York: Doubleday, 1955), 1:161; Stephen Hess, *Organizing the Presidency* (Washington, D.C.: The Brookings Institution, 1976), chap. 3; Transcript, Clayton Fritchey Oral History Interview, 1 July 1960, pp. 42–43, HSTL; Edwards, *Pulling No Punches*, 144ff.; Katie Louchheim, *By the Political Sea* (Garden City, N.Y.: Doubleday, 1970), 270; Cornelius P. Cotter and Bernard Hennessy, *Politics Without Power: The National Party Committees* (New York: Atherton Press, 1964), 82, 84; MacKenzie, *Politics of Presidential Appointments*, 11–15.

11. *New York Herald Tribune*, 20 November 1949, clipping, in folder "Women Voters," box 105, DNC papers, LBJL; Edwards, *Pulling No Punches*, 177, 186–187.

12. India Edwards to Harry S. Truman, 14 October 1949, in folder "General Correspondence, 1949," India Edwards papers, HSTL.

13. Diary of Eben A. Ayers, 14 September 1945, HSTL, (quoted in part in Robert J. Donovan, *Conflict and Crisis: The Presidency of Harry S. Truman, 1945–1948* (New York: Norton, 1977), 27.

14. Transcript, India Edwards Oral History Interview, 16 January 1969, pp. 84–85, HSTL.

15. Harry Truman to India Edwards, 6 October 1949, in folder

"General Correspondence, 1949," box 2, India Edwards papers, HSTL.

16. Martin Binkin and Shirley J. Bach, *Women and the Military* (Washington, D.C.: The Brookings Institution, 1977), 11–12; Department of Defense, press release, 11 August 1951, in folder "Press releases, DNC," box 3, India Edwards papers, HSTL; Mae Sue Talley, *Highlights of the DACOWITS: 25 Years of Service to the Department of Defense* (Washington, D.C.: Department of Defense, 1976), 1–3; Defense Advisory Committee on Women in the Services, minutes, 25th Anniversary Meeting, 14–18 November 1976, Washington, D.C., "DACOWITS, 1951–1976," D7.

17. George H. Gallup, *The Gallup Poll: Public Opinion, 1935–1971* (New York: Random House, 1972), vol. 1: *1935–1948*, pp. 322, 548–549, 659, vol. 2: *1949–1958*, pp. 837, 861; Edwin Coover, "Status and Role Change Among Women in the United States, 1940–1970: A Quantitative Approach" (Ph.D. diss., University of Minnesota, 1973), chap. 6.

18. Keesling and Cavanagh, "Women Presidential Appointees," 25–31; President's Commission on the Status of Women, transcript of the meeting of 2 October 1962, Washington, D.C., pp. 252–253, PCSW papers (Washington, D.C.); *New York Times*, 28 September 1952; "Women Listed in Government Organization Manual in Appointive Positions," in folder "Political Executives—United States," FE papers, PCSW.

19. E. Stevenson to Dr. Rosamonde Ramsay Boyd, 30 August 1952, in folder "Presidential Campaign 1952," box 2, India Edwards papers, HSTL.

20. American Association of University Women, statement, 18 September 1952, Portland statement, 7 October 1952, and Katherine Howard to "Co-worker," 24 October 1952, all attached to Katherine Howard to General Eisenhower, Governor Adams, Mr. Hauge, 29 October 1952, in folder "Letter to Women Leaders from Katherine Howard, October 24, 1952," box 6, Stephen Benedict papers, DDEL; "Campaign Statements of Dwight D. Eisenhower: A Reference Index," 277–281, DDEL.

21. Mrs. Charles W. Weis, Jr., to Hugh Scott, 11 January 1953, in folder "1936 (Women, 1952–53)," box 1058, WHGF, DDEL.

22. "Republican 'balance sheet' (as of December 1952)," Max Rabb to Governor Adams, 3 January 1953, in folder "109-A-1 1952–53(1)," box 476, DDEL; *Independent Woman*, January 1953, 7, March, 1953, cover. Hobby resigned in July, 1955.

23. MacKenzie, *Politics of Presidential Appointments*, 14–21.

24. Wes Roberts to Governor Adams, 4 March 1953, in folder "136 (women 1952–53)," box 1058, WHGF, DDEL.

25. Bertha Adkins entered political life after a career in college administration. Following a tenure as dean at Western Maryland College and Bradford Junior College, she became Republican National Committeewoman for the State of Maryland in 1948. In March 1950 the committee chose her to assume the post of executive director of the Women's Division of the RNC, and in January 1953 she was promoted to the post of assistant chairman of the committee and director of the programs for women's activities. Republican National Committee, "Miss Bertha S. Adkins," September 1956, biography file, SL; Transcript, Bertha Adkins Oral History Interview (Columbia University Oral History Project), 18 December 1967, pp. 1–5.

26. Republican National Committee, press release, 30 July 1953, in folder "General Correspondence, 1953–54," box 2, India Edwards papers, HSTL.

27. *Washington [D.C.] Post and Times Herald,* 30 May 1956, clipping, in folder "Louchheim, Mrs. Katie," box 149, DNC papers, LBJL.

28. *Newsweek,* 9 May 1955, 30–32, clipping, in folder "Women, General," box 105, DNC papers, LBJL.

29. White House, press release, 25 October 1956, reel 103, NWP papers (microfilm ed.); *Independent Woman,* October 1956, 3, 4, 34; Transcript, Bertha Adkins Oral History Interview, (Columbià University Oral History Project), 18 December 1967, pp. 46, 50.

30. Wheaton herself found out only that morning. Transcript, Anne Wheaton Oral History Interview, (Columbia University Oral History Project), 31 January 1968; *New York Times,* 4 April 1957; *Washington [D.C.] Post and Times Herald,* 4 April 1957, WBOF.

31. Republican National Committee, press release, 16 August 1958, in folder "109-A-1 Women 1958," box 477, WHGF, DDEL.

32. Keesling and Cavanagh, "Women Presidential Appointees," 28–36; "Women Listed in Government Organization Manual in Appointive Positions," in folder "Political Executives—United States," FE papers, PCSW; Republican National Committee, bulletin, 16 July 1961, in folder "Top women in government," Esther Peterson papers (in Peterson's possession); "Analysis of appointments of top women," n.d. [August, 1962], in folder "White House, 1962–63," box "Political (Dem. Campaigns)," Esther Peterson papers, SL.

33. Elsie L. George, "The Women Appointees of the Roosevelt and Truman Administrations: A Study of Their Impact and Effectiveness" (Ph.D. diss., American University, 1972), 297.

34. Mary Anderson, *Woman at Work: The Autobiography of Mary Anderson as told to Mary N. Winslow* (Minneapolis: University of Minnesota Press, 1951), 183–184.


CHAPTER 5

1. Herbert Parmet, *JFK: The Presidency of John F. Kennedy* (New York: Dial Press, 1983); David Burner and Thomas West, *The Torch Is Passed: The Kennedy Brothers and American Liberalism* (New York: Atheneum, 1984), chap. 3, 153–154, 186.

For discussions of America in the postwar period, see William Chafe, *The Unfinished Journey: America Since World War II* (New York: Oxford University Press, 1986); William E. Leuchtenburg, *A Troubled Feast: American Society Since 1945* (Boston: Little, Brown, 1982); James Gilbert, *Another Chance: Postwar America, 1945–1968* (New York: Knopf, 1981); and David Burner, Robert D. Marcus, and Thomas R. West, *A Giant's Strength: America in the 1960s* (New York: Holt, Rinehart & Winston, 1971).

2. Richard H. Pells, *The Liberal Mind in a Conservative Age: American Intellectuals in the 1940s and 1950s* (New York: Harper & Row, 1985), 381, 395–399.

3. Pells, *The Liberal Mind*, 398.

4. *New York Times*, 19 March 1961.

5. Parmet, *JFK*, 37, 84–85, 353; Burner and West, *The Torch Is Passed*, 151; Allen J. Matusow, *The Unraveling of America: A History of Liberalism in the 1960s* (New York: Harper & Row, 1984), chap. 1; Alonzo Hamby, *Liberalism and Its Challengers* (New York: Oxford University Press, 1985), chaps. 4 and 5; Charles Morris, *A Time of Passion: America, 1960–1980* (New York: Harper & Row, 1984), 2–5; Gilbert, *Another Chance*, chap. 8.

6. Burner and West, *The Torch Is Passed*, 4, 154 (quote), 186, 191.

7. Ibid., 48–50, 58, 152; James MacGregor Burns, *John Kennedy: A Political Profile* (New York: Harcourt, Brace & World, 1961), 96; William E. Leuchtenburg, *In the Shadow of FDR: From Harry Truman to Ronald Reagan* (Ithaca, N.Y.: Cornell University Press, 1983), 76–77, 95.

8. Chafe, *Unfinished Journey*, 207–216; Burner and West, *The Torch Is Passed*, 161–180; Parmet, *JFK*, chap. 11; Harvard Sitkoff, *The Struggle for Black Equality, 1954–1980* (New York: Hill & Wang, 1981).

9. Burner and West, *The Torch Is Passed*, 158–161, 180, 188–190; Chafe, *Unfinished Journey*, 215–217.

10. A great deal has been written concerning the personal attitudes

of John Kennedy toward women. Many writers contend persuasively that he indulged in numerous sexual liaisons outside of marriage, in inappropriate settings, leaving himself vulnerable to blackmail from FBI director J. Edgar Hoover and criminal figures. It is nonetheless my opinion that John Kennedy's public policy decisions concerning women sprang from his assessment of the social, economic, and political aspects of the situation, rather than from his personal views of women as sexual objects.

11.  Theodore Sorensen, *Kennedy* (New York: Harper & Row, 1965), 121, 136; Herbert Parmet, *Jack: The Struggles of John F. Kennedy* (New York: Dial Press, 1980), 159, 253; U.S. Congress, Senate, Committee on Commerce, *The Speeches of Senator John F. Kennedy: Presidential Campaign of 1960*, S. Rept. 994, pt. 1, 87th Cong., 1st sess., p. 959.

12.  Emma Guffey Miller to Lyndon Baines Johnson, 20 March 1968, in folder "Miller, Emma," name file, WHCF, LBJL; India Edwards to John F. Kennedy, 15 October 1960, in folder "Office of Women's Activities, DNC," box 2, India Edwards papers, LBJL; India Edwards to Harry Truman, 22 May 1960, in folder "Truman, Harry S., correspondence with," box 3, India Edwards papers, HSTL; Transcript, India Edwards Oral History Interview, 4 February 1969, pp. 17–25, LBJL; Transcript, Myer Feldman Oral History Interview, 10 April 1966, JFKL; Parmet, *Jack,* 462–464.

13.  The Governor to Adelaide Hart et al., 21 June 1960, in folder "Correspondence, May–July, 1960," box 4, Margaret Price papers, BHL; Transcript, Myer Feldman Oral History Interview, 27 March 1966, p. 225, JFKL.

14.  "Memorandum from Margaret Price," 28 July 1960, in folder "Correspondence, May–July 1960," box 4, Margaret Price papers, BHL.

15.  Margaret Price to Kenneth O'Donnell, 18 August 1960, in folder "Correspondence, August 1963," box 5, and Margaret Price to Robert F. Kennedy, 27 September 1960, in folder "Correspondence, August–September 1960," box 4, Margaret Price papers, BHL; Senate, *Speeches of Senator John F. Kennedy.*

16.  Letterhead, Committee of Labor Women, folder 90–22, Katherine P. Ellickson papers, ALUA; "Members of Women's Committee for New Frontiers," flyleaf of "Kennedy—60—New Frontiers: Report of the Women's Committee for New Frontiers," in folder "DNC campaign materials, reports, corr. 1960," box C10, Katie S. Louchheim papers, LC.

17.  Senate, *Speeches of Senator John F. Kennedy,* 663, 689, 901, 1241–

1249; U.S. Congress, Senate, Committee on Commerce, *The Speeches of Vice President Richard M. Nixon: Presidential Campaign of 1960,* S. Rept. 994, p. 2, 87th Cong., 1st sess., 1961, pp. 116–117, 319–320; Statement by the Vice-President on the Equal Rights Amendment, 2 September 1960, reel 106, NWP papers (microfilm ed.).

18. Margaret Price to John F. Kennedy, 8 December 1960, in folder "Women—role in government," box 1072, Prepresidential papers, JFKL.

19. Karen Keesling and Suzanne Cavanagh, "Women Presidential Appointees Serving or Having Served in Full-Time Positions Requiring Senate Confirmation, 1912–1977," Congressional Research Service Report 78–73 G, 23 March 1978, Library of Congress, Washington, D.C., pp. 36–38; Jim F. Heath points out that Kennedy ignored several of the transition reports (*Decade of Disillusionment: The Kennedy-Johnson Years* [Bloomington: Indiana University Press, 1975], 51).

20. *New York Post,* 20 December 1960, clipping, in folder "1960," box 1, India Edwards papers, LBJL.

21. Emma Guffey Miller to John F. Kennedy, 21 February 1961, folder PL9, box 696, WHCF, JFKL; Emma Guffey Miller to Victoria Gilbert, 21 February 1961, 24 March 1961, reel 106, NWP papers (microfilm ed.); Lawrence F. O'Brien to Emma Guffey Miller, 28 February 1961, folder HU3, box 374, WHCF, JFKL.

22. *New York Post,* 7 March 1961, clipping, in folder "Office of Women's Activities, DNC," box 2, India Edwards papers, LBJL.

23. Democratic National Committee, Office of Women's Activities, "Women Appointments, the Kennedy Administration as of November 1, 1961," in folder "DNC Office of Women's Activities, Reports of Director, 1955–1961," box C12, Katie S. Louchheim papers, LC.

24. Genevieve Blatt to Emma Guffey Miller, 5 December 1961, folder 68, box 4, Emma Guffey Miller papers, SL.

25. Clayton Fritchey to John F. Kennedy, 22 July 1963, folder HU3, box 374, JFKL.

26. Emanuel Celler to John F. Kennedy, 21 September 1961, and Lawrence O'Brien to Emanuel Celler, 20 September 1961, folder HU3, Box 374, JFKL.

27. Keesling and Cavanagh, "Women Presidential Appointees." Oveta Culp Hobby served as secretary of health, education, and welfare from 1953 to 1955, and Frances Perkins held the position of secretary of labor from 1933 to 1945. President's Commission on the Status of Women, transcript of the meeting of 2 October, 1962, pp.

252–253, PCSW papers (Washington, D.C.); Democratic National Committee, "Women Appointees of the Kennedy Administration as of February 19, 1963," uncatalogued papers of Esther Peterson, SL.

28. Keesling and Cavanagh, "Women Presidential Appointees."

29. India Edwards, *Pulling No Punches: Memoirs of a Woman in Politics* (New York: Putnam, 1977), 231–232, 252.

30. Emma Guffey Miller to Katie Louchheim, 26 January 1963, in folder "Department of State Letters of Congratulations, M-Z, 1962," box C17, Katie S. Louchheim papers, LC.

31. Sorensen, *Kennedy*, 124–125, 251–257; G. Calvin MacKenzie, *The Politics of Presidential Appointments* (New York: Free Press, 1981), xvii, 23–33. Myer Feldman, a Kennedy aide, has asserted that Margaret Price and President Kennedy "enjoyed an excellent relationship," but her influence with regard to women remains obscure (Myer Feldman to Cynthia E. Harrison, 3 October 1979). Note also that by the time Price took over as vice-chairman of the DNC, the Women's Division had been abolished as a separate entity.

32. Kennedy did not, however, neglect appointments of blacks nearly so much as of women (Carl Brauer, *John F. Kennedy and the Second Reconstruction* [New York: Columbia University Press, 1977], 68–70).

33. MacKenzie, *Politics of Presidential Appointments,* 23–33, 84, 198.

34. Telephone interview with Dan Fenn, Jr., 15 May 1981 (Boston, Mass.).

35. MacKenzie, *Politics of Presidential Appointments,* 255–259.

36. Dan Fenn to Ralph Dungan, 31 July 1962, in file Office of Education(?), Ralph Dungan papers(?). This item is on display at the Kennedy Library in Boston, Massachusetts.

37. Telephone interview with Dan Fenn, Jr., 14 May 1981 (Boston, Mass.).

38. Interviews with Esther Peterson, 4 October 1974 (telephone), 27 February 1978, 10 June 1978 (Washington, D.C.); Interview with Edith Green, 18 December 1978 (Portland, Oreg.); Interview with Maurine Neuberger, 15 December 1978, (Portland, Oreg.). For testimony that Kennedy did not take women seriously, see transcript, Mary McGrory interview, 4 August 1964, p. 48, JFKL; and Laura Bergquist, "What Women Really Meant to JFK," *Redbook,* November 1973, 54.

39. Bill Lawrence, *Six Presidents, Too Many Wars* (New York: Saturday Review Press, 1972), 227–228.

40. Sorensen, *Kennedy*, 124–125; India Edwards to John F. Kennedy, 8 April 1962, in folder "Office of Women's Activities, DNC,"

box 2, India Edwards papers, LBJL; Edwards, *Pulling No Punches,* 252; Katie S. Louchheim, *By the Political Sea* (Garden City, N.Y.: Doubleday, 1970), 135; Kenneth O'Donnell to India Edwards, 10 April 1962, in untitled folder [1960 clipping material and correspondence], box 1, India Edwards papers, LBJL; *New York Times,* 23 May 1962, clipping, in folder "Newspaper clips, 1962," box 10, Margaret Price papers, BHL.

41. MacKenzie, *Politics of Presidential Appointments,* 84, 196–197, 209; Burns, *John Kennedy,* 233–236, 266.

42. Frieda S. Miller to Mr. Moran, 17 August 1945, in folder "Women's Bureau," box 420, RG 174 (Schwellenbach), NA.

43. Judith Sealander, *As Minority Becomes Majority: Federal Reaction to the Phenomenon of Women in the Workforce* (Westport, Conn.; Greenwood Press, 1983).

44. Sylvia Beyer to Frieda Miller, 18 February 1947, in folder "FSM at ILO," box "Women's Bureau Statements and Press Releases, Correspondence," Frieda Miller papers, SL; "Meeting of the Labor Advisory Committee," 9 January 1947, in folder "Labor Advisory Committee, January 1947," box 943, RG 86, NA; "Meeting of the Labor Advisory Committee," 3 February 1947, in folder "Women's Bureau, Labor Advisory Committee, 1950–53," box "Committees, Women's Bureau," Frieda Miller papers, SL; "Meeting of the Labor Advisory Committee," 3 October 1947, in folder "Labor Advisory Committee, October 3, 1947," box 943, RG 86, NA; Frieda S. Miller, biographical notes, August 1956, SC 1104, WSHS; Barbara Sicherman and Carol Hurd Green (eds.), *Notable American Women: The Modern Period* (Cambridge, Mass.: Belknap Press, 1980), 478–479.

45. Department of Labor, press release, 11 December 1952, in folder "1953, Women's Bureau," box 9, RG 174 (Mitchell), NA.

46. Selma Borchardt to James P. Mitchell, 30 June 1954, and "Hearings before the Subcommittee of the Committee on Appropriations, House of Representatives, March 1954, Women's Bureau," folder 92–6, Katherine P. Ellickson papers, ALUA; Department of Labor press release, 30 September 1954, folder 3, and General Order no. 80, January 1955, folder 4, Alice K. Leopold papers, SL (General Order no. 80 officially established Leopold's position); *New York Times,* 30 September 1954; Telephone interview with Alice A. Morrison, 11 February 1981 (Alexandria, Va).

47. "John F. Kennedy, Voting Record on Measures of Interest to Labor," and William Green to John F. Kennedy, 22 August 1952, folder 37, Box 29, Legislative Reference Files, Meany Archives.

48. Parmet, *Jack,* 184–186; Burns, *John Kennedy,* 76–79.

49. Parmet, *Jack*, 388–393, 423–433; Burns, *John Kennedy*, 224–229; Hyman Bookbinder to Andrew Biemiller, 11 September 1959, folder 39, and George Meany to John F. Kennedy, 31 August 1960, folder 40, box 29, Legislative Reference Files, Meany Archives; *Washington Post*, 10 July 1960.

50. Transcript, Myer Feldman Oral History Interview, 6 August 1966, p. 379, 21 September 1968, pp. 19, 38, 45, 23, January 1966, p. 36, JFKL; Theodore Sorensen, *Decision-Making in the White House* (New York: Columbia University Press, 1963), 77; Tom Wicker, *JFK and LBJ* (New York: Morrow, 1968), 139; David Halberstam, *The Best and the Brightest* (New York: Random House, 1972), 71; AFL-CIO Executive Council, minutes, August 1962, folder 12, box 11, Executive Council Reference Files, William F. Schnitzler papers, Meany Archives; Telephone interview with Arthur Goldberg, 17 September 1985 (Washington, D.C.).

51. Mrs. Esther Peterson, biography, April 1964, in packet "Secretary of Labor Conference for Labor Editors," Esther Peterson papers (in Peterson's possession); *National Business Woman*, March 1961, 5; Esther Peterson interview with Kathy Kraft, 17 May 1975, SL; Transcript, Esther Peterson Oral History Interview, 1978, pp. 19–21, SL and University of Michigan; Interview with Esther Peterson, 4 October 1974 and 27 February 1978 (Washington, D.C.); Sorensen, *Kennedy*, 123–124; Draft transcript, Esther Peterson interview, 18 May 1966, pp. 1–3, JFKL; Draft transcript, Esther Peterson Oral History Interview, 22 January 1970, p. 16, JFKL; Transcript, Myer Feldman Oral History Interview, 23 January 1966, p. 36, JFKL; Parmet, *Jack*, 186, 422–423, 496–498, *Ashtabula [Ohio] Star-Beacon*, 9 June 1961, and *Tucson [Ariz.] Star*, 7 June 1961, clippings in folder "Labor's influence, news clippings," *Boston Record*, 15 February 1961, clipping, in folder "U.S. Department of Labor, Women's Bureau, Appointment, news clippings re: JFK appointees," box "NWCCR, Appointments to Women's Bureau, Assistant Secretary of Labor," Esther Peterson papers, SL; Sorensen, *Kennedy*, 53.

52. Sorensen, *Kennedy*, 277; Draft transcript, Esther Peterson interview, 18 May 1966, pp. 22–61, JFKL; [Esther Peterson] to Advance Teams, n.d., in folder "1960 correspondence with Labor," box "Political (Dem. Campaigns)," Esther Peterson papers, SL; Esther Peterson to Senator Kennedy et al., 23 September 1960, in folder "Peterson, Esther," box 202, DNC papers, JFKL.

53. Mary Anderson et al. to John F. Kennedy, 2 December 1960, in folder "Lists of Supporters," box "NWCCR, Appointments to Wom-

en's Bureau, Assistant Secretary of Labor," Esther Peterson papers, SL.

54. Mrs. Paul Douglas to John F. Kennedy, 13 December 1960, in folder "Appointments: government," box 1066, Prepresidential papers, JFKL; Elizabeth A. Magee to Louise Stitt, 8 December 1960, Esther Peterson papers, Giant Foods (Landover, Md.); Draft transcript, Esther Peterson interview, 18 May 1966, pp. 61–62, 22 January 1970, pp. 24, 27, JFKL; Esther Peterson to John F. Kennedy, 17 August 1961, in folder "John F. Kennedy, 1960–61," box "Political (Dem. Campaigns)," Esther Peterson papers, SL; *Washington Post*, 27 March 1961, clippings, Esther Peterson papers, Giant Foods (Landover, Md.); Arthur Goldberg to Pierre Salinger, 21 April 1961, in folder "1961 White House, President, April," box 24, RG 174 (Goldberg), NA; John F. Kennedy to the President of the Senate and the Speaker of the House, 4 May 1961, folder LE/FG 150-LE/215, box 473, WHCF, JFKL; Statement of Assistant Secretary of Labor George C. Lodge before the Education Subcommittee of the House Committee on Education and Labor on H.R. 6822, 15 May 1961, in folder "Assistant Secretary of Labor, 1961," box "NWCCR, Appointments to Women's Bureau, Assistant Secretary of Labor," Esther Peterson papers, SL; U.S. Congress, House, 87th Cong., 1st sess., 9 August 1961, *Congressional Record* 107: 15258–15264; U.S. Department of Labor, press release, 17 August 1961, Esther Peterson papers, Giant Foods (Landover, Md.).

55. Mrs. Esther Peterson, biography, April 1964, in packet "Secretary of Labor Conference for Labor Editors," Esther Peterson papers (in Peterson's possession).

56. Emma Guffey Miller to Katie Louchheim, 26 January 1962, in folder "Department of State, Letters of Congratulations, M–Z, 1962," box C17, Katie S. Louchheim papers, LC.

57. *Economist*, 11 August 1962, clipping, in folder "Edith Green, legislation, equal pay," box 62-12, Edith Green papers, OHS.

58. John W. Leslie to Pierre Salinger, 24 August 1962, folder FG 737, box 206, WHCF, JFKL.

CHAPTER 6

1. Valerie Kincade Oppenheimer, *The Female Labor Force in the United States: Demographic and Economic Factors Governing Its Growth and Changing Composition* (Westport, Conn.: Greenwood Press, 1976), 6, 11, 14, 21, 159–162, 167–168; Deborah S. Kligler, "The Effects of the

Employment of Married Women on Husband and Wife Roles: A Study in Culture Change" (Ph.D. diss., Yale University, 1954), 2, 3; Karen Anderson, *Wartime Women* (Westport, Conn.: Greenwood Press, 1981), 175.

2. *Wall Street Journal,* 30 October 1963, clipping, in folder "Women, General," box 105, DNC papers, LBJL.

3. Kligler, "Effects of Employment"; Morris J. Levitt, "Political Attitudes of American Women: A Study of Work and Education on Their Political Role" (Ph.D. diss., University of Maryland, 1965); U.S Department of Labor, Women's Bureau, "Background Facts on Women Workers in the United States," January 1962, Document VI-39, PCSW papers (Washington, D.C.).

4. James P. Mitchell to Sam Rayburn, 13 January 1961, in folder "1960, National Legislation, Department of Labor Draft Bills (1)," box 183, James P. Mitchell papers, DDEL; Frances A. Ambursen to Mrs. Morrison, 1 February 1961, Alice A. Morrison to Mrs. Peterson, 24 February 1961, Esther Peterson to Arthur Goldberg, 28 February 1961, and Alice A. Morrison to Esther Peterson, 28 February 1961, reel 59, DOL papers, JFKL.

5. Arthur Goldberg to Mr. Donahue, 13 March 1961, folder WA-3, box 92, RG 174 (Goldberg), NA; Alice A. Morrison to General Files, 9 March 1961, in folder "Equal Pay," box 1196, RG 86, NA.

6. "Meeting in Esther Peterson's office on equal pay bill Thursday, March 2, 1961, 2:00 P.M.," folder 92-11, Katherine P. Ellickson papers, ALUA; Esther Peterson to George P. Riley, 8 March 1961, in folder "Equal Pay," box 1196, RG 86, NA.

7. J. A. Beirne to Arthur Goldberg, 15 February 1961, reel 59, DOL papers, JFKL.

8. Arthur Goldberg to J. A. Beirne, 4 March 1961, folder WA-3, box 92, RG 174 (Goldberg), NA. See, for example, Esther Peterson to Margaret Mealey, 16 March 1961, in folder "Equal Pay," box 1196, RG 86, NA; Esther Peterson to Lois Frazier, 17 March 1961, Esther Peterson to Robert Simmons, 17 March 1961, draft letter to state labor departments, 16 March 1961, Esther Peterson to John Livingston, 21 March 1961, and Esther Peterson to Emily Chervenik, 4 April 1961, reel 59, DOL papers, JFKL.

9. Telephone interview with Morag M. Simchak, 14 August 1974 (Washington, D.C.); Interviews with Pearl Spindler and Sandra Bollhoefer, 15, 16, 17 July 1974 (Washington, D.C.); Bernice Sandler to the Editor, *Washington Post,* 24 September 1978; Interview with Esther Peterson, 27 February 1978 (Washington, D.C.).

10. John P. Earner, "Equal Pay for Equal Work: Federal Legisla-

tive Activity, 1945 to 1962," pp. 12–13, Legislative Reference Service, Library of Congress, in folder "Labor-Equal Pay for Equal Work," box 15, Maurine Neuberger papers, University of Oregon; Mary T. Norton to John F. Kennedy, 10 May 1951, and John F. Kennedy to Mary T. Norton, 6 June 1951, in folder "Equal Pay for Equal Work," box 3, Prepresidential papers, JFKL; "Deficiencies in Labor record of Senator Kennedy," 8 November 1960, in folder "1960 Political (November–December)," box 193, James P. Mitchell papers, DDEL; "Legislative Items Recommended by the President," 22 January 1962, in folder "Papers of the Democratic National Committee, 1960–1962," box 20, Margaret Price papers, BHL.

Journalist Nancy Dickerson claimed that John Kennedy "thought it ridiculous" to pay women the same wages as men and refused to hire her on his staff for that reason (Dickerson, *Among Those Present: A Reporter's View of Twenty-five Years in Washington* [New York: Random House, 1976], 19, 63).

11. George Riley to Esther Peterson, 22 March 1961, Esther Peterson to George Riley, 28 March 1961, and "Meeting of the National Committee on Equal Pay and the Women's Bureau," 6 April 1961, reel 59, DOL papers, JFKL.

12. "Bill W." to "Arthur," 4 May 1961, attached to Secretary of Labor to David Bell, 14 July 1961, folder LL-2-1, box 75, RG 174 (Goldberg), NA.

13. Esther Peterson to George Riley, 27 July 1961, folder 8, box 17, Legislative Reference Files, Meany Archives.

14. Administration bills were H.R. 8898, introduced 24 August 1961, and S. 2494, 30 August 1961; Dorothy A. Carroll to Esther Peterson, 18 August 1961, in folder "Equal Pay," box 1196, RG 86, NA; U.S. Congress, Senate, 87th Cong., 1st sess., 30 August 1961, *Congressional Record* 107: 17574-17576.

15. *Washington Star,* 13 February 1962, clipping, folder 91-5, Katherine P. Ellickson papers, ALUA; the President's Commission on the Status of Women, transcript of the meeting of 13 February 1962, Washington, D.C., p. 109, PCSW papers (Washington, D.C.).

16. *Washington Star,* 13 February 1962, clipping, folder 91-5, Katherine P. Ellickson papers, ALUA.

17. Laura H. Dale to Alice Morrison, 19 July 1961, in folder "Equal Pay," box 1196, RG 86, NA.

18. Interview with Esther Peterson, 17 June 1980, (Washington, D.C.); Alice A. Morrison to Esther Peterson, 9 March 1962, reel 59, DOL papers, JFKL; Alice A. Morrison to Esther Peterson, 30 January 1962, in folder "Equal Pay," box 1220, RG 86, NA; "Equal Pay Clauses

in Union Contracts, 1956" and addendum, uncatalogued papers of Esther Peterson, SL.

19. Leila Rupp and Verta Taylor, *Survival in the Doldrums: The American Women's Rights Movement, 1945 to the 1960s* (New York: Oxford University Press, 1987), 175.

20. U.S. Congress, House, Committee on Education and Labor, *Equal Pay for Equal Work, Hearings Before the Selected Subcommittee on Labor of the Committee on Education and Labor H.R. 10266 . . .* , Part 1: *Hearings Held in Washington, D.C.,* Part 2: *Hearings Held in N.Y., N.Y.,* 87th Cong., 2d sess., 1962; President's Commission on the Status of Women, Committee on Civil and Political Rights, transcript of the meeting of 28 May 1962, Washington, D.C., pp. 13–19, PCSW papers (Washington, D.C.); *New York Times,* 28 April 1962.

21. U.S. Congress, House, 87th Cong., 2d sess., 14 June 1962, *Congressional Record* 108: 10501.

22. U.S. Congress, House, 87th Cong., 2d sess., 25 July 1962, *Congressional Record* 108: 14767-14771; Alice K. Leopold to Irma Piepho, 30 April 1957, in folder "Equal Pay 4, National Equal Pay Committee," box 1096, RG 86, NA.

23. *New York Times,* 26 July 1961; U.S. Congress, House, 87th Cong., 2d sess., 25 July 1962, *Congressional Record* 108: 14747-14782. Neither this vote nor any other on equal pay legislation was recorded. No one discussed the prospect of comparing jobs unlike in character for the purposes of determining wage rates.

24. *Wall Street Journal,* 10 August 1962; U.S. Congress, Senate, 87th Cong., 2d sess., 11 August 1962, *Congressional Record* 108: 16245; Eleanor Roosevelt, column "By Eleanor Roosevelt," 27 July 1962, file 3163, Eleanor Roosevelt papers, FDRL.

25. "Here's the Issue," 17 September 1962, Esther Peterson papers (in Peterson's possession).

26. Theron J. Rice to Patrick McNamara, 24 August 1962, in folder "S. 2494," box H43, Wayne Morse papers, University of Oregon; President's Commission on the Status of Women, Committee on Civil and Political Rights, transcript of the meeting of 24 August 1962, Washington, D.C., pp. 25–27, and President's Commission on the Status of Women, transcript of the meeting of 2 October 1962, Washington, D.C., pp. 321–322, PCSW papers (Washington, D.C.); "Notes for Equal Pay Meeting," 18 September 1962, in folder "Equal Pay Act, 1962" box "Women," Esther Peterson papers, SL; U.S. Congress, Senate, 87th Cong., 2d sess., 3 October 1962, *Congressional Record* 108: 22081–22085; Earner, "Equal Pay for Equal Work," 26.

27. Earner, "Equal Pay for Equal Work," 26; Beatrice McConnell

to June Cedarleaf, 12 October 1962, and Patrick McNamara to Esther Peterson, 16 October 1962, reel 59, DOL papers, JFKL; Esther Peterson to Patrick McNamara, 5 November 1962, in folder "Congress, June–December 1962," box "Political (Dem. Campaigns)," Esther Peterson papers, SL; "Congress to Get Bills on Equal Treatment for Women," *Congressional Quarterly*, 28 December 1962, 2298–2299, clipping, Esther Peterson papers (in Peterson's possession); "Equal Pay Act of 1962," in folder "Papers of the Democratic National Committee, 1960–1962," box 20, Margaret Price papers, BHL.

28. Esther Peterson to Charles Donahue et al., 13 November 1962, Memorandum, 15 November 1962, "Meeting in Mrs. Peterson's office, November 15, 1962 on Equal Pay Proposals for 1963," 15 November 1962, and "Major Differences Between Equal Pay Bill H.R. 11677 as it passed the House and the Department of Labor's 1963 Proposal," 13 December 1962, folder 1-30, Morag Simchak papers, ALUA.

29. William B. Cannon to Legislative Liaison Officer, 3 January 1963, Norman J. Simler to the Council, 4 January 1963, and Walter Heller to William B. Cannon, 7 January 1963, reel 41, Walter Heller papers, JFKL.

30. "Memorandum for the Files—Council of Economic Advisers position on Equal Pay Bill—Esther Peterson, 8 January 1963," in folder "Equal Pay 1963," Peterson papers (in Peterson's possession); Walter Heller to Esther Peterson, 10 January 1963, reel 59, DOL papers, JFKL.

31. Norman J. Simler to the Council, 4 February 1963, reel 41, Walter Heller papers, JFKL.

32. Walter Heller to Kermit Gordon, 7 February 1963, reel 41, Walter Heller papers, JFKL.

33. Esther Peterson to W. Willard Wirtz, 13 February 1963, in folder "Equal Pay," Esther Peterson papers (in Peterson's possession).

34. Sorensen said later that Heller headed the most influential Council of Economic Advisers in history (Theodore Sorensen, *Kennedy*, [New York: Harper & Row, 1965], 265, 395). Administration bills were H.R. 3861, introduced 18 February 1963, and S. 910, 25 February 1963; U.S. Department of Labor press release, 14 February 1963, in folder "Equal Pay Clippings and Reference," box 63-5, Edith Green papers, OHS; "Administration Equal Pay Bill Is Taken to Senate, House Leaders," typed from *Daily Labor Report*, 14 February 1963, in folder "Equal Pay Act, 1963, bills," box "Women," Esther Peterson papers, SL.

35. U.S. Congress, House, 88th Cong., 1st sess., 21 February 1963,

*Congressional Record* 109: 2714; "Equal pay bills in the 88th Congress," 26 February 1963, folder 1-32, Morag Simchak papers, ALUA; "Statement by the AFL-CIO Executive Council," 23 February 1963, in folder "Equal Pay," box 1238, RG 86, NA; Morag Simchak to Esther Peterson, 26 February 1963, in brown envelope, Esther Peterson papers (in Peterson's possession); Edith Green to Katherine P. Ellickson, 2 August [1976], folder 90-31, Katherine P. Ellickson papers, ALUA.

36. "Chamber Attacks Equal Pay Bill," typed from *Daily Labor Report,* 28 February 1963, in folder "Equal Pay," Esther Peterson papers (in Peterson's possession).

37. "Questions raised at a meeting with the Committee on Labor Relations of the Glass Container Manufacturers Institute relative to the Equal Pay Bill," 27 February 1963, in folder "Equal Pay Bill," Esther Peterson papers (in Peterson's possession).

38. Charles Goodell to author, 29 August 1974; "Thumb Nail— H.R. 5110," n.d., in folder "Equal Pay Act 1963 bills" box "Women," Esther Peterson papers, SL; Charles Goodell to William Belknap, n.d., in folder "Amend Fair Labor Standards Act . . . ," box 31, Charles Goodell papers, Rare Books and Manuscripts Division, NYPL, Astor, Lenox, and Tilden Foundations.

39. "Outline of Mrs. Peterson's equal pay testimony," folder 1-32, Morag Simchak papers, ALUA; Esther Peterson, briefing book, Esther Peterson papers (in Peterson's possession); U.S. Congress, Senate, Committee on Labor and Public Welfare, *Equal Pay Act of 1963, Hearings Before a Subcommittee of the Committee on Labor and Public Welfare, Senate, on S. 882 and S. 910,* 88th Cong., 1st sess., 1963.

40. U.S. Congress, Senate, Committee on Labor and Public Welfare, *Equal Pay Act of 1963, Hearings Before a Subcommittee of the Committee on Labor and Public Welfare, Senate, on S. 882 and S. 910,* 88th Cong., 1st sess., 1963; "Main objections to equal pay bill of 1963 made by witnesses at hearings—March 25 and 26," reel 43, DOL papers, JFKL.

41. Morag Simchak to Esther Peterson, 2 April 1963, in folder "Equal Pay, 11 June 1964, plans for conference," Esther Peterson papers (in Peterson's possession); Memorandum for the record, 18 April 1963, uncatalogued papers of Esther Peterson, SL.

42. Frank Thompson to Esther Peterson, 8 April 1963, and Morag Simchak to Esther Peterson, 18 April 1963, reel 59, DOL papers, JFKL; Thomas J. Rice to Wayne Morse, 1 May 1963, in folder "S. 1409," box H-49, Wayne Morse papers, University of Oregon; Untitled memorandum, 9 May 1963, folder 1-34, Morag Simchak papers, ALUA; U.S. Congress, Senate, 88th Cong., 1st sess., 17 May 1963, *Congressional Record* 109: 8916; U.S. Congress, House Committee on

Education and Labor, *Legislative History of the Equal Pay Act of 1963*, Pub. L. 88-38, 88th Congress, H.R. 6060 and S. 1409, Committee Print, 88th Cong., 1st sess., December 1963.

43. Esther Peterson to Edna M. Johnson, 9 May 1963, in folder "Equal Pay," box 1238, RG 86, NA.

44. Esther Peterson to David Lasser, 22 April 1963, reel 59, DOL papers, JFKL.

45. Andrew J. Biemiller to Dear Congressman, 22 May 1963, in folder "88th Cong., Education and Labor—Labor," box 43, Martha Griffiths papers, BHL.

46. U.S. Congress, Senate, 88th Cong., 1st sess., 28 May 1963, *Congressional Record* 109: 9192–9218.

47. Ibid., 9761–9762.

48. *Washington Post,* 11 June 1963, clipping, folder 1-26, Morag Simchak papers, ALUA; White House, press release, 10 June 1963, in folder "Press releases January 1961–November 1967," box 9, Margaret Price papers, BHL; List of invitees, in folder "Equal Pay White House," and Esther Peterson to Lawrence O'Brien, 31 May 1963, in folder "Equal Pay Bill," Esther Peterson papers (in Peterson's possession). Text of Equal Pay Act can be found in Appendix 1.

49. Fair Labor Standards Act of 1938, as amended, 29 U.S.C. sec. 206, subsec. d (1964); Patrick Tanabe, "Views of Women's Work in Public Policy in the United States: Social Security and Equal Pay Legislation, 1935–1967" (Ph.D. diss., Bryn Mawr College, 1973), 68–69.

50. Caroline Davis to Esther Peterson, n.d., reel 59, DOL papers, JFKL. See also remarks of Margaret Hickey, President's Commission on the Status of Women, transcript of the meeting of 27 May 1963, Washington, D.C., p. 16, PCSW papers (Washington, D.C.); Telephone interview with Alice A. Morrison, 11 March 1981 (Alexandria, Va).

51. Jo Freeman, *The Politics of Women's Liberation* (New York: McKay, 1975), 177. Judith Hole and Ellen Levine assert that "some activists consider the Equal Pay Act the only law dealing with sex discrimination that is anywhere near properly enforced" (Hole and Levine, *Rebirth of Feminism* [New York: Quadrangle Books, 1971], 29).

## CHAPTER 7

1. Esther Peterson Recorded Interview by Ronald J. Grele, 18 May 1966, p. 23, Recorded Interview by Ann M. Campbell, 20 January 1970, pp. 55–57, JFKL; Oral History Program; Interview with Esther Peterson, 10 June 1978 (Washington, D.C.); Eva vB. Hansl to Edith

Green, 6 January 1961, in folder "Working Widows," box 61-11, Edith Green papers, OHS; Eva vB. Hansl et al. to John F. Kennedy, 20 January 1961, in folder "PCSW background 1961," box "PCSW #1," Esther Peterson papers, SL; Transcript, Katherine P. Ellickson Oral History Interview, 15 December 1974, p. 27, ALUA; Katherine P. Ellickson, "The President's Commission on the Status of Women: Its Formation, Functioning, and Contribution," January 1976, ALUA; Telephone interview with Arthur Goldberg, 17 September 1985 (Washington, D.C.).

2. Kathryn McHale to Harry S. Truman, 10 May 1948 (summarized by William D. Hassett), file 120, box 534, HSTL.

3. Arthur M. Hill to the President, 29 June 1948, file 120, box 534, HSTL.

4. Althea Hottel to the President, 15 September 1950, file 120, box 534, HSTL.

5. National Manpower Council, *Womanpower: A Statement by the National Manpower Council with Chapters by the Council Staff* (New York: Columbia University Press, 1957), 6.

6. Alice K. Leopold to the Undersecretary, 15 April 1957, and "Summary of Comments by Miss Leopold and Mrs. Wickens on Recommendation Contained in the National Manpower Council's Report on Womanpower" (draft), 17 April 1957, in folder "Women," box 5, RG 174 (Cass), NA; Labor Advisory Committee, minutes of meeting, 13 November 1953, in folder "1-1-8-1 work materials for Advisory Committee," box 942, RG 86, NA.

7. Secretary of Labor to the Undersecretary, 29 March 1957, in folder "1957 Women's Bureau, General," box 193, RG 174 (Mitchell), NA; Aryness Joy Wickens to the Undersecretary, 29 March 1957 [n.b., there are two memos with this date, both of which are cited].

8. Eva vB. Hansl to Edith Green, 6 January 1961, in folder "Working Widows," box 61-11, Edith Green papers, OHS; Eva vB. Hansl et al. to John F. Kennedy, 20 January 1961, in folder "PCSW background 1961," box "PCSW #1," Esther Peterson papers, SL; Telephone interview with Arthur Goldberg, 17 September 1985 (Washington, D.C.); Transcript, Caroline Ware Oral History Interview, 27, 28, 29 January 1982, pp. 138ff., SL; Dollie Robinson to Esther Peterson, 31 March 1961, in folder "PCSW, Background 1951," box "PCSW #1," Esther Peterson papers, SL.

9. *Washington Post*, 13 February 1962.

10. Notes on meeting concerning plans for the President's Commission on the Status of Women, 20 December 1961, folder 91-17, Katherine P. Ellickson papers, ALUA; *Current Status* (bulletin of the PCSW),

November 1962, PCSW papers (Washington, D. C.); Katherine Ellickson, "Mrs. Eleanor Roosevelt's Contribution to the Status of Women, 1962," Ellickson file, Eleanor Roosevelt papers, FDRL; Herbert Parmet, *JFK: The Presidency of John F. Kennedy* (New York: Dial Press, 1983), 35–36; William E. Leuchtenburg, *In the Shadow of FDR: From Harry Truman to Ronald Reagan* (Ithaca, N.Y.: Cornell University Press, 1983), 71–81, 88–89, 92–96, 100–103.

11. Frances Ambursen to Esther Peterson, 6 September 1961, in folder "PCSW members," box "PCSW #1," Esther Peterson papers, SL; Esther Peterson, Recorded Interview by Ann M. Campbell, 20 January 1970, pp. 57–60, JFKL Oral History Program.

12. President's Commission on the Status of Women, *American Women,* (Washington, D.C.: GPO, 1963), 85; Marguerite Rawalt, *A History of the National Federation of Business and Professional Women's Clubs, Inc.,* vol. 2: *1944–1960* (Washington, D.C.: NFBPWC, 1969), p. 4; Susan Becker, "An Intellectual History of the National Woman's Party, 1920–1941," (Ph.D. diss., Case Western Reserve University, 1975), 251–252. For a discussion of the way in which administrations control presidential commissions by the selection of members, see Thomas R. Wolanin, *Presidential Advisory Commissions: Truman to Nixon* (Madison: University of Wisconsin Press, 1975), 75–81. The complete list of commission participants can be found in Appendix 3.

13. Executive Order 10980, 14 December 1961, 3 C.F.R. (1959–1963), 500–501 (text in Appendix 2).

14. Goldberg to John F. Kennedy, 13 December 1961, and White House, press release, 14 December 1961, in black looseleaf notebook, box 4644, Eleanor Roosevelt papers, FDRL.

15. Esther Peterson to Myer Feldman, 12 March 1963, in folder "Final Report Materials, Hilton," PCSW papers (Washington, D.C.).

16. U.S. President, *Public Papers of the President of the United States* (Washington, D.C.: Office of the *Federal Register,* National Archives and Records Service, 1961–), John F. Kennedy, 12 February 1962, item 43.

17. Transcript, "Prospects of Mankind #10" (23 May 1962), in folder "Mrs. Roosevelt—Prospects of Mankind," and President's Commission on the Status of Women, Committee on New and Expanded Services, transcript of the meeting of 24 January, 1963 Washington, D.C., PCSW papers (Washington, D.C.); Telephone interview with Esther Peterson, 4 October 1974 (Washington, D.C.); *Washington Post,* 13 February 1962; Esther Peterson to Myer Feldman, 12 March 1963, in folder "Final Report Materials, Hilton," PCSW papers (Washington, D.C.); Arthur Goldberg to Timothy J. Reardon, 18 January 1962, in

folder "1962 Commission PCSW (Jan.–March)," box 29, RG 174 (Goldberg), NA; Interview with Catherine East, 6 July 1978 (Arlington, Va.); President's Commission on the Status of Women, minutes of the fourth meeting, 1–2 October, 1962, in folder "PCSW report meeting, December 15,1962," Peterson papers (in Peterson's possession).

18. "Proposed guidelines on subcommittees," PCSW Doc. 11, 8 February 1962, in folder "Commission meeting, February 12–13, 1962," PCSW papers (Washington, D.C.); President's Commission on the Status of Women, minutes of the first meeting, 12–13 February, 1962, PCSW Doc. 18, box 4644, Eleanor Roosevelt papers, FDRL; Staff meeting, 17 December 1962, folder 93-13, Katherine P. Ellickson papers, ALUA. A full list of committee members can be found in Appendix 3.

19. John F. Kennedy to Alma Lutz, 11 February 1957, in folder "Equal Rights Amendment, December 5, 1956–January 28, 1958," box 690, Prepresidential papers, JFKL.

20. John F. Kennedy to Adele E. Moroney, 5 February 1958, in folder "Equal Rights Amendment, February 4, 1958–June 5, 1958," box 690, Prepresidential papers, JFKL.

21. John F. Kennedy memorandum, 22 June 1960, reel 106, NWP papers (microfilm ed.).

22. "Advance platform hearings of the Democratic National Committee," 27 June 1960, and "Statement of Mrs. Esther Peterson," 7 July 1960, in folder "ERA 1960–61," box "Women," Esther Peterson papers, SL.

Peterson later asserted that the views she expressed on protective labor legislation reflected the convictions of the AFL-CIO. Her own opinion, she said, was that the labor legislation that applied exclusively to women was no longer appropriate. Catherine East, who worked with Esther Peterson on the President's Commission on the Status of Women, supports this contention (Telephone interview with Esther Peterson, 23 September 1981 [Washington, D.C.]; Telephone interview with Catherine East, 31 July 1981, [Arlington, Va.]).

23. "Hearing on Equal Rights for Women plank in the Democratic Platform," National Democratic Convention, Los Angeles, California, 11–17 July, 1960, and "Mr. Chairman and fellow members of the Platform Committee," [7 July 1960], reel 106, NWP papers (microfilm ed.).

24. The Republicans continued to support the ERA in their platform, despite Peterson's testimony. Marjorie Longwell to Alice Paul (telegram), 7 July 1960, 13 July 1960, Emma Newton to Mary Sinclair Crawford, 24 August 1960, "Plank on Equality for Women in the

Republican Platform, adopted in Chicago, Illinois July, 1960," Emma Guffey Miller to Clara Wolf, 16 February 1961, and Marjorie Longwell to Alice Paul (telegram), 13 July 1960, reel 106, NWP papers (microfilm ed.); Emma Guffey Miller to Joseph Clark, 28 October 1963, folder 73, and Emma Guffey Miller to Clare B. Williams, 17 August 1960, folder 66, box 4, Emma Guffey Miller papers, SL; AFL-CIO, Industrial Union Division, press release, 20 July 1960, and "Statement of Mrs. Esther Peterson," 21 July 1960, in folder "ERA, 1960–61," box "Women," Esther Peterson papers, SL; Julia Thompson et al. to Walter Reuther, 25 July 1960, in folder "1960 Misc. Correspondence," box "Political (Dem. campaigns)," Esther Peterson papers, SL; Carl Hayden to B. Kay Walters, 28 November 1960, folder 4, box 268, Carl Hayden papers, Arizona State University; Donald B. Johnson (ed.), *National Party Platforms*, 2 vols. (Urbana: University of Illinois Press, 1978), 2:583, 589, 610, 614.

25. Marion Sayward to Walter Martin, 5 August 1960, and Marion Sayward to Marjorie Longwell, 9 August 1960, reel 106, NWP papers (microfilm ed.).

26. Herbert Klein to Emma Guffey Miller and Perle Mesta, 1 September 1960, and "Statement by the Vice President on the Equal Rights Amendment," 2 September 1960, reel 106, NWP papers (microfilm ed.); *Los Angeles Times*, 3 September 1960, in folder "ERA Special re: NWP, 1960," box "Women," Esther Peterson papers, SL.

27. Emma Guffey Miller to John Kennedy, 3 September 1960, folder 67, box 4, Emma Guffey Miller papers, SL.

28. "Letter from Kennedy to Emma Guffey Miller (Women's [sic] Party)," 28 September 1960," in folder "ERA Special re: NWP, 1960," box "Women," Esther Peterson papers, SL.

29. John Kennedy to Emma Guffey Miller, 28 September 1960, reel 106, (microfilm ed.) NWP papers; John Kennedy to Emma Guffey Miller, 28 September 1960 (typed copy with handwritten amendments), in folder "ERA Special re: NWP, 1960," box "Women," Esther Peterson papers, SL; John Kennedy to Emma Guffey Miller, 7 October 1960, and Mary Kennedy to Emma Guffey Miller, 12 October 1960, reel 106, NWP papers (microfilm ed.).

30. Emma Guffey Miller to John Kennedy (telegram), 11 December 1960, Miller to Victoria Gilbert (telegram), 11 December 1960, and Miller to William Green, 14 December 1960, reel 106, NWP papers (microfilm ed.).

31. *Washington Post*, 16 April 1961, in folder "ERA newspapers clippings," Women's Bureau, DOL (Washington, D.C.).

32. Miller pretended not to notice the discrepancy between Kenne-

dy's amended campaign letter and Goldberg's response in May 1961. Emma Guffey Miller to Mrs. Forrest, 18 April 1961, and Arthur Goldberg to Marjorie Longwell, 4 May 1961, reel 106, NWP papers (microfilm ed.); Esther Peterson to Myer Feldman, 12 May 1961, in folder "ERA, 1960–61," box "Women," Esther Peterson papers, SL.

33. National Woman's party, minutes of meeting, 16 September 1961, reel 115, NWP papers (microfilm ed.).

34. Emma Guffey Miller to Esther [?], 25 September 1961, reel 107, NWP papers (microfilm ed.); U.S. Congress, House, "Equal Rights for Women," 87th Cong., 1st sess., 30 August 1961, *Congressional Record* 107: 17644; Morag Simchak to Esther Peterson, 25 September 1961, in folder "PCSW, background, 1961," box "PCSW #1," Esther Peterson papers, SL; Emma Guffey Miller to James Eastland, 20 October 1961, S. J. Res. 142, Bill Files, Committee on the Judiciary, Records of the U.S. Senate, RG 46, NA.

35. Esther Peterson to Clara Dunn, 5 April 1961, and Eva vB. Hansl to Edith Green, 14 April 1961, in folder "Pending file—Equal pay for equal work," box 61-11, Edith Green papers, OHS; "Need for a commission on the status of women," 1 May 1961, and Katherine Ellickson to Esther Peterson, 5 May 1961, in folder "PCSW background 1961," box "PCSW #1," Esther Peterson papers, SL; "February 28 [1961] discussion with trade union women." folder 90-31, Katherine P. Ellickson papers, ALUA.

36. Mildred Barber to Esther Peterson, 21 March 1961, in folder "PCSW background 1961," box "PCSW #1," Esther Peterson papers, SL.

37. Esther Peterson to Myer Feldman, 6 June 1961 (plus attachments), in folder "PCSW background 1961," box "PCSW #1," Esther Peterson papers, SL; Draft, Secretary of Labor to the President, 17 July 1961 (plus attachments), folder FG 737, box 206, WHCF, JFKL.

38. "Statement by Esther Peterson," folder 91-12, Katherine P. Ellickson papers, ALUA; Arthur Goldberg to John Kennedy, 13 December 1961, and White House, press release, 14 December 1961, in black looseleaf notebook, box 4644, Eleanor Roosevelt papers, FDRL; Executive Order 10908, 14 December 1961, 3 C.F.R. (1959–1963), 500–501; Alice Morrison to Esther Peterson, 10 October 1963, in folder "Briefing 3," box "PCSW #1," Esther Peterson papers, SL.

39. Caroline Davis to Esther Peterson, 15 December 1961, in folder "Peterson's letters," PCSW papers (Washington, D.C.); Katherine Peden to Viola Hymes, 29 December 1961, in folder "PCSW alphabetical (Liaison Federal Government) (1 of 3)," BPW Archives (Washington, D.C.).

40. *Washington Post,* 26 December 1961.

41. *Christian Science Monitor,* 15 December 1961. Interview with Evelyn Harrison, 12 September 1978 (Washington, D.C.).

42. Emanuel Celler, press release, 15 December 1961, and Arthur Goldberg to Emanuel Celler, 15 December 1961, in folder "H. J. Res. 92-87(1) Legal Status of Women 3," box 408, Emanuel Celler papers, LC.

43. Emma Guffey Miller to Elizabeth Conkey, 15 December 1961, reel 107, NWP papers (microfilm ed.).

44. Alice Paul to Mary Seebach, 27 December 1961, and Miller to Richard Lester, 28 March 1962, reel 107, NWP papers (microfilm ed.).

45. Arthur Goldberg to Emanuel Celler, 6 February 1962, in folder "LL-2-2 Judiciary 1962," box 69, RG 174 (Goldberg), NA; Draft letter, Special Assistant to the President, National Federation of Business and Professional Woman's Clubs, n.d. [early 1962], in folder "ERA 1962," box "Women," Esther Peterson papers, SL; Estes Kefauver to Mrs. Franklin D. Roosevelt, 14 February 1962, attached to Esther Peterson to Katherine Ellickson, 27 February 1962, in folder "PCSW Correspondence with Congress and Cabinet," box "PCSW #1," Esther Peterson papers, SL; Carl Hayden, draft letter, n.d., folder 3, box 268, Carl Hayden papers, Arizona State University; "Summary of H.J. Res. 55—complete to February 11, 1963," in folder "ERA, 1963 sponsors," box 50, Katherine St. George papers, Cornell University; Estes Kefauver to Emanuel Celler, 18 March 1963 (and handwritten notes), in folder "Legislative file, H.J. Res. 92-87(1), Legal Status of Women no. 1," box 408, Emanuel Celler papers, LC.

46. Eva Parshalle to Emma Guffey Miller, March 1962, reel 107, NWP papers (microfilm ed.).

47. See folders "Potential members—Lists" (1) and (2), 90–21 and 90–22, Katherine P. Ellickson papers, ALUA; "Recommended list of people to be considered for members of the President's Commission on Women in American Democracy," Elizabeth Carpenter to Esther Peterson, 18 August 1961, Frances Ambursen to Esther Peterson, 6 September 1961, and [untitled lists], 3 August 1961, in folder "PCSW members," box "PCSW # 1," Esther Peterson papers, SL.

The commission chairman, Eleanor Roosevelt had opposed the Equal Rights Amendment until the 1950s, when she withdrew her objection. She never became an advocate of it, but in May 1962 she told the Lucy Stone League: "Many of us opposed the amendment because we felt it would do away with protection in the labor field. Now with unionization, there is no reason why you shouldn't have it if you want it." By the time the Commission took up the issue, in October 1962, the former first lady had fallen ill. She never participated in any of the Commission discussions on the ERA (*New York Times,* 6 May 1962).

48. The National Woman's party reciprocated Green's enmity; Alice Paul described Green as "probably the greatest opponent of the Equal Rights Amendment on the Commission next to Mrs. Peterson" (Alice Paul to Marjorie Longwell, 2 April 1962, reel 107, NWP papers [microfilm ed.]). Emma Guffey Miller to Katie Louchheim, 26 February 1962, in folder "Department of State, Letters of Congratulations, M–Z, 1962," box C17, Katie S. Louchheim papers, LC; Genevieve Blatt to Emma Guffey Miller, 27 March 1962, Emma Guffey Miller to John Kennedy (draft), n.d., folder 69, and Alice Paul to Emma Guffey Miller, 18 July 1963, folder 72, box 4, Emma Guffey Miller papers, SL; Stephen Shulman to T. J. Reardon, Jr., 12 March 1962 (plus attachments), in folder "Civil and Political Rights—correspondence, March–December 1962" box "PCSW #2," Esther Peterson papers, SL; Emma Guffey Miller to John Kennedy, 26 April 1963, and Esther Peterson to Claude Desautels, n.d., attached to draft of letter to Emma Guffey Miller, 7 May 1963, in folder "White House/PCSW, 1963–66," box "Political (Dem. campaigns)," Esther Peterson papers, SL.

49. Emma Guffey Miller to Elizabeth Stanton, 1 February 1963, reel 108, NWP papers (microfilm ed.).

50. Nina Horton Avery to Emma Guffey Miller, 13 July 1963, Nina Horton Avery to Lee White, 15 July 1963, and Lee White to Nina Horton Avery, 12 August 1963, reel 108, NWP papers (microfilm ed.); Esther Peterson to Lee White, 7 August 1963, attached to Nina Horton Avery to Lee White, 13 September 1963, folder HU3, box 374, WHCF, JFKL. For a fuller discussion of the character of the National Woman's party, see Leila Rupp and Verta Taylor, *Survival in the Doldrums: The American Women's Rights Movement, 1945 to the 1960s* (New York: Oxford University Press, 1987).

51. Esther Peterson to Daniel Patrick Moynihan, 3 April 1963, in folder "ERA, 1963," box "Women," Esther Peterson papers, SL.

52. Esther Peterson to Mary F. Anderson, 24 June 1963, in folder "Commission materials, folder 2," box 1, PCSW papers, JFKL.

53. President's Commission on the Status of Women, transcript of the meeting of 12 February 1962, Washington, D.C., pp. 51–53, PCSW papers (Washington, D.C.).

54. Rough draft, "Political and Civil Status," in folder "Biogra-

phies, Members of Committee, Civil and Political Rights," CPR papers, PCSW.

55. PCSW, *American Woman,* 77–78; Interview with Marguerite Rawalt, 9 November 1984 (Arlington, Va.).

56. "Court decisions determining the validity of laws which distinguish on the basis of sex," n.d., Doc. II-9, CPR papers, PCSW; see folder "Inquire Replies," PCSW papers (Washington, D.C.); see folder "Jury Compositions (CPR)," CPR papers, PCSW; "Information paper on civil and political rights of women," 5 February 1962, Doc. II-2, PCSW papers; Committee on Civil and Political Rights, minutes of first meeting, 28 May 1962, in folder "Materials used at May 28, 1962 meeting," CPR papers, PCSW; "Summary, matters dealt with by Political and Civil Rights Committee, meeting of May 28, 1962," Doc. II-4, PCSW papers (Washington, D.C.); Committee on Civil and Political Rights, "Report of meeting held August 24, 1962," Doc. II-8, PCSW papers (Washington, D.C.); "Summary of Activities, Political and Civil Rights Committee, October 1–2, 1962," Doc. II-7, PCSW papers (Washington, D.C.); Telephone interview with Pauli Murray, 12 November 1981 (Baltimore, Md.).

The committee decided not to discuss birth control laws. When Pauli Murray raised the issue, Florence Murray, a Rhode Island judge, warned: "You are walking right into the face of something that will kill this commission off" (Committee on Civil and Political Rights, transcript of the meeting of 28 May 1962, pp. 147–149, CPR papers, PCSW).

57. Committee on Civil and Political Rights, transcript of the meeting of 24 August 1962, pp. 81–83, CPR papers, PCSW. The "Brandeis brief," written by Josephine Goldmark and Louis Brandeis, was submitted to the Supreme Court in the 1908 case of *Muller* v. *Oregon* (208 U.S. 412). It devoted eighty-seven pages to anecdotal data culled primarily from reports of factory inspectors and testimony of witnesses before legislative investigating committees to show that long hours of work in factories and laundries resulted in ill health of women workers and their children. Brandeis argued that women suffered more from such conditions than men did because of their physical characteristics and that sexual differences justified legislation restricting the hours women could work. The Supreme Court agreed, validating state labor legislation for women for the first time. William A. Chafe, *The American Woman: Her Changing Social, Economic, and Political Roles, 1920–1970* (New York: Oxford University Press, 1972), 128; Judith Baer, *The Chains of Protection: The Judicial Response to Women's Labor Legis-*

*lation* (Westport, Conn.: Greenwood Press, 1978), 57–67; "Draft memorandum of applicability of the Fourteenth Amendment to state statutes and administrative or executive practices which distinguish on the basis of sex," 24 August 1962, CPR papers, PCSW.

58.  Katherine Ellickson to Pauli Murray, 4 October 1962, in folder "Pauli Murray—Correspondence," PCSW papers (Washington, D.C.); Pauli Murray to Katherine Ellickson, 13 October 1962, Pauli Murray papers, SL.

59.  "A proposal to reexamine the applicability of the fourteenth amendment to state laws and practices which discriminate on the basis of sex per se," December 1962, Doc. II-20, PCSW papers (Washington, D.C.). Marguerite Rawalt deeply resented Peterson's failure to let her know of her plans to ask Murray to make a presentation (Interview with Marguerite Rawalt, 9 November 1984 [Arlington, Va.]).

60.  Esther Peterson to Pauli Murray, 11 November 1963, in folder "Pauli Murray—Correspondence," PCSW papers (Washington, D.C.).

61.  See, for example, Mary Eastwood to Emma Guffey Miller, 8 February 1963, in folder "General Correspondence, Civil and Political Rights Committee," PCSW papers (Washington, D.C.).

62.  Pauli Murray to Edith Green, 24 February 1963, in box "Misc. Box A," Edith Green papers, OHS.

63.  Anna Rose Hawkes to Mary Eastwood, 26 February 1963 (plus attachments), in folder "Materials used at March 8–9, 1963 meeting," CPR papers, PCSW.

64.  "Statement of Mrs. Samuel Brown before the Committee on Civil and Political Rights of the President's Commission on the Status of Women," 8 March 1963, Doc. II-35, PCSW papers (Washington, D.C.).

65.  Margery Leonard to Emma Guffey Miller, 16 February 1963, reel 108, NWP papers (microfilm ed.).

66.  Miriam Holden to Anita Pollitzer, 16 February 1963, reel 108, NWP papers (microfilm ed.).

67.  Committee on Civil and Political Rights, transcript of meeting, 8 March 1963, pp. 1–130, CPR papers, PCSW.

68.  Mrs. Joseph McCarthy to Edith Green, 5 March 1963, in folder "Materials used at March 8–9, 1963 meeting," CPR papers, PCSW. The ACLU later supported Murray's plan enthusiastically (Dorothy Kenyon to Board of Directors, 28 March 1963, in folder "Equal Rights— Civil and Political Rights," PCSW papers [Washington, D.C.]).

69.  Committee on Civil and Political Rights, transcript of the meeting of 8 March 1963, p. 43, CPR papers, PCSW.

70.  Ibid., 183–184.

71. Ibid., 125, 146, 180–187.

72. Ibid., 193–194.

73. Ibid., 194–199.

74. Pauli Murray to Edith Green et al., 12 March 1963, in folder "White House, President's Commission on the Status of Women," box 63-2, Edith Green papers, OHS; "Tentative draft recommendation on protection of the rights of women under the Constitution," n.d. [19 March 1963], Doc. II-42, PCSW papers (Washington, D.C.); Judith Patterson, *Be Somebody: A Biography of Marguerite Rawalt* (Austin, Tex.: Eakin Press, 1986), 142.

75. Committee on Civil and Political Rights, transcript of the meeting of 5 April 1963, pp. 75–120, box 14, PCSW papers, JFKL; Patterson, *Be Somebody*, 143.

76. President's Commission on the Status of Women, transcript of the meeting of 23 April 1963, Washington, D.C., p. 151, PSCW papers (Washington, D.C.).

77. Ibid., 23 April 1963, pp. 151–194, 24 April 1963, p. 343.

78. Ibid., 23 April 1963, pp. 151–194, 24 April 1963, p. 343; President's Commission on the Status of Women, Revised draft no. 1, Recommendation 4, attached to Katherine Ellickson to Norbert Schlei, 18 April 1963, in folder "Recommendations, Civil and Political Rights Committee," CPR papers, PCSW.

79. President's Commission on the Status of Women, transcript of the meeting of 24 April 1963, Washington, D.C., pp. 460–462, PCSW papers (Washington, D.C.).

80. Ibid., 23 April 1963, pp. 80–83, 94–96, 125–136, 143–181 (see esp. 178–180), 190–195.

81. PCSW, *American Women*, 44–45.

82. Esther Peterson to Carl Hayden, 10 October 1963, folder 3, box 268, Carl Hayden papers, Arizona State University.

83. "Statement by the National Woman's Party with regard to the report just issued by the President's Commission on the Status of Women," [October 1963], reel 108, NWP papers (microfilm ed.); "Reports by the President's Commission on the Status of Women, analysis of the report by the National Woman's Party," n.d., reel 108, NWP papers. The NWP had itself tried in the past to finance test cases of this sort (Susan D. Becker, "An Intellectual History of the National Woman's Party, 1920–1941," [Ph.D. diss., Case Western Reserve University, 1975], 154).

84. Rupp and Taylor, *Survival in the Doldrums*, 438.

85. Alice Paul to Mary Kennedy, 23 October 1963, reel 108, NWP papers (microfilm ed.).

86. Carl Hayden to Hazel Harvey Quaid, 18 October 1963, reel 108, NWP papers (microfilm ed.).

87. Alice Paul to Mary Kennedy, 23 October 1963, reel 108, NWP papers (microfilm ed.).

88. Alice Paul to Carl Hayden, 30 October 1963, and Marjorie Greenbie to Emma Guffey Miller, 14 November 1963, reel 108, NWP papers (microfilm ed.); untitled minutes of meeting, 6 November 1963, in folder "General Correspondence, Civil and Political Rights Committee," PCSW papers (Washington, D.C.).

89. PCSW, *American Women,* 45.


## CHAPTER 8

1. Executive Order 10980, 14 December 1961, in President's Commission on the Status of Women, *American Women* (Washington, D.C.: GPO, 1963), 76.

2. *Washington Post,* 24 May 1962, clipping, folder 91-5, Katherine P. Ellickson papers, ALUA. The article quoted other cabinet wives expressing similar sentiments.

3. Draft reply for the signature of a special assistant to the president, in folder "General Correspondence, PCSW, 12/61–12/62," PCSW papers (Washington, D.C.).

4. "Notes by Mr. Bookbinder," 16 June 1962, in folder "General Correspondence," PCSW papers (Washington, D.C.).

5. Margaret Mealey to Esther Peterson, 8 March 1963, in folder "Background memo, Dr. Ware, folder 1," box 1, PCSW papers, JFKL.

6. President's Commission on the Status of Women, *Report of the Committee on Home and Community* (Washington, D.C.: GPO, 1963), 9.

7. President's Commission on the Status of Women, transcript of the meeting of 1 April 1963, Washington, D.C., pp. 11–12, PCSW papers (Washington, D.C.).

8. Ibid., 11 February 1963, pp. 91–92, 1 April 1963, pp. 5–6; Interview with Richard A. Lester, 22 March 1974 (Princeton, N.J.). At a meeting of the Civil and Political Rights Committee, Harriet Pilpel, a New York attorney, responded to Katherine Ellickson's assertion that the commission would be more likely to act on a resolution framed more generally than the one Pilpel had been proposing, by saying: "I am disinclined to state my view in view of what Mrs. Ellickson says. She knows what the Commission wants. If the Commission doesn't want it, I won't urge it" (Committee on Civil and Political Rights, transcript of the meeting of 9 March 1963, pp. 331–333, in box "Misc. Box A," Edith Green papers, OHS). Myer Feldman ob-

served, talking about the report of the Panel on Mental Retardation, that part of his job was to "avoid anything that would be embarrassing to the President." He therefore went over the panel's report to "make sure that there weren't any outlandish recommendations." Any such group, he said, was "not completely independent, except in very rare instances" (Transcript, Myer Feldman Oral History interview, 21 September 1968, pp. 8–10, JFKL).

See David Burner and Thomas West, *The Torch Is Passed: The Kennedy Brothers and American Liberalism* (New York: Atheneum, 1984), for a discussion of the liberalism of the Kennedy administration.

9. PCSW, *American Women*, 10, 16, 30.

10. Section 165, "Revised Statutes and Opinion of the Attorney General of September 17, 1934," Doc. IV-24, PCSW papers (Washington, D.C.).

11. J. Stanley Lemons, *The Women Citizen: Social Feminism to the 1920s* (Urbana: University of Illinois Press, 1975), 77–78; O. Glenn Stahl to the commission, 19 September 1957, file 38-2, CSC; "Background Information on Women in the Federal Government," December 1926, in folder "Women Executives—Federal Woman's Award Winners," FE papers, PCSW; Catherine East to John Macy, 13 June 1963, in black notebook "Debate—Section 165 Revised Statutes," FE papers, PCSW; U.S. Department of Labor, Women's Bureau, "In the Federal Service: Equal Opportunity and Equal Pay," January 1965, reel 16, DOL records, LBJL; J. Lee Rankin to Hon. Charles C. Diggs, Jr., 16 March 1955, in folder "ERA," box 57-3, Edith Green papers, OHS; Cindy S. Aron, *Ladies and Gentlemen of the Civil Service: Middle-Class Workers in Victorian America* (New York: Oxford University Press, 1987).

12. See citations in previous note.

13. See citations in note 11; Mary Anderson, *Woman at Work: The Autobiography of Mary Anderson as Told to Mary Winslow* (Minneapolis: University of Minnesota Press, 1951), 152–153.

14. U.S. Department of Labor, Women's Bureau, *Women in the Federal Service 1954*, pamphlet 4 (Washington, D.C.: GPO, 1957); *Civil Service Journal*, October–December 1960, 24.

15. The BPW came out against selection by sex in the civil service in 1944. Minnie L. Maffett to Harry B. Mitchell, 15 March 1944, and Harry B. Mitchell to Minnie L. Maffett, 22 March 1944, file 36-150, CSC. Civil Service commissioner Barbara Gunderson, working from within, tried to wrest a new interpretation of Section 165 from administration attorneys, but to no avail. Frustrated, she developed an awards program at least to recognize the contributions of women in the federal

service. Interview with Evelyn Harrison, 12 September 1978 (Washington, D.C.); Mary Seebach to Alice Paul, 27 June 1956 (plus attachments: *The Federal Employee*, September 1954, 7 [typed copy] and *Independent Woman*, May 1955, 163 [typed copy]), reel 102, NWP papers (microfilm ed.); George Stafford to H. Richard McCamant, 31 July 1954, and H. Richard McCamant to George Stafford, 22 July 1954, file 36–150, CSC; J. Rankin to Charles Diggs, Jr., 16 March 1955, in folder "Equal Rights Amendment," box 57-3, Edith Green papers, OHS; O. Glenn Stahl to the Commission, 19 September 1957, file 38-2, CSC; Harris Ellsworth to Thomas Murray, n.d., file 38-2, CSC.

16. *Civil Service Journal,* October–December 1960, 24.

17. U.S. Civil Service Commission, *77th Annual Report Fiscal Year Ended—June 30, 1960,* 26.

18. "Highlights of Federal Employment," January 1962, Doc. IV-28, PCSW papers (Washington, D.C.); Philip Hart to Lawrence O'Brien, 15 May 1961, folder HU3 (Exec.), box 374, WHCF, JFKL.

19. "Committee on Federal Employment Policies and Practices, Activities since April 9, 1962," 8 June 1962, in black notebook, box 4644, Eleanor Roosevelt papers, FDRL; Robert Kennedy to John F. Kennedy, 14 June 1962, Doc. IV-23, PCSW papers (Washington, D.C.); Catherine East to Margaret Hickey, n.d., in folder "Miss Hickey's Hyde Park Commission meeting notebook papers," FE papers, PCSW; John F. Kennedy to Eleanor Roosevelt, 15 June 1962, box 4526, and John W. Macy to Heads of Departments and Agencies, 24 July 1962, Doc. IV-31, PCSW papers (Washington, D.C.); President's Commission on the Status of Women, transcript of the meeting of 16 June 1962, Washington, D.C., pp. 86–87, PCSW papers (Washington, D.C.); Evelyn Harrison to Warren B. Irons, 20 June 1962, and O. Glenn Stahl to the Civil Service Commission, 20 July 1962, file 39-2, CSC; John F. Kennedy, Memorandum for Heads of Executive Departments and Agencies, 24 July 1962, Doc. IV-30, PCSW papers; (Washington, D.C ); FPM letter 30-1, 31 July 1962, Doc. IV-33, PCSW papers (Washington, D.C.).

20. John Macy to the President, n.d., [11 October 1963], in folder "Commission on Status of Women, August, 1963 to November, 1963," box 7, Myer Feldman papers, JFKL.

21. PCSW, *American Women,* 52.

22. "Analysis of appointments of top women. . . ," n.d., in folder "Political Executives," FE papers, PCSW; Margaret Hickey to Eleanor Roosevelt, 7 August 1962, in folder "Meeting of committee, September 21, 1962," FE papers, PCSW; Catherine East to Margaret Hickey, 28 August 1962, in folder "Meeting of committee, September 21,

1962," FE papers, PCSW; President's Commission on the Status of Women, transcript of the meeting of 2 October 1962, Washington, D.C., pp. 243–267, PCSW papers (Washington, D.C.); "Notes on meeting with Mr. Dan Fenn, Thursday, December 13, 1962," attached to Catherine East to John Macy, 14 December 1962, "Report on Political Executives to the Committee on Federal Employment Policies and Practices from the Chairman," 3 January 1963, in folder "Political Executives, U.S.," FE papers, PCSW.

23. Phillip S. Hughes to Lee White, 23 January 1962, in folder "Federal Equal Employment Opportunity Act, January 4–October 1962, 6/25/63," box 20, Lee White papers, JFKL; Clarence Mitchell to Edith Green, 21 January 1962, in folder "Equal Pay—Equal Rights, August 24, 1961–1962," box 61-3, Edith Green papers, OHS; James Roosevelt to Catherine May, 8 March 1962, in folder "H.J.R. 55," box 42, Katharine St. George papers, Cornell University.

24. Executive order 10925, 6 March 1961; Executive Order 11114, 22 June 1963; Frances Ambursen to Emily S. Wood, 13 June 1961, in folder "ERA letter 1961," Women's Bureau, DOL (Washington, D.C.); Interview with Catherine East, 6 July 1978 (Arlington, Va.); Interagency procurement policy committee, minutes of the meeting of 7 June 1962, in folder "General Correspondence, Committee on Government Contracts, #1 folder," PE papers, PCSW; Summary of federal interagency procurement policy committee meeting, 7 June 1962, Doc. 7, PE papers, PCSW. An employment discrimination bill was considered by the Subcommittee on Labor, House Committee on Education and Labor, early in 1962.

25. President's Commission on the Status of Women, transcript of the meeting of 12 February 1962, Washington, D.C., pp. 9–10, 24–25, PSCW papers (Washington, D.C.).

26. Committee on Private Employment, transcription of the meeting of 4 April 1962, pp. 25–28, 97–101, PE papers, PCSW.

27. Summary of federal interagency procurement policy committee meeting, 7 June 1962, Doc. 7, PE papers, PCSW.

28. Committee on Private Employment, minutes of meetings of 19 November 1962, Doc. 22, and 31 January 1963, Doc. 30, PE papers, PCSW.

29. President's Commission on the Status of Women, *Report of the Committee on Private Employment*, (Washington, D.C.: GPO, 1963), 7–8.

30. Ibid., 16–18.

31. "Confidential background paper on the PCSW," PCSW Doc. 4, December 1961, file 4644, Eleanor Roosevelt papers, FDRL.

32. President's Commission on the Status of Women, transcript of

meetings of 12 February 1963, pp. 307–340, 23 April 1963, pp. 260–273, and 27 May 1963, pp. 127–36, PCSW papers (Washington, D.C.); Richard Lester to Samuel Morgenstein, 21 February 1963, folder L, PE papers, PCSW; Esther Peterson to members of the Commission, n.d., folder 94-17, Katherine P. Ellickson papers, ALUA.

33. PCSW, *American Women*, 30.

34. Ibid.

35. Ibid., 27–34.

36. Committee on Protective Labor Legislation, summary of the meeting of 6 June 1962, Doc. VII-1, and transcript of the meeting of 6 June 1962, pp. 83–84, PCSW papers (Washington, D.C.); Summary report and recommendations, Committee on Protective Labor Legislation, 26 March 1963, in folder "Commission meeting, April 1–2, 1963," PCSW papers (Washington, D.C.).

37. Committee on Protective Labor Legislation, transcript of the meeting of 6 February 1963, pp. 63–69, PCSW papers (Washington, D.C.). (David quotes are on pp. 67–68).

38. Summary report of the meeting of the Committee on Protective Labor Legislation, 6 February 1963, Doc. 8, PLL papers, PCSW; Committee on Protective Labor Legislation, transcript of the meeting of 6 February 1963, pp. 63–74, PLL papers, PCSW; Draft outline—Preliminary report of Subcommittee of Committee on Protective Labor Legislation, 1 February 1963, Doc. VII-5, PCSW papers (Washington, D.C.); President's Commission on the Status of Women, *Report of the Committee on Protective Labor Legislation* (Washington, D.C.: GPO, 1963), 9–13.

39. President's Commission on the Status of Women, transcript of the meeting of 1 April 1963, Washington, D.C., pp. 153–204, PCSW papers (Washington, D.C.). (David statement is on p. 171).

40. Esther Peterson to Arthur Morley et al., 19 April 1963, in file "General Correspondence, January 1963–December 1963," PCSW papers (Washington, D.C.).

41. President's Commission on the Status of Women, transcript of the meeting of 24 April 1963, Washington, D.C., pp. 384–415, PCSW papers (Washington, D.C.).

42. PCSW, *American Women*, 9–12.

43. President's Commission on the Status of Women, *Report of the Committee on Education*, (Washington, D.C.: GPO, 1963), 31.

44. PCSW, *American Women*, 16.

45. Ibid., 15.

46. President's Commission on the Status of Women, *Report of the Committee on Civil and Political Rights*, (Washington, D.C.: GPO, 1963), 22.

47. PCSW, *American Women*, 48.

48. "The Status of Women Under the Old-Age Survivors' and Disability Insurance Program," 15 May 1962, Doc. VIII-2, p. 11, PCSW papers (Washington, D.C.); Elizabeth Wickenden to Martha Griffiths, 14 June 1962, in folder "88th Cong., Ways and Means, Social Security," box 50, Martha Griffiths papers BHL; Committee on Social Insurance and Taxes, transcript of the meeting of 29 June 1962, pp. 38–41, minutes of the meeting of 29 June 1962, Doc. VIII-28, transcript of the meeting of 29 January 1963, pp. 78–85, PCSW papers (Washington, D.C.); Eveline Burns to Esther Peterson, 5 February 1963, SIT papers, PCSW; President's Commission on the Status of Women, *Report of the Committee on Social Insurance and Taxes* (Washington, D.C.:GPO, 1963); 36–39; PCSW, transcript of the meeting of 1 April 1963, (Washington, D.C., pp. 60–65, PCSW papers (Washington, D.C.); PCSW, *American Women*, 40–43.

49. Recommendations on old-age, survivors', and disability insurance, n.d., Committee Doc. B-6, in folder "Committee meetings—January 29–30, 1963," SIT papers, PCSW.

50. Ibid.; PCSW, *Report of the Committee on Social Insurance and Taxes*, 3–10; PCSW, *American Women*, 40–43. A similar decision was made about civil service pension benefits for women.

51. PCSW, *American Women*, 69.

52. William Chafe, *The American Woman: Her Changing Social, Economic, and Political Roles, 1920–1970* (New York: Oxford University Press, 1972), 159–173, 186; "History of Daycare and Child Development Council of America," in folder "Daycare," box 3, Elinor Guggenheimer papers, SL; U.S. Department of Health, Education, and Welfare, Children's Bureau, and U.S. Department of Labor, Women's Bureau, *Day Care Services, Form and Substance: Report of a Conference, November 17–18, 1960* (Children's Bureau Publication, no. 393, 1961; Women's Bureau bulletin no. 281, 1961); Mildred Arnold to Miss Emery, 6 March 1959, in folder "1959, legislation, day care," Katherine B. Oettinger to Charles I. Schottland, 28 July 1958, in folder "1958, legislation, day care," box 27, acc. 72A-3008, Records of the U.S. Department of Health, Education, and Welfare, Federal Records Center (Suitland, Md.); Esther Peterson to Arthur Goldberg, 1 August 1961 (plus attachments), folder WA-1, box 92, RG 174 (Goldberg), NA; *New York Times*, 28 July 1962.

53. *New York Times*, 2 February 1962, 17 May 1963; "Use of Federal funds for day care of children," in folder "1963, legislation, daycare," box 29, acc. 72A-3008, Records of the U.S. Department of Health, Education, and Welfare, Federal Records Center (Suitland,

Md.); PL 87-543, 26 July 1962; Committee on Home and Community, transcript of the meeting of 25 May 1962, pp.148–156, summary of the meeting of 13 September 1962, Doc. 6, HC papers, PCSW; President's Commission on the Status of Women, transcript of the meeting of 1 October 1962, Washington, D.C., pp. 86–88, 95–96, PCSW papers (Washington, D.C.).

54. PCSW, *Report of the Committee on Home and Community*, 7.

55. President's Commission on the Status of Women, transcript of the meeting of 1 April 1963, Washington, D.C., pp. 287–292; PCSW papers (Washington, D.C.); PCSW, *Report of the Committee on Home and Community*, 7, 39–42; PCSW, *American Women*, 19.

56. PCSW, *American Women*, 18.

57. Ibid., 53–54. Esther Peterson did not favor the establishment of continuing bodies. She said later she intended the Women's Bureau to oversee the commission recommendation (Esther Peterson, Recorded Interview by Ann M. Campbell, 11 February 1970, p. 77, JFKL Oral History Program).

58. Betty Friedan, *The Feminine Mystique* (New York: Dell, 1974), 361.

59. Katherine Ellickson to Esther Peterson, 12 January 1962, draft letter, 31 January 1962, folder 90-27, and Evelyn Harrison to John Macy, 1 February 1962, folder 91-21, Katherine P. Ellickson papers, ALUA; Summary of meeting of 23 January, 1962, Esther Peterson to Mrs. Arthur L. Zepf, 10 August 1962, attached to Mrs. Arthur Zepf to Esther Peterson, 20 June 1962, and Mrs. Robert J. Phillips to Esther Peterson, 9 July 1962, in folder "Women's Organizations File, General, PCSW," PCSW papers (Washington, D.C.); Committee on Social Insurance and Taxes, transcript of the meeting of 29 June 1962, p. 8, PCSW papers (Washington, D.C.); Summary of meeting of 19 February, 1962, in folder "PCSW organization," box "PCSW #1," Esther Peterson papers, SL; Interviews with Catherine East, 6 July 1978 and 20 November 1978 (Arlington, Va.).

60. Governor John Swainson of Michigan had created the first state commission in September 1962, before the BPW began its campaign. Swainson did so on the advice of Mildred Jeffries, a close political associate of his, who had been the first director of the Women's Division of the United Automobile Workers, and who had been involved in the quest for a commission on women since the forties. Telephone interview with Mildred Jeffries, 23 October 1981 (Detroit, Mich.); President's Commission on the Status of Women, transcript of the meetings of 2 October 1962, pp. 400–401, and 24 April 1963, pp. 324–325,

PCSW papers (Washington, D.C.); Eleanor Coakley to Esther Peterson, 30 November 1962, in folder "General Correspondence, PCSW, 12/61–12/62," Minnie C. Miles to Esther Peterson, 30 November 1962, in folder "Organizations—Correspondence," PCSW papers (Washington, D. C.); Esther Peterson to Kenneth O'Donnell, 11 January 1963, in folder "Peterson, Esther," box 2174, WHNF, JFKL; Esther Peterson to Myer Feldman, 17 January 1963, "Memorandum of Conversation with the President and Dr. Miles and Miss Allen of the BPW, January 18, 1963," in folder "Governor's Commissions on the Status of Women," box "Women," Esther Peterson papers, SL; Albert D. Rosellini to the Members of the Governor's Commission on the Status of Women, 30 February 1963 (plus attachments), in folder "Commission and Committees, President's Commission on the Status of Women," box 7, Maurine Neuberger papers, University of Oregon; National Federation of Business and Professional Women's Clubs, press release, 18 January 1963, in folder "PCSW . . . (2 of 3)," BPW Archives; Interdepartmental Committee/Citizens' Advisory Council on the Status of Women, *Progress Report on the Status of Women October 11, 1963 Through October 10, 1964* (Washington, D.C.: GPO, 1964), 18–25.

61. Diana T. Michaelis to Esther Peterson, n.d., in folder "Meeting February 11–12, 1963," box "PCSW #1," and Esther Peterson to Pierre Salinger, n.d., in folder "PCSW, Misc., Mass Media," box "PCSW #2," Esther Peterson papers, SL; President's Commission on the Status of Women, transcript of media consultation, 19 March 1963, pp. 21–22, 85, PCSW papers (Washington, D.C.); President's Commission on the Status of Women, *Four Consultations* (Washington, D.C.: GPO, 1963).

62. Daniel Patrick Moynihan to Esther Peterson, 26 March 1963, folder 95-1, Katherine P. Ellickson papers, ALUA.

63. "Women in Minority Groups," 18 March 1963, in folder "Minority Groups," PCSW papers (Washington, D.C.); President's Commission on the Status of Women, transcript of minority consultation, 19 April 1963, pp. 3, 11, and passim, PCSW papers (Washington, D.C.); "Summary of Meeting on the Status of the Negro Woman," 19 April 1963, in folder "Minority Groups Meeting, April 19, 1963," PCSW papers (Washington, D.C.); PCSW press release, n.d., "Problems of Negro Women Discussed at Commission Sponsored Meeting," press release file, PCSW papers (Washington, D.C.); PCSW, *Four Consultations*, 29–38.

64. At the ceremony, the first row of commission members was filled, according to protocol, with cabinet members, who were of

course all male. Before the pictures were taken and the ceremony began, Kennedy rearranged the seating so that Senator Maurine Neuberger and Representative Edith Green shared the front row with the cabinet (Transcript, John W. Macy, Jr., Oral History Interview, 23 May 1964, p. 60, JFKL). Myer Feldman to Esther Peterson, 9 October 1963, "Thank you letters, PCSW report," PCSW papers (Washington, D.C.); John F. Kennedy to Esther Peterson, 22 October 1961, folder FG737, box 206, WHCF, JFKL; White House press release, 11 October 1963, in folder "1963 Commission—PCSW (May–Oct.)," box 52, RG 174 (Wirtz), NA; Arthur Schlesinger to Esther Peterson, 16 October 1963, Lyndon Johnson to Esther Peterson, 7 October 1963, and Walter Heller to Esther Peterson, 10 October 1963, in folder "Thank you letters, PCSW report," PCSW papers (Washington, D.C.).

65. *Wall Street Journal,* 6 November 1963, cited in Loeta Korns, "Treatment by Seven Newspapers of the Report of the President's Commission on the Status of Women," 9 December 1963, in folder "General Correspondence, PCSW, January 1964–," PCSW papers (Washington, D.C.).

66. *Washington Post,* 12 October 1963; *Washington Post,* 13 October 1963, and *Baltimore Sun,* 12 October 1963, clippings in folder "Publicity on presentation of report, October 11, 1963," PCSW papers (Washington, D.C.); *Milwaukee Journal,* 16 October 1963, clipping, in folder "Women—President's Commission on the Status of Women, reported October, 1963," box 105, DNC papers, LBJL; Ruth Holstein, "The Status of Women," *NEA Journal,* November 1963, 68; "The Status of Women" (editorial), *Catholic Nurse,* December 1963, 16–17; *The Guidepost* (American Personnel and Guidance Association), November 1963, 1–3, in folder "Appreciation letters—Report, American Women," PCSW papers (Washington, D.C.); *National Businesswoman,* November–December 1963, 16–18; Margaret Mead, "Do We Undervalue Full-Time Wives?" *Redbook,* November 1963, 22, 24, 26; Esther Peterson, "The Status of Women in the United States," *International Labour Review* 89 (May 1964): 447–460; *New York Times,* 12 October 1963, 2 November 1963.

67. Myer Feldman to John F. Kennedy, 9 October 1963, folder FG737, box 206, WHCF, JFKL.

68. Executive Order 11126, 1 November 1963; White House, press release, 1 November 1963, in folder "Continuing Leadership, Executive Order," PCSW papers (Washington, D.C.).

69. Esther Peterson to Arthur Goldberg, 2 June 1961, FG737, box 206, WHCF, JFKL.

## CHAPTER 9

1. For a brief discussion of the Johnson period, see William Chafe, *The Unfinished Journey: America Since World War II* (New York: Oxford University Press, 1986), chap. 8, and James Gilbert, *Another Chance: Postwar America, 1945–1968* (New York: Knopf, 1981), chap. 10.

2. Jo Freeman, *The Politics of Women's Liberation* (New York: Mc-Kay, 1975), 28–30.

3. Ibid., 30–43; Abbot L. Ferriss, *Indicators of Trends in the Status of American Women* (New York: Russell Sage Foundation, 1971), 143. Evidence indicates that black women did not experience the same relative deprivation with respect to black men. The economic opportunities for black women actually progressed compared with those for black men, and the black community expressed the belief that it was imperative to improve the status of black men relative to white men, and of black people generally. These views militated against black women feeling an acute sense of injustice vis-à-vis black men. See, for example, the consultation on the problems of Negro women held by the President's Commission on the Status of Women in April 1963 (chapter 8 above).

4. "The America Woman: Her Achievements and Troubles," special issue of *Life*, 24 December 1956; William J. Grace, "The Dilemma of Modern Woman: Can She Solve It?" *Catholic World*, April 1956, 16–23; Mary Clinch, "The Phenomenon of the Working Wife," *Social Order* 6 (October 1956): 362–366; Mirra Komarovsky, *Women in the Modern World* (Boston: Little, Brown, 1953); Margaret Mead, "Modern Marriage, the Danger Point," *Nation* 177 (31 October 1953): 348–350; Marya Mannes, "Female Intelligence: Who Wants It?" *New York Times Magazine*, 3 January 1960; Mary Freeman, "The Marginal Sex: America's Alienated Woman," *Commonweal* 75, no. 19 (2 February 1962): 483–486; *Harper's* 225 (October 1962): 117. For a fuller discussion of articles about women in popular magazines, see Cynthia Harrison, "Women and the New Frontier" (Master's thesis, Columbia University, 1974).

5. Betty Friedan, *The Feminine Mystique* (New York: Dell, 1974 ).

6. Freeman, *Politics of Women's Liberation*, chap. 1.

7. Ibid., 44, 52.

8. Margaret Mead and Frances B. Kaplan (eds.), *American Women* (New York: Scribner, 1965); Interdepartmental Committee on the Status of Women [hereinafter ICSW], Summary of the meeting of 20 January 1964, item 16, box 16, Papers of the Citizens' Advisory Coun-

cil on the Status of Women [hereinafter CACSW], NA (Record Group number not assigned).

9. Esther Peterson to Elizabeth Carpenter, 29 November 1963, attached to Esther Peterson to the Secretary, 29 November 1963, in folder "White House/PCSW, 1963–66," box "Political (Dem. campaigns)," Esther Peterson papers, SL; Lyndon Johnson to Margaret Hickey, 7 January 1964 (plus attachments), folder FG686/A, box 386, WHCF, LBJL; CACSW, Summary of the first meeting, 12 and 13 February 1964, item 17, box 5, CACSW papers, NA; *Washington Post,* 13 and 14 February 1964, and *Washington Star,* 12 and 14 February 1964, clippings, in folder "Education, federal programs" [obviously mismarked], PCSW papers (Washington, D. C.); "What the Administration has done for women," 20 April 1964, in folder "Panzer: women," box 5D4-503, WHCF, 489, LBJL; Transcript, Esther Peterson Oral History Interview, 25 November 1968, LBJL (Peterson's copy is in her papers at Giant Foods, Landover, Md).

10. First Annual Report of Interdepartmental Committee and Citizens' Advisory Council on the Status of Women, [ICSW/CACSW], *Progress Report on the Status of Women, October 11, 1963 through October 10, 1964* (Washington, D.C.: GPO, 1964).

11. Elizabeth Carpenter, rather than Margaret Price, proved to be the main conduit to the president in support of jobs for women. Carpenter, a journalist who realized that appointments for women made good press, contacted India Edwards, Katie Louchheim, and Margaret Price soon after Johnson took office. Carpenter quickly realized that Price was not effective in her job, and she advised Lyndon Johnson to replace her with India Edwards posthaste (advice Johnson did not take). Price, she explained, was "more ceremonial than workhorse," and something had to be done before the 1964 campaign ("Pending vacancies to which women might be appointed, [Carpenter]," 16 January 1964, folder PE2, box 7, WHCF, LBJL). Katie S. Louchheim to Elizabeth Carpenter, 4 December 1963, in folder "Carpenter, Elizabeth," box C2, Katie S. Louchheim papers, LC; President's Commission on the Status of Women, *American Woman* (Washington, D.C.: GPO, 1963), 52; Patricia Zelman, "Development of Equal Employment Opportunity for Women as a National Policy, 1960–1967" (Ph.D. diss., Ohio State University, 1980), chap. 3; Notes for cabinet meeting, 17 January 1964, appointment file (25 January 1964) (diary backup), box 3, LBJL; *Washington Post,* 18 January 1964; Elizabeth Carpenter to Lyndon Johnson, 20 January 1964, appointment file (25 January 1964) (diary backup), box 3, LBJL; Elizabeth Carpenter to Lyndon Johnson, 29 January 1964, folder PE2, box 7,

WHCF, LBJL; White House press release, 3 January 1964, folder PE4-2, "Peterson, Esther, 1964," box 190, RG 174 (Wirtz), NA; Ralph Dungan to Lyndon Johnson, 17 February 1964 (plus attachments), folder PE2, box 7, WHCF, LBJL; Transcript, India Edwards Oral History Interview, 4 February 1969, pp. 34–39, LBJL.

12. *Newsweek,* 16 March 1964, clipping, in folder "Panzer: Women," box 5D4-503, WHCF #489, LBJL; Ralph Dungan to Margaret Horgen, 20 March 1964, folder PE2, box 15, LBJL; *National Business Woman,* May 1964, 2–15; William J. Crockett to Ralph Dungan, 24 February 1964, in folder "Department of State, women and minorities in DOS Statistics, appointments, report, 1964," box C20, Katie S. Louchheim papers, LC; Elizabeth Carpenter to "Anyone interested in women," 24 February 1964, Ralph Dungan to Elizabeth Carpenter, 25 February 1964, and Elizabeth Carpenter to the President, 25 February 1964, folder PE2, box 7, WHCF, LBJL; Karen Keesling and Suzanne Cavanagh, "Women Presidential Appointees Serving or Having Served Full-Time Positions Requiring Senate Confirmation, 1912–1977," Congressional Research Service Report 78-73 G, 23 March 1978, Library of Congress, Washington, D.C., 36–43.

13. Zelman, "Development of Equal Employment Opportunity," 114.

14. Notes on meeting with John Macy, 2 March 1965, in folder "Papers 1965 re: DACOWITS," box 16, Margaret Price papers, BHL; CACSW, transcript of the meeting of 12 February 1964, p. 48, box 13, CACSW papers, NA; Mary Stack to John B. Clinton, 9 December 1964, in folder "1964—committee—ICSW (Jan.–May)," box 243, RG 174 (Wirtz), NA; Interview with Esther Peterson, 10 June 1978 (Washington, D.C.); India Edwards to Lyndon Johnson, 8 January 1964, attached to Mary Stack to Juanita Roberts, 19 March 1964, in folder "Selected names, E," box 17, LBJA, LBJL; Transcript, Esther Peterson Oral History Interview, 25 November 1968, LBJL (Peterson's copy); Walter Heller to Lyndon Johnson, 28 December 1963, FI, LBJL; Zelman, "Development of Equal Employment Opportunity," chap. 3; Transcript, Mary Keyserling Oral History Interview, 1–4 February 1982, pp. 174–179, SL.

15. Keyserling also took over, by virtue of her position as Women's Bureau director, the post of executive vice-chairman of the Interdepartmental Committee on the Status of Women, but Peterson arranged for a new Executive Order, signed in May 1965, that ultimately made Peterson vice-chairman, ranking her above Keyserling. Esther Peterson to the Secretary of Labor, 26 November 1963, in folder PE-4-2, "Peterson, Esther, 1963," box 101, Willard Wirtz to the

President, 9 January 1964, attached to Wirtz to Ralph Dungan, 9 January 1964, in folder "1964 White House President (Jan.–Feb.)," box 126, Esther Peterson to the Secretary, 6 January 1965, folder PE-4-2, "Peterson, Esther 1965," box 290, Willard Wirtz to Kermit Gordon, 26 February 1965, folder LL-2-1, "Budget Bureau (February) 1965," box 274, Willard Wirtz to Esther Peterson, 22 July 1965, in folder "1965 Committee ICSW July," box 244, RG 174 (Wirtz), NA; CACSW, transcript of the meeting of 28 July 1965, p. 23, box 13, CACSW papers, NA; *Federal Register* 30, no. 89 (8 May 1965): 6427; Abe Fortas to Jack Valenti, 20 February 1964 (plus attachments), folder PE-2, box 7, WHCF, LBJL; Interview with Esther Peterson, 27 February 1978 (Washington, D.C.). For an example of the different approaches Peterson and Keyserling took toward states abolishing protective labor legislation that applied only to women, see Esther Peterson to Hope Roberts, 18 January 1965, 26 February 1965, and Mary D. Keyserling to Hope Roberts, 26 January 1965, in folder "Governor's Commission on the Status of Women," reel 25, DOL microfilm, LBJL.

16. U.S. Equal Employment Opportunity Commission, *Legislative History of Title VII and XI of Civil Rights Act of 1964* (Washington, D. C.: GPO, n.d.), 9–10, 2001–2038.

17. "Resolution adopted unanimously by the National Council of the National Woman's Party . . . Regarding the proposed Civil Rights Bill (H.R. 7152)," 16 December 1963, reel 108, NWP papers (microfilm ed.).

18. Emma Guffey Miller to Marjorie Longwell, 24 July 1961, reel 107, NWP papers (microfilm ed.); Nina Horton Avery to J. Vaughan Gary, 8 January 1964, reel 108, NWP papers (microfilm ed.); Emma Guffey Miller to Edith Green, 20 January 1964, in folder "Judiciary Committee Civil Rights," box 64-3, Edith Green papers, OHS; Emma Guffey Miller to Members of the House of Representatives, 3 February 1964, folder 74, box 5, Emma Guffey Miller papers, SL. See also Carl Brauer, "Women Activists, Southern Conservatives, and the Prohibition of Sex Discrimination in Title VII of the 1964 Civil Rights Act," *Journal of Southern History* 49 (1983): 37–57.

19. Zelman, "Development of Equal Employment Opportunity," chap. 4; Howard Smith to Nina Horton Avery, 26 December 1963, Smith to Emma Guffey Miller, 10 January 1964, untitled report beginning "Reported Judiciary Committee of the House, November 20, 1963," reel 108, NWP papers (microfilm ed.); Telephone interview with Martha Griffiths, 27 November 1978 (Romeo, Mich.); Alice Paul oral history, pp. 616–636.

20. U.S. Congress, House, 88th Cong., 2d sess., 8 February 1964, *Congressional Record* 110: 2577–2584; Alice Paul oral history, pp. 616–636. An attempt had been made by a representative from Texas, acting at the behest of the National Woman's Party, to add sex to each title as it came up, but these efforts met defeat. The congresswomen decided to vest their efforts in Title VII.

Although much has been made of Smith's ridiculing the "sex" amendment, it is quite possible that he was sincere. His support would be in keeping with his advocacy of the Equal Rights Amendment and the notion that blacks should not have rights not granted to women. Also, given the nature of the amendment and its potential impact on business, he would be unlikely to have undertaken such a legislative move frivolously. Furthermore, he cited the achievement in his campaign literature (Smith brochure, 1968, folder 36, box 79, Legislative Reference Files, Meany Archives).

21. *New York Times*, 9 February 1964; Zelman, "Development of Equal Employment Opportunity," chap. 4; U.S. Congress, House, 88th Cong., 2d sess., 8 February 1964, *Congressional Record* 110: 2577–2584.

22. U.S. Congress, House, 88th Cong., 2d sess., 8 February 1964, *Congressional Record* 110: 2577–2584; Zelman, "Development of Equal Employment Opportunity," chap. 4. The exception was Ross Bass (D-Tenn.) (Zelman, p. 149). Jo Freeman concludes that Republican ERA supporters played a crucial role ("Title VII" [1987], 7).

23. Emma Guffey Miller to Martha Griffiths, 14 February 1964, Dorothy Meehan to Martha Griffiths, 10 February 1964, and Martha Griffiths to Lucille Beckwith, 14 February 1964, in folder "Civil Rights Bill," box 47, Martha Griffiths papers, BHL; *Washington Post*, 10 February 1964, clipping, in folder "Commission and Committee, President's Commission on the Status of Women," box 7, Maurine Neuberger papers, OHS; Edith Green, the lone holdout among congresswomen, confided to a friend that she was finding the "climate . . . a bit frigid" on the Hill (Edith Green to Peggy Roach, 15 February 1964, in folder "Judiciary Committee Civil Rights," box 64-3, Edith Green papers, OHS).

24. *Washington Post*, 11 February 1964, clipping, in folder "H.R. 1752(88), Civil Rights Administration Omnibus Clippings," box 462, Emanuel Celler papers, LC.

25. CACSW, transcript of the meeting of 12 February 1964, pp. 146–158, box 13, CACSW papers, NA.

26. Zelman, "Development of Equal Employment Opportunity," 156–57; Pauli Murray, "Memorandum in support of retaining the

amendment to H.R. 7152, Title VII (Equal Employment Opportunity) to prohibit discrimination in employment because of sex," 14 April 1964, in folder "Civil Rights Bill," box 47, Martha Griffiths papers, BHL; Carl Brauer, "Sex and Race: Title VII of the Civil Rights Act of 1964," unpublished paper, pp. 23–27 (I am grateful to Carl Brauer for permitting me to see a copy of this paper); Lyndon Johnson to Modell Scruggs, 23 April 1964 (draft), folder HU3 (Exec.), box 58, LBJL. The senators, however, received few letters from constituents about the sex amendment. See, for example, "Civil Rights," folders, box 12, Daniel Brewster papers, University of Maryland. (Brewster was a cosponsor of the Senate Civil Rights Bill.)

27. Emma Guffey Miller to Helen Bitterman, 22 February 1964, and Joseph Clark to Emma Guffey Miller, 10 March 1964, reel 108, [Alice Paul] to Mary Kennedy (draft), June 1964, reel 109, NWP papers (microfilm ed.); Zelman, "Development of Equal Employment Opportunity," chap. 4.

28. CACSW, summaries of first meeting, 12–13 February 1964, second meeting, 12–13 October, 1964, fourth meeting, 26–27 October, 1965, and fifth meeting, 31 May 1966, in folder "CACSW Summary of Meetings," and summary of third meeting, 28 July 1965, in folder "Summary CACSW meeting, July 28, 1965," box 5, CACSW papers, NA; ICSW, summaries of first meeting, 20 January 1964, item 16, second meeting, 18 May 1964, item 65, and third meeting, 23 February 1965, item 89, box 16, and summary of fourth meeting, 1 October 1965, item 97, box 17, CACSW papers, NA; ICSW, summary of fifth meeting, 14 October 1965, in folder "ICSW meeting, 17 January 1967," reel 25, DOL microfilm, LBJL; First Annual Report of ICSW/CACSW, *Progress Report on the Status of Women* (1963–1964); Second Annual Report of ICSW/CACSW, *Report on Progress in 1965 on the Status of Women* (Washington, D.C.: GPO, 1965); Third Annual Report of ICSW/CACSW, *Report on Progress in 1966 on the Status of Women* (Washington, D.C.: GPO, 1966); Report of the ICSW, *American Women 1963–1968,* (Washington, D.C.: GPO, 1968).

The CACSW also observed with pleasure in its 1965 report (p. 21) that the Federal Communications Commission had reduced interstate telephone rates after 8 P.M., obviously a great boon to American women.

29. Esther Peterson to Myer Feldman, attached to Myer Feldman to Jane Grant, 31 December 1963, folder LE/HU3 (General), box 72, LBJL.

30. Emma Guffey Miller to Lyndon Johnson, 29 August 1964, folder 75, box 5, Emma Guffey Miller papers, SL.

31. ICSW, Summary of First Meeting, January 20, 1964, item 16, box 16, CACSW papers, NA; Zelman, "Development of Equal Employment Opportunity," 209; Alice Paul to Mrs. Arthur Holden, 30 November 1963, and Emma Guffey Miller to Lyndon Johnson, 27 November 1963, reel 108, NWP papers (microfilm ed.); Myer Feldman to Women's Organizations (copy), 31 December 1963, in folder "CACSW & ICSW items," box 16, CACSW papers, NA; Alma Lutz to Emma Guffey Miller, 23 January 1964, reel 108, NWP papers (microfilm ed.); Elizabeth Carpenter to Lyndon Johnson, 18 May 1964, in name file folder "Miller, Emma," WHCF, LBJL; Emma Guffey Miller to Elizabeth Carpenter, 9 June 1964, folder 75, box 5, Emma Guffey Miller papers, SL; "Support for pending equal rights amendment to the U.S. Constitution by possible nominees for the presidency," 1964, reel 109, NWP papers (microfilm ed.); Emma Guffey Miller, memorandum, 11 August 1964, Ivan Sinclair to Elsie Hill, 24 July 1964, "Hearing before Panel III, Platform Committee program for speakers for equal rights for women amendment to the U.S. Constitution," 21 August 1964, speech by Mrs. Emma Guffey Miller, 21 August 1964, and Lyndon Johnson to Emma Guffey Miller, 4 September 1964, reel 109, NWP papers (microfilm ed.); Donald B. Johnson (comp.), *National Party Platforms*, vol. 2: *1960–1976* (Urbana: University of Illinois Press, 1978), 645.

32. Pauli Murray to Alma Lutz, 9 December 1965, reel 109, NWP papers (microfilm ed.); Esther Peterson to the Secretary, 28 December 1965, folder PE-4-2, "Peterson, Esther, 1965," box 290, RG 174 (Wirtz), NA; *White v. Crook*, 251 F. Supp. 401, 1966; Frank Wozencraft to Mary Dublin Keyserling, 21 October 1966, in folder "Government agencies," Women's Bureau Office Files, DOL (Washington, D.C.). Cf. *State of Mississippi v. Virginia Hall*, 187 So. 2d. 861 (1966).

33. CACSW, *White v. Crook*, 23 February 1966, item 102, in folder "*White v. Crook*, March 1966," box "Women," Esther Peterson papers, SL.

34. ICSW/CACSW, *Progress Report on the Status of Women* (1963–1964), *Report on Progress in 1965, Report on Progress in 1966;* ICSW, *American Women 1963–1968;* CACSW, Summary of Third Meeting, 28 July 1965, in folder "Summary CACSW Meeting, 28 July 1965," box 5, CACSW papers, NA; ICSW, Summary of Third Meeting, 23 February 1965, item 89, box 16, CACSW papers, NA.

35. ICSW/CACSW, *Progress Report on the Status of Women* (1963–1964), *Report on Progress in 1965, Report on Progress in 1966;* ICSW, *American Women 1963–1968;* Summary of the Proceedings of the Conference of Governors' Commissions on the Status of Women, 12 June

1964, in folder "CACSW & ICSW Items," box 16, CACSW papers, NA.

36. Summary of the Proceedings of the Conference of Governors' Commissions on the Status of Women, 12 June 1964, in folder "CACSW & ICSW Items," box 16, CACSW papers, NA; ICSW/CACSW, *Progress and Prospects: The Report of the Second National Conference on Governors, Commissions on the Status of Women*, 28–30 July 1965 (Washington, D.C.: GPO, 1966), 40–42, 45–46.

37. "Questions raised by the Civil Rights Act Title VII," 5 November 1964, in folder "Title VII," reel 17, DOL microfilm, LBJL; Mary Keyserling to Emma Guffey Miller, 8 January 1965, reel 109, NWP papers (microfilm ed.); ICSW, "Women and the Equal Employment Provisions of the Civil Rights Act," 20 February 1965, item 68, box 16, CACSW papers, NA; Esther Peterson to the Secretary, 3 March 1965, folder PE-4-2, "Peterson, Esther, 1965," box 290, RG 174 (Wirtz), NA.

38. Mary Dublin Keyserling to the Secretary, 5 May 1965, folder 4, reel 17, DOL microfilm, LBJL; Pauli Murray and Mary Eastwood, "Jane Crow and the Law: Sex Discrimination and Title VII," *George Washington Law Review* 34 (December, 1965): 253.

39. "Prohibition to discriminate in employment on the basis of sex, Title VII of the Civil Rights Act, address by Esther Peterson . . . July 8, 1965 [with amendments by Mary Dublin Keyserling], in folder "Title VII," reel 20, DOL microfilm, LBJL. See also note 13 above.

40. Secretary of Labor to Franklin Roosevelt, Jr., 9 August 1965, in folder "1965—Commission—Equal Employment Opportunity (August)," box 237, RG 174 (Wirtz), NA.

41. Margaret Hickey to members, CACSW, 11 September 1965, item 91, in folder "Citizens' Advisory Council on the Status of Women, 1," reel 25, DOL microfilm, LBJL; policy resolution adopted by the AFL-CIO 6th Constitutional Convention, San Francisco, California, December 1965, in folder "1967, Committee, (ICSW (Jan))," box 52, RG 174 (Wirtz), NA; Olya Margolin to Franklin Roosevelt, Jr., 30 July 1965, folder 1-20, Morag Simchak papers, ALUA; CACSW, "Equal Employment Opportunities for Women Under Title VII of the Civil Rights Act of 1964," 1 October 1965, item 91, box 17, CACSW papers, NA.

42. Excerpts from the remarks of Franklin D. Roosevelt, Jr., 30 July 1965, in folder "1965—Commission—Equal Employment Opportunity (January–July)," box 237, RG 174 (Wirtz), NA.

43. Frances Kolb, "The National Organization for Women: A History of the First Ten Years," p.109 (unpublished manuscript).

44. N. Thompson Powers to Willard Wirtz, 7 September 1965, in folder "1965—Commission—Equal Opportunity (September–October)," box 237, RG 174 (Wirtz), NA.

45. *Washington Post,* 23 November 1965, clipping, in folder "Title VII, Civil Rights Act of 1964, Legislation 1964–65," BPW Archives.

46. *New York Times,* 19 August 1965, 28 September 1965; Equal Employment Opportunity Commission, press release, 18 August 1965, in folder "1965—Commission—Equal Employment Opportunity (August)," box 237, RG 174 (Wirtz), NA.

47. Interview with Richard Graham, 31 July 1985 (Washington, D. C.)

48. Equal Employment Opportunity Commission, press release, 18 August 1965, in folder "1965—Commission—Equal Employment Opportunity (August)," box 237, RG 174 (Wirtz).

49. *New Republic,* 4 September 1965, clipping, in folder "General 1964–1966," box "Title VII," Catherine East papers (Arlington, Va.).

50. *Wall Street Journal,* 22 June 1965.

51. "Current appraisal of issues relating to the status of women" [author not indicated, but internal evidence suggests that it is Esther Peterson writing to John Macy], 18 July 1966, in folder "General, 1964–66," box "Title VII," Catherine East papers (Arlington, Va.).

52. *Wall Street Journal,* 22 June 1965.

53. Ibid.

54. Equal Employment Opportunity Commission press release, 22 November 1965, in box "Title VII," Catherine East papers (Arlington, Va.); *Federal Register,* 30 (2 December 1965): 14926–14928.

55. Richard Graham to Ruth Gage-Colby, 1 December 1965, reel 109, NWP papers (microfilm ed.).

56. *Washington Post,* 23 November 1965, clipping, in folder "Title VII, Civil Rights Act 1964, Legislation 1964–65," BPW Archives.

57. *New York Times,* 27 March 1966.

58. *Federal Register,* 31 (28 April 1966), title 29, part 1604.

59. Edelsberg quoted in Griffiths's speech, U.S. Congress, House, 89th Cong., 2d sess., 20 June 1966, *Congressional Record* 112: 13689–13694.

60. Esther Peterson to the Secretary, 8 April 1966, in folder PE-4-2, "Peterson, Esther, 1966," box 400, RG 174 (Wirtz), NA; *New York Times,* 29 April 1966; Zelman, "Development of Equal Employment Opportunity," 234–235.

61. U.S. Congress, House, 89th Cong., 2d sess., 20 June 1966, *Congressional Record* 112: 13689–13694.

62. Kolb, "National Organization for Women," 6.

CHAPTER 10

1. Betty Friedan, *It Changed My Life: Writings on the Women's Movement* (New York: Random House, 1976), 77.

2. Esther Peterson to the Secretary, 26 January 1966, folder PE-4-2, "Peterson, Esther, 1966," box 400, RG 174 (Wirtz), NA; Citizens' Advisory Council on the Status of Women, transcript of the meeting of 31 May 1966, pp. 93–96, box 13, CACSW papers, NA.

3. "How NOW Began, Background Memorandum on NOW from Betty Friedan," n.d. [1967], in folder "NOW," box "Women's Organizations," Catherine East papers (Arlington, Va.); Interview with Catherine East, 6 July 1978 (Arlington, Va.); Frances Kolb, "The National Organization for Women: A History of the First Ten Years," chap. 1 (unpublished manuscript); Friedan, *It Changed My Life*, 77–84.

4. Citizens' Advisory Council on the Status of Women, transcript of the meeting of 12 October 1964, pp. 30–35, box 13, CACSW papers, NA.

5. Friedan, *It Changed My Life*, 77–84; East interview, 6 July 1978 (Arlington, Va.); Friedan, "How NOW Began," in folder "NOW," box "Women's Organizations," Catherine East papers (Arlington, Va.).

6. Interview with Richard Graham, 31 July 1985 (Washington, D.C.); Richard Graham to Cynthia Harrison, 13 February 1987; Cynthia Harrison to Richard Graham, 27 February 1987 (with Graham's handwritten notes).

7. Friedan, *It Changed My Life*, 77–84; East interview, 6 July 1978; Friedan, "How NOW Began," in folder "NOW," box "Women's Organizations," Catherine East papers (Arlington, Va.).

8. Esther Peterson to John Macy, n.d., in folder "NOW," box "Women's Organizations," Catherine East papers (Arlington, Va.).

9. According to Clarenbach, Esther Peterson was more receptive to the idea of permitting resolutions than the others, but Peterson later explained that she could not side with Clarenbach because Keyserling opposed the plan and insisted that Peterson not usurp her authority at the conference (Interview with Esther Peterson, 17 June 1980 [Washington, D.C.]; Telephone interview with Kathryn Clarenbach, 22 June 1981 [Madison, Wis.]). Friedan, "How NOW Began," in folder "NOW," box "Women's Organizations," Catherine East papers (Arlington, Va.); Friedan, *It Changed My Life*, 77–84; *Washington Post* and *Washington Evening Star*, 1 July 1966, clippings, in folder "Publicity," drawer "1966 Conference," PCSW papers (Washington, D.C.); *U.S. News and World Report*, 4 July 1966, 61–62, clipping in folder "NOW," Esther Peterson papers (in Peterson's possession).

10. Mary Keyserling, "Report to the Secretary on the Third National Conference of Commissions on the Status of Women, June 28–29–30," 12 July 1966, in folder "1966—Committee—ICSW (June–July)," box 349, RG 174 (Wirtz), NA; Olya Margolin to Andrew Biemiller, 5 August 1966, folder 22, box 55, Legislative Reference Files, Meany Archives.

11. Kolb, "National Organization for Women," chap. 1.

12. *Chicago Tribune*, 3 July 1966, clipping, in folder "89th Congress, women, comments re: discrimination," box 118, Martha Griffiths papers, BHL; Charles Maguire to Mr. Kintner, 29 June 1966, folder FG655 (Exec.), and 12 October 1966, folder FG655A (Exec.), LBJL.

13. *Detroit News*, 13 November 1966, clipping, in folder "General 1964–66," box "Title VII," Catherine East papers (Arlington, Va.); Toni Carabillo, "A Passion for the Possible," *Do It NOW* 9, no. 9 (October 1976): 5–8.

14. Carabillo, "A Passion for the Possible"; Friedan, *It Changed My Life*, 83–85; Kolb, "National Organization for Women," 4, 23, 39–44; Judith Hole and Ellen Levine, *Rebirth of Feminism*, (New York: Quadrangle Books, 1971), 84.

15. Carabillo, "A Passion for the Possible," 5–8; National Organization for Women, "An Invitation to Join," September 1966, reel 110, NWP papers (microfilm ed.); National Organization for Women, "Statement of Purpose," in *Up From the Pedestal: Selected Writings in the History of American Feminism*, ed. Aileen S. Kraditor (Chicago: Quadrangle Books, 1968), 363–69.

16. Friedan, "How NOW Began," in folder "NOW," box "Women's Organizations," Catherine East papers (Arlington, Va.).

17. Esther Peterson to John Macy, attached to untitled memorandum beginning, "The specific events I have set forth. . . ," n.d., in folder "NOW," Esther Peterson papers (in Ms. Peterson's possession); Esther Peterson to John Macy, n.d., in folder "NOW," box "Women's Organizations," Catherine East papers (Arlington, Va.).

18. Kolb, "National Organization for Women," 19–33; National Organization for Women, "Targets for Action, 1966–67" (draft), 26 October 1966, in folder "NOW," box "Women's Organizations," Catherine East papers (Arlington, Va.).

19. Kolb, "National Organization for Women," 25, 30–31; Friedan, *It Changed My Life*, 84.

20. Kolb, "National Organization for Women," 20–21.

21. NOW, "Statement of Purpose," in Kraditor (ed.), *Up From the Pedestal*, 363–369.

22. Ibid.

23. Kathryn Clarenbach, Betty Friedan, and Caroline Davis to Stephen N. Shulman, Luther Holcomb, and Samuel Jackson, 11 November 1966, and Clarenbach, Friedan, and Davis to the President, 11 November 1966, and Clarenbach, Friedan, and Davis to Ramsey Clark, 11 November 1966, in folder "ICSW meeting, January 17, 1976, Room 102-A," reel 25, DOL microfilm, LBJL; Betty Friedan to John Macy, 24 January 1967, in folder "NOW," Esther Peterson papers (in Peterson's possession).

24. Kathryn Clarenbach, Betty Friedan, and Caroline Davis to the President, 11 November 1966, in folder "ICSW meeting, January 17, 1967, Room 102-A," reel 25, DOL microfilm, LBJL.

25. Betty Friedan to John Macy, 24 January 1967, in folder "NOW," Esther Peterson papers (in Peterson's possession); Stephen Shulman to Edith Green, 27 February 1967, in folder "EEOC," box 67-12, Edith Green papers, OHS.

26. Willard Wirtz to Betty Friedan, 25 November 1966, in folder "1966—Committee—ICSW (Nov.–Dec.)," box 349, and Kathryn Clarenbach and Betty Friedan to Willard Wirtz, 9 April 1967, in folder "1967—Committee—ICSW (meeting April 18, 1967)," box 53, RG 174 (Wirtz), NA.

27. Esther Peterson to the officers of NOW, 15 December 1966, in Betty Friedan papers, cited in Kolb, "National Organization for Women," 112.

28. Betty Friedan to Marvin Watson, 5 December 1966 (plus attachments) folder HU3 (General), box 58, LBJL.

29. Kolb, "National Organization for Women," 111.

30. Harry McPherson, Jr., to Kathryn Clarenbach, 20 March 1967, folder S2-3/1967/HU2/Pro/A–Z, box 90, LBJL.

31. Willard Wirtz to Esther Peterson, 26 July 1965 (plus attachments), Joseph Goldberg, note for follow-up, 5 August 1965, and Joseph Goldberg, memorandum for the files, 1 October 1965, in folder "Re: Labor," box "Engagements—Labor," Esther Peterson papers, SL.

32. Penelope H. Thunberg to Willard Wirtz, 14 April 1967, in folder "H.R. 643(2)," box "Women," Esther Peterson papers, SL; Attachment 2 to FPM letter 713-7, 13 October 1967, "Catherine East to Esther Peterson, 17 February 1967," in folder "Government—Federal Woman's Award, 1963, 1966–67," box "Correspondence Files," Esther Peterson papers, SL; Joseph Goldberg to Esther Peterson, 30 September 1966, in folder "NOW," Esther Peterson to the Secretary, 24 March 1967, [no folder], Esther Peterson papers (in Peterson's possession); Willard Wirtz to the President, 2 June 1967, attached to Wilfred Rom-

mel to Mr. Levinson, 21 June 1967, folder HU2-1 (Exec.), box 43, LBJL; Harry McPherson, Jr., to Kathryn Clarenbach, 20 March 1967, folder SP2-3/1967/HU2/Pro/A–Z, box 90, LBJL; Francena Miller to the President, 19 October 1967, folder HU3 (General), box 58, LBJL; White House press release, 28 February 1966, folder MA1/F, box 2, LBJL; White House press release, 10 October 1967, in folder "1967— Committee—ICSW(Oct.–Dec.)," box 53, RG 174 (Wirtz), NA; Betty Friedan, Report of the President, NOW Second National Conference, 18 November 1967, reel 110, NWP papers (microfilm ed.); U.S. Congress, House, 90th Cong., 1st sess., 16 and 17 October 1967, *Congressional Record* 113: 28948–28949, 29098–29099; Federal Woman's Award Study Group on Careers for Women, Progress Report to the President, 3 March 1967, in notebook "ICSW meeting, 18 April 1967," box 23, CACSW papers, NA.

33. Betty Friedan, Report of the President, NOW Second National Conference, 18 November 1967, reel 110, NWP papers (microfilm ed.).

34. Wisconsin Commission Resolution, 20 April 1966, in folder "1966—Committee—ICSW (Jan.–Apr.)," box 349, RG 174 (Wirtz), NA; Dorothy Height to Luther Holcomb, 28 July 1966, in folder "Women's Bureau, Interdepartmental Committee on the Status of Women," reel 25, DOL microfilm, LBJL; "Statement adopted by the Commissioners at meeting #123 of August 19, 1963," in folder "1967— Committee—ICSW (Feb.)," box 53, RG 174 (Wirtz), NA; Esther Peterson to Willard Wirtz, 9 December 1966, in folder "ICSW meeting, 17 January 1967," box 23, CACSW papers, NA; Summary of meeting with representatives of Consumers League, 4 January 1967, in folder "1967—Committee—ICSW (March)," box 53, RG 174 (Wirtz), NA; Mary Keyserling to Esther Peterson, 23 January 1967, in folder "Title VII," reel 17, DOL microfilm LBJL; Draft working paper, Title VII and State Protective Laws, in folder "Equal Opportunity (1)," reel 20, DOL microfilm, LBJL; Proposed Department of Labor position on state labor standards relating to the employment of women and their relationship to Title VII of the Civil Rights Act of 1964, 14 March 1967, in folder "Title VII," reel 17, DOL microfilm, LBJL; Department of Labor position on state labor standards laws relating to the employment of women and their relationship to Title VII of the Civil Rights Act of 1964, 16 March 1967, in folder "Labor Standards," reel 16, DOL microfilm, LBJL; Draft position paper on inter-relationship of state labor legislation and Title VII of the Civil Rights Act of 1964, 2 February 1967, attached to Title VII and State Protective Laws, draft working paper, n.d., attached to Briefing for meeting with representatives

of the National Consumers League, 8 March 1967, in folder "1967—
Committee—ICSW (March)," box 53, RG 174 (Wirtz), NA.

35. Kolb, "National Organization for Women,"chap. 2; Equal Employment Opportunity Commission press release, 1 May 1967, reel
110, NWP papers (microfilm ed.); *Federal Register* 32 (11 July 1967):
10228; Stephen Shulman to the President, 23 March 1967, folder FG
655, box 380, LBJL; Jo Freeman, *The Politics of Women's Liberation*
(New York: McKay, 1975), 56.

36. Despite the new policy, the issue was finally decided by the
courts. Litigation, supported by NOW and other feminist groups organizing its wake, raised the matter repeatedly, and by 1971 federal
courts ruled consistently that hours laws and weight-lifting laws that
applied only to women were invalidated by Title VII. Citizens' Advisory Council on the Status of Women, "Summary of Equal Employment Opportunity Commission Hearings," 2 and 3 May 1967, item
141, box 17, CACSW papers, NA; National Federation of Business and
Professional Women press release, 3 May 1967, in folder "Title VII,
1967 Legislation," BPW Archives; Statement by Marguerite Rawalt, 2
May 1967, reel 110, NWP papers (microfilm ed.); U.S. Congress,
House, 90th Cong., 1st sess., statement by Martha Griffiths on 3 May
1967, 17 May 1967, *Congressional Record* 111: 13108–13110; Equal Employment Opportunity Commission, press release, 23 February 1968,
in folder "Equal Employment Opportunity, President's Commission
on," box 68-4, Edith Green papers, OHS; *Federal Register* 33 (24 February 1968): 3344, 3361; Hole and Levine, *Rebirth of Feminism*, 409; *Los
Angeles Times*, 11 September 1968, clipping, reel 111, NWP papers
(microfilm ed.); *Rosenfeld* v. *Southern Pacific*, 293 F. Supp. 1219 (C.D.
Cal. 1968), Aff'd, 444 F. 2d. 1219 (9th Cir. 1971).

37. CACSW, "Summary of Equal Employment Opportunity Commission Hearings."

38. Catherine East to Esther Peterson, 20 December 1966, attached
to Phineas Indritz to Officers and Directors of NOW, 6 December
1966, in folder "Advertising," box "Title VII," Catherine East papers
(Arlington, Va.); Petition to the EEOC to amend the Commission's rule
set forth in section 1604.4 of 29 Code of Federal Regulations, 19 December 1966, in folder "Equal Opportunity (2)," reel 20, DOL microfilm, LBJL; Stephen Shulman to Edith Green, 27 February 1967, and
Edith Green to Stephen Shulman, 14 February 1967, in folder "Equal
Employment Opportunity Commission," box 67-12, Edith Green papers, OHS; Stephen Shulman to Willard Wirtz, and Willard Wirtz to
Stephen Shulman, 26 January 1967, in folder "1967—Committee—
ICSW (Feb.)," box 53, RG 174 (Wirtz), NA; Esther Peterson to Clifford

Alexander, Jr., 9 September 1967, in folder "Title VII," reel 17, DOL microfilm, LBJL; U.S. Congress, House, 90th Cong., 2d sess., 30 September 1968, *Congressional Record* 114: 28819–28825.

39. Carabillo, "A Passion for the Possible," 5–8; Hole and Levine, *Rebirth of Feminism,* 40–44; Equal Employment Opportunity Commission press release, 6 August 1968, in folder "Equal Employment Opportunity, President's Commission on," box 68-4, Edith Green papers, OHS; *Federal Register* 33 (14 August 1968): 11539; Freeman, *Politics of Women's Liberation,* 76–79; Jacob Potofsky to Willard Wirtz, 7 March 1968, and Willard Wirtz to Jacob Potofsky, 29 April 1968, in folder "WA-3 Employment Advancement 1968," box 95, RG 174 (Wirtz), NA.

40. Freeman, *Politics of Women's Liberation,* 80–81; Jean Witter to Alice Paul, 15 April 1968, reel 111, NWP papers (microfilm ed.). Congress submitted the ERA to the states in March 1972. In 1982, when the ratification period expired, the ERA went down, having won approval from only 35 of the 38 states needed. It remains an important item on the feminist agenda.

41. The CACSW also adopted a recommendation to repeal criminal abortion laws in April 1968. Council member Viola Hymes responded initially to the makers of the motion, "Well, you have got a lot of guts" (Citizens' Advisory Council on the Status of Women, transcript of the meeting of 26 April 1968, pp. 168–204, box 13, CACSW papers, NA [quote, p. 169]). National Organization for Women press release, 20 November 1967, in folder "NOW" box 92, Martha Griffiths papers, BHL; Miriam Holden to Miss Newall, 1 February 1967, and Ernestine Powell to Alice Paul, 25 January 1968, reel 110, NWP papers (microfilm ed.).

42. Alice Paul oral history, pp. 530–535.

43. The CACSW endorsed the ERA in 1970. Freeman, *Politics of Women's Liberation,* 212; Citizens' Advisory Council on the Status of Women, notes for Mrs. Peterson, 2 and 3 December 1967, and notes for Senator Neuberger, 2 and 3 December 1967, in folder: "CACSW meeting, December 2–3, 1967," box 5, CACSW papers, NA; Interdepartmental Committee on the Status of Women, Summary of Eighth Meeting, 14 February 1968, in folder "Women's Bureau, Interdepartmental Committee on the Status of Women," reel 25, DOL microfilm, LBJL; Joseph Califano to Emma Guffey Miller, 11 April 1968, folder HU3·(General), box 58, LBJL.

In October 1967, Johnson did send Emma Guffey Miller a letter saying his Senate support for the ERA was unchanged. Miller's request for a statement had come through Deputy Press Secretary Robert Fleming and presidential assistant Will Sparks, who considered it a personal message and therefore did not send the inquiry to the Department of Labor to be answered as was the customary practice. Johnson's letter was an aberration, however, and subsequent letters from the White House were worded to avoid either reiterating support for the ERA or implying that the president's October 1967 letter was a mistake. Emma Guffey Miller to the President, 1 November 1967 (plus attachments), folder HU3 (Executive), box 58, LBJL; cf. Califano to Miller, 11 April 1968, and George Christian to Margery Leonard, 12 October 1967, folder HU3 (Executive), box 58, LBJL; Will R. Sparks to Cynthia Harrison, 11 December 1980.

44. Margery Leonard, "The Equal Rights Amendment in the New Hampshire Primary," telegram sent to all presidential candidates by Betty Friedan, 15 May 1968, National Organization for Women press release, 6 May 1968, George Wallace to Alice Paul, 20 July 1968, Statement by former Vice-President Richard M. Nixon on the Equal Rights Amendment, [July 1968], reel 111, NWP papers (microfilm ed.); *New York Times,* 7 May 1968; National Organization for Women press release, 6 May 1968, reel 111, NWP papers (microfilm ed.).

45. See Sara Evans, *Personal Politics: The Roots of Women's Liberation in the Civil Rights Movement and the New Left* (New York: Knopf, 1979).

46. See Cynthia Harrison, *Women's Movement Media* (New York: Bowker, 1975), for a contemporaneous compilation of the publications of the women's movement.

47. Freeman, *Politics of Women's Liberation,* 83–92, 145–151.

48. For discussions of the policy impact of the women's movement, see Freeman, *Politics of Women's Liberation;* Hole and Levine, *Rebirth of Feminism;* Irene L. Murphy, *Public Policy on the Status of Women: Agenda and Strategy for the 70s* (Lexington, Mass.: Lexington Books, 1973); and Joyce Gelb and Marian Leif Palley, *Women and Public Policies* (Princeton: N.J.: Princeton University Press, 1982).

CONCLUSION

1. Geoffrey Parsons, "Royal Commission," *Punch,* 24 August 1955, quoted in Harold Seidman, *Politics, Position, and Power: The Dynamics of Federal Organization* (New York: Oxford University Press, 1970), 23.

2. Joan Hoff Wilson, *Herbert Hoover: Forgotten Progressive* (Boston: Little, Brown, 1975).

3. Wolanin in fact underestimated the impact of commissions because he looked at the responses only to recommendations made in

final reports and not to those made during the life of the body (Thomas R. Wolanin, *Presidential Advisory Commissions* [Madison: University of Wisconsin Press, 1975], chap. 7).

4. Jo Freeman, *The Politics of Women's Liberation* (New York: McKay, 1975), chap. 2.

5. Ibid., chap. 7.

6. Ibid.

7. Evans goes on: "The existence of the commission and in subsequent years of state commissions on the status of women provided a rallying cry for professional women. Such commissions constituted a tacit admission that there was indeed a 'problem' regarding women's position in American society, that the democratic vision of equal opportunity had somehow left them out. Furthermore, they furnished a platform from which inequities could be publicized and the need for women's rights put forth. The President's Commission's report . . . was moderate in tone. Yet despite obeisance to the primacy of women's roles within the family, it catalogued in great detail the inequities in the lives of women, the discrimination women faced in employment, and the need for proper child-care centers" (Sara Evans, *Personal Politics: The Roots of Women's Liberation in the Civil Rights Movement and the New Left* [New York: Knopf, 1979], (16–17).

8. Frances Kolb, "The National Organization for Women: The First Ten Years," 16, (unpublished manuscript).

9. Freeman, *Politics of Women's Liberation,* 6, 151.

10. James Q. Wilson, *Political Organizations* (New York: Basic Books, 1973), 344.

11. Ethel Klein, *Gender Politics: From Consciousness to Mass Politics* (Cambridge: Harvard University Press, 1984), 39, 55, 73.

12. *New York Times,* 14 December 1967.

# Bibliography

### MANUSCRIPT COLLECTIONS

Dean Acheson. Harry S. Truman Library, Independence, Missouri.

Bertha Adkins. Dwight David Eisenhower Library, Abilene, Kansas.

AFL-CIO. George Meany Memorial Archives, Washington, D.C.

Mary Anderson. Schlesinger Library, Cambridge, Massachusetts.

Eben A. Ayers. Diary. Harry S. Truman Library, Independence, Missouri.

Stephen Benedict. Dwight David Eisenhower Library, Abilene, Kansas.

Daniel Brewster. University of Maryland, College Park, Maryland.

Emanuel Celler. Library of Congress, Washington, D.C.

Citizens' Advisory Council on the Status of Women. National Archives, Washington, D.C.

Clark M. Clifford. Harry S. Truman Library, Independence, Missouri.

Democratic National Committee. Lyndon Baines Johnson Library, Austin, Texas.

Democratic National Committee. John F. Kennedy Library, Boston, Massachusetts.

Helen Gahagan Douglas. Carl Albert Center Archives, University of Oklahoma, Norman, Oklahoma.

Catherine East. Arlington, Virginia.

India Edwards. Lyndon Baines Johnson Library, Austin, Texas.

India Edwards. Harry S. Truman Library, Independence, Missouri.

Katherine P. Ellickson. Archives of Labor and Urban Affairs, Wayne State University, Detroit, Michigan.

Myer Feldman. John F. Kennedy Library, Boston, Massachusetts.

Charles Goodell. Rare Books and Manuscripts Division, The New York Public Library, Astor, Lenox and Tilden Foundations, New York, New York.

Edith Green. Oregon Historical Society, Portland, Oregon.

Martha Griffiths. Bentley Historical Library, University of Michigan, Ann Arbor, Michigan.

Elinor Guggenheimer. Schlesinger Library, Cambridge, Massachusetts.

Carl Hayden. Arizona Collection, Hayden Library, Arizona State University, Tempe, Arizona.

Walter Heller. John F. Kennedy Library, Boston, Massachusetts.

John. F. Kennedy. Prepresidential papers. John F. Kennedy Library, Boston, Massachusetts.

Alice K. Leopold. Schlesinger Library, Cambridge, Massachusetts.

Katie S. Louchheim. Library of Congress, Washington, D.C.

Alma Lutz. Schlesinger Library, Cambridge, Massachusetts.

Patrick McNamara. Archives of Labor and Urban Affairs, Wayne State University, Detroit, Michigan.

Emma Guffey Miller. Schlesinger Library, Cambridge, Massachusetts.

Frieda Miller. Schlesinger Library, Cambridge, Massachusetts.

James P. Mitchell. Dwight David Eisenhower Library, Abilene, Kansas.

Wayne Morse. University of Oregon, Eugene, Oregon.

Pauli Murray. Schlesinger Library, Cambridge, Massachusetts.

National Consumers League. Library of Congress, Washington, D.C.

National Council of Negro Women. Washington, D.C.

National Federation of Business and Professional Women's Clubs, Inc. Washington, D.C.

National Woman's Party. Microfilm edition. Sanford, North Carolina: Microfilm Corporation of America, 1979.

National Woman's Party. Wisconsin State Historical Society, Madison, Wisconsin.

National Women's Trade Union League. Library of Congress, Washington, D.C.

Maurine Neuberger. Oregon Historical Society, Portland, Oregon; University of Oregon, Eugene, Oregon.

Katharine Norris. Schlesinger Library, Cambridge, Massachusetts.

Claude Pepper. Diary (in Mr. Pepper's possession). House Office Building, Washington, D.C.

Claude Pepper. Florida State University, Tallahassee, Florida.

Esther Peterson. Schlesinger Library, Cambridge, Massachusetts: Giant Foods, Landover, Maryland; Washington, D.C.

President's Commission on the Status of Women. John F. Kennedy Library, Boston, Massachusetts.

President's Commission on the Status of Women. U.S. Department of Labor, Women's Bureau, Washington, D.C.

President's Office Files. John F. Kennedy Library, Boston, Massachusetts.

Margaret Price. Bentley Historical Library, University of Michigan, Ann Arbor, Michigan.

Eleanor Roosevelt. Franklin D. Roosevelt Library, Hyde Park, New York.

Katharine St. George. Cornell University, Ithaca, New York.

Morag Simchak. Archives of Labor and Urban Affairs, Wayne State University, Detroit, Michigan.

Hattie Smith. Schlesinger Library, Cambridge, Massachusetts.

Robert A. Taft, Jr. Library of Congress, Washington, D.C.

U.S. Civil Service Commission. Washington, D.C.

U.S. Department of Health, Education, and Welfare. Federal Records Center, Suitland, Maryland.

U.S. Department of Labor. Lyndon Baines Johnson Library, Austin, Texas.

U.S. Department of Labor. John F. Kennedy Library, Boston, Massachusetts.

U.S. Department of Labor. Record Group 174. National Archives, Washington, D.C.

U.S. Department of Labor. Women's Bureau. Record Group 86. National Archives, Washington, D.C.

U.S. Department of Labor. Women's Bureau. Washington, D.C.

U.S. Senate. Judiciary Committee. Record Group 46. National Archives, Washington, D.C.

James W. Wadsworth, Jr. Library of Congress, Washington, D.C.

Lee White. John F. Kennedy Library, Boston, Massachusetts.

White House Central File. Dwight David Eisenhower Library, Abilene, Kansas.

White House Central Files. Lyndon Baines Johnson Library, Austin, Texas.

White House Central Files. John F. Kennedy Library, Boston, Massachusetts.

White House Central Files. Harry S. Truman Library, Independence, Missouri.

White House Official File. Franklin D. Roosevelt Library, Hyde Park, New York.

White House Staff Files. John F. Kennedy Library, Boston, Massachusetts.

Anne Whitman. Dwight David Eisenhower Library, Abilene, Kansas.

Women's Joint Congressional Committee. Library of Congress, Washington, D.C.

## GOVERNMENT DOCUMENTS

U.S. Bureau of the Census. *Statistical Abstract of the United States, 1975.* Washington, D.C.: GPO, 1975.

U.S. Civil Service Commission. *77th Annual Report Fiscal Year Ended June 30, 1960.*

————. *The Transition from War to Peace in Federal Personnel Administration: 63d [sic] Annual Report Fiscal Year Ended June 30, 1946.*

U.S. Congress. House. Committee on Education and Labor. *Equal Pay Act: Hearings Before a Subcommittee of the Committee on Education and Labor, House of Representatives, on H.R. 3861 and Related Bills.* 88th Cong., 1st sess., 1963.

————. *Equal Pay for Equal Work: Hearings Before the Selected Subcommittee on Labor of the Committee on Education and Labor, H.R. 10226.* Part 1: Hearings held in Washington, D.C.; Part 2: Hearings held in New York, N.Y. 87th Cong., 2d sess., 1962.

————. *Legislative History of the Equal Pay Act of 1963.* Pub. L. 88-38. 88th Cong., H.R. 6060 and S. 1409. Committee Print. 88th Cong., 1st sess., December 1963.

U.S. Congress. Joint Committees on Labor. *Women's Bureau: Hearings Before the Joint Committees on Labor on S. 4002, H.R. 1134, H.R. 12679.* 66th Cong., 2d sess., 1920.

U.S. Congress. Senate. *Labor Bureau Report on Condition of Woman and Child Wage-Earners in the United States, 1910–1913.* 19 vols. S. Doc. 645. 61st Cong., 2d sess., 1910.

U.S. Congress. Senate. S. Rept. 1576 to Accompany S. 1178. 79th Cong., 2d sess., 21 June 1946.

U.S. Congress. Senate. S. Rept. 1991 to Accompany S.J.R. 39. 84th Cong., 2d sess., 1956.

U.S. Congress. Senate. Committee on Commerce. *The Speeches of Senator John F. Kennedy: Presidential Campaign of 1960.* S. Rept. 994, part 1. 87th Cong., 1st sess., 1961.

————. *The Speeches of Vice-President Richard M. Nixon: Presidential Campaign of 1960.* S. Rept. 994, part 2. 87th Cong., 1st sess., 1961.

————. Committee on Labor and Public Welfare. *Equal Pay Act of 1963: Hearings Before a Subcommittee of the Committee on Labor and Public Welfare, Senate, on S. 882 and S. 910.* 88th Cong., 1st sess., 1963.

U.S. Department of Defense. DACOWITS. "Minutes, 25th Anniversary Meeting." 14–18 November 1976.

————. *Highlights of the DACOWITS: 25 Years of Service to the Department of Defense,* by Mae Sue Talley. [1976].

U.S. Department of Health, Education, and Welfare. Children's Bureau & U.S. Department of Labor. Women's Bureau. *Day Care Services, Form and Substance: Report of a Conference, November 17–18,*

*1960.* Children's Bureau publication no. 393. Women's Bureau bulletin no. 281. 1961.

U.S. Department of Labor. *Annual Report of the Secretary of Labor for the Fiscal Year Ended June 30, 1945.*

———. Women's Bureau. *Employment of Women in the Early Postwar Period.* Bulletin no. 211, 8 October 1946.

———. *Report of the National Conference on Equal Pay,* 31 March and 1 April 1952. Bulletin no. 243, 29 August 1952.

———. *Women in the Federal Service 1954.* Pamphlet 4. Washington, D.C.: GPO, 1957.

U.S. Equal Employment Opportunity Commission. *Legislative History of Title VII and XI of the Civil Rights Act of 1964.* Washington, D.C.: GPO, n.d.

U.S. Interdepartmental Committee on the Status of Women. *American Women, 1963–1968.* Washington, D.C.: GPO, 1968.

U.S. Interdepartmental Committee on the Status of Women / Citizens' Advisory Council on the Status of Women. *Progress and Prospects: The Report of the Second National Conference on Governors' Commissions on the Status of Women, July 28–30, 1965.* Washington, D.C.: GPO, 1966.

———. *Progress Report on the Status of Women, October 11, 1963 Through October 10, 1964.* Washington, D.C.: GPO, 1964.

———. *Report on Progress in 1965 on the Status of Women.* Washington, D.C.: GPO, n.d.

———. *Report on Progress in 1966 on the Status of Women.* Washington, D.C.: GPO, 1967.

U.S. Library of Congress. Congressional Research Service. *Women Presidential Appointees Serving or Having Served in Full-Time Positions Requiring Senate Confirmation, 1912–1977,* by Karen Keesling and Suzanne Cavanagh. Report No. 78-73G, 23 March 1978.

U.S. Office of War Information. Division of Public Inquiries. *United States Government Manual.* Washington, D.C.: GPO, [1944].

U.S. President. *Public Papers of the Presidents of the United States.* Washington, D.C.: Office of the *Federal Register,* National Archives and Records Service, 1945–.

U.S. President's Commission on the Status of Women. *American Women: Report of the President's Commission on the Status of Women.* Washington, D.C.: GPO, 1963.

———. *Four Consultations.* Washington, D.C.: GPO, 1963.

———. *Report of the Committee on Civil and Political Rights.* Washington, D.C.: GPO, 1963.

———. *Report of the Committee on Education.* Washington, D.C.: GPO, 1963.

———. *Report of the Committee on Federal Employment.* Washington, D.C.: GPO, 1963.

———. *Report of the Committee on Home and Community.* Washington, D.C.: GPO, 1963.

———. *Report of the Committee on Private Employment.* Washington, D.C.: GPO, 1963.

———. *Report of the Committee on Protective Labor Legislation.* Washington, D.C.: GPO, 1963.

———. *Report of the Committee on Social Security and Taxes.* Washington, D.C.: GPO, 1963.


BOOKS

Anderson, Karen. *Wartime Women.* Westport, Connecticut: Greenwood Press, 1981.

Anderson, Mary. *Woman at Work: The Autobiography of Mary Anderson as Told to Mary Winslow.* Minneapolis: University of Minnesota Press, 1951.

Aron, Cindy Sondik. *Ladies and Gentlemen of the Civil Service: Middle-Class Workers in Victorian America.* New York: Oxford University Press, 1987.

Baer, Judith A. *The Chains of Protection: Judicial Response to Women's Labor Legislation.* Westport, Connecticut: Greenwood Press, 1978.

Bailey, Stephen Kemp. *Congress Makes a Law: The Story Behind the Employment Act of 1946.* New York: Columbia University Press, 1964.

Baker, Elizabeth F. *Technology and Women's Work.* New York: Columbia University Press, 1964.

Banner, Lois W. *Women in Modern America: A Brief History.* New York: Harcourt Brace Jovanovich, 1974.

Becker, Susan. *The Origins of the Equal Rights Amendment: American Feminism Between the Wars.* Westport, Connecticut: Greenwood Press, 1981.

Binkin, Martin, and Shirley J. Bach. *Women and the Military.* Washington, D.C.: The Brookings Institution, 1977.

Brauer, Carl M. *John F. Kennedy and the Second Reconstruction.* New York: Columbia University Press, 1977.

Bremner, Robert H., and Gary W. Reichard, eds. *Reshaping America:*

*Society and Institutions, 1945–1960*. Columbus: Ohio State University Press, 1982.

Bureau of National Affairs. *Equal Pay for Equal Work: Summary, Analysis, Legislative History and Text of the Federal Equal Pay Act of 1963, with Summaries of Applicable State Laws*. Washington, D.C.: BNA, 1963.

Burner, David, Robert D. Marcus, and Thomas R. West. *A Giant's Strength: America in the 1960s*. New York: Holt, Rinehart & Winston, 1971.

Burner, David, and Thomas West. *The Torch Is Passed: The Kennedy Brothers and American Liberalism*. New York: Atheneum, 1984.

Burns, James MacGregor. *John Kennedy: A Political Profile*. New York: Harcourt, Brace & World, 1961.

——. *Roosevelt: The Lion and the Fox*. New York: Harcourt, Brace, 1956.

Campbell, D'Ann. *Women at War with America: Private Lives in a Patriotic Era*. Cambridge, Massachusetts: Harvard University Press, 1984.

Chafe, William. *The American Woman: Her Changing Social, Economic, and Political Roles, 1920–1970*. New York: Oxford University Press, 1972.

——. *The Unfinished Journey: America Since World War II*. New York: Oxford University Press, 1986.

Chambers, Clark A. *Seedtime of Reform: American Social Service and Action, 1918–1933*. Ann Arbor: University of Michigan Press, 1967 [1963].

Cotter, Cornelius P., and Bernard C. Hennessy. *Politics Without Power: The National Party Committees*. New York: Atherton Press, 1964.

Cronin, Thomas E., and Sanford D. Greenberg, eds. *The Presidential Advisory System*. New York: Harper & Row, 1969.

Cushman, Robert E., and Robert F. Cushman, eds. *Cases in Constitutional Law*. New York: Appleton-Century-Crofts, 1968.

DeCrow, Karen. *Sexist Justice*. New York: Random House, 1974.

Dickerson, Nancy. *Among Those Present: A Reporter's View of Twenty-five Years in Washington*. New York: Random House, 1976.

Donovan, Robert J. *Conflict and Crisis: The Presidency of Harry S Truman, 1945–1948*. New York: Norton, 1977.

Edwards, India. *Pulling No Punches: Memoirs of a Woman in Politics*. New York: Putnam, 1977.

Evans, Sara. *Personal Politics: The Roots of Women's Liberation in the Civil Rights Movement and the New Left*. New York: Knopf, 1979.

Ferriss, Abbott L. *Indicators of Trends in the Status of American Women*. New York: Russell Sage Foundation, 1971.

Filene, Peter Gabriel. *HIM/HER/SELF: Sex Roles in Modern America.* New York: Harcourt Brace Jovanovich, 1975.

Flexner, Eleanor. *Century of Struggle: The Woman's Rights Movement in the United States.* New York: Atheneum, 1974 [1959].

Freeman, Jo. *The Politics of Women's Liberation.* New York: McKay, 1975.

Freidel, Frank. *Franklin D. Roosevelt: Launching the New Deal.* Boston: Little, Brown, 1973.

Friedan, Betty. *The Feminine Mystique.* New York: Dell, 1974 [1963].

———. *It Changed My Life: Writings on the Women's Movement.* New York: Random House, 1976.

Gallup, George H. *The Gallup Poll: Public Opinion, 1935–1971.* New York: Random House, 1972.

Gelb, Joyce, and Marian Leif Palley. *Women and Public Policies.* Princeton, New Jersey: Princeton University Press, 1982.

Gilbert, James. *Another Chance: Postwar America, 1945–1968.* New York: Knopf, 1981.

Goldman, Eric F. *The Tragedy of Lyndon Johnson.* New York: Knopf, 1969.

Halberstam, David. *The Best and the Brightest.* New York: Random House, 1972.

Hamby, Alonzo. *Liberalism and Its Challengers.* New York: Oxford University Press, 1985.

Harrison, Cynthia E. *Women's Movement Media.* New York: Bowker, 1975.

Hartmann, Susan M. *The Home Front and Beyond: American Women in the 1940s.* Boston: Twayne, 1982.

Heath, Jim F. *Decade of Disillusionment: The Kennedy-Johnson Years.* Bloomington: Indiana University Press, 1975.

Hess, Stephen. *Organizing the Presidency.* Washington, D.C.: The Brookings Institution, 1976.

Hole, Judith, and Ellen Levine. *Rebirth of Feminism.* New York: Quadrangle Books, 1971.

Honey, Maureen. *Creating Rosie the Riveter: Class, Gender, and Propaganda During World War II.* Amherst: University of Massachusetts Press, 1984.

Johnson, Donald B., comp. *National Party Platforms.* 2 vols. Urbana; University of Illinois Press, 1978.

Kaledin, Eugenia. *Mothers and More: American Women in the 1950s.* Boston: Twayne, 1984.

Kanowitz, Leo. *Women and the Law: The Unfinished Revolution.* Albuquerque: University of New Mexico Press, 1969.

Klein, Ethel. *Gender Politics: From Consciousness to Mass Politics.* Cambridge, Massachusetts: Harvard University Press, 1984.

Komarovsky, Mirra. *Women in the Modern World.* Boston: Little, Brown, 1956.

Kraditor, Aileen, ed. *Up From the Pedestal: Selected Writings in the History of American Feminism.* Chicago: Quadrangle Books, 1968.

Lawrence, Bill. *Six Presidents, Too Many Wars.* New York: Saturday Review Press, 1972.

Lemons, J. Stanley. *The Woman Citizen: Social Feminism in the 1920s.* Urbana: University of Illinois Press, 1975 [1973].

Leuchtenburg, William E. *In the Shadow of FDR: From Harry Truman to Ronald Reagan.* Ithaca, New York: Cornell University Press, 1983.

———. *A Troubled Feast: American Society Since 1945.* Boston: Little, Brown, 1982.

Light, Paul. *The President's Agenda: Domestic Policy Choice from Kennedy to Carter.* Baltimore: Johns Hopkins University Press, 1983.

Louchheim, Katie. *By the Political Sea.* Garden City, New York: Doubleday, 1970.

McGlen, Nancy E., and Karen O'Connor. *Women's Rights: The Struggle for Equality in the Nineteenth and Twentieth Centuries.* New York: Praeger, 1983.

MacKenzie, G. Calvin. *The Politics of Presidential Appointments.* New York: Free Press, 1981.

Matusow, Allen J. *The Unraveling of America: A History of Liberalism in the 1960s.* New York: Harper & Row, 1984.

Mead, Margaret, and Frances B. Kaplan, eds. *American Women.* New York: Scribner, 1965.

Merriam, Eve. *After Nora Slammed the Door: American Women in the 1960s—The Unfinished Revolution.* Cleveland: World, 1964.

Morris, Charles R. *A Time of Passion: America, 1960–1980.* New York: Harper & Row, 1984.

Murphy, Irene L. *Public Policy on the Status of Women: Agenda and Strategy for the 70s.* Lexington, Massachusetts: Lexington Books, 1973.

National Manpower Council. *Womanpower: A Statement by the National Manpower Council with Chapters by the Council Staff.* New York: Columbia University Press, 1957.

O'Donnell, Kenneth P., and David F. Powers. *Johnny, We Hardly Knew Ye.* Boston: Little, Brown, 1972 [1970].

O'Neill, William. *Everyone Was Brave: The Rise and Fall of Feminism in America.* Chicago: Quadrangle Books, 1969.

Oppenheimer, Valerie Kincade. *The Female Labor Force in the United*

*States: Demographic and Economic Factors Governing Its Growth and Changing Composition.* Westport, Connecticut: Greenwood Press, 1976 [1970].

Pardo, Thomas C. *The National Woman's Party Papers, 1913–1974: A Guide to the Microfilm Edition.* Sanford, North Carolina: Microfilm Corporation of America, 1979.

Parmet, Herbert S. *Jack: The Struggles of John F. Kennedy.* New York: Dial Press, 1980.

———. *JFK: The Presidency of John F. Kennedy.* New York: Dial Press, 1983.

Patterson, Judith. *Be Somebody: A Biography of Marguerite Rawalt.* Austin, Texas: Eakin Press, 1986.

Phillips, Cabell. *The Truman Presidency: The History of a Triumphant Succession.* New York: Macmillan, 1966.

Rawalt, Marguerite. *A History of the National Federation of Business and Professional Women's Clubs, Inc.* Washington, D.C.: NFBPWC, 1969.

Rothman, Sheila M. *Woman's Proper Place: A History of Changing Ideals and Practices, 1870 to the Present.* New York: Basic Books, 1978.

Rupp, Leila J. *Mobilizing Women for War: German and American Propaganda, 1939–1945.* Princeton, New Jersey: Princeton University Press, 1978.

Rupp, Leila, and Verta Taylor. *Survival in the Doldrums: The American Women's Rights Movement, 1945 to the 1960s.* New York: Oxford University Press, 1987.

Sachs, Albie, and Joan Hoff Wilson. *Sexism and the Law: Male Beliefs and Legal Bias.* New York: Free Press, 1978.

Safilios-Rothschild, Constantina, ed. *Toward a Sociology of Women.* Lexington, Massachusetts: Xerox, 1972.

Scharf, Lois. *To Work and to Wed: Female Employment, Feminism, and the Great Depression.* Westport, Connecticut: Greenwood Press, 1980.

Schlesinger, Arthur, Jr. *A Thousand Days: John F. Kennedy in the White House.* Boston: Houghton, Mifflin, 1965.

Sealander, Judith. *As Minority Becomes Majority: Federal Reaction to the Phenomenon of Women in the Workforce, 1920–1963.* Westport, Connecticut: Greenwood Press, 1983.

Seidman, Harold. *Politics, Position, and Power: The Dynamics of Federal Organization.* New York: Oxford University Press, 1970.

Sicherman, Barbara, and Carol Hurd Green, eds. *Notable American Women: The Modern Period.* Cambridge, Massachusetts: Belknap Press, 1980.

Sitkoff, Harvard. *The Struggle for Black Equality, 1954–1980.* New York: Hill & Wang, 1981.

Sorensen, Theodore. *Decision-Making in the White House.* New York: Columbia University Press, 1963.

———. *Kennedy.* New York: Harper & Row, 1965.

Tolchin, Susan, and Martin Tolchin. *Clout: Womanpower and Politics.* New York: Coward, McCann & Geogegan, 1974.

Truman, Harry S. *Memoirs.* Vol. 1. New York: Doubleday, 1955.

Ware, Susan. *Beyond Suffrage: Women in the New Deal.* Cambridge, Massachusetts: Harvard University Press, 1981.

———. *Holding Their Own: American Women in the 1930s.* Boston: Twayne, 1982.

White, Theodore H. *The Making of the President, 1960.* New York: Atheneum, 1961.

Wicker, Tom. *JFK and LBJ.* New York: Morrow, 1968.

Wilson, James Q. *Political Organizations.* New York: Basic Books, 1973.

Wilson, Joan Hoff. *Herbert Hoover: Forgotten Progressive.* Boston: Little, Brown, 1975.

Wittner, Lawrence S. *Cold War America.* New York: Holt, Rinehart & Winston, 1978.

Wolanin, Thomas R. *Presidential Advisory Commissions: Truman to Nixon.* Madison: University of Wisconsin Press, 1975.


PERIODICAL LITERATURE


"The American Female: A Special Supplement." *Harper's* 225 (October 1962): 117–180.

"The American Woman: Her Achievements and Troubles" [special issue]. *Life,* 24 December 1956.

"The American Woman: A New Point of View" [special issue]. *Esquire,* July 1962.

Amlund, Curtis Arthur. "Executive-Legislative Imbalance: Truman to Kennedy." *Western Political Quarterly* 18, no. 3 (September 1965): 640–645.

"Are We Wasting Women?" [editorial]. *Life,* 28 July 1961, 36B.

Bacheller, J. M. "Lobbyists and the Legislative Process: The Impact of Environmental Constraints." *American Political Science Review* 71 (1977): 252–263.

Berger, Caruthers Gholson. "Equal Pay, Equal Employment Opportunity and Equal Enforcement of the Law for Women." *Valparaiso University Law Review* 5 (1971): 326–373.

Bergquist, Laura. "What Women Really Meant to JFK." *Redbook,* November 1973, 49–54.

Bernstein, Barton J. "The Truman Administration and Its Reconversion Wage Policy." *Labor History* 6, no. 3 (Fall 1965): 214–231.

Brauer, Carl M. "Women Activists, Southern Conservatives, and the Prohibition of Sex Discrimination in Title VII of the 1964 Civil Rights Act." *Journal of Southern History* 49 (1983): 37–57.

Brophy, Brigid. "Speaking Out: Women are Prisoners of Their Sex." *Saturday Evening Post,* 2 November 1963, 10, 12.

Burns, Catherine G., and John E. Burns. "An Analysis of the Equal Pay Act." *Labor Law Journal* 24 (February 1973): 92–99.

Byrne, Katherine M., et al. "The Redundant Housewife." *America* 104 (25 March 1961): 812–814.

Carabillo, Toni. "A Passion for the Possible." *Do It NOW* 9, no. 9 (October 1976): 5–8.

*Civil Service Journal,* October–December 1960.

Clinch, Mary. "The Phenomenon of the Working Wife." *Social Order* 6 (October 1956): 362–366.

*Commercial and Financial Chronicle,* 21 December 1944.

"Congress to Get Bills on Equal Treatment for Women." *CQ Weekly Report* 20 (28 December 1962): 2298–2300.

*Congressional Record,* 1945–1968.

Cott, Nancy F. "Feminist Politics in the 1920s: The National Woman's Party." *Journal of American History* 71 (June 1984): 43–68.

Cowan, Ruth Schwartz. "Two Washes in the Morning and a Bridge Party at Night: The American Housewife Between the Wars." *Women's Studies* 3, no. 2 (1976): 147–171.

Day, Lincoln H. "Status Implications of the Employment of Married Women in the United States." *American Journal of Economics and Sociology* 20 (July 1961): 391–397.

Drew, Elizabeth. "On Giving Oneself a Hotfoot: Government by Commission." *Atlantic Monthly,* May 1968, 45–49.

"Equality of Women." *America* 109 (26 October 1963): 473.

"Equal Pay Act." *CQ Weekly Report* 21 (14 June 1963): 978.

"Equal Pay Act for Women Enacted." *CQ Almanac* 19 (1963): 511.

"Equal Pay for Women." *American Federationist* 71 (July 1964): 14–17.

"Equal Pay for Women" [editorial]. *Commonweal* 78 (7 June 1963): 293–294.

"'Equal Pay' for Women: Its Effect." *U.S. News and World Report,* 15 June 1964, 91–92.

"The 'Equal Pay' Law: How It Will Work." *U.S. News and World Report,* 24 June 1964, 10–11.

*Equal Rights* (National Woman's Party), 1943–1954.

"Fairer Wages for the Fair Sex." *Business Week,* 6 June 1964, 74.

*Federal Register,* 1965–1968.

Fisher, Marguerite. "Equal Pay for Equal Work Legislation." *Industrial and Labor Relations Review* 2, no. 1 (October 1948): 50–57.

Foley, Paul. "Whatever Happened to Women's Rights?" *Atlantic* 213 (March 1964): 63–65.

Freeman, Mary. "The Marginal Sex: America's Alienated Women." *Commonweal* 75, no. 19 (2 February 1962): 483–486.

Gallup, George, and Evan Hill. "The American Woman." *Saturday Evening Post*, 22 December 1962, 15–32.

Gelb, Joyce, and Marian Lief Palley. "Women and Interest Group Politics: A Case Study of the Equal Credit Opportunity Act." *American Politics Quarterly* 5, no. 3 (July 1977): 331–352.

Gould, Beatrice B. "Appointments for Women." *Ladies' Home Journal*, January 1961, 64.

Grace, William J. "The Dilemma of Modern Woman: Can She Solve It?" *Catholic World*, April 1956, 16–23.

Hartmann, Susan. "Prescriptions for Penelope: Literature on Women's Obligations to Returning World War II Veterans." *Women's Studies* 5, no. 3 (1978): 223–239.

Holstein, Ruth. "The Status of Women." *NEA Journal*, November 1963, 68.

*Independent Woman* [later *National Business Woman*] (National Federation of Business and Professional Women's Clubs), 1945–1968.

Lear, Martha Weinman. "The Second Feminist Wave." *New York Times Magazine*, 10 March 1968, 24–25 +.

Lees, Hannah. "Women Should Not Play Dumb." *Saturday Evening Post*, 28 January 1961, 27 +.

McGlen, Nancy E., and Karen O'Connor. "An Analysis of the U.S. Women's Rights Movements: Rights as a Public Good." *Women and Politics* 1, no. 1 (Spring 1980): 65–85.

Mannes, Marya. "Female Intelligence: Who Wants It?" *New York Times Magazine*, 3 January 1960, 11 + ; letters, 17 January 1960.

Mead, Margaret. "Do We Undervalue Full-Time Wives?" *Redbook*, November 1963, 22, 24, 26.

———. "Modern Marriage, the Danger Point." *Nation* 177 (31 October 1953): 348–350.

Moran, Robert. "Reducing Discrimination: Role of the Equal Pay Act." *Monthly Labor Review* 93 (June 1970): 30–34.

Murphy, Thomas E. "Female Wage Discrimination: A Study of the Equal Pay Act, 1963–1970." *University of Cincinnati Law Review* 39 (Fall 1970): 615–649.

Murray, Pauli, and Mary Eastwood. "Jane Crow and the Law: Sex Discrimination and Title VII." *George Washington Law Review* 34 (December 1965): 232–256.

*National Business Woman.* See *Independent Woman.*

*New York Times,* 1938–1968.

O'Kelley, Charlotte G. "The 'Impact' of Equal Employment Legislation on Women's Earnings: Limitations of Legislative Solutions to Discrimination in the Economy." *American Journal of Economics and Sociology* 38, no. 4 (October 1979): 419–430.

"On Equal Pay for Women." *U.S. News and World Report,* 23 March 1964, 115–117.

Peterson, Esther. "The Status of Women in the United States." *International Labour Review* 89 (May 1964): 447–460.

"Pro: Should Congress Approve the Proposed Equal Rights Amendment to the Constitution?" *Congressional Digest* 22, no.4 (April 1943): 107–110.

Rostow, Edna G. "The Best of Both Worlds: Feminism and Femininity." *Yale Review* 51 (March 1962): 384–399.

Rupp, Leila J. "The Women's Community in the National Woman's Party, 1945 to the 1960s." *Signs* 10 (Summer 1985): 715–740.

Sanders, Marion K. "A Proposition for Women." *Harper's* 221 (September 1960): 41–48; letters, 221 (November 1960): 6.

"Shaping the '60s . . . Foreshadowing the '70s." *Ladies' Home Journal,* January 1962, 30–33.

Simchak, Morag. "Equal Pay Act of 1963: Its Implementation and Enforcement." *AAUW Journal* 61 (March 1968): 117–119.

————. "Equal Pay in the United States." *International Labour Review* 103 (June 1971): 541–557.

"The Status of Women" [editorial]. *Catholic Nurse,* December 1963, 16–17.

Tompkins, Pauline. "Change and Challenge for the Educated Woman." *Saturday Review* 46 (18 May 1963): 69 + .

*Wall Street Journal,* 1963–1968.

*Washington Post,* 1945–1968.

"When Women Get Paid as Much as Men." *U.S. News and World Report,* 3 June 1963, 97–98.

"The Woman in America," *Daedalus* (Spring 1964).

Young, Louise, ed. "Women's Opportunities and Responsibilities." *Annals of the American Academy of Political and Social Science* 251 (May 1947): 1–224.

## DISSERTATIONS

Aron, Cindy S. "'To Barter Their Souls For Gold': Female Federal Clerical Workers in Later Nineteenth-Century America." Ph.D. dissertation, University of Maryland, 1981.

Becker, Susan D. "An Intellectual History of the National Woman's Party, 1920–1941." Ph.D. dissertation, Case Western Reserve University, 1975.

Blahna, Loretta J. "The Rhetoric of the Equal Rights Amendment." Ph.D. dissertation, University of Kansas, 1973.

Cassell, Joan M. "A Group Called Women: Recruitment and Organization in Contemporary American Feminism." Ph.D. dissertation, Columbia University, 1975.

Coover, Edwin Russell. "Status and Role Change Among Women in the United States, 1940–1970: A Quantitative Approach." Ph.D. dissertation, University of Minnesota, 1973.

Daly, Sister John Marie, R.S.M. "Mary Anderson, Pioneer Labor Leader." Ph.D. dissertation, Georgetown University, 1968.

Dowd, Jane T. "An Investigation of the Image of American Women in Selected American Motion Pictures, 1930–1971." Ph.D. dissertation, New York University, 1975.

Elshtain, Jean Bethke. "Women and Politics: A Theoretical Analysis." Ph.D. dissertation, Brandeis University, 1973.

Florer, John Harmon. "NOW: The Formative Years. The National Effort to Acquire Federal Action on Equal Employment Rights for Women in the 1960s." Ph.D. dissertation, Syracuse University, 1972.

Gallagher, Mary Miles Frossard. "Women's Liberation: Social Movement in a Complex Society." Ph.D. dissertation, University of Colorado, 1973.

George, Elsie L. "The Women Appointees of the Roosevelt and Truman Administrations: A Study of Their Impact and Effectiveness." Ph.D. dissertation, American University, 1972.

Kligler, Deborah Schupper. "The Effects of the Employment of Married Women on Husband and Wife Roles: A Study in Culture Change." Ph.D. dissertation, Yale University, 1954.

Levitt, Morris Jacob. "Political Attitudes of American Women: A Study of the Effects of Work and Education on Their Political Role." Ph.D. dissertation, University of Maryland, 1965.

Makosky, Donald R. "The Portrayal of Women in Wide-Circulation Magazine Short Stories, 1905–1955." Ph.D. dissertation, University of Pennsylvania, 1966.

Morain, Thomas Jeffrey. "The Emergence of the Women's Movement, 1960–1970." Ph.D. dissertation, University of Iowa, 1974.

Mulligan, Joan Elizabeth. "Three Federal Interventions on Behalf of Childbearing Women: The Sheppard-Towner Act, Emergency Maternity and Infant Care, and the Maternal Child Health and Mental

Retardation Planning Amendments of 1963." Ph.D. dissertation, University of Michigan, 1976.

Ondercin, David George. "The Compleat Woman: The Equal Rights Amendment and Perceptions of Womanhood, 1920–1972." Ph.D. dissertation, University of Minnesota, 1973.

Sealander, Judith. "The Women's Bureau, 1920–1950: Federal Reaction to Female Wage Earning." Ph.D. dissertation, Duke University, 1977.

Straub, Eleanor F. "Government Policy Toward Civilian Women During World War II." Ph.D. dissertation, Emory University, 1973.

Strobel, Marian Elizabeth. "Ideology and Women's Higher Education, 1945–1960." Ph.D. dissertation, Duke University, 1976.

Tanabe, Patricia Anne White. "Views of Women's Work in Public Policy in the United States: Social Security and Equal Pay Legislation, 1935–1967." Ph.D. dissertation, Bryn Mawr College, 1973.

Zelman, Patricia. "Development of Equal Employment Opportunity for Women as National Policy, 1960–1967." Ph.D. dissertation, Ohio State University, 1980.


                                    INTERVIEWS

Bertha Adkins Oral History Interview. 18 December 1967. Columbia University Oral History Project, New York, New York.

Sandra Bollhoefer. 15–17 July 1974. Washington, D.C.

Hyman Bookbinder Oral History Interview. N.d. John F. Kennedy Library, Boston, Massachusetts.

Elizabeth Carpenter. Interview with Patricia Zelman, 20 September 1977. Austin, Texas.

Kathryn Clarenbach. Telephone interview, 22 June 1981. Madison, Wisconsin.

Catherine East. 6 July 1978, 20 November 1978, 12 February 1981; telephone interview, 31 July 1981. Arlington, Virginia.

India Edwards. Interview with Patricia Zelman, 10 November 1975. Austin, Texas.

India Edwards Oral History Interview. 16 January 1969. Harry S Truman Library, Independence, Missouri.

India Edwards Oral History Interview. 4 February 1969. Lyndon Baines Johnson Library, Austin, Texas.

Katherine P. Ellickson Oral History Interview. 15 December 1974. Archives of Labor and Urban Affairs, Wayne State University, Detroit, Michigan.

Myer Feldman Oral History Interview. 23 January 1966, 27 March

1966, 10 April 1966, 6 August 1966, 21 September 1968. John F. Kennedy Library, Boston, Massachusetts.

Dan Fenn, Jr. Telephone interview, 15 May 1981. Boston, Massachusetts.

Betty Friedan. Telephone interview, 21 January 1975. New York, New York.

Clayton Fritchey Oral History Interview. 6 June 1970. Harry S Truman Library. Independence, Missouri.

Elizabeth R. Gatov Oral History Interview. 25 June 1969. John F. Kennedy Library, Boston, Massachusetts.

Arthur Goldberg. Telephone interview, 17 September 1985. Washington, D.C.

Richard Graham. 31 July 1985. Washington, D.C.

Edith Green. 18 December 1978. Portland, Oregon.

Martha Griffiths. Telephone interview, 27 November 1978. Romeo, Michigan.

Evelyn Harrison. 12 September 1978. Washington, D.C.

Mary Hilton. Telephone interview, 11 February 1981. Washington, D.C.

Mildred Jeffries. Telephone interview, 23 October 1981. Detroit, Michigan.

Mary Keyserling Oral History Interview. 1–4 February 1982. Women in Federal Government Project, Schlesinger Library, Cambridge, Massachusetts.

Helen Lempart Oral History Interview. March 1966. John F. Kennedy Library, Boston, Massachusetts.

Richard A. Lester. 22 March 1974. Princeton, New Jersey.

Katie Louchheim Oral History Interview. 24 April 1968, 14 June 1968, 13 September 1968. John F. Kennedy Library, Boston, Massachusetts.

Mary McGrory, Peter Lisagor, George Herman Oral History Interview. 4 August 1964. John F. Kennedy Library, Boston, Massachusetts.

Marie C. McGuire Oral History Interview. 3 April 1967. John F. Kennedy Library, Boston, Massachusetts.

John Macy Oral History Interview. 23 May 1964. John F. Kennedy Library, Boston, Massachusetts.

Alice A. Morrison. Telephone interview, 11 February 1981. Alexandria, Virginia.

Pauli Murray. Telephone interview, 12 November 1981. Baltimore, Maryland.

Maurine Neuberger. 15 December 1978. Portland, Oregon.

Maurine Neuberger Oral History Interview. 12 February 1970. John F. Kennedy Library, Boston, Massachusetts.

Alice Paul. "Conversations with Alice Paul: Woman Suffrage and the Equal Rights Amendment." An oral history conducted 1972–1973 by Amelia R. Fry. Regional Oral History Office, The Bancroft Library, University of California, Berkeley, 1976.

Esther Peterson. 27 February 1978, 10 June 1978, 17 June 1980; telephone interviews, 4 October 1974, 23 September 1981. Washington, D.C.

Esther Peterson. Interview with Kathy Kraft, 17 May 1975. Schlesinger Library, Cambridge, Massachusetts.

Esther Peterson Oral History Interview. 25 November 1968. Lyndon Baines Johnson Library, Austin, Texas. (Draft transcript in Peterson's possession).

Esther Peterson Oral History Interview. 1978. Schlesinger Library, Cambridge, Massachusetts / University of Michigan, Ann Arbor, Michigan.

Esther Peterson Oral History Interviews. 1976–1983. Columbia University Oral History Project, New York, New York. (Copy in Peterson's possession.)

Esther Peterson Recorded Interview. 18 May 1966, 20 January 1970, 4 February 1970. John F. Kennedy Library, Oral History Program, Boston, Massachusetts.

Marguerite Rawalt. 9 November 1984. Arlington, Virginia.

Morag Simchak. Telephone interview, 14 August 1974. Washington, D.C.

Pearl Spindler. 15–17 July 1974. Washington, D.C.

Anne Wheaton Oral History Interview. 31 January 1968. Columbia University Oral History Project, New York, New York.

UNPUBLISHED MANUSCRIPTS

Freeman, Jo. "Title VII." 1987.

Kolb, Frances. "The National Organization for Women: A History of the First Ten Years." In progress.

# Index

| | |
|---|---|
| Compositor: | Huron Valley Graphics, Inc. |
| Text: | 11/13 Baskerville |
| Display: | Baskerville |
| Printer: | Maple-Vail Book Manufacturing Group |
| Binder: | Maple-Vail Book Manufacturing Group |